Growing Up in a Divided Society

Growing Up in a Divided Society:

The Contexts of Childhood in South Africa

Edited by Sandra Burman
and Pamela Reynolds
With Forewords by Archbishop Desmond Tutu
and Robert Coles

Northwestern University Press   Evanston, Illinois

Northwestern University Press
Evanston, Illinois 60201

Printed in the United States of America

Library of Congress Cataloging-in-Publication Data

Growing up in a divided society : the contexts of childhood in South
    Africa / edited by Sandra Burman and Pamela Reynolds ; with
    forewords by Desmond Tutu and Robert Coles.
            p.   cm.
        Reprint. Originally published: Johannesburg : Ravan Press, 1986.
        Includes bibliographical references.
        ISBN 0-8101-0860-7. — ISBN 0-8101-0861-5 (pbk.)
        1. Children—Africa. 2. Apartheid—South Africa.   I. Burman,
    Sandra. II. Reynolds, Pamela.
    HQ792.S6G76   1990
    305.23'0968—dc20   90-6715
                                                                        CIP

The paper used in this publication meets the minimum requirements of
American National Standard for Information Sciences—Permanence of
Paper for Printed Library Materials, ANSI Z39.48-1984.

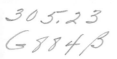

Contents

Acknowledgements

The idea of compiling this book was generated by our separate research conducted under the auspices of the Centre for African Studies and the Department of Anthropology at the University of Cape Town, the University of Zimbabwe, and the Centre for Cross-Cultural Research on Women at Queen Elizabeth House, Oxford. In these investigations we have been funded by the Human Sciences Research Council and the Anglo-American Chairman's Fund Educational Trust, to whom we should like to express our thanks.

When we compared notes on our findings we realized that we had independently reached similar conclusions about the urgent need to draw attention to the role of children in the family and society in South Africa. The Ford Foundation made the realization of this project possible by providing a grant, for which we are most grateful.

The book would never have been produced without the enthusiastic and patient editorial assistance of Martine Huvers and Marlene Powell. The latter was also responsible for compiling the index. Friends and colleagues have generously assisted us with encouragement and advice — especially necessary in an interdisciplinary book of this nature — and we are particularly indebted to Mr Sean Archer, Mr Emile Boonzaaier, Professor Colin Bundy, Dr Jacklyn Cock, Dr Brenda Cooper, Professor Dennis Davis, Professor Peter du Preez, Ms Sally Frankental, Professor Hermann Giliomee, Mr Keith Gottschalk, Dr Kenneth Hughes, Ms Patricia Langton, Professor Walter Loening, Dr Vanessa Maher, Mr Richard Mendelsohn, Dr Christopher Molteno, Mr Tony Morphet, Ms Shirley Moulder, Dr Norman Reynolds, Dr Mary Roberts, Professor Michael Savage, Ms Mary Simons, Dr Robert Thornton, Professor Martin West, Professor Eleanor Preston-Whyte, Dr Timothy Wilson, and Dr Nigel Worden. We are most grateful to all of them.

Sandra Burman and Pamela Reynolds
March 1986

The Contributors

Paul Alberts has worked as a writer and photographer on various newspapers in South Africa. In 1981 he founded the Gallery Press, a company dedicated to the publishing of social documentary photography. He currently serves as its director. His work has appeared in magazines and books in South Africa and abroad, and four collections of his photographs have been published. He has exhibited extensively in one-man shows in Cape Town and Johannesburg, and has contributed to a number of group exhibitions in South Africa and abroad.

Gina Buijs lectured in social anthropology at the Universities of Durban-Westville and Natal, and is currently Senior Lecturer at the University of Venda. She has done research into kinship and religion among Indian South Africans and has recently completed a study of migrancy in South Africa, dealing with African female workers from the Transkei.

Sandra Burman is a Research Fellow at Queen Elizabeth House, Oxford University, and is currently a Visiting Research Fellow at the University of Cape Town while conducting a socio-legal research project on family break-up in South Africa. She is author or editor of a number of books and articles on southern African and British topics. After qualifying as an advocate in South Africa, she graduated from the University of Oxford with a degree in philosophy, politics, and economics, and a doctorate in history, and was a Senior Research Officer at the Centre for Socio-Legal Studies, Wolfson College, Oxford.

Frank Chikane is the General Secretary of the Institute for Contextual Theology, Johannesburg. He was Pastor of the Apostolic Faith Mission of Africa at Kagiso in Krugersdorp from 1976 to 1981. He is now resident in Soweto, and is the Deputy President of the Soweto Civic Association.

Jacklyn Cock graduated from Rhodes University with a doctorate in sociology and is a Senior Lecturer in the Sociology Department, University of the Witwatersrand. Her publications include a book on domestic workers in South Africa and her current research is in the sociology of education.

Erica Emdon graduated from the University of the Witwatersrand with an honours degree in industrial sociology. She is at present studying law.

Don Foster studied at the Universities of Stellenbosch, Cape Town, London, and Cambridge. He is an Associate Professor in the Department of Psychology at the University of Cape Town, and has a particular interest in psychological aspects of South African society.

Sally Frankental is Director of the Kaplan Centre for Jewish Studies and Research at the University of Cape Town, where she was formerly a Lecturer in the Department of Social Anthropology. She is a graduate of the University of Cape Town, and her doctoral research is on migration and ethnicity.

Rebecca Fuchs has degrees from Cornell University and the University of Texas. She is a practising lawyer working in commercial litigation. While a student, she spent some time working as a research assistant to Sandra Burman.

Maurice Kibel is the Stella and Paul Loewenstein Professor of Child Health at the University of Cape Town, a post he has held since 1979. Prior to that he was in Consultant paediatric practice in Zimbabwe.

Barbara Klugman graduated from the University of the Witwatersrand with an honours degree in development studies. She was employed at the Health Information Centre for three years, during which time the research on child care and working mothers was completed, and is at present a Lecturer in the Department of Social Anthropology at the University of the Witwatersrand. Her current research is on contraception and family life among urban Africans. She is co-author of a book on African women's lives under apartheid.

Pieter le Roux is Professor of Development Studies and Director of the Institute for Social Development at the University of the Western Cape. Previously he was Senior Lecturer in Economics at the Rand Afrikaans University. He trained in economics at the Universities of Stellenbosch and Cambridge and has published, *inter alia*, in the fields of mathematical and labour economics, political sociology, and the philosophy of science.

Jennifer Louw is employed by the University of Natal as Secretary to the Director of Academic Planning. Soon after joining the staff she registered (part-time) for the B.Soc.Sc. degree, majoring in history and social anthropology, and completed the degree in 1983.

Kay McCormick is a Lecturer in English Language and Literature at the University of Cape Town. Her chapter in this volume is from work for her doctoral dissertation in sociolinguistics, and other articles from that research are currently in the press.

Fiona McLachlan is a practising attorney in Johannesburg with a particular interest in civil rights and family law, including the legal rights of children, who are seldom independently represented in the South African legal system. She is the author of reports on children in South African prisons and on children's courts and institutions in South Africa, researched for Defence for Children International, a children's rights organization based in Geneva.

Christopher Molteno is a Senior Specialist at the Red Cross War Memorial Children's Hospital and Senior Lecturer in the Department of Paediatrics and Child Health, University of Cape Town. He heads the Developmental Assessment Clinics at the hospital, which are concerned with the management of handicapped children. He is also involved in the treatment of abused children. His research interests include growth and development of children, neurodevelopmental sequelae of perinatal complications, services for handicapped children, and childhood mortality.

Bill Nasson is a Lecturer in Economic History at the University of Cape Town and has published work on South African education and history. He is currently completing a book on African participation in the Anglo-Boer War and co-editing a volume on poverty and education in South Africa. He was educated in South Africa and in Britain at the Universities of Hull, York, and Cambridge, where he completed his doctorate. After working in aid and voluntary agencies in Britain, he held posts as Research Assistant and Research Officer at the Universities of Cambridge and Cape Town, and was a Visiting Fellow at Yale University.

Marlene Powell holds an honours degree in discourse studies and is presently attached to the Department of Comparative and African Literature at the University of the Witwatersrand, where she is researching developments in popular media discourse in South Africa in the 1970s and 1980s. Prior to her present research she worked as a Research Assistant at the University of Cape Town.

Eleanor Preston-Whyte is Associate Professor of Social Anthropology in the Department of African Studies at the University of Natal. The results of her research amongst English, Afrikaans, and Zulu South Africans have been published in various books and journals. She is currently involved in work on African women and the informal sector in KwaZulu and Natal, with particular emphasis on the production and distribution of crafts and curios. The chapter in this volume combines her interests in research and in stimulating students to become actively involved in fieldwork as part of their training in social anthropology.

Pamela Reynolds is a Senior Research Fellow in the Faculty of Agriculture at the University of Zimbabwe, where she is currently studying child labour in Harare and the Zambezi Valley. Her doctoral thesis for the University of Cape Town was on the cognitive development of seven-year-old children in Crossroads, South Africa, and her subsequent work has included a study of the transmission of knowledge between indigenous healers and children in Mashonaland, Zimbabwe. She holds degrees in social anthropology and education from the Universities of Cape Town, Rhodesia (Zimbabwe), Harvard, and Delhi.

Mary Roberts is at present a Community Health Registrar at the University of Cape Town Medical School. Since graduating in medicine from the University of Edinburgh in 1957, she has worked in child health and family planning in South Africa and Australia, including many years of work in the squatter camps around Cape Town. She has published various papers on family planning there.

Ina Roux graduated from Rhodes University, Grahamstown. Her areas of study are psychology and anthropology, and she is currently a Junior Lecturer in the Psychology Department. She was one of the contributors to *The Surplus People Project* study, for which she wrote the section on life histories.

Wilfried Schärf is a Lecturer in the Institute of Criminology at the University of Cape Town. After he qualified as an advocate, his career included a short spell with a firm of attorneys and research for a graduate degree in criminology. His work includes studies of farm labour and the tot system in the Western Cape, and illicit liquor distribution by street gangs operating through shebeens. He is currently investigating informal courts in African townships.

Milton Shain is a Lecturer in the Department of Hebrew and Jewish Civilization at the University of Cape Town, where he teaches Jewish history. He holds degrees in history and education from the Universities of South Africa and Leeds. His publications include a book on Jewry and society in the Cape Colony, and his doctoral research is on the image of the Jew in South Africa from *c.* 1870 to 1945.

Charles Simkins is a Senior Lecturer in the School of Economics at the University of Cape Town. His chapter in this volume draws on his doctoral thesis for the University of Natal. He has published a number of influential articles on labour economics, income distribution and poverty, and demography.

Edgar Thomas taught at Zeekoevlei Senior Secondary School for three years and later served as housefather at the Homestead Activity Centre (for vagrant children) in Cape Town for a year. During 1985 he was employed as a researcher at the Institute of Criminology at the University of Cape Town.

Helen Zille is a freelance journalist, researcher, and editor. She was formerly the political correspondent of the *Rand Daily Mail* and

Associate Editor of *Frontline*. She was also Research Coordinator of the Second Carnegie Inquiry into Poverty and Development in Southern Africa and is currently editing a book of research material arising out of the Inquiry.

Foreword

I once read an extended article or perhaps it was a series of articles in *Time* magazine, devoted to a study of what happens to children who live and grow up in war-torn areas. That reading left me devastated. I heard how children learn to cope with having known nothing but violence and terrorism since they were born, and that the prospects were very bleak that they would know much peace and stability for the rest of their lives. It was horrifying to hear how children accepted that human life was dirt cheap. I recall another occasion, listening to a church assembly debate in Northern Ireland on Youth Work. One of the speakers described how a group of girls belonging to one faction of that strife-torn land had used bricks to pound to death a girl belonging to the opposite side. That was bad enough. But what shocked the Assembly was when the speaker went on to describe how those girls, showing not a trace of remorse, then went to a pub for a drink as if they had just come from a picnic.

The collection of essays in this book seeks to describe as scientifically as possible what it means to be born into an apartheid society where there is a ruthless social stratification and caste system. Depending on your pigmentation, you are placed high or low on the social pyramid; and where you are or, rather, where your parents are, determines so many things for you. It will decide, with a rigidity unknown even in the strictest Calvinistic predestination, where you are born and where you can live. It will determine what sort of health care is available to you; indeed, it will determine your chances of survival or whether you will become part of the dismal infant mortality statistic. It will determine the probability that you will succumb to kwashiorkor, be potbellied, or suffer from easily preventable deficiency diseases. It will determine what sort of education you are likely to get and how well you can be expected to perform at school (assuming you are fortunate enough to get into one, if you are at the bottom end of the scale). It will determine whether you can in fact hope to have a decent, stable home environment where father is not a migrant worker separated for eleven months of the year from his loved ones, who are expected to eke out a miserable existence in poverty-stricken, barren 'homeland' resettlement camps. It will determine whether you can ever hope to be treated as a human person of infinite worth because you have been created in the image of God.

The anthology catalogues the colossal harm a divided, fragmented, caste-ridden, and polarized society is doing to its most valuable resource — its young people, the hope of the future. It cannot make for pleasant reading. It is not meant to be a nightcap. It is meant to shock us out of our complacency. Some of us have encountered the bitterness that injustice and oppression have evoked in black youth. We have also seen how cheaply black life was regarded on occasion by white youths whose fingers rested on the trigger in the unrest that has claimed so many lives — mostly young black lives — unnecessarily. Because these young people have been separated, they have never learnt to know each other. They do not understand each other's ambitions. From their earliest years fear of each other is instilled into them. In defence of their privileges some have been taught to hate and to kill and the others are learning to hate and to kill. Our country, our beautiful country, cannot afford the carnage. We cannot afford to reap the whirlwind.

This book is meant to shake us out of our lethargy and imagined impotence, to do something to save our children, to save our land, before it is too late. I devoutly hope that many South Africans will read it. They may then be spurred to get on with the job of working for justice, peace, and reconciliation, for the new South Africa where black and white will live as God intends us to live — as members of one family, God's family, the human family.

Bishop Desmond Tutu
Bishop of Johannesburg
20 March 1986

Foreword to the American Edition

As I read the essays in this book, and thought of similar work in other countries seized by social and political turmoil, I began to wonder whether the social sciences, in a strange fashion, don't really come to life under "normal" circumstances—whether, in fact, social observation and social reflection aren't enriched enormously by the impact of a crisis on everyone in a given world, the observer and the observed alike. One of the editors, ironically though understandably, worries about the desirability of such a book as this one, even the studies that go to make it up, given the political crisis which now obtains in South Africa. At the very beginning we are told this: "Although children have been conspicuous in South Africa's current civil strife, while this book was being compiled we were often asked, 'why study children, and especially in South Africa today?'" Further along one is told: "In the view of our interrogators, therefore, to investigate childhood is a luxury for tranquil societies, able to indulge their interest in marginal groups and topics of peripheral importance."

But the editors and authors of the essays which make up this fine volume know better—know that children in many respects are the heart of the problem for a conflicted nation such as South Africa: what they are, a nation will soon enough be, one way or the other. This book, in that sense, tells us what South Africa is like—and is all too likely to be like ten years hence, unless the "divided society" that it is somehow goes through a transformation.

Such a change, were it to be significant, would certainly have to affect the millions of children whose fate is described in this book.

Their difficulties and tragedies are amply documented: the poor health; the faulty education; the unstable family life; various tragedies connected to the social, economic, political consequences of apartheid—a racial policy, yes, but one which affects the minds, hearts, and souls of each and every person in a particular nation, not excluding the Afrikaner young, as Pieter le Roux makes quite clear in his instructive essay "Growing Up an Afrikaner." My own work with Afrikaner children made me more aware than ever of the price such boys and girls must pay morally and spiritually for their undoubted advantages, a lesson I first began to learn in our American South in the early 1960s, when I studied white as well as black children in *our* "divided society." I suppose the "interrogators" the editors mention would insist that in view of the terrible, objective deprivation, the pain and sadness and constant jeopardy, the bleak prospects for the overwhelming majority of a nation's young, it is a bit much (maybe even a scandal) for us to be concerned for those children whose parents are running the show, whose parents have in their hands money, power, the franchise—everything important politically, economically, socially. Yet, even on a practical basis, never mind the ironies involved, it is important for those who want a society changed to understand the learned assumptions of those who own it, rule it, control it through the ways laws are written.

I doubt many readers will be surprised by the thrust of this book— the essays which, collectively, tell an old story, alas, of suffering and deprivation passed from generation to generation. But many readers may well be surprised—indeed, impressed—by the thoroughness of this book's scope: the study of children in prison; children's use of language in certain racial neighborhoods; the paper on the so-called "strollers" or streetchildren; the description of the way South African Jews grow up; and, of course, the examination by several writers of the medical and educational and familial consequences of apartheid. This is not a polemical book, not an explicitly political book—and yet its cumulative message is disheartening, dismaying, searing to the memory and to the Christian heart.

I must also remark upon the *documentary* nature of these essays; they offer direct observations, rendered in clear and affecting prose. There is, too, an affecting photographic section (children of various racial and socioeconomic backgrounds pictured in a variety of situations). There is no cluttered or opaque or pretentious social science jargon—such as we must endure so commonly in America (talk about "a luxury for tranquil societies"). It is as if each writer has no patience with self-important and pretentious abstractions—but rather wants to help the reader get down to the bare bones of a particular world, as it determines the way children eat, dress, talk, dream, get their schooling, and as it gives shape to their hopes and fears and worries. One can only hope and pray that one day all the essays will prove to be thoroughly outdated—that a generation of children in Cape Town and Johannesburg and Port Elizabeth and Durban and countless towns and villages all over "the beloved country" will no longer have to endure the circumstances these essays have to document so carefully and thoughtfully.

Robert Coles

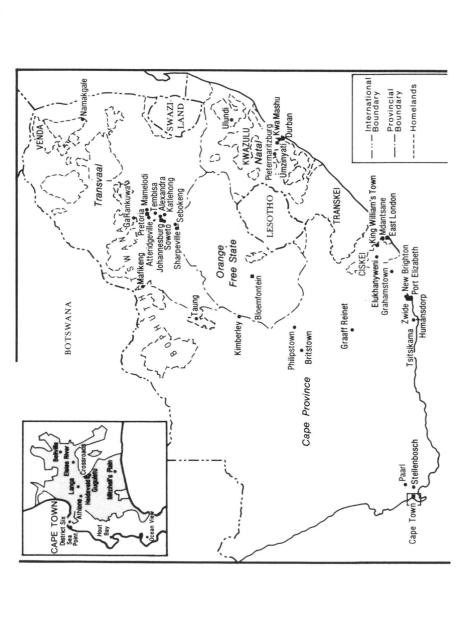

BOTSWANA

VENDA

Namakgale

Transvaal

SWAZI-
LAND

Ulundi

KWAZULU
Natal

Pietermaritzburg
Umzinyati• Kwa Mashu
• Durban

GaRankuwa
Mamelodi
Pretoria Tembisa
Atteridgeville• Alexandra
Johannesburg• Katlehong
Soweto• Sebokeng
Sharpeville

LESOTHO

Mafikeng

B
O
P
H
U
T
H
A
T
S
W
A
N
A

*Orange
Free State*

TRANSKEI

King William's Town
Mdantsane•
East London

CISKEI

Taung

Bloemfontein

Elukhanyweni• New Brighton
Grahamstown• Port Elizabeth
Zwide
Tsitsikama• Humansdorp

Kimberley

Philipstown•
Britstown•

Graaff Reinet

Cape Province

International
Boundary
Provincial
Boundary
Homelands

Paarl•
•Stellenbosch

Cape Town

CAPE TOWN
District Six
Sea
Point
Hout
Bay
Bellville
Elsies River
Crossroads
Langa
Athlone
Heideveld Guguletu
Mitchell's Plain
Ocean View

The Contexts of Childhood in South Africa: An Introduction

Sandra Burman

Although children have been conspicuous in South Africa's current civil strife, while this book was being compiled we were often asked, 'Why study children, and especially in South Africa today?' After all, the questioner implied, adults make the policy decisions in society; children are merely appendages until they become adult. Children's views are unformed or uninformed, their actions without consequences of importance until such time as they are old enough to take their place in the social machinery. In the view of our interrogators, therefore, to investigate childhood is a luxury for tranquil societies able to indulge their interest in marginal groups and topics of peripheral importance. Where a society is on the threshold or, indeed, in the throes of transformation, priorities are different. Scholars should be studying those groups whose existence and actions have a major impact on the shape of the nation and its future direction.

We agree on the necessity of studying such groups in a society like South Africa, and it is for that very reason that this book has been compiled. In the pages that follow we outline the reasons for our view that it is of crucial importance to study children *as children*, not simply as future adults, and that this particularly applies in South Africa today.

The Importance of the Invisible

It is true that children are often invisible socially and seem to be so unimportant in the progress of a nation that they do not appear at all in the pages of most history books. The obvious reason is that historical investigations are governed by the documents available and children do not appear in those. As Peter Laslett (1965: 104-105) points out,

> crowds and crowds of little children are strangely absent from the written record . . . . There is something mysterious about the silence of all these multitudes of babes in arms, toddlers and adolescents in statements men made at the time about their own experience. Children appear of course, but so seldom and in such an indefinite way that we know very little indeed about child nurture in pre-industrial times . . . We cannot say whether fathers helped in the tending of infants . . . . Nothing can as yet be said on what is called by the psychologists toilet training, and reckoned by them to be of great importance in the formation of personality . . . It is in fact an effort of mind to remember all the time that children were always present in such numbers in the traditional world, nearly half the whole community living in a condition of semi-obliteration . . .

Various explanations have been offered for this silence. Edwin Ardener (1972) and, subsequently, Charlotte Hardman (1973), for example, first drew attention to the way that both women and children form 'muted groups', unperceived and elusive, for anyone viewing a society. The cause, it is suggested, is not that they are uninfluential but that they are socialized to be deferential and submissive, in conformity with male attitudes. As a result of this, the models of society which are articulated are men's models, incorporating male values and priorities. There is also the factor that at certain periods and in certain societies childhood is so circumscribed as to be almost or completely defined out of existence. The historian Phillippe Ariès, for example, believes that 'there was no place for childhood in the medieval world' (1962: 31) and that in medieval society the idea of childhood did not exist (1962: 36). But the failure to record the effect of children in society does not necessarily prove that they were unimportant; it may merely prove that the society and those who recorded it failed to recognize a range of crucial influences at work. We suggest that a similar blindness afflicts those who believe children to be merely footnotes, if that, in a respectable study of social and political developments in South Africa today.

At the most superficial level, the very existence of children, no matter how muted or invisible, has a very visible effect in the nation's balance sheets. In the 1984-1985 national budget, for example, almost a fifth was set aside for education (*White Paper* 1985: 32), and government pronouncements since then indicate that the amount cannot but escalate sharply in the near future. The nation also budgets for children's needs in many other areas such as clinics and other medical provision for maternity and child health, crèches and child care facilities, state maintenance for children where the parents cannot provide for their basic needs, social workers for children in need of care, probation supervision and other investigations: the list accounts for a large chunk of society's finances which ultimately must be produced by adult work. Children also account for many adult jobs. Furthermore, although no independent figures on child labour in South Africa are available, it is clear that it plays a role in the nation's productivity and the survival of many families (Anti-Slavery Society 1983). For these reasons alone a study of children in the society — their needs and provision — is important for anyone investigating or planning for a present or future South Africa.

However, at a more basic level, most adult women in society, and a high proportion of adult men, are affected for a large part of their lives by their apparently invisible offspring. Except for the wealthy, the existence of children dictates how men as well as women must order their lives to care for their children — or, at the very least, to avoid those who would otherwise make them do so. We would suggest that considerations of affection usually play a role in this adaptation of life style and priorities, as well as considerations of investment in the future; but whatever the reasons, adults devote much effort to socializing and providing for their offspring. The family in its various forms is still the main agent of socialization in South Africa.

Further, to view this process as one in which adults and society at large imprint their mark on passive children is to misunderstand what occurs. As Giddens points out (1979: 130),

> *The unfolding of childhood is not time elapsing just for the child:* it is time elapsing for its parental figures, and for all other members of society; the socialization involved is not simply that of the child, but of the parents and others with whom the child is in contact, and whose conduct is influenced by the child as the latter's is by theirs in the continuity of interaction. Since the newborn human infant is so helpless, and so dependent on others, normally its parents, it is easily forgotten that children 'create parents' as well as parents creating children. The arrival and development of a child reorders the lives of the adults who care for it and interact with it. The category 'mother' is given by the arrival of the

child, but the practice of enactment of motherhood involves processes of learning that stretch back before and continue after the birth of the child. Socialisation is thus most appropriately regarded not as the 'incorporation of the child into society', but as the *succession of the generations.*

More even than this, if we accept Piaget's theory that children reinvent knowledge, then not only do they transmit the values of the society, but they change with time and in the process they alter society's understanding and consciousness. As Dryden (1886: 262, part 3, 1.392) said, 'And thus the child imposes on the man.' In this way children, *as children,* by their very existence affect the patterns of behaviour and attitudes of the older generations, as well as acquiring and mutating existing ones which they carry into the future.

The Influence of the Visible

In South Africa today children have also emerged from the shadows to invade the arena and the history books usually reserved for adults. The phenomenon is neither new nor unique to South Africa: examples range from the Children's Crusade of 1212 to the Cambodian children of the Khmer Rouge, who seized the 're-education' initiative from the seniors of their society and took control of their own lives and those of many adults. The influence of such children's movements has arguably been relatively fleeting in the long-term though of great moment for those affected by the chaos of the events at the time. It remains to be seen what importance the revolt of the schoolchildren in South Africa will have when viewed retrospectively in future decades. A strong argument may be made, as by Chikane in his examination of the issue in this book, that more than the immediate political repercussions must be assessed. The indirect effects on attitudes of both the adult and rising generations may well prove to be the deciding factor in making the schoolchildren's revolt a permanent landmark in South African history. Certainly, at present any examination of current political developments and influences in South Africa must include children as an active and visible force, quite apart from their less visible but more deep-rooted effects discussed in the preceding section.

South African Peculiarities

Children, then, inevitably if inconspicuously have a major effect on the economy, social policy, way of life, and attitudinal developments, with all that the last implies. They may also have a more obviously direct effect on the course of political events. The importance of examining the role of children in society is, however, further increased in South Africa by a series of features peculiar to the society, as the studies in this book show. In what follows we discuss three of the most critical, before broaching the subject of how such research might be undertaken.

1. Social engineering and socialization

Since 1948 the South African government has placed more faith than is usual in most countries in the use of direct legal intervention to organize the most personal details of people's lives. The Population Registration Act, No.30 of 1950, together with Proclamation 123 of 1967, introduced no less than nine categories into which everyone in the country had to be classified. The main divisions, in current terminology, are 'white', 'Black' (that is, African), and 'Coloured', with 'Asians' (subdivided into Chinese and Indians) as the main subdivision of 'Coloured'. In terms of the Group Areas Act, No.41 of 1950 (as amended), each group may live only in separately allocated areas. Except for private schools, children may be educated only with members of the same 'race', unless special permission has been received to attend a school with children of another 'race'. White children may be educated only in their official home language. The nature of white children's education in government schools is further prescribed: it is to be 'Christian' and 'National', as defined by the government.[1] At the time of writing, Africans may not stay in an urban area for more than seventy-two hours unless they qualify for one of the categories of exemption, which depend on birth in an urban area, 'legal' work there, or marriage to a man with permission to be there who also has an approved house. Until 1985 both marriage and sexual relations between whites and members of other groups was forbidden, with sexual transgressions followed by prison sentences. A host of other regulations and laws bolster these divisive controls. In addition, forced population relocations have taken place on a scale more massive than that conducted by the USSR under its Deportation of Nationalities

Policy (Conquest 1970; Surplus People's Project 1983). As a result, while the concept of race has been thoroughly discredited as a meaningful biological classification system, it has acquired a pseudo-reality because of its socio-political consequences. Generations of children have now grown up within this system, with uniquely different experiences and attitudes from and about each other despite being members of one nation.

The implications for the future of this type of social engineering must be a major concern of social and political planners. The legacy for the future is twofold: the material deprivation suffered by underprivileged groups, and the attitudes with which children are imbued. A number of chapters in this book concentrate on the provision made for children of different groups; others focus on questions of socialization, although the two aspects are closely interconnected. In the latter category, different disciplines are brought to bear on specific aspects of socialization and on how different groups are socialized. For example, Foster's survey of research in this and other countries on the development of racially oriented attitudes among children examines the psychological literature on the subject, while anthropologists, sociologists, and linguists bring different approaches to the topic. By looking at children these studies hold up an enlarging mirror to society's attitudes and policies, and highlight the problems and contradictions within them.

Various interlinked themes emerge. The first is the extent to which the desired aims of the government's separation and socialization policies have been realized and what factors have contributed to failures. While the overwhelming evidence of the studies is of how isolated from each other the children of different communities are, there are also interesting sidelights on breakdowns in the attempts to inculcate approved government attitudes. Thus McCormick, for example, shows how political and social pressures are leading to increased bilingualism in her sample of coloured children as their parents, for non-academic reasons, fight to have them taught in English rather than Afrikaans. A second and related theme emerging from the studies concerns inherent contradictions of the apartheid system as it affects children. One type of contradiction is that between the forms of socialization desired by the government and some of its policies; another is that between government policies and different groups' own interests or ethics. Thus, for example, Nasson on education in general, Le Roux on the experience of Afrikaner children,

Roux on children of the resettlement camps, and Chikane on the children's revolt all illustrate in different ways the two-edged nature of education which teaches critical ability. As they demonstrate, it may be subversive of Afrikaner-approved ethics but not usually of Afrikaner politics when provided for Afrikaans children, while simultaneously having a very different effect when provided for African and coloured youth. Similarly, the Le Roux paper provides an interesting contrast to that by Frankental and Shain on Jewish children, illustrating as they do the interaction of the educational system with different ethical ideals to produce rather different effects.

To reveal how far the socialization of children buttresses power and domination is not, we would argue, peripheral to studies of the place of children in society. In his efforts to reformulate the analysis of power, Foucault (1980) argues that attempts to think in terms of a totality of power have proved a hindrance in research. He suggests that we ask, rather, what are the various contrivances of power operating at different levels of society. We should seek to describe power, he suggests, in 'the manifold forms of domination that can be exercised within society . . . [and] the multiple forms of subjugation that have a place and function within the social organism' (1980: 96). He recommends that the analysis of domination should be concerned with power at the point of its direct and immediate relationship with its target. In his view power should be examined from the bottom up, rather than the top down, starting from its infinitesimal mechanisms and traced through the net-like organization wherein individuals are the vehicles of power, up through the ever more general mechanisms to forms of global domination. In the investigation, he stresses, one should not neglect the apparatuses of knowledge evolved, organized and put into circulation by the subtle mechanisms of power. To view capitalist society, he suggests that we dismantle the formula of a generalized bourgeoisie and identify the agents responsible for control in society — those which consitute the immediate social entourage, such as the family, parents, and doctors. They enable mechanisms of power to function. Phenomena of repression or exclusion have their instruments and their logic at the effective level of the family, of the immediate environment, of the most basic units of society.

If his suggestions are correct, then to understand control in South Africa we must examine power in the basic units of society: the family, the classroom, the playground, the clinic, the street corners, the prison cells. Children are dominated and learn to dominate — and to resist —

within these units. They carry their knowledge with them into adulthood. Ezekiel Mphahlele in his autobiography (1965: 17) illustrates the point very clearly.

> We learned a great deal at the fireplace, even before we were aware of it: history, tradition and custom, code of behaviour, communal responsibility, social living and so on.

The studies of the effects of social engineering and socialization found in this book should be viewed within the framework advocated by Foucault. We suggest it is a framework particularly useful for understanding the true import of domination in South Africa. Apartheid ideology is usually analyzed so exclusively in abstract terms that there is a tendency to ignore the actual mechanisms through which government policy becomes social reality for the smallest building blocks in society: the family, the home, and the children.

2. Definitions and divisions

Analysts of South Africa are also usually too preoccupied with the chaos created by the use of racial and citizenship definitions to consider the role other definitions of social groups play in this very divided society. Yet the different concepts utilized in defining who are classified as children have a number of important social and policy implications for South Africa.

The criteria used in defining groups, as Ardener (1978) has shown in *Defining Females*, can themselves reveal as much as they qualify. Ariès (1962) points out that the concept of childhood varies widely in different periods of history and at different places. A range of criteria may be used to distinguish the transition from childhood to adulthood. For some societies, for example, marriage has been regarded as the marker; in others some *rite de passage*; or, as in South African civil law, age may define who is and who is not a child. But in even so apparently unambiguous a definition as age are hidden many other assumptions. The stated justification for a definition of childhood by age is a socio-biological one — that people under a certain age are in general incapable or only partially capable of responsible judgement, and therefore cannot be held responsible or fully responsible for their actions and must be protected by society. Until the age of seven, for example, a child is presumed to be completely without criminal capacity, while until the age of twenty-one a person cannot be held to have contractual capacity if unassisted by his or her guardian — with five minor exceptions created by statute (Boberg 1977: 568-70). The concept of adolescence, discussed by Molteno, Kibel, and Roberts in the chapter on child health, comes within this sphere of thought. The adolescent is a half-formed adult and so should be treated as partially responsible but also afforded some protection by society, not simply classed as an adult. Current scientific research supports this and the law therefore sounds eminently reasonable until one examines it more broadly. For example, eighteen is the minimum age for voters in South Africa and the age at which young white men become liable for military service. The implication is that at eighteen people are responsible enough to help decide the fate of their country and to kill, but not to order their own affairs unassisted. And are these voters and killers to be regarded as adults or children?

Another example of the ambiguity of the apparently unambiguous criterion of age is supplied by the state welfare system — a branch of the law. It provides that state maintenance for white and coloured children shall terminate when they reach eighteen years of age, while for African children it stops when they turn sixteen. One implication is that Africans are responsible and mature enough to finish school and enter the labour market two years before the rest of the nation's children. Welfare officials, when asked to justify this apparent anomaly, explain that Africans are not considered dependent at that age — so it would appear that financial dependence rather than irresponsibility is the legal criterion for deciding whether someone is immature enough to require financial support. This still begs the question, however, of what makes Africans of sixteen more independent than white or coloured children of that age. And what if the African aged sixteen is patently not self-supporting and unable to become so, being unskilled in an over-supplied market for unskilled labour? It makes no difference; the state maintenance grant stops. It would therefore seem that some other concept is involved when defining what causes an African to be treated as an independent adult at sixteen, while those who are white or coloured are not. While this finding may hardly surprise the reader, its policy implications are important for future governments pledged to equal treatment for children.

As the papers in this book show, clashes between criteria used in defining childhood are not found only in the broader legal system. South Africa has a population with a richly varied assortment of values, traditions, religions, and ways of life. Not surprisingly, therefore, different criteria are in use among different groups. Sometimes these do not cause problems. Frankental and Shain describe how a Jew becomes classified as an adult after his or her barmitzvah or batmitzvah at the age of thirteen. However, it is clearly understood by all concerned that this reception into the adult community pertains only within a religious context, and that claims to be treated as an adult in any other would be given short shrift. In contrast, however, boys who have undergone initiation ceremonies in certain African communities, with examples ranging from the Transvaal to the Cape, are regarded as men within those societies and may no longer be disciplined by women, irrespective of the boys' physical age. Some are as young as six years of age; many are in their mid-teens. Yet, apart from exceptional cases of the type described by Schärf, Powell, and Thomas in their chapter on street children, there is no question of most initiates becoming financially or legally independent of their families. They remain at home, under the control of the head of the family. But, as discussed in several chapters, an increasingly prominent feature of African society is the number of female-headed households. The combination of these facts has serious implications for South African society in terms of socialization.

The studies in this volume talk of children from birth to reproduction and reflect a number of definitions of childhood, either explicitly or implicitly. There are, however, many more in use in South Africa. Our purpose is, in part, to draw attention to their implications and invite close examination of preconceptions about childhood that shape the nation's institutions.

3. *Children and Change*

The third particular feature of South Africa which makes the study of its children so important is that it is a society in the throes of major and rapid social change. The argument is not that it is unique in this respect: many societies have experienced large-scale urbanization; mass immigration on a scale greater than South Africa's has been a feature of several countries; some have found their national incomes soaring; others have seen the majority of their society discarding one way of life and set of values in favour of another, as has happened in South Africa with the 'detribalization' of a large section of the population. But the scale and combination of these factors, together with the effects of such social engineering measures as mass population removals and influx control, puts South Africa high on the list of societies in the midst of basic social change. In addition, there are the extensive effects of political unrest.

In such a situation the discontinuities of experience between children and their parents or grandparents rob the younger generation of the role models so essential for the transmission of values and experience which have been found useful for dealing with their world. The most extreme example presented in these studies is that of the resettlement camps, where as Roux shows the transition from rural farming community to camp slum renders the accumulated expertise of the adult useless and thus liable to be rejected by the younger generation. However, changes in occupation and income can have much the same effect on a lesser scale. Buijs's chapter on the Indian children of a Natal sugar mill demonstrates this phenomenon, which had occurred a generation earlier for many Jewish and Afrikaans children. Moreover, conditions resulting from urbanization and the effects of apartheid may disrupt family life to such an extent that old values and modes of behaviour can no longer be followed. The description by Preston-Whyte and Louw of the behaviour causing and resulting from a Zulu teenage pregnancy illustrates this. In other cases the normal role model may be removed from the child's life either by family break-up and the effects of apartheid, as described by Burman and Fuchs, or by the child's reactions to an unbearable home situation, as Schärf, Powell, and Thomas show in their examination of street children who have run away from home. The recurrent theme of all these papers is how children in many situations in South Africa are having to work out their own destiny, values, and life style to an extent far greater than is usual in more settled societies. The result, as Chikane's and Roux's papers show, is an increase in the importance of the peer group in the process of socialization. The potential repercussions for South Africa both at present and in the future pressingly require examination if social policy is not to run aground on false assumptions.

Research Problems and Goals

We have argued that research on children in South Africa is urgently needed. Indeed, in compiling this book our choice of papers was constricted not only by limitations of space but also by the dearth of research on children. However, some problems should be noted for those undertaking it. The study of childhood has traditionally been the preserve of certain disciplines: health, psychology, and sociology in particular. The danger in this insulation is twofold: first, that analysts may fail to place studies of childhood in the context of the wider society; and, second, that they may fail to take advantage of relevant theoretical advances in other disciplines. To talk of the clinical problems of malnutrition, for example, without taking cognizance of the social causes that frustrate its prevention, is indeed an academic luxury of narrowed vision which South Africa cannot afford. Similarly, no discipline is so suited to understanding the place and problems of childhood as not to need the insights of other approaches. Interdisciplinary work is indeed fraught with many problems, but the price of staying in a safe academic alcove is a much narrower understanding of the subject, in this case one as varied and important as the children of the society. The need is rather to break the seals and persuade experts in a wide variety of disciplines to focus on the concerns of childhood in relation to the encompassing social, political, and economic issues. One of our aims in compiling this collection of papers into a book was to encourage people who do not normally focus their expertise on the sphere of childhood to do so. Hence, for example, we have a paper by an economist and demographer, Charles Simkins, a political sociologist, Pieter le Roux, and three lawyers, Fiona McLachlan, Rebecca Fuchs, and Sandra Burman. In time such studies, read and combined together, should provide deeper insights into the multi-faceted problems South Africa faces.

For example, Simkins's analysis of structural change provides a backdrop against which the findings of microstudies can be evaluated. He documents changes in marital status patterns. Between 1970 and 1980 in every population group change was away from the married state. The context of childhood must have been affected. Marriage, says Simkins, was rendered least stable among Africans and the instability coincided with the effective imposition of modern mobility controls and a restrictive urban housing policy. The highest incidence of female-headed households occurs among Africans: in the 'homeland' areas it reaches nearly 60 per cent. He estimates that in 1980 twenty-seven per cent of African husbands lived away from their wives and that 17 per cent of children lived away from their mothers. Burman and Fuchs, in their study of what happens to children on the break-up of marriages, provide an analysis of how the South African socio-legal system promotes this pattern in the event of family break-up, why it varies between different population groups, and how it is increasing the differences in the way South African children of each group experience family life.

The effect of these social patterns becomes clearer when juxtaposed with studies from other disciplines. In the survey by Molteno, Kibel, and Roberts on childhood health, for example, the results are given of 5 000 interviews of rural African families conducted by Dr Trudy Thomas. She found that the most important determinant of the nutritional health of the child was the organization of his or her home life. Some of her findings may be briefly listed.

The Social Background of Children

| | Percentages | |
	With Kwashiorkor	Well-nourished
Illegitimate	62	26
In the personal care of their mothers	33	78
Fathers were migrants	86	-
supporting the family financially	14	71
deserted the family	60	5
Children lived where breadwinner worked	1	21
Children lived in a family group	24	83

Similarly, Molteno, Kibel, and Roberts also cite research by Fincham and Thomas (1984) to show that in the commercial farming area of Diaz, where the nutrition of children is good, 73 per cent of the fathers are employed at home and 86 per cent of the mothers stay at home. As they point out, the likelihood of malnutrition is greater in homes where the mother is the chief breadwinner.

To understand, however, what these macro-patterns mean at the micro-level, it is necessary to turn to two other studies in the book, both by anthropologists but using different techniques. Preston-Whyte and Louw examine a female-headed household in the making, from the point of view of grandmother, mother, and child. They show the implications of these policy developments for individuals with whom one can identify, putting flesh on the statistics and bringing them alive. And finally, in a detailed study of how seven-year-old children view their relatives, Reynolds looks up from a child's perspective at the complex and changing world of the family in a squatter camp. In examining with linguistic tools their view of kinship, she allows them to 'speak' of how fluid their social surroundings are and who figures large in it.

These five studies illuminate each other. For example, they raise such questions as whether, with female-headed households becoming the norm in some areas, the legal and welfare systems should be adapted to relate to such households as the norm and not as instances of social pathology. Similarly, the study of child care by sociologists Cock, Klugman, and Emdon permits a more detailed understanding of the problems outlined in the socio-legal study of family break-up; Zille's study of childbirth fills out the statistical picture provided by the study of child health; the studies of street children and the children's revolt paint in the background to McLachlan's stark picture of children in jail. In this way it is hoped to generate new questions and fresh insights into the problems which await today's children in the future.

Finally, it is necessary to remember that tomorrow's policy makers in many political, social, and economic spheres are likely to be drawn from today's students. Children are too important both as children and as future adults to be relegated to specialist study at graduate level or the occasional lecture on developmental psychology. Under-graduates in economics, for example, hear about poverty but need to be shown how it can be transmitted from mother to child. They also need to learn how discrimination against women discriminates against the growing number of children who are wholly dependent on their mothers as breadwinners. Similarly, law students need to realize that the family is not neatly encompassed within the field labelled 'family law'. Such subjects as administrative, criminal, and constitutional law all have crucial implications for the family unit and the children it is meant to nurture. The results of the research on children which we have advocated should be incorporated into undergraduate teaching in all social sciences, and disseminated to the public at large. The situation of many children today is threatened and thus endangers the next generation, too; but if enough people are made aware of the problem, perhaps something can yet be done to salvage tomorrow.

Notes

1. These terms were defined by the Minister of Education, Arts and Science in 1967 during the debate on the National Education Policy Act, No.39 of 1967: 'my interpretation of the "Christian character of education" is that education shall build on the basis of the traditional Western culture and view of life which recognize the validity of the Biblical principles, norms and values . . . . By "national" it is understood that education shall build on the ideal of the national development of all citizens of South Africa, in order that our own identity and way of life shall be preserved, and in order that the South African nation may constantly appreciate its task as part of Western civilization' (*Hansard* 6 col. 2011). Pieter le Roux, in his chapter in this volume, discusses some implications of the policy.

Household Composition and Structure in South Africa

Charles Simkins

1. Framework of this Study

This study has quite a narrow focus. The five variables with which it is centrally concerned are: *age*; *sex*; *marital status*; *kinship* (as Gilbert (1971) has shown, it is possible to build up a complete kinship network if for every individual one knows the identity of the father, mother, next oldest sibling (or oldest if the individual is the youngest), spouse or spouses, and first child); and *incidence of household headship*.

From these variables, inferences can be made about the distribution of households by: *size* and *type*. Hammel and Laslett (1974) advocate the use of a typology of households which uses the broad categories: single, no family, simple, extended, and multiple.

Clearly there are other variables to which these can be related, and the set selected for attention will be discussed below. But there is a whole series of issues in the sociology of the family which will not be dealt with here at all. To use a checklist extracted from Steyn (1982), these are: the functions of the family in society; child abuse; the changing roles of husband and wife; counselling; and the structure of authority in the family.

Why then is this study worth doing? The household is the crucial mediating institution between personal income and expenditure. Income levels are set in factor markets[1] for the most part; they are also defined by opportunities for non-marketed production and state transfer rules. Incomes accrue to individuals, yet these incomes are aggregated within households and decisions about labour supply, consumption, and savings are taken on a household basis. The analysis of income distribution and poverty also involves the study of households. Households may be poor because of inadequate sources of income; the inadequacy may also be because of household composition and structure. In many countries, distinct relationships between household size, type, and headship on the one hand, and poverty on the other, have been found. Consideration of the relationship between individual and household is a goal of this study.

A second reason is that, in a period of rapid social change, a study of changing household structure may provide useful indices of the extent of social change. As Van den Berghe observes, there is a correlation between 'social organisation variables' and 'kinship organisation variables' (Van den Berghe, 1979: chapter 4), though to erect functionalist arguments on the basis of an imperfect correlation would be unwise. The interesting question at the present stage of South Africa's history is this: given the extent and progress of industrialization and the increasing involvement of everyone in this development, how far has there been a convergence of household structure between groups of people who were (or more accurately, who might have been) in very different positions in earlier times? South African data are, of course, always organized on a racial basis, so an empirical investigation must proceed by interracial comparison. In some respects this would in any case be the reasonable way to proceed; in others not, as will be indicated below.

A third reason is that, while qualitative aspects of the sociology of the family will not be discussed here, this does not mean that findings in these fields cannot be illuminated from studies of structure. Indeed, without a sense of structural change, this or that development or problem turned up by microstudies cannot be evaluated properly with respect to likely incidence and therefore significance. Perspective on problems is not as useful as finding solutions to them; nonetheless, it helps.

Every society, or every culturally homogeneous segment of a society, contains notions about desired marriage, fertility, and household composition patterns. These notions are not equally developed in every adult, nor is there complete consistency in the notions that do exist. Nonetheless, it is usually possible to construct from these notions ideal-types in the forms of consistent sets of rules. There have been such ideal-typical constructions in relation to segments of South

African society and these will be considered shortly.

In relation to these ideal-types, one can also discern disorganizing factors. Of these the first two are universal.

(i) *Divorce and desertion.* Under most systems of rules (perhaps not quite all) marriage is intended for life and quite often is hedged about with exchanges of property and other practices to ensure that the will of the parties involved is not the only basis of its continuance. Associated with divorce and desertion, quite apart from psychological burdens, are frequently to be found problems of support for a part of a formerly unified family.

(ii) *Illegitimacy.* One essential component of a rule system is a set of rules specifying when births are legitimate and when they are not. These rules are usually associated with marriage rules, though sometimes in complex ways.

(iii) The third disorganizing factor has universal aspects but is more usefully discussed specifically in relation to South Africa. Certain sets of rules presume certain kinds of arrangements about co-residence and housing, which may come to be inappropriate as settlement patterns change. Ways of forming households in the country may be quite impossible to follow in the city where housing is provided on entirely different assumptions. One may be able to maintain traditionally accepted housing densities (perhaps low in relation to urban densities) on a self-build basis on cheap land but not on a rented basis in expensively built housing on high-price urban plots. For certain groups of people housing availability functions as a constraint on building up large households; for other groups, shortages may frustrate desires to live on a more nuclear basis.

(iv) The fourth factor is more specific still and applies only to Africans in South Africa. Influx and labour control laws oblige large numbers of men and some women to live apart from their families. As will be shown, this has massive effects on African household structure. The pathologies associated with these institutions have often been listed (see e.g. Wilson 1972). Survey evidence collected by Moller and Schlemmer suggests that not all such split families would be reunited if the laws permitted free choice of place of residence and work (see Moller and Schlemmer 1977: 17-25). The effects of decades of this system could therefore be expected to survive (in diminished or probably attenuated form) the demise of the system itself.

This section concludes with definitions. Particular definitions of the household and family are used in the sources from which the data for this study are drawn. A household is primarily a *co-residential* group. All the South African evidence shows that co-residents in a household are, on average, nearly all related, usually by the closest kinship links. Some sources require households to have a *common budget*; this is the case in the Bureau of Market Research's studies for example. But there is an element of vagueness in this criterion and, in any case, it is not applied in the major government sources.

A family, as defined in the 1970 Population Census, has one of four structures: husband and wife; father, mother, and children; father and children; and mother and children. This is the most elementary definition possible.

The classification of households by type is not so simple. Typologies used by analysts are not uniform, as will become clear in Section 3. Most typologies are, however, variations on the five types given here.

(i) *Solitary* i.e. 1 person households. Even here, difficulties of interpretation arise. A married person living on his or her own might be regarded as an incomplete nuclear household.

(ii) *No family.* These household units consist of two or more people who are unrelated or who are related in such a way as to prevent them from being regarded as nuclear, extended, or multiple households. Unmarried siblings living together would be an example.

(iii) *Nuclear.* These households consist of a single family as defined above, with no other members present.

(iv) *Extended.* These households consist of one family nucleus plus at least one other relative (such as a grandmother or an uncle).

(v) *Multiple.* These households have at least two family nuclei, with or without extensions.

In cases (iii), (iv), and (v) non-family members such as lodgers may be present.

As an example of the difficulties which may arise, consider a widow with two daughters, one of whom is married. Both daughters have children. If the widow, her son-in-law, her daughters, and all her grandchildren form a household, it is a multiple household. If, for example, the unmarried daughter and her children move away, it is an extended household. But what if we are speaking of an African family in a 'homeland' and all the middle generation are away from home most of the year, working elsewhere? Then we are left with a grandmother and grandchildren, some of whom are each others' siblings, while others are cousins. One way of describing the situation is to call such a household an incomplete multiple household. Another way would be to describe it as a no-family household, since there is no nuclear unit in it. The former is more in line with the spirit of the classification, but in this case and a number of others there is room for disagreement, making comparisons of results a matter for caution.

2. *South African Households: Ideal Types*

(i) *Whites*

There is very little material on white household structure. The regulating ideal is widely taken to be that of the nuclear family with a substantial proportion of unmarried but adult children forming single households on their own. Evidence in support of the nuclear family ideal was found by Van der Merwe (1969), who studied attitudes in four Afrikaans communities in the 1960s. On average, the following percentages of respondents *disapproved* of:

Parents living with a nuclear family	86
Married children living with their parents	95
Other kin living with a nuclear family	95

(Van der Merwe, 1969: 19)

and one would expect similar attitudes among English-speakers, except possibly those with close links with Mediterranean countries and their former colonies.

(ii) *Asians*

Discussions of the ideal-type among Indian South Africans have tended to centre on the concept of the joint family (see, for instance, Jithoo 1978). The discussions have been derived from analysis in India itself. The joint family consists of two or more male-headed elementary families joined together by patrilineal ties between the married males, the relationship of these men usually being that of brothers. As well as these genealogical aspects, the joint family is, according to Jithoo, distinguished by three other features: co-residence; commensality, the sharing of meals; and implicit 'shares' which certain family members have in property that is jointly owned (Jithoo 1978: 88-89).

The joint family, then, is associated with a quite specific structure which can be looked for in the statistical evidence. It should also be noted that it underpins a certain form of economic organization: that of the small enterprise based on family labour.

(iii) *Africans*

Patrilineality and patrilocality were dominant features of society in South Africa prior to colonization. The social importance of the lineages is given a summary exposition by Steyn and Rip (1968: 502):

> The Bantu tribe [*sic*] only exhibits a limited amount of labour specialization and every household is to a large extent economically self-supporting with a strict division of labour based on sex. Each household is a replica of all the others, and mutual economic dependence does not serve as a basic principle for the joining together of the different households. Instead consanguinal bonds branch throughout a group and bind everyone together who claims descent from a common ancestor.[2]

When she marries, a woman leaves her natal home and goes to live with her husband's kin. She retains her membership of her father's lineage, but her children belong to that of her husband. The marriage is accompanied by the transfer of bridewealth from her husband (or husband's family) to her parents. Families are formed in the elementary way; each family has its own possessions and provisions. Polygyny is permitted; where this occurs, each wife lives in a separate dwelling.

Urbanization, and then denser forms of settlement in many parts of the 'homelands', has much modified this pattern. First, polygyny has almost entirely disappeared. Second, the limitations of housing supply transform simple two-generation families into extended two-generation and three-generation families. Third, the high incidence of illegitimacy results in a large number of female-headed households of two or three generations. These themes will be explored below when the survey and statistical evidence on African households is considered. An interesting question is the assessment of the regional variation in patterns.

(iv) *Coloureds*[3]

It would be a foolhardy analyst who tried to formulate a coloured ideal-type. A category composed of descendants of the Khoi and San, Malay slaves, and white-African unions in an assortment of social contexts could hardly be imagined to be following the same set of rules at any stage in its history. One consequence of this situation, which does not seem to have been sufficiently appreciated in the literature, is that there is a problem of deciding exactly what 'coloured marriage' is. A rather restrictive definition of either civil or religious is used (as opposed to civil, religious, and traditional for Africans) leading to low reported marriage rates and high reported illegitimacy rates. This will be discussed further below. One is obliged to proceed here on a strictly empirical basis, as the Theron Commission (1976) found.

3. Survey Evidence

(i) Whites

Argyle (1977) has published the results of a survey of 225 mixed working- and lower-middle-class white households in Durban. Predominantly English-speaking and adherents of mainstream churches, these households supplied sufficient information for Argyle to classify them in terms of the Hammel-Laslett typology. He found the distribution of households by type to be:

Solitaries	6%
No family	5%
Simple	67%
Extended	10%
Multiple	12%

(Argyle 1977: 108)

The interesting thing about these findings is that over a fifth of the households had an extended or multiple structure. Compared with historical data drawn from Laslett (1972), this proportion is high as is the proportion of three-generation households. Accordingly, Argyle cautions us against accepting 'the myth of the elementary family' in relation to white household structure.

Argyle offers two explanations for his findings. An older couple, widow, or widower may control more accomodation than they need and may therefore offer a home to a recently married child and its family, or to a divorced, widowed, or deserted child and its family. Alternatively, a young couple may take in one or more parents of either spouse if the parent(s) are no longer capable of looking after themselves.

Both of these explanations suppose that, for at least a substantial part of the white population, housing and acceptable services for the care of the old are sufficiently scarce and expensive to induce departures from nuclear organization. Argyle speculates that high white divorce rates may contribute significantly to this departure, a divorced mother and her children finding it difficult to live on their own. Data presented below will enable us to assess this claim.

(ii) *Coloureds*

Whisson (1976) reported the results of a study carried out in Ocean View near Simonstown in 1971 and 1975. He was able to put forward, for that community, an ideal developmental cycle:

> The ideal is that a young couple will set up house together at marriage, independent of either sets of parents. They will rear their children until all are independent and they will move in for their last few years with a daughter (preferably) who has space in her home for the elders. Such an ideal arrangement implies that the only exceptions to the general rule of two-generation family households should be in the case of elderly grandparents. Variations on the basis of wealth would be such that poor families might retain their children at home for a longer period, possibly leading to three-generation families at two periods of the cycle rather than only at the end (Whisson 1976: 258).

Whisson holds that his empirical findings confirm the general validity of this norm. His 197 households had the following distribution of structures:

Normal (i.e. simple or nuclear)	68%
Three generation	13%
Older kin present	14%
Non-kin present	5%

(Whisson 1976: 259)

These categories are not all directly comparable with those of Argyle; insofar as comparisons can be made, there is considerable similarity between the two samples. The main difference is that there are no 'solitary' nor 'no family' households present in the Ocean View sample. This can be ascribed to housing policy: Whisson reports that 'there is no place for persons living alone nor, in theory, for unrelated single people living together' (Whisson 1976: 257). Once allowance is made for this, the similarity becomes more striking. One should not, however, be misled into over-interpreting it. The samples are medium-sized and refer to particular, limited localities and the underlying demographic magnitudes (fertility, mortality, nuptiality) are substantially different for the two groups.

One should also bear in mind that Ocean View at the time of the study was a relatively new residential area. Many inhabitants had been displaced from elsewhere and extended families were split in the process. There had been relatively little time for new ones to form, so it is likely that the proportion of nuclear families was higher than in older urban settlements.

Two special features found by Whisson need to be noted here. The first is the existence of 'matrifocality', especially in the poorest sector. Whisson identified a hierarchy of residential-rights holders in the household group. At the core is the householder — a woman, even if most tenancies are held by men — and her dependent children. In the case of unregistered unions, in particular, the rights of women are established administratively as well as economically and socially. The rights of men are more tenuous if they are not official tenants.

The second feature is that the avoidance of conflicts between young single adult men and the rest of the household is achieved by these men returning home only to eat and sleep. The desire for independence which might, in more affluent circumstances and ones in which single accommodation is more easily available, give rise to single households is to some extent accommodated by younger men spending much of their non-working time with peer groups outside the home.

(iii) *Indians*

Butler-Adam and Venter (1984) have recently studied Indian household composition and structure as part of a housing study in Durban and Pietermaritzburg. They refer to Meer's 1969 finding that the joint family pattern was characteristic of between 30 per cent and 50 per cent of all families and that the percentage at that date was below that in earlier years (Butler-Adam and Venter 1984: vol. I, 87).

The distributions of households by type found were as follows:

	Durban(%)	*Pietermaritzburg(%)*
Solitary/no family	1	—
Simple or extended simple	79	87
Multiple (2 families)	16	10
Mutiple (3 or more families)	3	2
Sample size	1036	452

(Butler-Adam and Venter 1984: vol.I, 91 and vol.III, 89.)

Again, incompatibility of classification categories make precise cross-racial comparisons difficult, but there appears to be, in Durban at least, a higher proportion of multiple households than in the white or coloured samples. If one counts by elementary families rather than households, a third of families lived in multiple households in Durban and just under a quarter in Pietermaritzburg. There has probably been a decline in the incidence of the joint family in the fifteen years between Meer's study and that of Butler-Adam and Venter.

This impresson is substantiated by the finding that 90 per cent (in Durban) and 84 per cent (in Pietermaritzburg) of the multiple households were generational in nature 'consisting of the basic families of parents and a married son or daughter — in most cases a married son (or sons)' (Butler-Adam and Venter 1984: vol. I, 91). While some of these households could be regarded as joint families, others would not fit the description. Seven per cent and ten per cent respectively consist of families of brothers and/or sisters and the remainder are both generational and sibling units. While the joint family hypothesis clearly still has some explanatory power, these household forms could also be explained by the operation of factors discussed in relation to white and coloured households.

Equally revealing are findings on attitudes. Simple and multiple households were studied separately. In Durban 90 per cent and in Pietermaritzburg 95 per cent of simple households said they lived that way because they preferred to. The situation in the case of multiple households was more complex, as shown below.

Reason for Living in Multiple Household	*Durban(%)*	*Pietermaritzburg(%)*
Preference	5	4
Tradition	69	70
Shortage of accomodation	23	20

(Butler-Adam and Venter 1984: vol. I, 94 and vol. III, 92)

Further reasons for wanting to live in multiple households are mutual family help and economic commitments. Butler-Adam and Venter conclude that there are two reasons for a move away from the joint family: the pattern of public housing provision (which is mainly designed for nuclear families) and penetration of the nuclear family norm at the cultural level. Buijs's chapter in this volume illustrates some of the complexities of these developments. Yet planners must continue to take into account a minority preference for multiple family living.

(iv) *Africans*

There have been a number of studies of African household structure. Geographically, these have been mostly of conditions in the cities with some attention being paid to the reserves. It is of interest to compare conditions in the cities with those in the towns and in the rural areas outside the 'homelands'; such a comparison is possible and will be undertaken in the next section. Here an account will be given of some of the classic studies.

Marwick (1978) studied 500 households in the Nguni section of a Reef township in 1961. Ninety per cent of household heads were male and the households were distributed across categories as follows:

Solitary	8%
Couples without children	9%
Single parent and children	6%
Couple with children	48%
Extended and multiple households	27%
Others	2%

(Marwick 1978: 42)

What particularly interested Marwick was the analysis of extended relationships. He showed that if the extension involved the head of the household's generation, it was likely to be through a male. If the extension involved the children of the household, it was likely to be through a female, which was 'attributable to the greater frequency with which illegitimate children of daughters rather than sons are included in the household' (Marwick 1978: 45).

Marwick concluded that, among a significant proportion of households, matrifocalism had become the organizing principle, with the mother-child relationship being of principal importance and the role of the father peripheral. Nonetheless, he observed that over two-thirds of households had an essentially 'modern' form.

Pauw (1973) made a study of East London households in the early 1960s. His households were distributed across categories as follows:

Simple

Father-mother-children	21%
Mother-children	7%

Extended and Multiple

Male-headed multigeneration	17%
Female-headed multigeneration	19%
Father-mother-children extended	11%
Mother-children extended	11%
Other	17%

(Pauw 1973: 145)

Pauw's sample indicates that, by contrast with Marwick's Reef sample, simple or nuclear households were in a minority in East London. On the other hand, he observed, 'although so many households consist of multi-generation families, they usually do not grow into three or four generations along the traditionally important patriline' (Pauw 1973: 145). This can be inferred from the fact that 34 per cent of all households were female-headed nuclear, extended and multiple households; many of the heads had never been married. And most of the male-headed multigeneration households consisted of a married couple with husbandless daughters and their children, the majority of these daughters being unmarried mothers.

In the end, Pauw proposed that all the variants of household structure can be composed from only two basic types:

> the household consisting of or based on an elementary family during its earlier phase of growth — this being the major type — and a minor type based on the group consisting of an unmarried mother and her children. Both have the tendency to develop a multigeneration span, while the major type often loses the male head at an early stage (Pauw 1973: 154).

Pauw agrees with Marwick about the substantial incidence of matrifocalism (indeed, it is better attested in the Pauw sample), but denies that the husband-father *when present* plays only a marginal role in the household. He attributes this to the persistence of patrilineal and patriarchal values, although these have been undermined by a changing economic structure. His findings suggest that a distinction should be made between patrilineal and patriarchal *ideals*, which still command great support, and patrilineal and patriarchal *organization* which, the evidence suggests, is not the only form of organization there is.

Schlemmer and Stopforth (1974) found, on the basis of a survey conducted in the early 1970s, that 69 per cent of households in Namakgale, Phalaborwa, had a simple, nuclear structure. This, they observe, is unusually high and compares with Reader's (1966) estimate of 44 per cent based on the 1951 Population Census counts in several Zulu wards. One explanation they offer for this is the short period of residence of many Namakgale households. Interestingly, Pauw found a drop in multigeneration households when he compared Mdantsane (where many residents of Duncan Village, the site of his first survey, were moved in the 1960s) to Duncan Village. He concluded that the move had split a number of households into their nuclear components. The general hypothesis would then be that (other things being equal) the newer the African settlement, the higher the proportion of nuclear households.

4. Statistical Evidence

In principle, statistical evidence drawn from the Population Censuses and the Current Population Survey should serve to make more precise and to universalize the accounts developed so far. In practice, however, the data are fragmentary and presented in forms unsuited to our purposes, so that important questions will have to be left unresolved quite often. Nonetheless, a degree of clarification and illumination is possible.

(i) Fertility and Mortality

Table 1 presents measures of fertility and mortality for each race in 1980.

Table 1: Fertility and Mortality, 1980

	Whites		Coloureds		Asians		Africans	
Fertility								
Total fertility rate	2.05		3.35		2.85		5.21	
Mortality	M	F	M	F	M	F	M	F
Infant mortality rate	20	15	103	88	32	24	96	76
Life expectancy at five yrs	64.5	70.1	52.8	60.1	59.4	63.2	55.8	61.8

Source: Grobbelaar 1984

Notes: 1. The total fertility rate is a period rather than a cohort concept. It refers to a particular year. It is the average number of children a woman would have if successfully exposed to the probabilities of live birth in each cohort in the year in question. Usually the age limits of the fertile period are taken as 15 to 44, so that the total fertility rate is the number of children which would result from five years' exposure to the probabilities of live birth to women aged 15-19 plus those resulting from five years' exposure to the probabilities aged 20-24 plus . . . up to 40-44. No actual cohort of women has average fertility equal to any total fertility rate.

2. Fertility rates can be measured in a number of ways. As noted in the chapter by Burman and Fuchs in this volume, a recent President's Council report put the rates at 963 female children born per 1 000 white women, the respective rates for coloureds, Asians and Africans being 1 427, 1 278 and 2 500. These are at most only a little different from the total fertility rates cited.

3. Infant mortality rate refers to deaths within a year of birth per 1 000 live births.

4. Foreign Africans excluded.

The total fertility rates vary greatly across the races and these differences are the most important determinants of differences in average household size, far more important than differences in mortality or household organization. Differences in infant mortality offset, to a slight extent, difference in fertility, since fertility is highest among races with the highest infant mortality. From the point of view of the numbers of children who survive infancy, a high fertility rate accompanied by high infant mortality is equivalent to a somewhat lower fertility rate accompanied by low infant mortality.

Life expectancies, combined with average differences in age between married men and married women and remarriage probabilities, control the incidence of widowers and widows in the older age cohorts. Except in the case of Asians, there is a difference of more than five years in male and female life expectancies and this factor alone explains much of the high proportion of widows to widowers.

(ii) *Marriage*

Neither the 1970 nor the 1980 Population Censuses have published satisfactory cross-tabulations of marital status by age and sex. From the published data and an unpublished comparable tabulation for Africans, Table 2 can be compiled.

Table 2 shows that the proportion of persons married and living together in each age cohort is generally highest in the case of whites,

Table 2: *Persons Married or Living Together per 1 000 in Each Age Cohort, 1970*

Age	Male				Female			
	Whites	Coloureds	Asians	Africans	Whites	Coloureds	Asians	Africans
0-20	2	1	1	2	18	7	24	14
20-24	294	196	199	172	598	332	525	421
25-34	807	651	748	580	883	712	784	706
35-64	902	850	933	848	808	765	739	713
65+	775	693	719	803	326	349	229	360
Average age of married and 'living together' people	44.8	42.7	41.0	43.0	41.7	39.9	36.1	37.7
Average male/female difference	3.1	2.8	4.9	5.3				

Note: 1. These rates have been calculated from raw figures and no attempt has been made to correct them for 'spouse leak' — the fact that the number of married men enumerated does not quite match the number of married women enumerated.

2. 'Living together' figures are available only by race and sex. They have been allocated to age cohorts *pro rata* to the distribution by age of married persons.

3. Foreign Africans are included.

intermediate in the case of Asians and lowest for coloureds and Africans. The exception to the rule is in the sixty-five plus age cohort where the internal age distribution varies considerably by race; an adequate interpretation here would require a disaggregation impossible to execute on the basis of the published data.

The racial variation in marriage rates coincides with the racial variation in average income per head. On that account one may judge a considerable part of the variation revealed by the figures as accurately reflecting reality. Marriage, in every society, has to be afforded. On the other hand, some of the variation may be merely apparent, in that it is harder to decide just what African marriage is; given this, there is likely to be a degree of under-enumeration of persons as 'married'.[4]

The average age of married people varies within a fairly narrow range for men (between forty-one and forty-five) and women (between thirty-six and forty-one). The average age difference between man and wife is about three years for whites and coloureds and about five years for Asians and Africans.

Have marriage patterns changed since 1970? Table 3 sets out the distributions of marital status by race and sex in 1970 and 1980.

Table 3: Distribution of the Population by Marital Status, 1970 and 1980 (%) (All ages)

MALES	Whites		Coloureds		Asians		Africans	
	1970	1980	1970	1980	1970	1980	1970	1980
Never married	51.7	48.3	70.1	68.1	65.1	60.4	69.0	69.7
Married	45.4	47.3	24.1	26.4	33.0	37.5	27.7	26.0
Living together	0.3	1.2	3.9	3.7	0.7	0.8	1.9	3.2
Widowed	1.4	1.4	1.5	1.3	1.0	1.1	1.0	0.8
Divorced	1.2	1.8	0.4	0.5	0.2	0.2	0.4	0.4
FEMALES	Whites		Coloureds		Asians		Africans	
	1970	1980	1970	1980	1970	1980	1970	1980
Never married	45.3	42.2	66.5	64.3	60.7	54.8	62.4	66.7
Married	44.9	45.6	24.1	25.7	32.6	37.3	27.5	23.3
Living together	0.3	1.2	3.9	3.9	0.7	0.7	2.5	3.3
Widowed	7.7	8.1	4.7	5.0	5.4	6.3	6.7	5.6
Divorced	1.8	2.9	0.8	1.1	0.6	0.9	0.9	1.0

Source: 1970 and 1980 Population Censuses

Notes: 1. Computed from raw figures with no correction for 'spouse leak'.

2. Foreign Africans included.

3. Transkei, Bophuthatswana, Venda excluded in 1980.

On the three minority statuses, Table 3 tells us that there was an increased propensity among whites both to 'live together' and to be divorced; and that there was an increased propensity among Africans to 'live together', more clearly discernible from the male figures.

In interpreting changes in the broader pattern, changing age compositions have to be borne in mind. Had age-specific distributions of marital status remained constant from 1970 to 1980, the proportion of white males married would have been 48.6 per cent, the corresponding proportion for females being 47.1 per cent. Comparison with realized figures suggest a slight drop in the propensity to marry. Expected figures for coloureds would have been 26.2 per cent and 27.0 per cent, also above realized figures. For Asians, the figures would have been 37.0 per cent and 36.7 per cent, suggesting very little change.

I have carried out a more detailed analysis of the position in respect of South African born Africans since 1960 elsewhere (Simkins 1984a) and reproduce my conclusions here:

> The things to notice . . . are:
>   (i) a drop over time in the widow/widower rates . . .
>   (ii) a rise from very low levels of divorce rates as one might expect.
>   (iii) most interestingly, a rise in the never married rates, especially for women but also for men. This rise is powerful enough to more than counteract the effect of dropping widowhood rates on marriage rates, which therefore also drop.
>
>   The rise can be dated from about 1960 since the 1951 and 1960 marital status schedules are considerably closer to one another than those for 1960 and 1970 or 1970 and 1980. Its start therefore coincides with the effective imposition of modern mobility controls on Africans; this coupled with a restrictive urban housing policy is likely to have made marriage more difficult and less rewarding (Simkins 1984a: 199).

To summarize: underlying marital status patterns were highly stable between 1970 and 1980 in the case of Asians, somewhat less so in the cases of coloureds and whites, and least stable in the case of Africans. All change was away from the married state.

Finally, illegitimacy rates are of interest. Rates in 1980 were:

Whites	5%
Coloureds	52%
Asians	15%
Africans	43%

Source: Department of Statistics, *Report* 07-01-08, 1983; Simkins 1984a: 208.

The coloured illegitimacy rate is based on a restricted definition of marriage and, as will be seen, is not as serious as it looks. The African illegitimacy rate estimate is closer to a reasonable reflection of the situation. As has already been suggested, it conditions African household structure to a marked extent.

(iii) *Household Structure: Whites, Coloureds and Asians*

The 1970 Population Census published material on families and dwellings. While the form of the published data is poorly suited to our interests, some progress will be made by reviewing it. Table 4 summarizes the information on families.

Table 4: Data on Families: Whites, Coloureds, and Asians, 1970

	Whites			Coloureds			Asians		
Total population	3773282			2050699			630372		
Non-family persons	334867 (9.7%)			188735 (10.1%)			21953 (3.6%)		
Family persons	3438415			1861964			608419		
Families by Type									
Husband and wife	227738 (24.7%)			38353 (10.7%)			11126 (9.2%)		
Father, mother and children	629612 (68.2%)			248618 (69.1%)			93854 (77.4%)		
Father and children	9448 (1.0%)			10873 (3.0%)			2867 (2.4%)		
Mother and children	55832 (6.1%)			61686 (17.2%)			13459 (11.1%)		
Total families	922630			359530			121306		
Average Composition	M	F	M + F (%)	M	F	M + F (%)	M	F	M + F (%)
Head/wife	0.9	1.0	53	0.8	1.0	35	0.9	1.0	38
Children under 10yrs	0.4	0.4	22	0.9	0.9	35	0.7	0.7	28
Children over 10yrs	0.5	0.4	25	0.8	0.8	30	0.9	0.8	34
Total av. family size	3.7			5.2			5.0		

Note: Although the source does not specifically say so, the terms 'mother' and 'father' are certain to include 'stepmother' and 'stepfather'.

One becomes a 'non-family' person by living on one's own or with unrelated persons or by living in a household where one is neither the head, part of a married couple, or a parent or child. The incidence of non-family persons is small; in the case of whites, persons living on their own (either young or old) probably make up a considerable proportion of non-family persons. In the case of coloureds, tenants probably make up a large part of this group. In the case of Asians, the tightness of family organization would account for the very low figure.

Turning to the analysis of elementary family units by type, one notes that the proportion of husband and wife pairs is considerably higher for whites than for coloureds and Asians. This is a reflection both of lower fertility (so that newly married white couples wait longer for their first child) and the greater ability to live alone of older couples whose children have left home. The other interesting variation is in the proportion of mother-and-children units. This reflects illegitimacy rates; the 1980 illegitimacy figures (and those for earlier years) corroborate Table 4. Divorce and widowhood are contributory factors, though they are only secondary. Notice that in the case of coloured people, despite a reported illegitimacy rate of 52 per cent, 69 per cent of elementary family units are of the father-mother-children type and 3 per cent more are headed by a father.

The average composition figures demonstrate the importance of fertility for the elementary family unit and therefore household size. Coloured and Asian fertility in 1970 was considerably higher than in 1980 and the difference between coloureds and Asians on the one hand and whites on the other is apparent in the row marked 'children under 10'.

Table 5 combines information about dwellings with data from Table 4.

The housing densities in Table 5 reflect the relative economic statuses of the three groups, coloured housing density being just over three times that of whites in 1970. More interesting is the last row of Table 5, which suggests the following interpretation.

First, there is a significant degree of multi-occupancy among whites, suggesting a significant incidence of multiple households. The evidence of Table 5 suggests that Argyle's findings (1977) are of general applicability, even though the incidence of extended and multiple households recorded in his sample may be marginally higher than the national figure in 1970.

Second, the degree of multi-occupancy among coloureds is considerably higher than for whites. This suggests that Whisson's Ocean View study probably yields a proportion of multiple households somewhat below the 1970 national average. Certainly, the evidence of Table 5 suggests a greater contrast between white and coloured

Table 5: Data on Dwellings: Whites, Coloureds, and Asians, 1970

		Whites	Coloureds	Asians
Houses:	Number	771745	282970	71332
	Average no. of living rooms	4.85	2.38	3.64
Flats:	Number	201490	12413	14570
	Average no. of living rooms	2.70	2.60	2.92
Other dwellings:	Number	11018	22139	1847
	Average no. of living rooms	2	2	2
Total living rooms (million)		4.309	0.750	0.306
Housing density: persons per living room		0.88	2.73	2.06
Total dwellings		984253	317522	87749
Families		922630	359530	121306
Non-family persons living on their own		133947	18873	4391
Total families and solitaries		1056577	378403	125697
Families and solitaries/dwelling (million)		1.073	1.192	1.432

Note: There are some assumptions in this table. Each 'other dwelling' is assumed to have two living rooms. In view of the small proportion of 'other dwellings' in the total some inaccuracy here does not matter much. More importantly, an assumption has had to be made on the proportion of non-family persons living on their own; I have based the calculation on 40 per cent in the case of whites, 20 per cent in the case of Asians, and 10 per cent in the case of coloureds. The ordering of these magnitudes, at least, seems plausible.

multiple household rates in 1970 than suggested by a comparison of Argyle's and Whisson's findings.

Third, in the case of Asians the degree of multi-occupancy is very high, even though the housing density is well below the coloured housing density. Here the influence of the joint family ideal is very clear; the evidence of Table 5 is consistent with Meer's estimates. There has probably been greater change here for Asians than for whites and coloureds since 1970.

Information on the composition of coloured and Indian households in Cape Town and Durban respectively has been reported by the Bureau of Market Research. Table 6 summarizes the relevant results.

Table 6: Composition of Coloured and Indian Households, 1980

	Coloured (Cape Town)	Indian (Durban)
Average size	4.54	5.05
Made up of: head	1.00	1.00
wife	0.84	0.92
children under 10yrs	1.06	1.17
children 10yrs and over	1.43	1.55
other members	0.21	0.41
Percentage of heads female	15	7
Percentage of members 'other members'	5	8
Percentage of sample aged 20 and over	48	50
Pecentage of heads	22	20
Percentage of heads among persons aged 20 and over	46	39

Source: Tables A1 and A2 of University of South Africa, Bureau of Market Research, Research Projects 94.2 and 94.5 (1981).

Table 6 confirms what we have already found. The larger average household size and the lower incidence of headship among persons aged 20 and over suggest a higher proportion of multiple households among Indians than among coloured people. The higher incidence of 'other members' also suggests a greater incidence of extended households among Indians. On the other hand, there is a considerably greater incidence of female-headed households in the coloured sample.

(iv) Household Structure: Africans [5]

The focus here is regional. How does structure vary between households in the following five categories: people living in metropolitan areas (the cities) outside hostels, compounds, backyard shacks, and other forms of single accomodation; people living in towns outside the 'homelands', other than people in single accommodation; people living in rural areas outside the 'homelands'; 'homeland' urban residents; and 'homeland' rural residents?

Table 7 sets out the proportion of household heads that were female in 1980 and the distribution of households by type in that year.

The first thing to note from Table 7 is the high incidence of female-headed households. Households have been considered on a *de facto* basis: that is, migrants are *not* counted as part of households (though

Table 7: Household Headship and the Distribution of Household Type

Region	Source	% Heads Female	Distribution of households by type (%) 1980					
			Single	Incomplete nuclear	Complete nuclear	Incomplete extended	Complete extended	Compound
Metropolitan	CPS	30	7	7	41	20	19	6
	BMR	18						
Urban	CPS	20	6	9	43	19	18	5
Rural	CPS	25	2	8	37	15	24	14
Homelands								
Urban	CPS	47						
	BMR	36						
Rural	CPS	59						
	BMR	53						
Male-headed	CPS		2	4	52	7	25	10
Female-headed	CPS		2	46		39	3	10

Sources: CPS — Unpublished tabulations from the Current Population Survey

BMR — Income and expenditure surveys of African households (UNISA, Bureau of Market Research.)

Notes: The detailed versions of the type headings are as follows:

1. Single persons.
2. Nuclear households not headed by a complete married couple.
3. Nuclear households headed by a complete married couple.
4. Extended households not headed by a complete married couple.
5. Extended households headed by a complete married couple.
6. Compound households (i.e. households containing two or more complete or incomplete married couples).

simulation[6] methods enable the links to be made). Even under the fairly undisturbed conditions of small towns and farms outside the 'homelands', female headship runs at 20-25 per cent. In the metropolitan areas it is a little higher. In 'homeland' urban areas it is higher still and in the 'homeland' rural areas it reaches nearly 60 per cent. All these levels are higher than those for the other races. The highest levels testify to the massive influence of influx control, but the chapter by Preston-Whyte and Louw in this volume illustrates other causes of such households.

The second point of importance is the essential regional similarities of distribution of households by type. Between 45 and 56 per cent of the households are nuclear (complete or incomplete); between 32 and 42 per cent are extended (complete or incomplete). Together with the high incidence of female headship, these statistics suggest that the transformation of African household structure, discussed by Marwick (1978) and Pauw (1973) in the case of urban areas, has penetrated the entire society. Simulation work suggests that this transformation had been largely completed at least as far back as 1960. Between 1960 and 1980 there has been a modest drop in marriage rates and a modest rise in illegitimacy; but the impact on household structure has been limited.

Simulation also enables us to estimate the proportion of husbands living away from their wives, and children under 15 away from their mothers. The former was 27 per cent and the latter 17 per cent in 1980; while some of these separations can be attributed to the degree of divorce and desertion which would have happened in the absence of influx control, most can be attributed to influx control. A few of the children separated from their mothers live with their fathers; most will live with other kin, especially grandparents.

5. Conclusions

One can identify four main determinants of household structure: tradition, class, housing policy, and influx control.

The role of *tradition* can be seen most clearly among Indian people where a quite specific preference for a certain form of household organization still has an influence on household structure. It can also be seen in African society where, although traditional patrilineal, patrilocal organization (and, to a lesser extent, ideals), are much diminished in influence, the principle of widespread downward extension (now largely through unmarried daughters) continues as a major determinant of household structure. Traditions can be eroded by cultural interpenetration, and public policies may frustrate their expression, but they cannot be ignored as a distinct explanatory factor when accounting for household structure.

The factor of *class* has two important aspects. The first is income, which determines what can be spent on housing, whether it is necessary to extend one's household to finance housing costs, whether young, unmarried adults can think of having a place of their own, whether households have to accommodate elderly kin, and so forth. One may conjecture that the income elasticity of expenditures[7] designed to create more space for oneself, or to live on one's own or in a nuclear rather than an extended family, is greater than one. That is, other things being equal, rises in income will lead to a drop in the proportion of complex households. For most South Africans, incomes are still too low to allow effective expression of these desires.

The second aspect is the influence of factors tending to produce household disorganization, either imposed or chosen. Ragged and rough working-class environments are ones in which economic misfortunes can easily lead to household disorganization. Given the extent of this disorganization, chosen actions such as desertion may be more readily tolerated than in respectable working-class or middle-class circles.

In a context where housing is limited and largely provided in terms of state *housing policy*, accommodation for single people and small households will be particularly hard to find. This will prevent such households emerging. It may also be hard to accommodate large multiple households if houses are designed to suit nuclear families. Private building of housing, whether in formal housing estates or in site and service areas, will remove these rigidities. Then the effective constraints become the budgets of households.

The restructuring of the principles of African household organization has taken place in a period when *influx control*, in one form or another, has been operative. Even if such controls were lifted, a variety of economic factors (such as the possession of assets in places far from centres of employment) and the persistence of habits built up over the decades would ensure that African household structure changed relatively slowly. Split households could be expected to continue as a substantial proportion of all households. Low marriage rates and high illegitimacy might well persist, though perhaps not to their present extents.

Will the distributions of household structure become more uniform across the races? The first problem is that of deciding on the pattern to which the distributions might converge. Demographers in the United States are wrestling with the description of a new form of family: husband and wife with the children from their respective former marriages. New perspectives open up when divorce is regarded not as a dysfunction but as a central institution in lives of 'serial monogamy'.[8] As Burman and Fuchs point out in this volume, divorce rates, already high in certain segments of South African society, might lead to a substantial incidence of new, complex household structures, models for which might be found in strata (defined largely by race and class) where desertion is a common occurrence.

A second, related issue involves sexual ethics and the meaning of marriage. Dubb observes: 'Africans, generally, take a pragmatic view of sex: it is a natural urge which everyone is entitled to satisfy within socially defined limits' (Dubb 1979: 147). These limits have become more tolerant for some groups during the twentieth century : external intercourse among the unmarried has been replaced by full intercourse, extramarital relationships are frequent and, in relation to widowed people, the levirate and sororate have fallen into disuse in favour of the freedom to enter any relationship. Perhaps these changes can be defended in terms of Dubb's crystallization of the African principle; what is certain, however, is that the spread of more tolerant sexual ethics is not confined to African society. Moreover, the observation can be made that the spread of Christianity has led to the adoption of a stricter ethic by many Africans. Also, ethical developments have to be related to changes in social structure. The issues here are complex and by no means fully understood.

Accordingly, there are questions about the prospect of uniformity in South African household structures, an important issue for a book which considers children's experiences and opportunities in a very diverse society. In relation to the operation of the four determinants identified above, certain observations may be made.

It is probable that greater cultural interpenetration in the coming years might further reduce the force of differing traditions. African tradition is likely to be the most resistant, while a greater degree of uniformity might be expected among whites, coloureds, and Asians.

Income gaps between the races are still very wide, although they can be expected to narrow. The very unequal housing densities shown in Table 5 can be expected to become somewhat more equal. More smaller households, insofar as they are desired, will be affordable. While middle classes will grow, substantial working classes will remain, particularly among coloured people and Africans.

Housing policy is moving in the direction of more private provision, which will allow more scope for the realization of desired household structures. The precise effect of this is uncertain and will depend on developments in tradition and class structure.

Influx control will probably be abolished or erode, perhaps rapidly, in the coming years. The impact of this on African household structure, for the reasons discussed, will probably be slow to work itself out, though it must be acknowledged that our ability to make predictions here is limited.

Perhaps just over half of South African households are nuclear in structure; most of the rest are extended or multiple. If there is a trend towards the nuclear household, it is a very weak one. More complex forms will be distributed in varying measure and to a very substantial degree throughout South African society for as far ahead as one can see.

Notes

1. Factor markets refer to markets in the factors of production — labour and capital. The labour market can be disaggregated in various ways, notably by education and occupation.
2. As will be demonstrated, the use of the present tense is much less appropriate than use of the past would be. In addition, the degree of strictness of division of labour by sex probably varied across African society even during the pre-colonial and early colonial periods.
3. Objections to the term 'coloured' are noted, understood, and sympathized with. The text has not been littered with quotation marks or the qualifier 'so-called' in the interests of plain exposition.
4. Marriage may take the following forms in South Africa: civil; religious, according to the rites of most of the major religions of the world — Judaism, Christianity, Islam, Hinduism, and occasionally others; African traditional marriage, in which bridewealth is transferred from the bridegroom or his family to the family of the bride.

   In addition, although not recognized as marriage by any system of law in South Africa, there are long-standing (non-African) unions where the couple regard themselves as virtually married — a relationship sometimes referred to as a 'common law union', to which a few of the legal consequences of marriage attach. See the chapter by Burman and Fuchs for the statistical problems resulting from this multiplicity of forms. In particular, in the case of African traditional marriage, it is often difficult to tell quite when a marriage has taken place, and the perceptions of the parties involved and their kin may differ. The response 'living together' may sometimes be given in such uncertain circumstances. It is unlikely that my enumeration would use entirely consistent criteria for distinguishing between the various marital statuses. People may, of course, be married in more than one way.

5. This section is drawn from Chapter 6 of Simkins (1984).

6. Simulation in this context refers to the generation of hypothetical individuals on the computer from demographic schedules, and the arrangement of these individuals into households. The methods used are discussed in Chapters 5 and 6 of Simkins (1984).

7. The income elasticity of expenditure on a particular item is the relation of the proportional rise in expenditure to the proportional rise in income, when it occurs. What is being suggested here is that if incomes rise by one per cent, expenditures designed to create more space etc. will rise by more than one per cent.

8. Serial monogamy refers to a situation where a person has more than one spouse during his lifetime, but never more than one at a time.

Childhood Health in South Africa

Christopher Molteno, Maurice Kibel, and
Mary Roberts

Introduction

Children are our most precious asset. A generation of robust, vigorous
children augurs well for the future. A secure, well-nourished child
who has the opportunity to learn and develop within a family, school,
and community has the best chance of becoming a confident adult able
to contribute to the happiness and welfare of society. Poorly nourished,
unhealthy children, on the other hand, may fail to reach their full
potential and place a burden on the nation's resources. Health is defined
in the constitution of the World Health Organization as a state of
physical, mental, and social well-being and not merely the absence of
disease or infirmity. It may also be defined as a state of well-being and
effective functioning satisfactory to the child and its environment. The
aim of the practice of child health is to achieve this well-being and optimal functioning for all children in South Africa from conception to
adulthood.

In South Africa there are approximately 10 million children of
whom 8 million are African, and 70 per cent of these live in rural
areas. Health is closely related to race, for it is racial legislation which
determines nutrition, medical care, education, housing, community
resources, employment and often family cohesion. The population
comprises groups classified as white, coloured, Asian and black
(or African). In addition, children may be categorized according to
the setting in which they grow up, for example rural 'homeland', rural
farm, urban, and peri-urban. Each of these settings is associated with

specific health problems as well as difficulties regarding the delivery of health care. There is a wide discrepancy between the health of the affluent and that of the poor, both urban and rural. The health of the white and affluent coloured and Indian children is on par with that of children in the major industrialized countries. On the other hand, the health of rural African and under-privileged coloured and Indian children in some areas is similar to that in the poorest developing countries.

Because of this contrast and consequently the inbuilt system of comparison, we have the opportunity to examine the whole spectrum of child health. We should also be under an obligation to put right those defects which may come to light.

Assessing Child Health

Statistical data

An important requirement for getting to know the children of South Africa is to collect demographic data, such as their numbers and ages, vital events in their lives and environments, and the prevalence of disease among them. The main sources of this information are discussed below.

In this country the national Population Census is taken every ten years, although in 1985 a census was carried out after five years. This gives the number, age, sex, marital status, residential area, income, occupation, educational level, and house occupancy rates of all people in the country. An accurate census provides the denominator base for calculation of important health indicators. Unfortunately, because of influx control legislation, the census returns are often incomplete and this results in misleading figures.

All births, deaths, marriages, and in- and out-migrations must be recorded to get a picture of the health of each region. However, at present the accuracy of the vital events record varies from region to region. In addition there are problems regarding the classification of Muslim, Hindu, and African customary marriages.

Disease notification, the health records of local authorities, hospital records, and research data give information on the incidence of disease and environmental factors that adversely affect health. In squatter areas, where disease rates are highest, the data are often least accurate.

The information that is available for assessing the health of South African children comes from government statistics, hospital records, and annual reports of local authorities, as well as from a large number of research studies. The latter studies have by and large been quite uncoordinated, so that there is a shortage of data on which comparisons between different areas can be made. Almost invariably such research is 'cross-sectional' — that is, the sample of children is viewed only at the time when the study is carried out. Virtually lacking have been longitudinal studies which follow the same children over a period of time as they grow and develop. Such studies yield an enormous amount of information. A further frequent deficiency is lack of precise knowledge about the denominator — we often do not know for certain the number of infants or children who form the population we are testing for a particular health measurement. There is little information about handicapped children, children 'in need of care', child abuse and neglect, child adoption, fostering, or children's homes and Places of Safety. In addition First World definitions are often applied to whites only and this leads to differing standards of care. In many areas, such as the current status of women, the functioning of the family, the experience of giving birth, and mother/child bonding, we need more writing by South African women either as objective research or from subjective experience. There is little written from the viewpoint of the child about early memories of mother, father, family, school, adolescence, culture, or community. We need to encourage people to record these experiences and researchers to study childhood in depth to build up a picture of the health of children.

Child health can be assessed by looking at the following indicators: mortality rates, acute and chronic illness, growth, intellectual and emotional development, frequency and nature of major handicaps, provision and utilization of health services, and functioning of the family. It is important to have reasonably accurate information and to realize that situations applying to one group which is well documented should not be assumed to apply to all groups.

Childhood mortality

Mortality is considered an important indicator because of its finite nature and the general availability of mortality rates. The infant mortality rate (IMR = the number of deaths during the first year of life per 1 000 live births) is widely used in international comparisons of child health. In 1981 South Africa, with a rate of 90/1 000 live births, ran sixtieth out of 130 nations in order of descending IMR and fell in the group of high IMR countries (Grant 1985). Perinatal mortality (stillbirths and first week deaths) tends to reflect the standard of medical care, as avoidable factors are usually medical or due to lack of medical facilities. Postperinatal avoidable deaths (from the second week until the end of the first year), on the other hand, are generally 'socially' determined.

Until 1978 there was no national record of African deaths, but only figures for selected urban magisterial districts. The figures which we have since then show that age-specific death rates among white children are similar to those in First World countries and differ significantly from Third World patterns of childhood deaths, typified by African and coloured rates. Wyndham (1984a), when analyzing the leading causes of death among children less than five years of age, found that coloured and African children had the causes typical of developing countries (ranked in order of prevalence: gastro-enteritis, pneumonia, immaturity, 'ill-defined', malnutrition, measles). For white children the causes resembled those found in Western developed countries (immaturity, anoxia, pneumonia, gastro-enteritis, congenital heart disease, accidents). Further analysis of deaths over the period 1968 – 1977 showed dramatic improvements in coloured children, with marked reductions in mortality from gastro-enteritis and malnutrition. Unfortunately, during the same period there was no improvement in mortality rates for tuberculosis, measles, or pneumonia in coloured or white children.

Rip and Tibbit (1984), using a cross-linkage process, found in the Western Cape metropolitan area that the white population had a birth weight distribution and IMR comparable to that of developed countries. The African group, on the other hand, had a similar birth weight distribution but a significantly elevated postneonatal mortality rate. The coloured cohort had a marked negatively skewed birth weight distribution with a high incidence of low birth weight and an infant mortality comprising more neonatal than postneonatal deaths.

In rural Transkei, Irwig and Ingle (1984) found, for the year 1980, a one in five risk of children dying before the age of five years. The greatest risk was in the first year, when the IMR was 130 per 1 000, about 75 per cent of deaths occurring in the postneonatal period.

In a study of a rural Western Cape region, Molteno *et al* (1985) found that coloured infants who died were more often malnourished, less frequently breast-fed, and more likely to have been incompletely immunized than children in a matched control sample. The risk of dying in infancy also correlated with single parent families, poor parental education and occupation, social problems, and sibling deaths. Gastro-enteritis was the most common cause, and fully 80 per cent of deaths were from preventable diseases.

A retrospective study of non-natural deaths in children in greater Cape Town (Knobel *et al* 1984) highlighted the problem of road traffic accidents, especially in older children.

Acute and chronic illness

For a major segment of the South African child population, morbidity patterns still reflect inadequate protection from the environment. There are basic deficiencies in water supply, sanitation and housing. Often the family's water supply is completely untreated and water must be transported laboriously for long distances. Sewerage disposal in the modern sense may be non-existent. Under these conditions, water- and food-borne infections flourish. Episodes of diarrhoea are common in the young child and comprise a major cause of death in infancy. Infestation with intestinal parasites, particularly round worm, is widespread and serves to increase the nutritional drain. Nutrition is the crucial factor in the formula for ill health (Ebrahim 1983).

There is an important relationship between nutrition and infective illness. Just as the poorly nourished child is predisposed to infections and has a poor capacity to fight them, so also infective illness — especially diarrhoea — contributes to deterioration in the state of nutrition. It is thus not surprising that at the national level, diarrhoeal disease still accounts for the majority of deaths in the first years of life (Wyndham 1984a). Such conditions are not unique to the 'homelands' or underdeveloped areas. They may still be seen in some of our most productive farming areas due to the living conditions provided for farm labourers. In the Western Cape region studied in 1983, thirty children out of every 1 000 live births still died of diarrhoeal disease in the first year (Molteno *et al* 1985).

Lack of water for bathing, a common disadvantage in African homes in South Africa, is an important factor in such skin diseases as impetigo, scabies and scalp infections. Many important water-related, vector-borne diseases also occur when communities derive their supply from untreated water or live close to natural water bodies. Two are of importance in South Africa. Bilharzia, particularly of the bladder, is widespread among African children in parts of Natal and the northern and eastern Transvaal (Pitchford 1981). Malaria, though much less widespread than in former years, is still an intermittent seasonal scourge in the north of the country.

Overcrowding, an unrelenting fact of life in all countries with burgeoning populations and a drift to the cities, is a particular problem among our own urban poor. Airborne infections are common in these conditions. Tuberculosis, viral and other respiratory illnesses, meningitis, and rheumatic fever all owe their high prevalence to housing congestion. Lower respiratory infection is the most common cause of morbidity among urban children and the most common cause of death in those under one year of age. Important contributing factors in the overcrowded environment are cigarette smoking and smoke from the oil, wood, and coal fires needed for cooking and warmth in many African homes. In South Africa tuberculosis is a particularly serious problem. Greatest in the 'homeland' territories of the Transkei and Ciskei, the continual traffic (largely due to migrant labour and influx control measures) of infected individuals to and from the towns makes adequate treatment and case detection difficult.

Evidence from the Department of Health (Epidemiological Comments 1985) shows rising trends in tuberculosis among the coloured population of the Cape over the past five years. A particularly tragic aspect is the number of young children who die or are permanently maimed by tuberculous meningitis (Deeny *et al* 1985). In the six-year period 1979 – 1984, 195 coloured children below the age of five years were affected by this disease in the Western Cape health region — a rate of 20.5 cases per 100 000. (The Western Cape health region is one of three health regions of the Cape Province and serves a population of almost three million.)

The national vaccination programme provides children with a measure of protection against six important infections — tuberculosis, measles, diptheria, tetanus, whooping cough, and poliomyelitis. In 1984 the Department of Health (Epidemiological Comments 1985) estimated coverage of susceptible children in six of the seven health regions for the year 1983. BCG vaccination against tuberculosis was virtually complete. Eighty-four per cent of children had received full vaccination against poliomyelitis. However, full vaccination against measles reached only 40 per cent of children and in the case of diptheria, pertussis and tetanus only 39 per cent. The suboptimal effectiveness of this preventive health programme is illustrated by a recent measles epidemic in Port Elizabeth (Fisher 1984). Over a period of eight months in 1983, 19 025 cases were notified and there were 295 deaths, giving a case fatality of 15,3 per cent. Eighty-eight per cent of the cases and 91 per cent of the deaths occurred in the African population coming mainly from the township of Zwide and the squatter area of Soweto/Veeplaas. The latter had an average shack occupancy of 10,8 persons and 56,6 per cent of housing units accommodated more than ten people. There was a high incidence of malnutrition in the children. Thirty-seven per cent of those with measles, including most who died, fell below 60 per cent of expected weight-for-age. In half the households, incomes were less than 50 per cent of the average in the better-off nearby African township of New Brighton. Because the population of the area had been grossly underestimated, one clinic serviced 330 000 people.

Accidents remain an important source of illness, disability and death in children. Economic factors certainly contribute to the causes and have an effect on outcome. Perhaps the two most important accidents in our poor communities are head injuries and burns.

Initial findings from a large, multidisciplinary study on head injuries presently being carried out in Cape Town (Jacobs 1984) showed that 1 800 children were admitted to hospital with head injuries over a fifteen-year period. A further 1 000 died at the site of injury or *en route* to hospital. There are indications that the poor child in Cape Town is not only at greater risk from head injury but also, following such injuries, has constraints on his or her access to appropriate rehabilitation and educational facilities. Of the 1 127 burns and scalds seen at the Children's Hospital Trauma Unit in the past year, a disproportionate 41 per cent were suffered by African children. This reflects the overcrowding and unsafe heating methods so prevalent (Child Safety Centre 1984).

Among the more privileged, where nutrition, housing, water supply and sanitation meet adequate standards, morbidity in children is now determined largely by social environment and personal lifestyles. Despite optimal services, there will always be those who do not make use of what is available, are inadequate rearers of children, or are not amenable to counselling. It is clear that much unnecessary illness and death occurs among these families.

A composite picture of the extent of childhood illness in South Africa is yet to emerge. It will only be seen when information on population surveys, records of hospital in-patient notification of certain conditions such as infectious diseases, congenital malformations, and child battering can be properly coordinated. Already groups of children requiring special attention such as the 'street children' have come to notice.

Physical growth

Growth begins soon after conception and consideration of fetal growth forms an important part of the overall assessment. During the last three months of pregnancy rapid fetal growth takes place. This period, together with the first eighteen months of postnatal life, represents the time of maximum brain growth. Malnutrition during this phase will cause severe and persistent developmental retardation. In developing countries depletion of maternal resources due to diminished food intake, closely-spaced pregnancies, and anaemia contribute to low-birth-weight infants. However, not all groups are equally affected; in South Africa, small-for-gestational-age infants are a particular problem in the coloured population (Rip and Tibbit 1984).

Growth is a product of the interaction of heredity and environment. An optimal environment will theoretically allow the inherited potential to be fulfilled. Sub-optimal nutrition leads to sub-optimal growth. Growth as defined in terms of body measurements (anthropometry) is often used as an indicator of nutritional status, either as an estimator of the prevalence of malnutrition (comparison between groups of children) or as surveillance (comparison of the same children at different times). A number of anthropometric indices are used, such as weight-for-age, height-for-age, weight-for-height, head circumference, skinfold thickness and mid-upper arm circumference. The weight-for-age is a good global indicator as it includes the height-for-age and weight-for-height.

As regards reference values, statistics representing optimal growth can be calculated from large samples of children drawn from well-to-do populations. Ethnic differences in growth potential are small. The reference values of the American National Center for Health Statistics (Hamill et al 1979) are currently widely used in South Africa.

Hansen (1984), in an extensive review of over thirty growth studies in South Africa, reports that, whenever the official survey figures of the Department of Health and Welfare or research data are used, the results show that approximately a third of African, coloured, and

Indian children below the age of fourteen years are underweight and stunted for their age. In some areas a figure of 60-70 per cent is reached. Elsewhere, for example the urban areas of Cape Town and Soweto, where more income is available to households, the incidence of underweight children has shown marked improvement in recent years. In addition it appears that the severe forms of malnutrition (kwashiorkor and marasmus) may occur in up to three per cent of the pre-school population in rural areas, leading to a high admission rate to hospitals (5-30 per cent of admissions) and considerable morbidity.

Intellectual and emotional development

Development refers to a progressive series of changes in an orderly, coherent pattern (Hurlock 1972). Such changes may involve motor, language, conceptual, emotional, or social skills and behaviour. Unfortunately, in contrast to somatic growth, there are no satisfactory objective measures of assessment. For example, mental ability or learning capacity is always related to the particular culture of the child. From a pragmatic point of view, however, developmental tests used for comparisons between sub-groups within a population are legitimate. Many investigations into the relationship between malnutrition and cognitive development have been conducted. Two long-term South African studies have gained wide recognition with regard to the association between malnutrition and behavioural development. Stoch and Smythe (1976) followed marasmic children from infancy until early adult life and Evans *et al* (1980) reported on the outcome of children with kwashiorkor. These studies and others from other parts of the developing world indicate that cognitive development is significantly impaired in marasmic children but not in those with kwashiorkor. This is probably because marasmus has its onset during a period of rapid brain growth and is usually more chronic than kwashiorkor. Gross pathological malnutrition is generally accepted as being detrimental to the developmental progress of the young child. Less severe forms of under-nutrition, as evidenced by slow growth, are far more common in disadvantaged children, but the developmental consequences have not been well documented. In a study of pre-school development of coloured children in Cape Town, Molteno (1985) found that during infancy milestones corresponded to those found in First World countries. Later, however, there was a developmental fall-off which coincided with the influence of the socio-economic environment. Just prior to school entry social factors far outweighed growth indices as predictors of developmental outcome.

In industrialized countries survey data show that behavioural problems are common in young children, but such studies have not yet been carried out in this country. A London survey (Richman *et al* 1982) found that 14 per cent of three-year-olds had mild generalized behaviour problems, and 7 per cent had more severe difficulties. A considerable number of these problems persisted through to school age. Social stress, parental mismanagement, family factors, especially discord and mental illness, and life events such as hospitalization and birth of a sibling may all play a part in producing such early childhood problems. Current levels of social stress in South Africa are bound to have negative effects on the country's children.

Accelerated motor development of African infants is widely recognized in South Africa and elsewhere. It has been ascribed to specifically taught skills, traditional methods of child care, physical contact between mother and child, a more permissive attitude to child rearing, to social class and to innate racial differences. Neither the causes of this phenomenon nor whether it carries any advantages for the child are known (Super 1976).

Handicap — prevalence, facilities, and management

Growth, maturation and development are continuous and dynamic processes in the healthy child from fetal life until adulthood. Interference with the normal developmental progress of a child constitutes a handicap. A handicapped child has been defined by Sheridan (1968) as one who suffers from a continuing disability of body, intellect, or personality which is likely to interfere with normal growth, development or capacity to learn.

The incidence of handicap in South Africa is largely unknown, but some data is available from urban populations. In 1977 Power found an administrative prevalence of mental retardation of 2:6/1 000 in a school-aged coloured sample in Cape Town. Similarly, Friedlander and Power (1982) recorded a figure of 2:5/1 000 for the coloured residential area of Heideveld. These figures agree with those reported from other countries. Down's syndrome accounts for a quarter of mentally retarded children and occurs in approximately 1/600 live births. In 1981 Smart found an incidence in the Peninsula of 1/750 whites, 1/180 coloured and 1/1 170 Africans.

There is currently a debate as to whether the incidence of cerebral palsy is falling in developing countries. We do not know the incidence in South Africa but have reason to believe, according to Arens *et al* (1978) that there has not been a decline in recent years. Arens *et al* found a high incidence of post-natally acquired cerebral palsy, particularly in coloured children, due to trauma and infection, especially cerebrovascular accidents associated with gastro-enteritis. However, in the study of Friedlander and Power (1982) in the middle-class coloured suburb of Heideveld in Cape Town, a relatively low incidence (1:25/1 000) was found. A large study on screening for neural tube defects in Natal (Grace *et al* 1981) gave some idea of the incidence of spina bifida. The purpose of the study was to report on the feasibility of screening for the condition. However, in over 12 000 pregnancies screened the detection rate was 1:520 for whites, 1:1 130 for coloureds and 1:2 500 for Indians. Spina bifida is relatively uncommon in Africans.

In South Africa, education and training facilities are officially segregated and may not be shared by those classified into different racial groups. A paper on the management of handicapped children in the Cape Peninsula (Molteno *et al* 1982) evaluated facilities for the mentally retarded, cerebral palsied, visually impaired, hearing impaired, spina bifida, autistic, multi-handicapped, and children with musculo-skeletal defects. The evaluation considered such matters as early diagnosis, early treatment and evaluation, and placement in special schools, training centres, and facilities for special care. This led to the conclusion that the mentally retarded are most in need of additional services, and particularly Africans, who had no residential care facilities and only limited day care facilities. African children were most in need of additional services, with coloured children slightly better off, and the white children reasonably well catered for.

Friedlander and Power (1982) looked at the provision of health, welfare, education, and community services for severely mentally-retarded coloured children in Cape Town. They found half of the children received no day care at all, and three quarters of those who received care did so at normal schools. They found that counselling and social welfare services were adequate.

The past ten years have seen a proliferation of special schools and other facilities for handicapped children in all major centres. However, there remains a tremendous lack of facilities for those who live in more peripheral areas. In addition, many handicapped African children in the Western Cape have to go to the Transkei or Ciskei for facilities. These were not provided in the Western Cape because it was considered a 'coloured labour preference area'.

Provision of health services

The Health Laws Amendment Act, No.36 of 1977, founded a National Health Policy Council which framed the Health Facilities Plan of 1980. This proposed health facilities plan has six levels. The first level consists of the provision of safe water, adequate sanitation, housing, and nutrition for all people. This is a huge task, and there are no signs that the relevant government departments are even beginning to make inroads on the enormous needs countrywide.

The most important of these basic amenities is adequate nutrition, since the cost of growth failure in a child is incalculable in the long term. It is much cheaper for the state to supplement the child's diet with protein and energy food, than to offer treatment in hospital once kwashiorkor or marasmus have developed (Whittaker *et al* 1985). The second level of the Health Facilities Plan makes provision for nation-wide health education. The Department of Health has been active in the preparation and dissemination of health education literature. The third level provides for community health centres for Primary Health Care. While much progress has been made in providing 'grassroots' health care — the Day Hospitals in the Cape are an excellent service — gross deficiencies in numbers of clinics and staff exist. Such facilities are also not truly comprehensive, as envisaged in the Act, in the sense than they do not provide curative and preventive/promotional health services under one roof. The fourth, fifth, and sixth levels are the provision of different categories of hospitals. Much of the total provincial health budget is expended on 'sixth level' highly sophisticated hospitals in large cities, often to the detriment of the provision and upgrading of lower level hospitals. In the cities curative and preventive services for children of all groups are, nevertheless, of a high standard since not only hospitals and laboratories but most of the private practitioners — general practitioners and specialists — are concentrated there. Well-off families, and those covered by medical aid schemes, are served by the private sector. The remainder, representing the great majority, obtain their medical care at state-run clinics. A charge is made on a sliding scale depending on income, but indigents receive free treatment. Preventive/promotive care is rendered without charge.

While health care is theoretically available to all, it becomes less readily accessible to children in African and coloured communities and progressively less so with increasing distance from the towns. For example, many clinics are not open at night or over weekends, necessitating long and expensive journeys to hospitals. The 'fee for service' health system of private practice in South Africa is a perfect example of the 'Inverse Care Law': those most in need of the service are in the worst position to receive it.

A feature of the health services is their fragmentation. The Department of National Health and Population Development provides community (or chronic) psychiatric services, school health services for Africans, and family planning motivation services. The provincial authority provides curative services, including specialist treatment for all acute illnesses except infectious and communicable diseases like tuberculosis, antenatal and maternity services, district nursing services, and ambulance services. Promotive and preventive health services are provided by the state, which delegates the work to local authorities where they exist. These services are antenatal care, midwifery, child welfare clinics and home visiting, immunization services, tuberculosis and communicable disease control, dental, family planning, and psychiatric care (Robertson 1980). The lack of coordination is illustrated by the example cited by Wilson (1984). Before a child is one year old, a mother in Soweto may have many different sets of records relating to antenatal and routine care, to family planning and child welfare, and also to acute illness.

Under the new constitutional dispensation of 1984, the problem of fragmentation will become even more severe, as health is to be administered by five new, separate bodies — the white, coloured, and Asian 'Houses of Parliament', African local authorities and, under 'General Affairs', the white House of Assembly in Parliament and the President's Council — in addition to the 'homeland' health authorities. Since there is no African representation in parliament in white South Africa, African health outside the 'homelands' will be run by local community councils. This new arrangement will further fragment and duplicate health services. There is talk of basic amenities being provided for all but also of Africans having to raise their own revenue for health. This would be detrimental since the central government is the only body able to pay for health services for the poorest section of the community.

School health services for white children are provided by the medical staff of the Provincial Educational Departments in conjunction with the Provincial Hospital Services. The Department of Health, through school nurses attached to regional offices, provides a school health service for Asian and coloured children. This service is still largely inadequate. In 1982 only 384 out of 1 333 schools in the Western Cape region were visited by a school nurse (Cameron 1984). School health nurses have been provided for some African schools recently by the Department of National Health and Population Development, but even fewer of these schools receive visits than those of other groups.

The services for the chronically ill and handicapped are unequal, being of a reasonable standard for whites but almost non-existent for Africans. In the African 'homelands' the health and welfare services are integrated, with comprehensive community-based hospitals and clinics embracing preventive, curative, and rehabilitative care (Robertson 1980). However, by combining health and welfare allocations in an already limited budget, both services suffer. Pensions are too low and often arbitrarily administered.

In South Africa, 94 per cent of the health budget is spent on curative services, while the major need is for basic health services at primary care level (Cooper *et al* 1984: 483-84). Hospital beds are allocated according to the race classification of the patient. The average number of people per hospital bed is 61.3 for whites, 504.8 for Asians, 346.1 for coloureds and 337.4 for Africans. The average hospital expenditure per patient per day varies from R75,76 to R107,47 for whites, coloureds and Indians, whereas for African hospitals it ranges from R20,54 to R41,56 (Moosa 1984). Thus separation of facilities according to race classification works heavily to the detriment of the poorest section of the population.

Functioning of the family

The state postulates that the family is a primary social unit and that children are born and nurtured within it until such time as they grow into adults, ready to found their own families. It is supposed that family members interact with each other according to prescribed social and cultural mores, thus sharing amenities, generating family bonds and maintaining a common culture. The family is seen to act in pursuit of the satisfaction of biological and socio-cultural needs. It is assumed that it provides the child's genetic endowment, as well as nourishment, protection against environmental hazards, emotional security and cultural nurturing. The family is also regarded as the principal mediating agent between the child and society. Because the family is generally seen as a functional unit, major family dysfunction has profound consequences.

Crises which threaten its existence may come from within, such as marital disharmony or violence, or from without, such as poverty. Alternatively, the very structure may be damaged, for example by the migrant labour system, which results in fathers having to spend most of their working lives away from home. A number of studies in both rural and urban areas have shown a high incidence of family problems.

Dr Trudy Thomas (Fincham and Thomas 1984) found in 5 000 interviews of African families that the most important determinant of the nutritional health of the child was the organization of his or her home life. Looking at the social background of children with kwashiorkor, she found 62 per cent were illegitimate, and only 33 per cent were in the personal care of their mothers. Eighty-six per cent of the fathers were migrants, of whom only 14 per cent were supporting the family financially and 60 per cent had deserted. Only 1 per cent lived where the breadwinner had work, and only 24 per cent lived in a family group — nuclear or extended. When she investigated the homes of well-nourished children, she found by contrast that 78 per cent of the children were in the care of their mothers, and 71 per cent of the migrant fathers supported their child. Eighty-three per cent of the well-nourished children lived in a family situation, and 21 per cent lived with their breadwinner. Only 5 per cent of the fathers had deserted their children, and 26 per cent of the children were illegitimate. Research (Fincham and Thomas 1984) has shown that in the commercial farming area of Diaz, where 73 per cent of the fathers are employed at home and 86 per cent of the mothers stay at home, the nutrition of the children is good. The likelihood of malnutrition is greater in homes where the mother is the chief breadwinner. Family size is a factor causing malnutrition in the towns (Hansen 1984).

In a study of coloured pre-school children in Cape Town, Molteno *et al* (1980) found poor maternal education, low incomes and overcrowding to be particular risk factors in child health. Sixty-five per cent of the mothers were not educated further than primary school level and over half of the families were living below an effective minimum level of income. Similarly, over half the families lived in grossly overcrowded conditions.

Child abuse is both a cause and consequence of major family crises and is usually indicative of family malfunctioning. A transcultural study in Cape Town (Robertson and Hayward 1976) found that the incidence of child abuse was relatively high among whites, moderate among coloureds, and low among Africans. Factors such as differences in child rearing practices, mistrust of Western doctors, and inadequate child welfare services could have accounted for the few African children seen. Similarly, the high incidence among whites could indicate greater use of child welfare agencies by this group. However, the white children tended to be amongst the most severely injured. Coloured children, who made up most of the burn cases, were often conceived out of wedlock and were cared for during the day by caretakers. Child abuse in coloured families is often part of a widespread, ever-present level of family violence associated with poverty, overcrowding, and alcohol abuse. In Natal Loening (1981) reported a number of cases in Zulu families. He claimed that industrialization and westernization were causing changes in the lifestyle of the Zulus that had led to the breakdown of traditional culture which had not been replaced by adequate social support structures. The social ills of the First World were then compounded by persistent beliefs in witchcraft. As in many other countries, the problem of sexual abuse has become apparent in recent years in South Africa (Westcott 1984).

The Needs of Children

Secure family environment

There should be a firm commitment by all concerned to maintain and strengthen the child-rearing unit. The problems of poverty, unemployment and overcrowding as a result of influx control and migrant labour must be addressed. In African rural areas, lack of employment means food shortages and poor child health. Consequently breadwinners leave these areas for the cities, and the family unit is physically disrupted. Employment for the breadwinner where his or her family can stay together is thus one of the first requisites for having healthy children in this country. This requires greater urbanization, an end to resettlement schemes, and positive rural development.

Public works campaigns are needed to provide employment. These employment schemes are used in many developing countries and have many developmental advantages (Reynolds 1984). Efforts to maintain effective family functioning, such as marriage guidance and education for parenting, need to be encouraged. Furthermore, such children themselves require preparation for parenthood. These efforts should be directed at satisfying the child's basic needs: biological (nutrition and protection); psychological (such as emotional and mental development); socio-cultural (such as socialization, which includes the acquisition of language, and the formulation of culturally acceptable behaviour); and economic (the acquisition of resources for present and future use).

Fertility control

In his now classical study Morley (1973: 300) wrote that 'medical workers when caring for a mother and her young child will come to realize that delaying the next conception and extending the interval between births are quite as important a part of health care as seeing that the latest child is adequately immunized.' Vigorous efforts need to be made to implement effective family planning in South Africa. However, the issues involved go beyond the biological and encompass sociological and political aspects. Family planning programmes must be fully integrated into a comprehensive primary health care service. Moreover, they must not be seen as a state-inspired attempt 'to keep down the African population in favour of the white'.

Contraception has both side effects and a significant failure rate, and two important additional measures need to be considered. These are sterilization and easily accessible, safe, and humanely-conducted early abortion. It is estimated that there are at least 75 000 illegal abortions performed each year in South Africa (Cooper *et al.* 1984: 499). Clearly the demand for proper abortion services has been demonstrated.

Family planning is widely available in South Africa at all hospitals and clinics. However, many men will not allow women to use contraception because of the need to prove fertility before marriage, or so that parents will have children to care for them in their old age. Furthermore, the use of contraception is thought to promote 'unfaithfulness'. In order to prevent teenage pregnancies, young women need to feel that there is a role for them in their society, over and above motherhood. They need to be educated so as to become economically self-supporting and independent. Children will be healthier if their mothers plan for motherhood. The education of girls is one of the best health investments which a developing country can make. Recent research (Kemp 1984) suggests that, far from being merely a reflection of living standards, maternal education acts as a powerful independent force in reducing the number of infant and child deaths.

Perinatal health — pregnancy and birth

Adequate nutrition throughout pregnancy is a vital ingredient of normal growth in the fetus. The first need, therefore, is to lessen the percentage of infants who are born undernourished or underweight. The last three months of pregnancy, labour, and the first week after birth are the most hazardous periods of a child's life. Complications are common and result in significant mortality and long term disability. It is well established that perinatal services organized on a regional basis will improve the outcome of pregnancy. The aim of regionalization is to improve access of the high risk mother-fetus and infant to the appropriate level of technology but at the same time to recognize all social, cultural, and family determinants. The implementation of regionalization involves education, communication and transportation. These principles apply in both a sophisticated urban setting and an underdeveloped rural environment. Even in those areas where many deliveries are conducted by traditional midwives, education has a role to play, while communication and efficient transportation are vital when complications develop. There is clearly a need for regional perinatal health services in South Africa.

Another aspect of child health which warrants attention at this stage is the preparation for breastfeeding. In a study on infant-feeding practices in a socio-economically disadvantaged community in the Cape Peninsula, Hoffman *et al* (1984) found that subjective dissatisfaction with the quantity and quality of milk was the main reason why mothers stopped breastfeeding. Since contact between the local authority and mothers often took place after breastfeeding had been discontinued, they felt that concentrating on education and support during the perinatal period could prevent the disturbing trend away from breastfeeding.

Health care for the under fives: GOBI-FFF

The United Nations International Children's Emergency Fund (Grant 1984) has adopted four recommendations which provide remarkably cost effective protection to young children in poor communities. Together they are referred to by the mnemonic GOBI. These recommended measures (listed below) together offer a combined effect several times greater than a simple addition of their advantages in combating the infection-malnutrition spiral which takes such a high toll of children in this vulnerable and vital period of life.

Growth monitoring: every newborn baby should be provided with a Health Card on which to plot growth from birth to five or six years, and which serves as a home-based medical record.

Oral rehydration: teaching mothers how to make a simple solution of water, sugar, and salt to combat diarrhoeal disease.

Breastfeeding: its active encouragement and promotion for the first two years of life.

Immunization: against six common and important diseases — tuberculosis, poliomyelitis, diptheria, tetanus, whooping cough, and measles.

Three further strategies are also emphasized.

Family spacing: integrated into comprehensive health care.

Female education: placing emphasis on teaching girls the health needs of children and skills for earning power.

Food supplements: two forms of food supplementation are of great importance. First, supplements for pregnant women can provide vital calories to improve the growth of the fetus. Second, supplementing diets with specific nutrients can protect children's lives and growth. Three important examples are iron in the prevention of anaemia, iodine supplements in preventing goitre and cretinism, and Vitamin A supplements in preventing blindness. In addition, children who show growth failure at any time from birth to the end of primary schooling should be given food supplements.

While the four key components of GOBI-FFF are nothing new, the innovative features of the concept are still insufficiently understood in South Africa. These require full community understanding of the benefits, and active implementation at grassroots. Instructional and educational programmes at a suitable level are thus an essential component. When used in this way the total effects of the GOBI package can exceed the value of the individual components in favourably influencing the health of young children. A shining example is to be found at Elim and in the Gelukspan district of Bophuthatswana. 'Care groups' of specially trained members of the community are used to promote and supervise the use of health cards, oral rehydration, etc. It is of vital importance that adequate resources be set aside for the above strategies.

Pre-school education

The need for pre-school education is increasingly recognized. According to Short (1984) there are two basic approaches. The one is posited on the compensatory education philosophy of the 1960s and aims at the preparation of economically disadvantaged children to reach limited short-term goals. The second approach regards the young child as a whole and has a broad concept of child development, focussing attention on life-long learning and the development of human potential. Of the two approaches, the second is more comprehensive but also more difficult to apply. A combination of approaches may be required, tailored to the specific needs of pre-school children in South Africa.

The school child

The purpose of a school health service should be to ensure that every child is able to derive full benefit from his or her education (Bamford 1980). This entails the prevention of disease in healthy children, making certain that all children get appropriate treatment, caring for handicapped children, and bringing medical expertise to learning problems. The extent to which the school health services for coloured and African children fall short of even the most minimal standards mirrors or exceeds the overall disparity in the respective educational systems referred to elsewhere.

Adolescent health

There is a dearth of data on the health state of our adolescent population (Kibel and Epstein — forthcoming 1986). Adolescence is widely regarded as a period of infinite energy and robust health, yet in the major industrialized countries mortality rates in the second decade are actually rising. As in these countries, the major causes of death in

South African teenagers are related to accidents, poisoning, and violence, motor vehicle accidents being the most important entity. There is evidence to show that the mortality rates from these causes are three times higher in South Africa than those in England and Wales (Wyndham 1980), and substantially higher than those in Israel (Marshalkowitz 1985). Recent papers have also called attention to the extent and importance of teenage pregnancy (Editorial 1985) and drug abuse (South African Conference on Dagga 1983). Today all these are major sources of morbidity in adolescence.

It is clear that behavioural dysfunction is at the root of much of this mortality and disability. However, this is not the whole picture. 'A love of risk taking' is a feature of the age (Mahler 1985). Cigarette smoking, drug usage, drinking of alcoholic beverages, and un-protected sexual intercourse, all part of the changes that have occur-red in the lifestyle of youth in recent years, generally begin as experimentation. It has been established that there is a strong inter-relationship between these various behavioural patterns in young people (Tamir *et al* 1982; Epstein *et al* 1984). The Israeli studies cited found that youths who indulged in such behaviour had certain characteristics, and that the behaviour placed them at risk both in terms of their health (adolescent pregnancy, venereal disease, respiratory disease, etc.) and in their social functioning, such as early school dropout. Relatively little is known of the extent of these behavioural patterns in South African youngsters and there is a great need for similar studies.

A second deficiency relates to health services for adolescents: we have hardly begun to address this question. Few clinics are available which cater specifically for the comprehensive health care of an age group which has unique physical and psycho-social needs. The sick or injured adolescent needing admission to hospital but too old for the paediatric ward will be accommodated with adults, usually in a corner where he will cause least disturbance or embarrassment. This deficien-cy is even more obvious in the ten per cent of children who come into adolescence with chronic illness or physical disabilities. The often complex nature of the disorder may result in the child's care being in the hands of a sub-specialist clinic, with no regular primary care to cater for his or her general and preventive health requirements.

Many European and North American cities (admittedly those without population growth problems) provide the optimal services for which South Africa should begin to strive (Resnick *et al* 1980).

Adolescent in-patient units are rapidly multiplying. They are age-related rather than speciality-orientated and due attention is given to setting and furnishings, food and recreation. Adolescent health centres have sprung up, often with strong community links. Open at suitable hours, they offer confidential counselling and health care by health professionals with a special interest and training in this field. They provide the service link between the organic disease problems and the manifestations of risk behaviour of this age group.

This points to a third deficiency in our own setting: the need for appropriate medical training in the 'new' discipline of adolescent medicine. While family practitioners are the logical providers of such care, not all are temperamentally suited or adequately qualified to deal with teenagers, and the need for specialists and consultants in the field has become increasingly evident.

The child with special needs

In any society there are children whose needs exceed those of the majority. They can usually be divided into the handicapped and those who are likely to be found 'in need of care'.

Comprehensive care for the handicapped involves early diagnosis and a multidisciplinary assessment, followed, when indicated, by neuro-developmental therapy. Depending on the diagnosis, genetic counselling may be necessary. All families with a handicapped child require general counselling and support, especially during times of crisis. In addition, single-care grants must be arranged for those who qualify. The management of these patients also includes appropriate placement on reaching school age.

Successful comprehensive programmes should include developmental screening at community health clinics and regional assessment centres attached to major hospitals; adequate special schools, training centres and special care centres; and residential care for children who cannot be looked after at home. Agencies catering for the various types of handicap must provide country-wide service. As stated previously, the facilities for the handicapped are patchy and in some areas non-existent. Obviously, therefore, there is a need to establish or expand such facilities where indicated.

Children found to be 'in need of care' are provided for in the Childrens Act No.33 of 1960. Such children require adequate protection services. These include timeous recognition of physical or mental abuse or neglect, and removal to a place of safety. Thereafter, a Children's Court should decide on further management for the child which could be foster care, placement in a children's home, or a return to the parents under the supervision of a social work agency. Such agencies must be able to provide supervision and support for families in crisis. Unfortunately, at present the child protection services are poor and often non-existent for many coloured and African children.

Conclusion

The enormous disparities in child health standards, which we have attempted to describe, are not unique in South Africa. They are a feature of most Third World countries. In 1981 the World Health Organization adopted twelve global indicators which were regarded as the minimum prerequisites for such countries to reach the goal of 'health for all by the year 2 000'. The plan included a declaration of commitment by the Head of State, allocation of adequate resources equitably distributed, and a high degree of community involvement. South Africa has the resources to achieve these goals, but fundamental political changes would be required to bring this about. Vast allocations are needed for basic amenities — water supply, housing, and sanitation. Implementation of strategies to involve the community in its own health care with programmes such as GOBI-FFF come next. Immediate benefits would flow from the unification of the various services under one authority — a single health service for all races.

The Care of the Apartheid Child: An Urban African Study[1]

Jacklyn Cock, Erica Emdon and
Barbara Klugman

Our central argument is that this society has failed to recognize the social needs and rights of women as mothers and as workers: as a result it has failed to meet the needs of their children. Among African urban working-class women economic necessity generates a fusion of the mother/worker roles. 'Motherhood' here is a role which emphasizes the satisfaction of a child's basic physical needs — obtaining the cash income necessary to pay the rent and buy food. Given the massive disorganization of African family life in contemporary South Africa, mothers are often forced to go back into wage labour soon after birth. The inadequacy of crèches and other formal child care arrangements means that this is often done at enormous physical and emotional cost. It involves a cost to the mothers who are subjected to considerable strain and anxiety. It also involves a cost to the young children who are left alone, or in the care of aged and infirm grandmothers, or with older children whose education is disrupted for this purpose, or with ill-equipped and often expensive childminders.

Take the case of 'Sophie'.

Profile

'Sophie' is a forty-five year old African woman living in Katlehong. She is a wage worker and the mother of six children, one of whom is five years old. Sophie was born in Pimville location (Johannesburg) and was looked after by her own mother when she was a child. She is now widowed, having given birth to a total of eight children. One died at the age of twenty, and the other after eleven days.

Sophie earns R138 a month. 'I work in the kitchen at the barracks. There are twelve of us. We prepare food and menus. I started this work four years ago after giving birth to my last child. I did not go back to my old job. It was hard work. We did spot-welding. Yes, I lost benefits when I left that job because they did not register us at the Pass Office. They robbed us. I started this job because of the hardship. My eldest son, who was a breadwinner, was killed. I sold liquor but was not getting enough. I am fortunate because I foot it to work. It's near-by. We get over an hour off daily. There are dishwashers and the prisoners clean the floors. I work seven days a week from 7 a.m. until 2 p.m. I even have to work on Christmas Day. We get four weeks' leave, though. When I'm sick I send a message. They get satisfied when I come with a doctor's certificate. They pay us off when we are sick. But there are cases where money is deducted from our salaries. We don't know the reason. But there are no deductions when we are off sick. I noticed a deduction in my first salary. I questioned it but there was no explanation given me.

'I leave my young child with the other children whom I haven't been able to afford to keep at school. He spends most of his day playing. He's fond of pushing wheels. I would like there to be a crèche at work. Although I get enough food from work, the older children are lazy. They do not feed the young one properly. They don't give him enough to eat. I often wish I could take him to work with me. My children are irresponsible; they roam in the township during the day when I am at work. I suppose it's because of lack of supervision. They should eat food but they only eat bread. They only eat proper food when I'm home. I have thought of sending the young one to a crèche. But I have my doubts about it because of his age. He should go to school later. The older children are missing school. It makes me very unhappy, especially when I see other children coming back from school. But there's nothing I can do at the moment to remedy the situation. I wish I had the money to send the older children to a boarding school where they would be cared for and where they would get education. I'm not at all happy about leaving the children alone. I wish I could get an old lady to look after them. My mother is busy. She is a witchdoctor. They are alone for about six hours. I have not been able to find the right person to look after them. Besides, I can't afford it at this stage.

'I get up at 5 a.m. and make fire and cook porridge before leaving for work. When I get home I usually do some washing or ironing, then I cook supper. I do all the cooking. I usually go to bed between 10.30 and 11 p.m. If I go to bed earlier I don't sleep but start brooding. On weekends I do cleaning and washing. If I had more spare time I would like to improve myself, go to night school, or do some correspondence course. As a child I thought I'd be a nurse but my family was poor.'

Sophie has lived in the same house since 1964. She lives with her eldest daughter, her boyfriend, her daughter's two children, and five other children of her own. Altogether there are ten people in her household, and expenses are shared. Her oldest daughter earns R124 a month, and the man who stays with her contributes R60-R100 a month, 'but he is a widower with his own children'. Sophie has to work for economic reasons. 'My family wouldn't have enough to live on because my brothers and sisters do not help me although they are well off. I do prefer to work anyway because it helps me avoid all the township gossip and so on. My main complaint is that I earn very little money. That's why my children are not at school. As soon as I get my pay it's gone.'

Low wages are a major source of strain for the many African women in contemporary South Africa who are both mothers and workers. Much of this tension surfaces around the issue of child care. At the macro level child care may be viewed as an 'indexical issue': as a crucial indicator of the level of organization among women, the standard of living of the working class, and the state's concern with the reproduction of labour power. The neglect of child care in South Africa points to the state's lack of concern for the conditions under which African labour power is reproduced generally. State under-expenditure on child care is thus linked to a pattern of state neglect in policy areas such as housing, education, health, pensions, and welfare services.

The outcome, rendered all the more certain by extremely low wages for Africans, is that increasing numbers of African working women like Sophie are engaged in a struggle for daily survival which has devastating consequences for themselves and their children.

Women as Workers and Mothers

In our national sample of African working women the vast majority are mothers as well as workers.[2] Ninety-six per cent have children, and well over half of the sample (66 per cent) have pre-school children. These findings suggest that one cannot assume a fixed and invariant relation between having pre-school children and women's participation in wage labour. It is widely believed that the first acts as an obstacle or brake on the second. Instead we would argue that in our sample the need for employment is possibly amplified by the responsibility of supporting pre-school children.

This pattern contrasts with the ideological prescription that 'a woman when she becomes a mother should withdraw herself from the world, and devote herself to her child.'[3] This is clearly an option for women of the dominant classes in South Africa, and for white women who have access to cheap domestic servants,[4] but not for many African women in the urban areas. A paediatric social worker maintains that 'most mothers have to go back to work when their children are less than three months old. The children are not breast-fed and can suffer from malnutrition'.[5] In our national sample it was found that 20 per cent of the mothers went back to work when their last child was less than two months old, 62 per cent when their last child was one year old or younger, and half (52 per cent) when their last child was six months old or younger.

It is clear to us that economic necessity propels most of these African women into wage labour — often reluctantly. As one informant stated, 'It's hard. I feel it's important that a mother looks after her own children. Money shouldn't come first. But what can we do?' Several informants emphasized the absence of choice because 'prices are up' or 'times are bad'. Rising inflation, linked to rural collapse and the massive disorganization of African family life, lies behind the increasing employment of both our sample and black women generally. This increase was especially dramatic (52 per cent) between 1973 and 1981.[6] These women are mainly located in the service and agricultural sectors in the least skilled, lowest paid, and most insecure jobs.[7]

Many of them are subject to a 'dual shift', a double load of work inside and outside the home. Inflation increases the burden of domestic labour which working-class women have to bear in order to stretch the wage further. Consequently, they suffer a continual drain of resources and energy, born of tension, conflict, and sheer overwork — the last a constant feature of the experience of working-class women in other cultural and historical contexts. For black working-class women in South Africa the dual shift, and the strain of combining the roles of worker and mother, are compounded by racial oppression.

The daily routine of most of the women interviewed in depth in our small Johannesburg sample began around 5 a.m. and included very little leisure time, or even sufficient rest. Few had time or energy to participate in trade unions or community organizations. The majority of these women worked between 16 and 18 hours a day; nine of them had only six hours sleep on average a night. Their time at home is spent largely on domestic labour: 'I boil water, do cleaning, cooking, washing and ironing, when I get home in the evenings. On weekends, I do my big household chores — mostly cleaning and washing clothes.'

The typical pattern which emerged from our study was one of unremitting work in the household as well as in the place of employment, which left one informant 'exhausted to the point of death'. Relief from this treadmill depends on the access women have to other forms of support, usually in the form of an extended family structure in which other female members of the household provide a support network for the woman who is both a mother and a worker (Mullins 1982: 62; Becker 1983: 58-59). While most of the women prepared breakfast and supper for themselves, and in no single instance did their husbands help with the preparation of food, there was some sharing of household tasks, especially child care, among the women members.

While our research does not provide us with a comprehensive understanding of the nature of the urban African working-class household, a number of themes have emerged. First, this household does not refer to the small, relatively isolated monogamous unit termed 'the nuclear family'. Many households comprise a number of generations and the acute housing shortage manifests itself in excessively overcrowded homes. Most women in our Johannesburg sample reported a household size of 8 to 10 people. There also seems to be an increasing number of women living outside stable marital relationships. A large number of women were single (30 per cent) and many (78 per cent) of these were mothers of pre-school children.

It is possible that the marriage relationship is increasingly being questioned by African women. For example, an informant told Mullins: 'Of course, I want children, but I don't want to get married. I think I'm happy without a man. Some men think that they must marry you and then you sit in the house and they can go all around by themselves' (Mullins 1982: 74). One source of resistance to marriage may be the sexual division of labour within the household, which seems to be widely viewed as natural and immutable. Clearly, there is no single pattern of urban African family life, and it is equally certain that the disorganization of the family has demanded qualities of strength and resilience from African women. As Angela Davis has written of black women in America, 'Black women could hardly strive for weakness; they had to become strong for their families and their communities needed their strength to survive' (Davis 1982: 231).

In this daily struggle for survival, children are an important source of joy and meaning to many African women. As one of Malcolm's informants expressed it, 'even if it is expensive, children are making us happy' (Malcolm 1983: 57). However, in what follows our aim is to demonstrate how the struggle that this irreducible joy makes bearable is rooted in the state's failure to mediate the tension between African women's roles as mothers and workers, and how capital exploits this tension.

The Response of the State

We have argued that in South Africa among African working-class women there is a fusion of the mother/worker roles; that having pre-school children propels many mothers into wage labour; and that this has important implications for the physical and emotional health of both mother and child. In terms of protective legislation covering employees in the retail trade and the clothing industry from which our national sample was drawn, there is a prohibition on the employment of women so soon after their confinement: our findings, however, point to the ineffectiveness of such protective legislation in South Africa. Failure to implement the law extends to maternity rights, protection from working in an environment specifically dangerous to women, and restrictions on overtime and nightwork, all issues which arise specifically from the fact that working women usually carry responsibility for child care and family life.

Protective legislation is intended not only to protect the health, family life, and social needs of a mother and baby, but also to guarantee women's protection within the sphere of employment by preventing discrimination in employment practices on the basis of sex and pregnancy. In South Africa working women have never been protected from dismissal during pregnancy. Moreover, the law forbids employment immediately before and after confinement. Section 23(2) of the Factories, Machinery and Building Work Act, No. 22 of 1941 and

Section 13(2) of the Shops and Offices Act, No.75 of 1964, prohibit a pregnant employee from working between the period commencing four weeks before and ending eight weeks after the confinement. There are exemptions from this constraint in the event of still birth, or death of the child before the end of the eight week period. Clearly the intention of this law is good: the protection of the health of mother and child; but it does not consider the broader social imperatives, like the need to retain one's job.

This is not to argue that women should have to work during pregnancy. Two factors, the health of the individual woman and possible health hazards at work, should determine whether or not pregnant women work. In either case, the right to a substantial period off work after the child is born and the right to return to work should both be guaranteed.

Another important issue is maternity benefits obtainable under the Unemployment Insurance Fund.[8] At present, maternity benefits, like all other UIF benefits, are available to a select few of the working population.[9] For those who are eligible, the maximum benefit obtainable from UIF is 45 per cent of the weekly earnings. But women can only claim one week's benefit for every six weeks' employment, so that they are eligible for the full twenty-six weeks' benefits only if they have paid three years' worth of UIF. This means that to claim the full amount a woman could have a baby only at intervals of four years. In addition, says Cloete (1983: 24), 'due to the inefficient bureaucratic machinery, women mostly receive their money after the three month period'.

It was in this context that the Wiehahn Commission sat in 1979 to evaluate the state of labour relations in South Africa. One of the many issues it investigated was that of the position of working women. The Study Group on Women in Employment gave evidence to the Commission in which they compared pregnancy with military leave, saying that just as Defence Act No.44 of 1957 ensured that employees might not be dismissed from work during short periods away on military service, so pregnant women too should be guaranteed security in their jobs.[10]

The findings of the Wiehahn Commission on the question of maternity leave reflected a full cognizance of the position of working women. Its recommendations were as follows (Wiehahn Commission 1981):

5.15.6   the relevant sections of the Shops and Offices Act and of the Factories, Machinery and Building Work Act be amended so as to provide for —
  (i) the raising of the period of pre-confinement leave from four weeks to six weeks (paragraph 5.14.19);
  (ii) the raising of remuneration during approved leave due to pregnancy to 60 per cent of the employee's normal earnings (paragraph 5.14.19);
  (iii) provision be made in these Acts for prohibiting the termination of employment on account of pregnancy and that employers be required to reinstate female employees at the end of the approved absence from work (paragraph 5.14.19);

5.15.7   similar provisions to those in paragraph 5.15.6 be included in any future legislation that deals with fair employment practices (paragraph 5.14.19 (iii));

5.15.8   all applicable legislative measures to be such as to require an employer to assign light duties to pregnant women where questions of health and safety are relevant (paragraph 5.14.19);

5.15.9   the attention of the appropriate authorities be drawn to the need to streamline administrative procedures in connection with the payment of maternity benefits (paragraph 5.14.20).

The commission's argument — that the needs of women and thereby of society in general were being severely impaired by the present lack of maternity protection — fell on deaf ears. The government White Paper on confinement responded that, 'The prescribed four weeks pre-confinement leave has to the Government's knowledge not created any undue hardship and, in the absence of any sound reason why the period of leave should be increased to six weeks the Commission's recommendation in this regard cannot be supported' (1981: paragraph 4.63:657). On the issue of remuneration, responsibility was laid at the door of the Unemployment Insurance Board to look into the matter (paragraph 4.63:657-58).

On the retention of employment, the response was:

The Government cannot support the Commission's recommendation in paragraph (iii) that the termination of employment of female workers as a result of pregnancy be prohibited in terms of the relevant two Acts and that employers be required to reinstate the employees at the end of the approved absence from [work]. Such a provision would result in serious complications for employers, especially for the small employer who has to employ substitute labour when an employee takes maternity leave and who cannot afford to increase his labour complement by reinstating the employee concerned. The government would nevertheless urge employers to give cases of this nature their most sympathetic consideration and where possible to act in the spirit of the recommendation (paragraph 4.63:658).

As regards light work, the White Paper (paragraph 4.65:658) argued that the legislation 'and the administration of such legislation are not considered feasible and the recommendation can therefore not be accepted. The government is aware that this procedure takes place in practice in some cases. It urges all employers to implement this recommendation on their own accord.'

This refusal to legislate maternity protection was rationalized in terms of production losses, and failed to give serious consideration to the most critical needs of working mothers today. Granting maternity leave, protection from dismissal, and 60 per cent of a salary for the period of absence were all seen in terms of their cost to the employer or the state. The gains for individual women, families and society were not the primary issue. The fact is that it would cost the employer extra money to reserve a job for a woman since this might involve training, paying a substitute, and possibly continuing pension fund contributions and even perhaps part of the wage payments of the absent worker.

The White Paper manifested government priorities even more clearly on issues such as overtime and night work. The Factories, Machinery and Building Work Act provides that women cannot work between 6 p.m. and 6 a.m. The maximum overtime is two hours a day, on not more than three consecutive days and not more than sixty days a year in total. The Act also prevents women from working at night after 6 p.m., as does the Shops and Offices Act. (Many exemptions to this were nevertheless granted to employers.)

Both these protective laws were promulgated in recognition of the dual shift. If women were kept late at work, or expected to work at night, they would be unable to carry out their household duties. The importance of this cannot be overstated. Since women take full responsibility for the household, their days are tightly scheduled to ensure that household chores are done before and after work hours. If these hours were altered, the tenuous balance between work and home would be threatened.

Unfortunately, the evidence on these issues given to the Wiehahn

Commission took up contemporary debates in Western Europe where some countries are suggesting that the prohibition of overtime and nightwork discriminates against women, whereas all individuals should have the right to choose a job in terms of their needs and abilities. The government White Paper took up this idea by removing the meagre protection provided in the Acts described above. It wrote: 'In view of the necessity for the optimal utilisation of manpower and in order to remove any differentiation on the basis of sex, the prohibition of the Factories, Machinery and Building Work Act, 1941, and the Shops and Offices Act, 1964, on the employment of women on night work after 18h00 will be repealed . . . . The circumstances which led to the introduction of these protective measures decades ago have in the meantime changed to the extent that such protection is no longer necessary' (paragraph 4.62:657). The White Paper does not document how these 'circumstances' have changed. As we shall go on to see, the burden of child care remains squarely on the shoulders of the working class, and on women in particular. In addition, night work raises more specific problems since women would require twenty-four hour crèches plus transportation to and from work. Neither facility exists anywhere for African women at present. The net effect of all these deliberations on protective legislation is that, with the replacement of the Factories Act and the Shops and Offices Act by the Basic Conditions of Employment Act, No.3 of 1983, working women have lost the little protection that they formerly enjoyed.

Wiehahn's recommendations that women should be protected from heavy work and dismissal during pregnancy have not been implemented. We can understand this to some extent within a critique of the state's so-called 'reform' strategy. On the ideological level we find the Wiehahn Commission making proposals which conform with present practices in Europe, suggesting the importance of guaranteeing women's rights to work. The state, however, chooses to implement only those aspects which suit the needs of production and which do not fundamentally threaten apartheid. The state's suggestion to employers that they should deal sympathetically with pregnant women is also indicative of this broad policy towards the reproduction of the working class. In relation to all aspects of reproduction — health, housing, child care, etc. — we hear murmerings of 'reform'. But in every case reform is in fact part of a drive by the state and capital to improve conditions for a small part of the working class, in an attempt to incorporate this segment at an ideological level, whilst continuing or increasing the levels of control and oppression of the majority, who are left to carry the burden of reproduction on their own.

From the point of view of women, given the sexual division of labour in the home and the dual shift, Mullins argues that 'withdrawing such protective legislation cannot alleviate women's oppression but merely serves to exacerbate it. The only way out then, is for demands to be made that those protections won for women be extended to include all workers. The abstract right for workers of both sexes to be equally exploited at work, in effect, places an intolerable burden on women workers' (Mullins 1982: 29).

The Response of Capital

We now focus on management practices and policies relating to the tension experienced by many women in their roles as mothers and workers. On the basis of thirty interviews with employers,[11] three themes may be identified.

(i) *Women are widely viewed by management as temporary and intermittent workers because of their child bearing and child rearing roles.*

This is widely used as a justification for not training and promoting women. Pregnancy and child care create discontinuous work patterns, and contribute towards women workers being concentrated in the lowest paid and most unskilled jobs. The stratification applies even where there is an explicit company policy as regards non-discrimination on the basis of sex. For example, an informant from the Johannesburg head office of a large insurance company reported that 60 per cent of their total workforce of 450 were women, and that they were employed in the full spectrum of jobs from clerks to section heads and managers. However, closer questioning established that there were only two women managers out of a total of forty; the Human Resources Manager attributed this to the fact that 'very few women are totally career oriented'. Black women are located in the most subordinate jobs even where there is an explicit company commitment to non-discrimination on the basis of race. In one company where there is such an explicit commitment, the reality is 'management is white and the workers are black'. Another personnel officer reported with pride that 'we are a colour blind company' and said they employed a number of black women in 'management positions'. However, the examples cited were 'industrial nurse' and 'home economist'. Several informants described women in 'top positions' as 'single', or with diminished domestic responsibilities.

While we came across no instance of any explicit company policy as regards the employment of women with young children, 'domestic arrangements' were often probed during pre-employment screening. In one instance, we came across an informal block on the employment of women with pre-school children. The informant, the chief personnel officer of a company employing 30 000 people (approximately 12 per cent of whom are women) described how the exclusion operated: 'When I interview young white women I ask them about how many children they have, their ages, and who looks after them. I don't believe in maids . . . there should be continuous care by the mothers for the first years. Once the kids are at school it's O.K. But I steer clear of a young married woman with small children'. This exclusion was not applied to black women because 'their family structure is better. With coloured people especially, the culture is different, the families are willing to dig in. They have this family set up which is so much closer than ours.' The assumption here is that the isolation of the 'white' nuclear family created a particular tension between women's roles as workers and mothers. This tension was assumed to be diluted in the case of Africans, who were believed to exist within an extended family structure which could incorporate child care arrangements more easily in a support network.

(ii) *The tension between women's roles as mothers and as workers surfaces as a lacuna in management policy.*

'There is no policy on pregnancy', as one informant expressed it. The absence of explicit policy regarding maternity rights and maternity leave in the name of 'discretion' and 'flexibility' increases the insecurity of women workers of child-bearing age. We came across very few instances where companies have an explicit commitment to 'maternity rights', including leave and a guarantee of reinstatement after a fixed period. At the same time, we also came across few instances where management stated that pregnancy was an automatic ground for dismissal. The most common policy was to grant unpaid maternity leave, after which returning to work depended on individual negotiations governed by the following criteria: the nature of the job, particularly the skills and training invested in the worker; length of service; and the supervisor's assessment of the woman involved. However, we have heard of women workers trying to conceal their pregnancies for as long as possible so as to retain their jobs. Cloete reports an African cleaner who lost her baby when she was eight and a half months pregnant due to her efforts to conceal her condition by strapping herself down tightly (Cloete 1983: 83).

Without maternity protection a woman may be fired either as soon as the employer discovers she is pregnant, or at any point thereafter. In effect, many women workers have been faced with a choice: to be a worker or a mother. The usual upshot is that the woman loses her job, gives birth, and goes out in search of another job soon after. At a time of acute unemployment, women are increasingly in an either/or situation. To quote an African worker interviewed, 'They expect you to say, "Please Sir, can I have a baby this year?"'

Cleaners, hotel staff, waitresses and shop assistants seem to be particularly vulnerable to dismissal on the ground of pregnancy. A representative of management in the hotel trade reported that 'having pregnant women toddling around would ruin our image'. Women are automatically dismissed at their sixth month of pregnancy since 'it is not considered desirable for these women to be in the public eye'. In a few instances, pregnant women are given alternative work; 'once they start bulging they are sent into back rooms', but this is not common. Women workers are easily replaced. As one employer stated, 'there is no need to make concessions as there is a large working group to choose from'.

Management expressed a general resistance to any notion of maternity rights or guaranteed job reinstatement. This was justified on the grounds that it was 'impracticable', and 'would undermine productivity. Giving a guarantee that a job would remain open would remove some of the incentive'. However, many informants were at pains to stress that, despite the lacuna in company policy, in practice most women are re-employed after three to six months' unpaid maternity leave. This applied particularly to skilled white women workers. For example, an informant from a large insurance company reported that 'a clerk is sacked and immediately replaced; but supervisors get their jobs back nine times out of ten'. In the few instances where arrangements were made by management to cover a worker's job while she was absent on maternity leave, this involved the employment of temporary workers, part-time workers, rearranging shifts, and/or job sharing among the remaining employees.

The size of the workforce and the degree of union organization are the critical variables determining whether pregnancy is grounds for automatic dismissal.[12] From our interviews with management, it emerged that the most common policy was to grant unpaid maternity leave. In all cases where this applied, the duration of maternity leave varied from three to six months, after which the woman was dismissed if she did not report for work. The time limit involved was often 'loose' and this was justified on the grounds of flexibility. 'We try to steer clear of hard and fast rules'. In very few instances does a woman retain unconditionally benefits that normally accrue to employees for continued service. In the case of the few women in management positions, such benefits are usually retained if certain contributions, such as those to pension and medical aid funds, are maintained. For women in non-management positions, maternity leave is regarded as interrupted service and they lose benefits as well as reduce their prospects of promotion.

We did not come across a single instance of a company within our sample supplementing maternity benefits, obtainable for some women workers under UIF, from a special fund.

(iii)*While motherhood was central to management's conceptions of women, there is widespread resistance to the practical implications of this, such as the provision of crèches in the workplace.*

Management perceptions of the problems for their workers involved in child care depended on how close the informant was to workers on the shop floor. An industrial nurse at a manufacturing company in Johannesburg identified child care as 'an enormous problem'. She maintained that almost all of the one hundred women workers at the factory were 'young mothers' whose pre-school children were cared for by grandmothers during their absence at work. In her view, these grandmothers were 'very old' and 'incapable of giving adequate care'. Another industrial nurse at a different company reported that pre-school children are often left alone while their mothers are at work. In her view, such neglect was both psychologically and physically hazardous to the children: 'children get burnt and run over'. By contrast, the Human Resources Director of a large insurance company reported that the introduction of flexitime in his company had eased the burden of women workers 'specifically as regards fetching arrangements and child care'. However, it transpired that the lowest paid and most unskilled section of his workforce, 'the restaurant ladies', did not work flexitime.

None of the representatives of management interviewed reported that they provided crèches for their workers at the workplace. The general tendency was to see child care as either the responsibility of individual parents, or of the state. 'The state should be more involved in the provision of social services generally'. However, four informants expressed the view that employers should be involved in the provision of child care for their workers. 'Women with small children can't abdicate their responsibility when they come to work'. The Director of Personnel of one of South Africa's largest groups of companies, with a 1982 turnover exceeding R3 billion and employing 56 500 workers, commented, 'If a large number of women workers are employed, then employers have a social obligation to pay attention to the problem'. This group of companies at the time of the interview did so through financial contributions to crèches in Soweto, Tembisa, Claremont (Pinetown) and District Six, although these crèches were not specifically for their own employees.

There was a general resistance by all management informants to the provision of nursery facilities and crèches at the workplace, mainly on economic grounds. 'Child care is an expensive commodity. It would be too costly for an individual employer'. This informant suggested cost sharing among a number of different companies. Another pleaded the present recession. 'The focus now is on maintaining employment and avoiding retrenchments rather than on extending benefits'. However, this informant maintained that a crèche would be a good way of creating a positive image of the company in the black community: 'It would help to avoid strikes and consumer boycotts'. Another spokesman stressed disruption of productivity. 'I'm sure it would cause a disruption in the work, as don't you think the mothers would keep wanting to go to their kids?'

Other reasons given were impracticability as regards transport arrangements, where workers are drawn from a wide geographical area; restricted benefit ('A workplace crèche would only cater for a small section of the workforce': this informant had previously estimated that approximately a quarter of his workforce of 700 women had pre-school children); and that there was no demand for crèches from trade unions.

There has been such a call from organized workers in other capitalist societies. However, the demand is only meaningful in a society where women have maternity rights and guaranteed reinstatement after maternity leave. At present, in South Africa, the achievement of such rights for women workers appears to be remote. We have attempted to show that child bearing and child rearing are central to most management perceptions of women. Yet there is no recognition in either policy or practice of the tension between the roles of mother and worker. This lacuna amplifies the insecurity and exploitation of women workers who are treated as cheap and easily replaceable. We now go on to discuss the various options open to these women who are also mothers of young children.

Child Care Arrangements

The mothers of pre-school children (two-thirds of our national sample) adopted various strategies within the limits set by state policies and management practices. Almost 40 per cent of the women left their children with adult relatives, particularly grandmothers, and 10 per cent left their children with older siblings. Thus the main form of child care amongst working-class women was the extended family. However, a significant 50 per cent of the women in our sample are using forms of child care *outside* their own family, suggesting that access to support in the form of the extended family is declining. We have found that once women have to start looking outside their own families for day care, their options are limited and often severely inadequate.

A small proportion of our sample were leaving at least one of their pre-school children alone, implying a chronic lack of facilities; 9 per cent were leaving their children with neighbours; 14 per cent with childminders; 14 per cent were using crèches and 6 per cent had hired domestic servants to care for their young children. Women leaving their children with grandmothers tended to be younger and, more often than not, single.[13] Grandmothers, like childminders, are old. In our small Johannesburg sample, the average age of grandmothers involved in child care was sixty-three years. Grandmothers, however, have more access to support networks in the home than childminders, and look after on average less children (usually one or two). Other than these differences and the obvious emotional advantages of intra-familial care, grandmothers care for children in essentially similar conditions to childminders.

Neighbours tend to provide an intermediary form of child care between grandmothers and childminders. The arrangements women make with neighbours are similar to those they make with their own mothers. In both cases they pay them and have fairly informal arrangements with them over hours and accessibility. However, like childminders, they are not kin and tend to be unemployed women.

Of all these methods of child care, only crèches receive financial assistance or subsidization. In our national sample, 86 per cent of women workers with pre-school children used child care options which involved either their own families or informal township networks. As extended family assistance becomes less accessible, the care of young children increasingly gets taken over by neighbours and childminders, who then become part of the elaborate network of self-help, informal-sector activities which tend to emerge in working-class areas. These child care systems are not cheap. In Soweto, for example, we found that a crèche costs considerably less than a childminder.[14]

At the moment, the state is not providing even day care on a reasonable scale for African women. A report on day care published in 1983 found that of a pre-school population of over four million African children, only 0.37 per cent were looked after in crèches (Reilly and Hofmeyr 1983: 73). In our study of Soweto, we found that only 4 per cent of the overall pre-school population were being catered for in crèches. These crèches are predominantly funded by fees and subsidies from private welfare groups, rather than the state.

Thus, not only does the state provide almost no day care for working-class women, but the small amount of day care that does exist is funded by non-state finance. The small welfare subsidy which the Department of Co-operation and Development used to give to African crèches was withdrawn during 1983. At the time of writing the only government subsidies that African children in day care centres receive are grants-in-aid from the different local authorities and community councils, and a *per capita* subsidy of R100 per child over five years but only in crèches registered by the Department of Education and Training, whose conditions of registration are so stringent that very few crèches comply.[15]

Nor, as we stated earlier, do employers directly contribute to the provision of day care for their women workers. Numerous large companies give financial assistance to welfare groups like the African Self Help Association in Soweto, but this is indirect and not always regular. In recession, cutbacks occur and welfare bodies are inevitably among the first groups to be adversely affected. The only direct employer involvement in providing women employees with day care benefits white women workers, and this too is exceptional. Thus the workplace crèches we found during our research covered white women shift workers at ISCOR and the steel and engineering employers' federation (SEIFSA) head-office. Neither crèche had plans to extend the service to include black staff.

The Wiehahn Commission report has been the only official document in the past few years to recognize that day care is linked to women's participation in the labour market. It recommended that the provision of day care be revised to increase the number of day care centres, to raise the subsidization of day care, and to extend subsidization to welfare, church, and other private groups involved in providing day care. In contrast with the De Lange Commission's view, it recognized the importance of day care as a right to which working parents were entitled.

The De Lange Commission, set up by the Human Sciences Research Council in 1980 to investigate educational reform, did not view the issue of day care from the perspective of working parents but purely in instrumental terms relating to the costs and benefits that intervention into pre-school education would have on the formal education system. It stated (Human Sciences Research Council 1981: 92):

> The most important single reason for poor utilization of formal education is to be found in inadequate preparatory learning experiences before starting school and inadequate support from the home during the years of schooling.

To this end, the De Lange report did not recommend that the government provide more nursery schools or crèches, but simply a one-year bridging programme in *existing* primary schools. It said, furthermore (Human Sciences Research Council 1981: 108),

> In terms of expense and manpower it is unrealistic to recommend any comprehensive provision of these institutions at state expense. However it is recommended that, in addition to private welfare initiative, there should be limited development of these institutions on department initiative, but in restricted areas where the needs of small children are greatest.

No change in state involvement has resulted from these recommendations. Furthermore, subsidization is seen purely in terms of the educational needs of the child. This, while in itself laudable, ignores both the wider needs of the child and the needs of the working mother. State policy seems to be informed by the assumption that pre-school children are cared for at home; that child care is the responsibility of the family and not the state.

When looking at the situation of crèches in Soweto in more detail, we found that the way the small amount of state subsidization works in practice is highly elitist. The six West Rand Administration Board (WRAB) crèches are the only crèches in Soweto receiving significant state subsidization. They receive about R379 000 per annum from the council, which means that they are of an excellent standard. The salaries of the staff at these crèches are high compared with the others in Soweto.[16]

The high level of state involvement in the six WRAB crèches has far-reaching implications. Of a pre-school population of 192 000 children in Soweto, only 720 are in these institutions. This constitutes 0.37 per cent of children in Soweto. Private crèches in Soweto which used to receive subsidization from the Johannesburg City Council before 1973 and then from WRAB until 1982, are all experiencing a reduction of subsidization since 1983, when the Soweto Council began allocating the money. It seems that the six showpiece crèches are receiving inordinately high financial assistance, while other groups which used to receive reasonable subsidization are now receiving less.

Despite this, they run reasonable child care centres. The 4 per cent of children in Soweto who attend crèches constitute an elite group. In all crechès the diet children receive is nutritious and well-balanced,[17] and all crèches run relatively good daily programmes. The WRAB crèches offer somewhat higher quality care as most of their staff are trained and receive more money. Nevertheless, all crèches provide various educational activities, and all have had some input from the in-service programmes being run by different groups in Soweto.[18] The ratios of children to staff are sometimes high. In our sample of Soweto crèches the average ratio was 1:29, which is far above the official limit.

The physical conditions of crèches are uniformly high, as the requirements for registration as a crèche are fairly rigorous. All the crèches we visited in the course of the research had rooms opening onto verandahs and outdoor play areas. All had climbing equipment and sandpits, running water, child-sized lavatories, low basins, stoves and large rooms. On a physical level, they can therefore give the children more than adequate care. Certainly, if one considers the conditions of the average township house, with its lack of space and light, the crèches offer a pleasant, spacious alternative. The gardens of almost all crèches were grassed and well cared for — some with large shady trees and many with vegetable gardens.

To run crèches is costly and to initiate them is expensive, which partly explains why there are so few. It was estimated, even in 1982, that the cost of building a crèche which complied with the fairly strict standard laid down by the Children's Act, No.33 of 1960, was R130 000 (African Self Help Association 1982: 3).[19]

In terms of the Childrens Act, all pre-school facilities catering for more than six children must register with the relevant Department of Welfare, which then requires certain standards to be met, such as the amount of space per child and the provision of child-sized lavatories. This means that for a pre-school care facility to be legal, there must either be only six or fewer children attending it or more than R130 000 must be available in order to comply with the official standards. This leads to the situation where no pre-school which does not conform to these high standards is recognized by law.

As a result, a whole range of intermediary forms of child care have come into existence. These fall outside the scope of the Children's Act and therefore are subject to no control or monitoring. Also, many of these arrangements are in fact 'illegal' in terms of the Act. Any childminder who takes in more than six children is considered to be acting illegally as is any enterprising woman who converts her garage and takes groups of children into an informal mini-crèche. Yet because of the chronic shortage of facilities, childminding has become a major form of child care in working-class areas.

Another reason why alternative types of child care flourish is that women in many sectors of employment cannot use crèches because of factors such as unstable and unpredictable working hours.[20] Crèche hours should therefore accord with the needs of working mothers, allowing them to deliver their children yet not be late for work, and to commute from work to the crèche in time to fetch them. This is certainly not the case in Soweto, where most working women commute to Johannesburg daily. Only two crèches in our sample opened at 6.30 a.m. and only one stayed open until 5.30 p.m. Most were open for shorter hours. Thus a number of women cannot use crèches unless older children and neighbours are available to help: according to crèche supervisors the former do most of the taking and fetching. Childminders cater more fully to the needs of working-class women in terms of flexibility and accessibility.

We estimate that as many as 17 500 pre-school children in Soweto are being cared for by childminders.[21] Very little is known about this community activity. Intervention by welfare groups has been limited.[22] In Soweto, the average age of the childminders interviewed was sixty-one years. Many were sickly, having spent a long, physically exhausting life in wage labour.[23] Almost half (47 per cent) had come into childminding through illness or having experienced stress in previous employment. Given their age, it is not surprising that the majority (68 per cent) of the childminders we interviewed never took their children out.

In the totally different context of Britain, a study found that many childminders tended to see their role in passive, custodial terms, 'space is not being made for the child — the child is simply, in its most passive sense, being minded' (Jackson and Jackson 1979: 165). In our sample this was largely the case. Many childminders made the following kinds of comments when asked what the children in their care did all day: 'They play around in the yard'; 'They stay inside'; 'They play around all day. I wash nappies'; 'They sleep a lot because I must clean'; 'They play in the yard and sleep and wash'. It is likely that the physical world of many young African children is extremely restricted.

We found that each childminder in our small Sowetan sample was caring for an average of seven children. The average age of the children was one year, eight months. Almost half (47 per cent) of the childminders were caring for babies under one year. The average charge was R25 per month per child. Most (94 per cent) of these children were receiving milk daily and nearly half were fed starch and vegetables. Among our sample of twenty childminders, the ratio of children to adults was 7:1, but according to our informants even this number of children involves some strain if one is sixty to seventy years old. The limitations on energy imposed by age are exacerbated by the inadequacy of facilities in the childminders' houses. Over a third (37 per cent) of our sample had no running water in their homes. The remainder had water but only 44 per cent had hot water. The others had to heat water, if they had a stove. A proportion (16 per cent) had no stoves, and only 43 per cent had indoor toilets. Clearly, it is not easy in these conditions to keep bottles sterile, nappies dry, and children clean.

These stark and almost Dickensian conditions must be qualified by the personal attributes of the childminder herself. The women who mind children are not a homogeneous group of people and child-minding should not be characterized in crude, monochromatic terms as either good or bad. While one may find the physical amenities of a particular childminder's house very inadequate, it may be that the childminder herself is a warm, affectionate person who provides a great deal of emotional support, security, and stimulation to her charges.

Many childminders said they enjoyed childminding as it meant they were not lonely. As one woman said, 'I am used to it. I appreciate it. If they're not here weekends, I feel so sad. It's so quiet.' As it happens, this particular childminder was a highly energetic and communicative woman, giving the children comparatively good care.

Childminders are being used by increasing numbers of working-class women because they are accessible and are prepared to look after children and babies in a manner which suits the mothers. They take babies from as young as one month old and are prepared to have the children for long hours or extra days if the mother has to work over-time. They fit into the lives of working-class women in a flexible manner. Many childminders have themselves been in wage employment and can empathize with the insecurities and unstable hours which the mothers of their charges experience. Nevertheless, women interviewed are sometimes suspicious of childminders, and as a system it is open to abuse as long as its practitioners remain isolated from one another.

The Politics of Child Care

It is clear that child care arrangements are often a source of con-siderable anxiety to the mothers involved, and do not always provide their children with the optimal level of care. These private anxieties need to be translated into public issues through a politicization of the whole question of motherhood. It follows that child care should be conceptualized in political terms to generate demands on the state for more adequate child care provision and demands on capital for mater-nity rights and benefits. The working class, through trade unions and community organizations, will have to take the initiative in the struggle to achieve this. A distinction needs to be drawn here between short and long-term goals. 'As a short term demand, the provision of sufficient child care facilities is an important one which can free women from the home and open the way for women's involvement in political struggle. It is a means of uniting women to organize around a common problem, challenge authority, and learn the value of collective action, but for it to have a long-term political significance, it must be demonstrated how it is connected to the rest of society and the mainstream political struggle' (Hill 1983: 88).

Mainstream political struggles in South Africa have frequently articulated a demand for child care provision. For example, the Federation of South African Women (FSAW), formed in 1954, drafted a women's charter setting out 'what women demand' for the Congress of the People in 1955. The demands included nurseries and child welfare centres. The demand for paid maternity leave for working mothers was incorporated into the Freedom Charter adopted by the Congress of the People meeting in 1955 (Kimble and Unterhalter 1982: 26).

'We are the women who know the joy of having children and the sorrow of losing them. We know the happiness of rearing our children and the sadness caused through illness and ignorance'.[24] Walker comments, 'This statement, issued in 1955 by the Federation of South African Women, formed part of an appeal for the support of all women of South Africa. The call for solidarity was not merely rhetorical, nor a cynical political stratagem, but flowed out of the recognition that for most women motherhood is a central and unifying experience in their lives' (Walker 1982: 2).

Child care is an issue which takes us beyond the workplace and the household and raises fundamental questions about how our society is structured. It is an issue which involves shifting the boundaries between the 'private' and the 'public' spheres. At present, child care is a site of struggle built into the problem of daily survival for many African women. It is not a struggle on the larger social terrain involving collective effort but one often conducted by women alone within the hidden, isolated arena of the household. It is often a struggle of desperate dimensions — a struggle of a deeply moving kind.

Notes

1. This paper is based on a 300 page report of the same title submitted to the Second Carnegie Inquiry into Poverty and Development in South Africa in February 1984. It should be stressed that this project was conceptualized in exploratory terms. We set out to identify the difficulties experienced by a sample of working women in contemporary South Africa in relation to

the care of their pre-school children. Given the limited time and resources at our disposal, we do not claim to have produced anything near a comprehensive, definitive account of what is a large and complex social issue. Our report is the outcome of part-time work conducted by the three of us over a twelve-month period. The fact that we have worked collectively is significant, given the privatized, isolated nature of much social research. We hope that the project is a much richer document than any single one of us could have produced alone during this time.

2. Our data was obtained from interviews and questionnaires administered to 885 African women throughout South Africa. These samples were drawn from two different 'catchment areas': the workplace and the household. Our largest sample involved a total of 835 African women workers employed in the retail trade and the clothing industry. Questionnaires were administered to all the women employed by a large retail organization in a total of 62 towns throughout South Africa. These 835 women are referred to as our 'national sample population'. The remainder of our workplace sample was drawn from the clothing industry, this being the only industry in which African women constitute the majority of the workforce. We chose three different clothing factories in Johannesburg which an official from the Garment Workers Union assured us covered a range of work situations. We administered questionnaires to all their African women workers. Another 'network' sample of 50 African women was drawn from three communities in the Johannesburg area: Soweto, Alexandra, and Katlehong. We interviewed these women in depth for two reasons: first, we wanted to obtain a fuller, richer picture of their experience as mothers and as workers, and the options open to them in regard to the care of their pre-school children. We wanted to try to ascertain precisely why they had chosen these options and how they felt about them. Thus, the stress in these interviews was on the women's own subjective perceptions and experiences. Second, we wanted to explore the relation between child care and women's participation in wage labour. Do pre-school children act as an obstacle or an impetus to African women's employment? What kind of employment options are open to them? How does pregnancy interfere with their work patterns? Our interest in these questions precluded us restricting our sample to the workplace, to women presently engaged in wage labour. In our report these women are referred to as our 'small Johannesburg sample'. From these two sample populations, we hoped to illustrate the different dimensions — in both qualitative and quantitative terms — of problems relating to the care of their pre-school children experienced by African women in different urban communities, work situations, and household arrangements. One parameter

of our research is thus women who belong to the urban African working class, which implies the exclusion of the majority of African women in South Africa living in the rural areas. Given the diminishing number of black South Africans who have access to employment, accommodation, and rights to be in a 'white' urban area, we have focussed on a 'privileged' section of the African working class.

3. Quoted by Stellman 1977: 13.

4. For a discussion of the particular contradiction motherhood involves in South Africa, see Cock 1980 and 1981.

5. Quoted in *The Star*, 18.04.83.

6. Calculated from National Manpower Surveys by M. Favis. Cited by Favis 1983: 5.

7. For a more detailed account of African women's place in wage labour in South Africa, see Yawitch 1983.

8. Maternity benefits paid out under UIF increased from R5.5m in 1971 to R22.2m in 1981 (Randall 1982: 75). In 1982, they increased to R29.2m (interview with Department of Manpower official conducted by Marian Cloete, May 1983).

9. Amongst those excluded are agricultural employees (except in forestry), seasonal workers, pieceworkers, domestic servants employed in private households, and people employed on the 'fixed establishments' of the Civil Service.

10. Study Group on Women in Employment, 'Memorandum on Women in Employment', February 1978: 42-43. Amongst our management interviews, only one informant, from a large retail organization employing 1 500 workers (78 per cent of whom are black women), believed that women workers should have their jobs kept open for them and that maternity leave should be regarded as 'analogous to military service'.

11. Thirty interviews were conducted with different employers in the Johannesburg area, where women form a significant proportion of the workforce. The interviews were loosely structured and the information given often labelled as 'highly confidential', a condition which, of course, we have taken pains to respect. We attempted to cover all sectors where women workers are concentrated and a widely divergent scale of operations. Management representatives were interviewed at companies ranging from a clothing factory employing 500 workers (79 per cent of whom were women) to a large group of companies employing 226 000 workers (20 per cent of whom were women).

12. Eighteen of the women interviewed in depth in our small Johannesburg sample believed that many women were fired from their jobs because of pregnancy. One woman commented, 'Bosses get fed up with pregnant women'. This is an issue where union membership may provide some protection. A laundry worker who 'had forgotten' the name of her

union said, 'I have noticed that since we joined the union they no longer fire pregnant women'.

13. In our national sample, half of the women in the under twenty-five age group left at least one of their pre-school children with their mothers. Only 21 per cent of the older women (between thirty-five and forty-nine years old) did so.

14. We found that the average crèche cost R15 a month per child. (It went up to about R18 while the research was in progress.) Childminders, on the other hand, were charging on average R25 per month *excluding* food, and some were charging as much as R60. Furthermore, women using adult relatives to look after their young were paying them between R16 and R30 a month on average.

15. The way this subsidy has been offered in Soweto, for example, has in fact made it inaccessible to the vast majority of African day care centres. In Soweto, at least 90 per cent of crèches take children under three years of age. As these crèches are fulfilling a need in the community by taking children from two years and upwards, they are loath to raise the subsidy, which is given at crèches only where the age of acceptance is three. A spokesperson for the African Self Help Association in Soweto (ASHA) said that this Department of Education and Training subsidy was useless for their crèches as they would have to employ expensive, qualified teachers to run the five to six year old groups in order to qualify for the subsidies. She said this expense would virtually cancel out the small subsidy of R100 per child aged five to six years, making for a complete farce.

16. Teachers were earning over R250 per month compared with teachers at some ASHA crèches, who were earning less than R150 a month.

17. All the crèches we visited gave children milk and porridge for breakfast and lunch; all included starch, protein, one vegetable and occasionally salads. All gave children milk or cocoa with bread.

18. For instance, the following groups have run in-service training for the staff at Soweto crèches: Entokozweni Early Learning Centre, Johannesburg City Health Department, the Department of Education and Training, RAU, World Vision, and the Johannesburg Early Learning Society.

19. In an interview with another crèche informant it was estimated that the cost of building a crèche was much higher — R240 000.

20. Women in domestic work who sleep at their place of employment, for instance, would not be able to use crèches unless they had some help in taking and fetching their children to and from the crèche. Women who are employed in any work in which overtime has to be performed, night shift workers, and women working in any establishment operating outside normal hours would be in a similar position.

21. We estimate that there are about 2 500 childminders, each caring for about seven children in Soweto.

22. There are seven childminding schemes operating in Soweto and Alexandra. These schemes are mostly assisted by private welfare agencies. About 400 children, cared for by approximately 70 childminders, fall under such schemes. Mostly the schemes have some form of bulk buying offer, some training for the childminders, and some monitoring of the conditions under which they are working.

23. We found that 18 per cent of our sample of childminders had been garment workers; 29 per cent had been informal sector workers, sewing and selling goods; 42 per cent had been domestic servants or employed in the service sector; and 11 per cent had been professional, that is, teachers or nurses. We interviewed twenty childminders in Soweto altogether. Our additional data on the providers of child care services were obtained from thirty interviews with key informants, including donor agencies, social workers, union organizers, and educationalists, and twenty interviews and observation visits to selected crèches in Soweto, Alexandra, and Meadowlands.

24. Meeting of the Congress of Mothers, 7 August 1955. Treason Trial exhibit G838 p.2 cited by Walker (1982: 2).

Perspectives on Education in South Africa [1]

Bill Nasson

It was the end of a school day where we left our initials, hurt and momentous, in the wooden desk and schoolteacher (old Knobbleknees) rubbing off chalk from the blackboard like a nasty day from the calendar (Abse 1982: 11).

An Image of Apartheid Schooling

A Cardiff education of the 1930s may be light years away from a Soweto one of the 1980s, but we can of course still take our literary sources where we will. Whatever the point in history, there are clear and obvious connections between the quality of a culture and the quality of the system of education it provides for its children. The shadowed schoolhouse door represents a universal symbolic structure in mass schooling systems; behind it lies the sorting and grading process so intrinsic to organized learning in both capitalist and socialist societies. In one important sense, the common adolescent culture of the classroom is the pupils' own. It consolidates peer comradeship and shared moral and cultural meanings which serve their interests; their desks are their own, their satisfactions and customary practices are their own. The 1985 Student Representative Councils in coloured high schools of the Western Cape are the pupils' own. Their views of life are their own — in particular, traditions of adolescent contempt for overbearing adult authority. Those who are schooled may create a common generational identity, binding the British schoolboy who cheekily essays 'I hate Margaret Thatcher and all the Tories', to the anonymous Soweto school rebel who daubs 'Biko lives' on a classroom wall.

However, this developing classroom identity, comprising what one might call the mini-politics of educational rebellion, acquires real significance and meaning only within a particular organization of social and educational relations. In these relations it is adults who wield the most power. Therefore, an independent pupil consciousness anywhere has to function under adult control. One cannot hope to begin to understand what it is to be schooled, what is most important about educational reproduction, or how the world of schoolchildren is defined internally, unless one takes account of the controls and divisions of adult authority. Childrens' desires for, and responses to, education, are inescapably part of a sphere of relations in which school, community, state, and educational ideology all perform roles intrinsic to that system within characteristic limits defined by it. It is very difficult, for example, to live in South Africa today and be unaware of the depth of the crisis in relations between black schoolchildren, their communities, and the state. It is equally evident that there are limits to what might be achieved by such current childrens' struggles. At one level there are the limits to what is politically achievable, and also, at another level, limits to what is culturally and intellectually possible.

What best defines South African education in the end is not a picture of separate black and white systems, but a tense kind of connection. By way of illustration, let us conjure up a concrete image. The racism and class oppression which characterizes life in white farming areas is epitomized by rigid school segregation, and notorious inequalities of educational provision between black farm schools and white rural schools (Nasson 1984). But in their comings and goings, blazered white pupils are but a breath away from labourers' barefoot children. On weekdays, they might pedal or rumble past, inches away from fellow primary school pupils, slogging it out on foot to their farm school. Buses shuttle white secondary school boarders past ragged and hungry black pupils tramping ten or twelve kilometres each schoolday. At weekends, these children might sometimes share a motorized journey to the nearest rural market town: children of farmers or managers encased in the cabin of the truck, while those of the workers bounce about in the open, a metre or so away in the rear. Sharp racial division there certainly is, but there is also a visible unequal relation of coexistence.

To appreciate the critical realities of a South African childhood and education, one needs first some general grasp of the working of the dominant cultural system, and the growing degree to which it is disputed and contested by schoolchildren rebelling from below. Second, one needs to be continually aware of the importance of seeing education as a whole. In so divided a society, a satisfactory total picture of its educational systems is extremely difficult to obtain. One or other sectional African, coloured, or white account of South African schooling does not provide an adequate sample of the whole. The worst error is to suppose that if one piles up sufficient educational texts, from the apartheid orthodoxy of J.C. Coetzee (1975) to the radicalism of the recent Peter Kallaway collection (1984a), one can add them up to obtain a view of the whole body of education. One cannot.

In general, the key to making sense of South African schooling is to see the learning system in terms of interaction between its varying practices and responses. Moreover, to isolate South Africa's segregated schooling networks (Bantu Education, Christian National Education, Coloured Teaching and Education) from one another completely, is unrealistic; in practice, they interact with each other. To construct any authentic imagery of childhood and education, one needs to move into the complex worlds of divided children, with their own consciousness, social relations, and inherited expectations. It is the essential aim of any exercise of this kind to relate the realities of living as a child to the structure and spirit of the education he or she encounters. One truth about South Africa, it would seem, is to be found in understanding the relationship between its unequal systems of formal learning and its systems of early generational nurturing. A fundamental of this evolution is a teaching and an early learning about human polarization, pain, injury, power, and powerlessness.

For in childhood settings there occurs a fusing of power and privilege on the one hand, with the subordination and deprivation on the other, which closely prefigures divided adult experience. Schooling reproduces patterns of class and racial identity as well as working skills and life opportunities. Thus, the most radical differences in childrens' learning experiences are tied as closely to social class as they are to race. As a universal system of domination, injury, constraint, and social recognition, class inequality is, as Williamson (1982) has illuminated, always confronted first in the shaping experience of childhood.

Our thinking on South African schooling is perhaps still too much dominated by blanket categories. For the sake of clarity, writers, the present included, have dealt in segregationist labelling: white education, black education, liberal (white) educational history, radical (black) educational history, and so on. Without such perspectives, educational differences would naturally be impossible to define, and comparisons and contrasts regarding such factors as expenditure, pupil-teacher-ratios, and dropout rates, impossible to make. But, over and above such considerations, there is a compelling need to consider a type of analysis more accommodating to the idea of education having a single and inclusive pattern of action. Apartheid education most emphatically has a dual social and political character. We speak of, and argue about, education primarily in terms of black schooling and white schooling. But the actions of black and white schooling are continuously working upon each other in a kind of symbiosis. For to study, say, Indian education, is at once to study its relations with coloured and African education systems. To know one is to raise questions about the other.

Perhaps, as adults too preoccupied with the various branches of apartheid schooling, we stand in need of lessons from schoolchildren. Their responses to their own segregated schooling systems are not as hemmed in by conventions from the past. The greatest achievement of the post-1970s black schools rebellion has been in setting radical new terms for educational debate. Discontented school students have not simply been pressing for racial parity or equality of expenditure, but have been raising questions of educational democracy and accountability. They have clamoured for abolition of the leaving-age and corporal punishment, and for unrestricted community access to school facilities. In calling for a unitary and equal education system, any system of segregated schooling has been spurned. Thus, as set down characteristically by the Mitchell's Plain Students' Action Committee in October 1985, the cry from boycotting Western Cape high school students is for an 'equal, democratic, and non-racial education for all' (*Argus* 21.10.85). In these terms, a transformation of schooling conditions for black children can take place only on the basis of challenging the educational order as a whole.

In its provision of differing life chances for black and white children, the contradictions of that order are complex. It is apparent, as Morris (1985) among others has argued, that the image of white schooling as a simple, uniform process for the profit of the dominant class, and that of black schooling as producing a mass of subordinate workers, is misleadingly simple. Childrens' learning capacities and opportunities also depend vitally on their class origins, as 'colour is not by any means the sole determinant of the achievement of pupils or the "quality" of schooling obtained.' (Morris 1985: 24)[2] Not all black children are educated to be production line workers; not all white children end up as managers. The constraints within which children learn are those of a capitalist as well as an apartheid society.

Some Dimensions of Educational Inequality

For anyone considering schooling conditions in the 1980s, the present status and future direction of education can scarcely be adequately understood without some basic grasp of the inequalities which characterize the established order. What are the dimensions of a racially discriminatory allocation of resources?

Table 1: Percentage Distribution of Some Racial Inequalities in Educational Attainment in the Republic of South Africa

	African	*White*	*Coloured*	*Indian*
School-leavers passing final year Standard Ten Certificate (1983)	50	80	72.5	86
School-leavers obtaining university entrance (1984)	12.25	49	14.9	40

Table 2: Pupil Enrolment, 1982

	African	*White*	*Coloured*	*Indian*
All classes	3 603 039	975 414	767 340	224 322
Standard One	480 511	84 818	95 875	21 724
Standard Ten	41 127	55 216	10 844	8 576

Table 3: Pupil-Teacher Ratios, 1983

African	42.7: 1
White	18.2: 1
Coloured	26.7: 1
Indian	23.6: 1

(Omond 1985: 78-80; Nasson 1983b: 16; McIntyre 1984: 18.)

How is state policy confronting these distortions? What are we to make of promises of serious effort to end a discriminatory system? First, there is a continuing commitment to narrow the enormous gap between educational provision and educational need in black schooling by achieving what my fellow contributor Charles Simkins (1984) has termed elsewhere 'a much more defensible fiscal configuration'. Second, the principle of 'equal schooling' has been accepted and propagated as part of some steady and general advance towards a more democratic and politically legitimate society. The government is committed to what the then Prime Minister and now State President, P.W. Botha, called in 1980 'the goal of equal education for all population groups' (Omond 1985).

A point much stressed in a recent and growing body of analytical literature on South African eduction is that this policy of schooling expansion is directed, in the end, to larger purposes: more and better learning resources for black children are seen as providing a convincing basis for the growth of the good equal opportunity society of the future. Clearly there has been some quantitative growth, especially in urban black schooling provision. The budget of the department responsible for African education rose by a little over 600 per cent in the period 1972 – 1982, and by a further hike of 18 per cent in 1983 – 1984, to the benefit of African pupils in 'white' South Africa. Estimated expenditure per African pupil rose from R41.80 in 1975 – 1976 to R192.34 by 1982 – 1983. Things certainly seem to have moved forward a little since the niggardly years of Dr Hendrik Verwoerd and Bantu Education in the 1950s.

But it remains as essential as ever to keep a sense of proportion about signs of increased budgeting for black children. Spending on white pupils rose from R644 in 1975 – 1976 to R1 385 per pupil by

1982 – 1983. We might also reflect upon the fact that, while in 1983 African school enrolment was 3.6 million and white 982 276, in the most recent 1985 – 1986 budget R917 million has been allocated to African schooling out of the total education expenditure of R5 044 million, a proportion of only eighteen per cent (Omond 1985). So, while few observers would dispute the reality of expansion and the fact that, to quote Chisholm (1984: 387), 'the South African education and training apparatus is clearly in a process of transition', abnormally large inequalities remain in force. Provision of unequal shares is a habit passed down from the past. And habits to which South Africa's rulers have become addicted have a tendency to cling.

Schooling and Equality

In response to the school revolts of 1976 – 1977 and 1980, when black schooling systems began visibly falling apart, official attempts have been made to rescue black education from its Cinderella status, and to lower the temperature of school-centred political and social conflict. In the 1980s we have seen an orchestrated strategy by government and its interests to push the idea of education reform as a central element in social progress and the common good of children. The earlier aim was the maintenance of an explicitly discriminatory social order: one thinks of Verwoerd's obscene declaration in the 1950s that an African child should be schooled for servility since 'there is no place for him in the European community above the level of certain forms of labour' (Christie and Collins 1984: 173). The new purpose of education has been defined as creating conditions for a fairer society. Schooling on a basis of equality of opportunity, rather than for graded needs according to race, would help to conciliate black and white interests, and would assist incremental advancement and welfare among black children. With capitalist ways of thinking emphasizing the growth of a market order in which educational and skill inequalities between people will narrow, a reformed schooling system provides the lower rungs of a ladder for a child to make an individual climb from poverty and disadvantage. Children can expect to grow up in an increasingly meritocratic South Africa in which greater equality in knowledge, skill, and effort will lead to greater individual competition.

Pretoria's diplomats, if not yet her discontented black schoolchildren, are flocking to bleat their exhilaration at improving schooling and living standards. Characteristically, one Washington embassy official advised an American audience in November 1984 that:

> dramatic upgrading of black education has occurred . . . . From 1970 to 1980, the number of black high school students has jumped from 105 000 to 550 000 and blacks' share of total personal income rose from 25 percent to 40 percent, while the white share dropped from 75 percent to 60 percent. In short, things are changing, and for the better. Unlike other government programs, the education budget was not curtailed in the most recent budgetary provisions. For the first time it exceeded that for defence in 1983 – 1984. (*New Haven Register*, 14.11.84)

British viewers have been similarly enlightened, being informed in April 1985 that the percentage share of state expenditure on white education has been declining progressively since 1970 (ITN 18.04.85). There have been crumbs for domestic consumption as well. The number of African pupils in the 1984 matriculation year exceeded that of whites (*Cape Times* 2.05.84). Moreover, differential expenditure on white and black children has been freely conceded as unjust and indefensible by the Minister of Education and Training. He has a mind for equality of schooling expenditure, if not yet the muscle (*Sunday Times* 31.08.84).

One ought never to take apartheid apologists too literally in their moral accountancy. How credible is the premise that, under conditions of sustained economic growth, increased investment in education and rising levels of school certification will enlarge the future shares of deprived children at the bottom of every unequal life distribution? Such human capital arguments have had a long run since the 1960s, but it is time to turn our backs on them. The lessons of Plowden in the United Kingdom and Project Headstart in the USA (both influential committees of investigation on educational disadvantage) are that any notion that schooling has some innate capacity to set right disparities of wealth, welfare, and opportunity between children is highly questionable. If one accepts that what is really required to improve the life prospects of poor children are high economic growth conditions coupled to a massive redistribution of income and wealth, then the case for enlisting schooling in the battle does not appear to be a particularly strong one. An impressive range of comparative studies worldwide continue to show us, in empirical terms, the limitations of policies and programmes that attempt to ameliorate the educational disadvantages of children from impoverished backgrounds.[3] The roots of such childhood hardship lie outside of schooling, in a system of economic power and privilege in which class and racial oppression play crucial, determining roles.

It is commonly recognized that while a strategy of equal opportunity schooling can bring individual benefits and advantages to resourceful children from deprived backgrounds, it is significant that at the more critically important community level, equal educational opportunity has not greatly aided the prospects of disadvantaged children as a *group*. Thus in thinking about achieving an equitable educational order in which children might have genuine freedom and rights to benefit from this schooling choice or that schooling opportunity, the realities we have to confront include not so much its benefits for individuals as its limitations. Building classroom 'equality' between black and white youth is clearly less tricky than grappling with the unequal distribution of childhood life chances, in which the long term survival prospects of the most subordinated and very poorest are defined by the privileged and the strong.

A further point to note is the persistence of thinking that economic growth will help to reduce inequalities for children. First, growth does not guarantee conditions of social justice. Such authoritative commentators as Greenberg (1981: 21), for instance, have pointed out that 'there is little prospect that economic growth, even under the most optimistic assumptions, will fundamentally alter the economic inequalities characteristic of South Africa.'[4] Second, the reality of the mid-1980s is that of deepening recessionary slump. It is very far from certain that on present evidence, and given likely developments, the direction and rate of growth of the economy will guarantee a steadily rising standard of educational provision for all children. Government spokesmen have already indicated that a speedy equalization of educational opportunity and schooling provision at present levels would entail unacceptably high levels of public expenditure. For example, Joop den Loor, the immediate past Director-General of Finance, has already ruled out the chance of achieving educational parity between black and white within the next decade (*Cape Times* 13.08.84). Against this background, and with tens of thousands of black schoolchildren clamouring in the streets rather than in their classrooms, can one realistically foresee a dominant white community exercising disinterested self-restraint to redistribute significant resources to the poor and downtrodden? Equally, what of the additional dimension of inequality between growing towns and stagnating countryside? For the making of a common educational provision some of the contradictions seem inherently destructive.

Reformed Schooling in the 1980s

One central factor in current educational thinking is, as we have noted, an ideological transformation of schooling. This has two dimensions. One is the inextricable connection between official thinking and conservative free market doctrines, now as ascendant in South Africa as in Britain and the USA. Boiled down to basics, the key concern of market thinking is that agreed ends ('freedom', 'opportunity', 'equality') might be best achieved through the free economic activity of individuals in a market order, rather than through public investment, public enterprise, and public planning. It neatly relieves the state of full responsibility for adequate public provision of social resources.

What are the implications for children's educational welfare? As part of 'equal' welfare expenditure under South Africa's new constitution, the state will provide 'only a very basic level of social services' (Simkins 1984b: 17). The educational consequences of this strategy are far-reaching. Most fundamentally, there is the proposed ending of free education. Apparently, 'parents of all races can expect to pay school fees from 1986, bringing to an end free education in South Africa for all' (*Cape Times* 14.06.84). Not only black but poorer white working-class households will be pinched. Government education funding will meet only a minimal universal norm. While differentiated school fee limits and subsidy allocations may draw some of the sting for low income families, the state is cheating on a basic educational principle for which generations have been struggling. There is, moreover, a further, divisive implication. Prosperous communities or individuals — irrespective of colour — whose aspirations for their children outrun the minimal provision of the public school system, will be able to make up deficiencies and increase the quality of facilities by endowing those local schools which serve them. Those groups able to afford to do so, will be able to purchase better levels of public education. In practice, declared educational objectives of 'equal standards' and 'equal opportunities' for 'everyone irrespective of race, colour, creed, or sex' can become the basis of new forms of competition and social class inequality, as divided parents invest in a divided future for their children.

As in other societies, we habitually speak of work as the 'labour market' and argue about schooling in terms of the 'needs of the economy'. Such imagery in South African education is especially strong. One important consequence is the greatly expanded role of private sector investment in the provision of urban technical and vocational schooling and training. Professor J.P. de Lange, chief architect of the Human Sciences Research Council's influential and expansionary 1981 *Report on Education Provision in the RSA*, has given his personal support for this development, arguing that 'as the whole trend in South Africa in recent years has been towards . . . the involvement of private enterprise . . . I don't see why education should be excluded' (*Sunday Times* 24.06.84). South African capitalists, gripped by anxiety over skill shortages and rising youth unemployment, are evidently falling over themselves to invest in new industrial, technical, and commercial education systems for young people (Kallaway 1984b; Davies 1984; Gardiner 1984; Nasson 1983a, 1984d). In a version of partnership between government and business drawn up by one prominent industrialist, it is seen as 'essential for the private sector to accept its responsibility to supplement basic education', for 'private enterprise and government must work together to sell the system' (*Cape Times* 13.07.84). Another has set definite limits to what the state educational spending can and should accomplish, arguing that 'financing of education can no longer be borne by the taxpayer in South Africa's traditional state socialistic [sic] system' (*Sunday Times* 18.03.84). It is, of course, natural for dominant groups to think in this way, and to see the schooling and instruction of children in terms of perpetuating rather than transforming the stratified basis of society. Therefore, education is seen as an investment in the future legitimacy of a capitalist social order.

However, the real question is whether a majority of black pupils will ever be persuaded that such an educational order can serve their needs fairly. The degree to which the capitalist state retains the odour of racial repression and class privilege will surely create quite exceptional difficulties in achieving a society sufficiently legitimate to be crossed and dotted by the pens of restive students. It is one thing to offer children certain meanings and values. It is another to have these convincingly displayed in practice. To quote Williams's concise reflection (1965: 139), 'children, while at school, learn from their whole social environment as well as from the particular curriculum, to say nothing of the fact that when they leave school they have to compare what they have learned with the actual practices of their society.'

This is perhaps a most appropriate point at which to turn to South African education's adoption of a universal, liberal vocabulary. In contrast to the 1950s, 1960s and early 1970s when, as we have seen, explicit racial inequality formed the core of policy and practice, 'equal educational opportunities' has been erected as a new totem for an increasingly strained society, desperately cultivating hope for its children. The meaning of equality of opportunity seems a very different thing from real social equality in education. There is already some tentative argument that in certain instances educational outcomes between coloured and white children may now be cutting right across the usual analysis by race, introducing questions which cannot easily be negotiated within our ordinary categories of segregated schooling. Thus, in terms of traditional academic excellence, a sample of coloured high schools in Cape Town with a predominantly middle-class enrolment were shown in 1983 (a year of educational peace) to have been doing as well, if not better than, a cluster of white high schools with pupil enrolments roughly equivalent in size and social class origin. Equally importantly, the results of such coloured schools outpaced a sample of white schools with lower-middle- and working-class enrolments (Morris 1985). To anyone familiar with the ways in which contemporary British education reinforces inherited class inequality, this should hardly come as a complete surprise. Here, very clearly, is a major challenge for progressive South African educationists. If we do ultimately end racial inequalities in schooling distribution, do we then leave children to learn in the shadow of increasing class inequality?

We have to face the hard fact that equality of opportunity in learning is an elusive enough objective, without even considering the political challenge of real social equality. Schooling reform, as we have seen again and again in other societies and in past periods, invariably expresses a compromise between inherited interests and the emphasis of new ones. Thus, far from representing any meaningful break with segregationist thinking, the 1981 De Lange Commission report and the 1983 *White Paper on the Provision of Education* do not advocate the abandonment of racially differentiated schooling. What children have been offered is a sanitized version of apartheid schooling, with the promise that resources for black pupils need no longer be grossly substandard or lacking in prestige. The painfully long haul towards parity in expenditure and a more unitary system of national schooling is contained within the shell of older forms of inequality. Even in the totally unforeseeable event of schooling for black children being exactly equal to that of whites, any official standard of 'separate but equal' is likely to meet with continuing incomprehension or derision from those young people it is most intended to beguile. For, in signalling that 'each population group should have its own schools', government policy continues to shackle the future of South African children in racial chains.

For those trying to make an adequate response to the human needs, energies, and rights of all children, the system of learning proposed by the De Lange reforms is unlikely to be a windfall. What we see is yet another grading model to order and magnify inequalities between children. The report (Human Sciences Research Council 1981: 100) calls for a tripartite schooling system, weighted towards basic education as its core. Curricula are to cover 'reading, writing, arithmetic, listening, and a technical orientation'. The end of the first stage will lead either to non-formal education or to secondary schooling. The first phase consists of provision for six years of universal, compulsory schooling, with the post-basic level operating for a further three years. The principle of pupil ability 'streaming' at all levels to eliminate 'wastage' is eagerly embraced. Treatment of the 'equal and compulsory' objective merits some caution. It is envisaged that education will be 'free' and compulsory for the first six years, during which period pupils will be the beneficiaries of full state funding, with the provision. as we have already noted, of a parental fee levy. Thereafter, there are some rather large question marks. Children who make the grade for formal secondary education will be more expensively schooled in facilities which may be endowed by additional funding from wealthier communities and individual parents. If, on the other hand, children proceed to some form of vocational education, the pickings will be leaner. It is important to stress that post-basic education is viewed as compulsory learning for a further three years, but not necessarily 'education' in the common sense of the term. In short, pupils may find themselves being streamlined into technical or 'career orientated' education from the astonishingly tender age of twelve. The early ending of general schooling will force children to decide between many hard options and choices which would be difficult decisions to make even if the learning context preceding them were quite satisfactory. In practice, while middle-class children will monopolize access to formal secondary schooling, it will be working-class, overwhelmingly black, children who find themselves being shunted into narrow, non-formal work training, heavily financed by private capital. This inevitably means that for the great mass of South African children there will be a contraction in the length of formal learning in favour of hurrying them into the wage labour market as young workers with narrow skills and a limiting basic education. One recent estimate suggests that up to eight per cent of black pupils could be affected (McIntyre 1984). It is true that the idea of linking education with work, and schooling with employment, can be an admirable strategy against youth unemployment and alienation. There is nothing intrinsically suspect about the promotion of on-the-job learning and technical and vocational education for young students (Chisholm 1982). However, it is difficult, in terms of the De Lange Commission's capitalist frame of reference, to see the proposed link between education and work doing anything other than entrenching divisions of labour (Nasson 1983a: 60; 1984d: 12; Chisholm 1984: 401-402).

Dependence and Rebellion

In giving broad consideration to childrens' educational fortunes, two initial realities need to register in one's mind. First, that few if any children have a chance to grow, explore social relationships, and form an identity unencumbered by a prescribed racial classification. Perhaps in special, circumscribed contexts, one might see pre-school years as a kind of moratorium on colour differences, a moment in which some children can briefly be free to realize their common relation to a social world. On, say, white farms, with their small-scale, face-to-face paternalist relations, the young children of white owners and managers might eagerly and instinctively seek the friendship and companionship of black children. The spontaneous behaviour of some very young rural white children might be seen as not unlike that of masters' offspring in the American South under slavery, displaying 'the generous impulses of human beings not yet hardened to the possibilities for oppressing others' (Genovese 1976: 519).

Yet these are but brief moments. With the onset of formal education, children lose much potential capacity to shape their own common relations, and to achieve a common general respect. Schooling becomes a disinheritance of the instinctive social communication of early childhood. Since education is a crucial layer of experience for the majority of children, its racial and class categories impose themselves to leave an early, formative imprint. Being moulded as an Afrikaner, African, coloured, or Indian pupil is to live within barriers of thought and experience.

Second, there are the extremities of the educational spectrum. Without trying to suggest that all white children experience high quality schooling and all black children a low grade kind, we know that a lot of the latter is in virtually every respect the negative image of the former. In general terms, white schoolchildren go off to school better dressed, better fed, with better transport. The homes they leave are less cramped and better fitted with useful learning facilities and comforts. The schools they enter are well endowed. They are less crowded, more peaceful, and better serviced. They have better provision for learning, health care, and leisure. With black children long denied full rights to formal learning, their deprivation has served as the condition for the accumulation of resources to advantage white pupils. To suggest that the accelerating numerical growth of the black pupil population is the real problem behind the backlog of facilities is to muddle the critical issue, which is one of educational redistribution.

If we are to look for a few rough, simplifying parallels between the layers of black childhood experience and that of children elsewhere, some are perhaps to be found in the class structure and emotional fibre of elementary schooling in Victorian and Edwardian Britain. Attitudes, images, and values sometimes contain that sense of hierarchy and division. The consciousness of mass schooling experience might well have been plucked from the pages of Dickens's *Nicholas Nickleby* (1839). We see, for example, the survival of familiar kinds of human grading: the instructed and the uninstructed; the washed and the unwashed; the included and the excluded; the rewarded and the deprived; the powerful and the puny. To these we might add: those with sports shoes on turf and those running barefoot on sand; those with a taught tradition of white cultural domination and those widely denied access to traditions of struggle and resistance. However, the latter group do not fail to make the link between mental and material deprivation. Arguing for access to all reading material that is available in South Africa, one 1985 African matriculant has been moved to remark, 'I always wonder how it came, the white people to rule over the black people — but we demand it [access to reading material] as our right. That is why I have that desire, to have the emphasis on black history, because we should know what our rights are' (Malherbe 1985).[5]

What is no less striking is the fact that for very many poorer children, predominantly rural but urban as well, schooling is as yet nowhere near a major influence. At present half of African and coloured pupils drop out of school with four years or less of education, and are thus functionally illiterate (Pillay 1984: 7; Omond 1985: 81). In agricultural communities especially, irregular or non-attendance means that the determining experiences of childhood lie far beyond classroom walls (Nasson 1984c). The idea of schooling as a customary dividing line between childhood and adult life is of little relevance in *platteland* areas where children's labour is needed as early as possible to make an essential contribution to the income of poor households. It is plain that whatever aspect we might care to examine, in education we are compelled to confront the importance and meaning of town and country experience.

It is, however, difficult to select any single group of the young as the most deprived of formal education or the poorest. At one extreme, there are the knots of urban children surviving by their own energies and wits on and off city streets, in a cycle of child destitution reminiscent of Henry Mayhew's London street 'arabs' of the 1860s, or of the sweeps of Kingsley's *Water Babies* (1863). As an accompanying chapter on street children in Cape Town points out, numbers of very young school dropouts, freed from parental influence or other control, are living on the street by begging, stealing, or other survival strategies. At another extreme, numbers of rural children, squeezed by the demands of work and family need, can expect to spend their early years cutting, fetching and carrying, rather than behind a desk.

Where children *are* schooled, it is in rural areas that the differences in educational opportunities, expectations, and prospects are most sharply highlighted. The lives of rural white children, salting away years of cultural capital in boarding schools, could not be more remote from the wretched uncertainties of life as experienced by those children of farm workers who daily tramp country roads. In many encounters of everyday life, farm school children are often creatures of caricature. Inequalities in urban and rural facilities produce wide differences in status and perception which take their meaning from relationships of superiority and inferiority. Many people living in cities view country children as the dense and inarticulate, with a low level of knowledge and culture. Rural working-class children have their station in life painfully imprinted on them. It is important to remember that in numbers these pupils form a large constituency. African farm schools account for some three-quarters of all Department of Education and Training schooling, and instruct over two-thirds of all registered pupils (*White Paper* 1983: 19).

The learning environment could scarcely be more unfavourable. Farm schools make no provision for education beyond an elementary Standard Five, and a 1983 sample study revealed that approximatey fifty per cent of children dropped out before reaching even this minimal level (Nasson 1984a). The minority who manage to clamber to a precarious secondary school place will often find themselves defined by the image of rural 'degeneration', bovine intelligence, and pauperism. Subjective feelings of being characterized as a dunce, living out in the sticks as a *plaasskool kind* (farm school child) cannot but be cruelly numbing. They shape the child's sense of personal worth, limiting already meagre expectations and possibilities. As one rural primary teacher has remarked:

> Look, if you're a *plaasskool* pupil, life can be very difficult. There is a genuine stigma attached to coming from a farm school, believe me. Some of our kids who've made it to town secondary schools don't have an easy time there. There are ignorant pupils in those schools who look down on farm children. They think they are stupid, growing up and living on a farm. Even some of the teachers have a negative attitude. They make the kids feel inferior, treating them like slum children who can't be expected to do well at school. Would you like to be called *penkop* [pencil-head] or *plaasjapie* [country-yokel] in the classroom? (Nasson 1984b).

We can have but the barest glimmer of how these schoolchildren live in comparison to the adolescent and adult world of urban secondary education. How do they cope with the injuries of social inferiority and a *plaasskool* pedigree? What do these pupils feel about rural learning, and its relation to the education, leisure, and work lives of their town counterparts? Take, for instance, the influence of school values. The lack of inherited educational culture is costly, especially in places where the young are commuting from farms to urban schools. In schools where pupils are judged for neatness of dress as well as cleanliness, punctuality, and learning performance, it is inevitable that customary values will sharpen distinctions between 'rough' and 'respectable' children. In classroom rituals, the differences that often really matter are those between clean and dirty hands, and bare feet and shoes and socks. Schoolchildren are rarely indifferent to those classroom distinctions which cut them off from others. Many, desirous of something of their own, end up being exploited by farm employers. For example, one farmer's wife who was interviewed disclosed that in return for laundry work and domestic cleaning, she would supply sweaters and blazers, pointing out, 'I'm a great believer in helping whenever I can, but not in giving something for nothing. I try to teach them the importance of earning things they want. It doesn't do to let our workers' kids grow up thinking the world owes them a living, now does it?' (Nasson 1984b). Some farmers have even argued that preventing children from working to meet their consumption wants would not only be detrimental to their moral fibre, but would put pressure on their family household income, and thus compound poverty (Nasson 1984b). In such circumstances, the habits of personalized giving and supplicatory receiving develop quite freely within the world of the school. The effect on poorer childrens' work and cultural strategies is clearly profound.

How do such children experience the relationship between class and age within the school? Born of poor and unskilled households, many rural children encounter the bonds, deprivations, and pain of a class society simultaneously with those of age. Insofar as pupil's feelings register a low sense of self-esteem and alienation in relations with urban pupils and punitive teachers, their experience will, to borrow and adapt a phrase from Sennett and Cobb (1972), continue to reflect 'the hidden injuries of class'. Added to this are corrosive feelings of racial subordination. Do we see here the classic divisions of one kind of South African childhood? Farm schooling highlights that constant factor in South African education, namely, that childhood is a shifting concept. White children are today receiving full-time compulsory schooling when many of their black counterparts have been dropouts for years. Here, also, is the question of compulsory schooling. As against compulsory school attendance up to the age of sixteen for white, coloured, and Indian pupils, there are only four years of compulsory schooling for African children (Pillay 1984: 4). Extended compulsory education is not systematically enforced. Approximately 183 000 pupils, or less than three per cent of the total African school population of over three million, are at schools where individual local school committees have instituted compulsory education (*Argus* 8.01.86). Even at these schools, twenty-three per cent of pupils were reported to have dropped out well before the age of sixteen during 1981 – 1982 (Omond 1985: 78).

The reality of farm schooling is dependence on terms and limits set by powerful whites whose looming presence can reach down to the very threshold of learning experience. Classrooms may feel the daily weight of powerful external adult authority, expressed in the delivery of homilies on misbehaviour, obedience, and cleanliness, or in the removal of children for seasonal field labour during school hours (Nasson 1984c). God and Mammon are seldom far apart in South African schooling, and never closer than in black classrooms in 'white' farming areas.

For schoolchildren, everything in this particular world makes sense only in relation to surrounding ownership and authority. The perceived world is generally experienced as the only possible world. There are no wider, visible, and readily accessible alternative cultural traditions upon which children might draw. Children, then, invariably perceive the world during their schooling years with little real idea of the range of alternative social realities present. They absorb deferential attitudes, produced by encounters with teachers, farmers, or similar significant others. Highly confining, such schooling is mainly learning a place within the disciplinary social order and closed culture of the rural working world. What we perhaps see here is an extremely inhibiting kind of adult power, successfully infecting education with a paternalist and authoritarian tone. In such a cramping environment, children are mostly denied the power and experience to challenge or transcend the social deference taught by their elementary schooling experience.

We may stress the capacity of rural schooling to impress upon groups of children the command to conformity and natural respect for constituted authority, yet educational networks elsewhere are subject to overwhelming pressures and tensions from within. Schools in towns and schools in the countryside appear to enforce visibly and radically different experiences. The perspective which has been employed here suggests a closing reflection on the connection between education and prospects for the young. As Tapper and Salter (1978) have argued, one critically important paradox about mass schooling systems is that, while they can control children, they also have the potential to equip them for revolt. It is true that in the deference and stagnation of rural living, where a coloured childhood is experienced in the shadow of white landlordism, a subordinating schooling may reinforce within young minds notions of inferiority which their cultural experience is powerless to challenge. But schooling is both controlling and liberating: that is the source of its tension and contradiction. One should, therefore, never exaggerate the power of apartheid education to shut out the children's traditions, memories, and daily experience outside school hours. Schooling in Soweto, Sebokeng, Atteridgeville, Athlone, or Mitchell's Plain can be nurtured by threads of learning experience quite distinct from those imposed by official Social Studies or Civics curricula. These experiences, ideas, relationships, and beliefs are conveyed by both oral and literate means; or expressed in symbolism, such as politically and socially determined language preference for English over Afrikaans.

As a result, the dominant ideas of South African society do not find unchallenged space on every blackboard. Discussion of education reform and expansion is not taking place with black schoolchildren listening quietly outside the windows. In the 1980s, many of them are taking a full-throated part in it. The Azanian Students' Organization Education Charter Campaign and the Congress of South African Students' United Action for Democratic Education did not wait upon the outcome of deliberations in the Department of Education and Training. Educational relations in urban areas are more messy and volatile, less subject to total control, than farm learning. With vast numbers of schoolchildren, including some from rural towns, actively protesting the bankruptcy of their educational systems, schools are today, more than ever, areas of conflict and contradiction. Children, sometimes independently, sometimes in mutual alliance with parents, teachers, and community organizations, are able to make and remake a cultural idiom not only separated from, but also opposed to, much of the dominant educational culture. The Congress of South African Students may have been banned by the state in 1985, but its energies are surely finding new forms. There is thus a yawning chasm between the culture of Carter Ebrahim, Minister of Education and Culture, and that of coloured secondary school students. Ministerial definitions of student representative councils as bodies to arrange tea parties with school staff and to serve refreshments at official functions could not be more at odds with the wants of increasingly politicized pupils.

As a generational response to political repression, educational inequality, and spiralling unemployment among school-leavers, the traumatic schools crisis shows every indication of rolling through the 1980s and beyond. Significantly, the challenge of black schoolchildren has fanned out increasingly to take in such grievances as housing, employment, earnings, and other life prospects in a caste and class discriminatory society. The widespread dissent and raging revolt of the new young generation of black children is not just against over-crowded classrooms and equipment shortages, but is directed against the whole system of apartheid and capitalism. In the process, such children are almost completely disabling a system of mass state school-ing in various parts of the country, a phenomenon which is, to the best of one's knowledge, without any known precedent in history. The visibility and seriousness of school protests present an immediate and inescapable challenge for new and constructive policies to shape themselves directly to the energies and needs of children. But the future history of children's education cannot be predicted. It is in the making.

What of future prospects? With the casualty lists of the 1970s lengthening dramatically in the 1980s, large numbers of school-children are living through increasingly abnormal and frightening times. The unofficial alternative education programmes in class-rooms, mass school walkouts, and examination boycotts of 1985 are a reminder that many pupils have lost neither the will nor the inclina-tion to contest authority, even when faced with whips, teargas, or bullets. They may be seen by observers as premature or misguided revolutionaries, but there can be no argument as to the meaning of their courage and bloodshed. The utmost emphasis is not simply on more, 'equal', or better schooling, but on the qualitative construction of an education for a more democratic culture.

For the moment one can only hope that schoolchildren will find safe routes out of their threatened worlds, enabling them to grow old pur-suing the contradictions of a more just South African society. Possibly their continuing turbulence will go a long way towards realizing the intentions of those schoolfellows who have died violently in recent years. Whatever conclusions are reached as to their varying tactics and actual gains, there surely remains no doubt that children have been exposing what Edward Thompson (1980: 165) has called 'the nerve of outrage' against the injustices and inequalities of their society. It is perhaps not their youthful credulity but the inertia of adults which makes the rapid fulfilment of the schoolchildren's intentions appear to be a Utopian endeavour.

Notes

1. I am most grateful to Sandra Burman and Pamela Reynolds for their helpful criticism and comments on earlier drafts of this paper.
2. My thanks to Alan Morris for permission to quote from this paper.
3. For a literature survey, see Nasson (1984d).
4. My thanks to Stanley Greenberg for permission to quote from this paper.
5. My thanks to Candy Malherbe for permission to quote from her oral transcript collection.

When Families Split: Custody on Divorce in South Africa

Sandra Burman and Rebecca Fuchs

No-fault divorce was introduced into South Africa in July 1979 by the Divorce Act, No.70 of 1979. This act incorporated the existing law on custody allocation on divorce (Hahlo 1985: 390). Section 6 provides that a court shall not grant a decree of divorce until it is satisfied that the provisions made or contemplated with regard to the welfare of any child of the marriage are 'satisfactory or are the best that can be effected in the circumstances'. Our study is an investigation of the reality which results from this provision: how the welfare of the child is interpreted for purposes of custody allocation and what effect the socio-legal context has, both in determining allocations and on their subsequent effects.

The Numbers and Categories of Children Involved

The basic tenet of the South African government's apartheid policy is that each state-defined 'population group' should live and 'develop' separately. A plethora of acts differentiates and governs the lifestyle of each group. A different ministry handles each group's affairs, with the result that statistics in South Africa are usually collected for each population group separately. As we deal extensively with official documents and statistics in this chapter, we have been forced to adopt their categories.

The South African divorce rate has shown such a sharp upward trend over the past few years that at least one section of the population

— the white — appears to have one of the highest divorce rates in the world. Between 1978 and 1982 it increased by 47 per cent (Department of Statistics 1982). The white population forms 18.1 per cent of the total population (1980 census). In 1982, the last year for which, at the time of writing, extensive official divorce calculations exist, figures showed that, were existing divorce rates to remain the same, the probability was that one in 2.24 marriages would end in divorce. Comprehensive data for the intervening years is not yet available, but the available figures show a drop in the divorce rate for 1983. However, on the evidence from other countries which have had no-fault divorce systems in operation for a decade longer than South Africa, such as the United States and the United Kingdom, small fluctuations in the divorce rate do occasionally occur but have only very temporarily halted the upward trend in their divorce rates. Furthermore, our interview data indicate that South African rural areas, as a result of such restraints as religious conservatism and social stigma, have a lower divorce rate than urban areas. If, as seems likely, any decline in the divorce rate in South Africa is merely a dip in an overall trend of increase, it is probable that approximately 50 per cent of white marriages in the urban areas (where most whites live) will end in divorce.

The median ages for whites at divorce were, in 1982, 34.4 years for men and 31.3 for women. Over two-thirds of the white couples divorcing in 1982 had minor children: a total of 22 224 children, which represented an increase of about a third since 1978 (Department of Statistics 1982). Thus, the number of white children involved in divorce increased at a slower rate than did the number of divorces. The fertility rates of different population groups in the country are relevant to this discussion, in that those groups with higher fertility rates will have proportionately more children involved in their divorces. By 1983 the intrinsic growth rate of the white population was negative, with only 963 girls (who could in turn reproduce) being born for every 1 000 women (*Cape Times*, 24.03.83, citing the President's Council demographic report). Thus, the very low fertility figure for white South Africans explains the declining rate of increase in the number of white children involved in divorces. It must be stressed, however, that the absolute number of children involved is still rising.

The divorce figures for other sections of the population are less clear-cut. The official coloured and Asian figures do not reflect the actual rate of divorce among these population groups, which contain many Hindus and Muslims who do not marry by civil law and whose marriages by their religious rites are not recognized as legal marriages. Coloureds and Asians together comprise 13.8 per cent of the South African population, and of this number at least 6.4 per cent of the coloureds and 80.2 per cent of the Asians — a total of 24 per cent of the two groups combined[1] — belong to religious dominations with leaders not usually appointed by the state as marriage officers.[2] Marriages performed by these leaders are not officially regarded as civil law marriages (which must be performed by a marriage officer), and do not therefore appear in the official statistics. In other words, approximately a quarter of all coloured and Asian marriages are not recognized by the state unless a separate civil law ceremony is conducted at a magistrate's court. While practices differ throughout the country, it would seem that the majority do not have a civil ceremony. This makes accurate statistics impossible to obtain.

The official figures showed a divorce ratio in 1982 of 1 in 4.5 marriages among coloureds and 1 in 8.8 for Asians (Department of Statistics 1982). However, according to the statistics, the divorce rates for these population groups are increasing at a much higher rate than are those for whites; the coloured and Asian fertility rates (1 427/1 000 and 1 278/1 000 respectively) are also considerably higher than for whites. This has resulted in a far higher percentage increase in the number of coloured and Asian children involved in divorce than has been the case with whites, and this is likely to continue unless the birth rate drops. Table 1 shows the official figures available on the number of children involved in civil law divorces over the five years from 1978 to 1982.

Table 1: Number of Children Involved in Civil Law Divorces

Year	White	Coloured	Asian
1978	14 849	2 908	479
1979	18 123	2 704	576
1980	21 039	3 775	731
1981	22 167	5 292	958
1982	22 224	5 802	1 050

Source: Department of Statistics, Report 07-02-16, 1982

Thus, over the five-year period from 1978-82, the number of coloured and Asian children involved in divorces doubled, while the figures for whites increased by half.

Even such inadequate figures as those available for coloured and Asian divorce rates are not provided for Africans, and what figures do exist are grossly misleading. Africans may choose to avail themselves of their indigenous customary law, but it will be overridden by the civil law where the two systems conflict. African customary unions, very common in rural areas though less so in most urban areas, are afforded some legal recognition but are not given civil law marriage status because they are potentially polygamous. There is no nation-wide register of customary unions and, furthermore, many non-customary law African marriages are not recognized either. Since the religious leaders of many of the Zionist and other smaller independent African churches are not appointed as marriage officers, marriages in these churches (which in 1980 served some 29.3 per cent of the African population within the area classified as the Republic of South Africa) are not included in the official figures. The same applies to the marriages of the 35 240 African Muslims, Confucians, Hindus, and Buddhists, who constituted 2.1 per cent of the total African population in the Republic of South Africa according to the census. Thus, in addition to customary unions, the marriages of between a quarter and a third of the African population in the Republic are not recognized by the state. Their divorces are therefore not reflected in the official statistics either.

To complicate matters further, South African courts claim jurisdiction only when the husband is domiciled within South African territory, or where a plaintiff wife has been ordinarily resident there for at least one year. The Transkei, Ciskei, Bophuthatswana, and Venda are now classified as independent as a result of South Africa's 'homeland' policy, and all migrant workers and 'illegal' urban residents emanating from these territories are held to be domiciled in them. As a result, many African civil law divorces may not be heard in South African courts and do not appear in the official figures, although the individuals concerned are in fact resident in South Africa.

Finally, for those South Africans who are formally married but who have no property (usually coloured or African citizens) and are not in dispute over custody, there is often little incentive to legitimize *de facto* family breakdown with an expensive formal divorce. While they may well regard themselves as divorced, they would not appear as such in the official statistics, except possibly in the census.

Compounding the problem of what African census respondents would regard as a marriage or divorce, there are various reasons people have for not answering census questions truthfully. It is therefore difficult to know what weight to attach to the 1980 census figures. Despite the fact that the African segment of the population is by far the largest (some 68.1 per cent within the Republic according to the 1980 census, and four times that of the white),[3] the census figure for divorced African people in South Africa was only 120 000, merely 20 per cent more than the white figure. Yet there is a considerable body of anthropological and sociological literature corroborating our own fieldwork findings of a very high rate of family breakdown, if not of state-recognized divorces, among the African population. The migrant labour system, urban 'influx control' legislation and the shortage of African housing grossly aggravate the forces for family breakdown inherent in a situation of stressful urbanization and cultural change such as is taking place in South Africa today.

The fact that the number of African children affected by this rate of family breakdown is probably very high is implicit in the revelation in the 1983 President's Council demographic report that the birth rate per 1 000 African women is 2 500 female offspring. However, while the number of African children from families where marriages have been dissolved is obviously larger than that of other population groups, there are no national figures on how many are involved in state-recognized divorces.

Interpreting the Law

In a society where different traditions within groups have been preserved and emphasized by legislation, as in South Africa, it is far from certain that all groups will agree on the role of children within the family, the nature of which may itself vary from group to group. The vast majority of the population does not have the vote or play any role in the formulation of policy or legislation, and the interpretation of what constitutes satisfactory provision for a child's welfare is likely to be dictated by the values of the legislators and/or the presiding officers in the relevant courts, all of whom are white. We therefore sought to ascertain what these values were, as enunciated in legal, official, and related pronouncements.

The law itself, which applies to all population groups with civil law marriages, has very little to say on the question of who should have the right to custody of the children after divorce. The law differentiates between two kinds of care for the children: guardianship and custody. Guardianship covers the administration of the minor's property and business affairs, while custody covers the care and control of the minor's person. During the subsistence of the marriage, guardianship rests with the father (although the mother has certain rights in this sphere) and custody is shared by the parents, with the father having over-riding authority in cases of differences of opinion (Spiro 1971).[4] On divorce, sole guardianship may be awarded to either parent to the exclusion of the other, otherwise (as is usually the case) the father retains his guardianship. However, if sole guardianship is not awarded against her, a mother's consent remains necessary for the legal marriage of minor children, and she cannot be excluded by testamentary disposition from becoming guardian of the children on the death of the father. Sole custody is usually awarded to one or other parent, though the court may give custody first to the mother and, when the child has reached a certain age, to the father, or it may award custody of some children to one parent and some to another. There is no legislated preference in favour of either party as regards the custody of the children. Hahlo, an eminent legal authority in this area of the law, citing a large number of cases, wrote (1975: 461):

> As a rule, the custody of young or handicapped children and of girls of any age will be given to the mother. It is a truism that a mother's affection is better adapted to the care of a young child than a father's. But where the mother's character or past conduct is such as to render it undesirable to leave the children in her care, or where the home and circumstances of the father are more satisfactory than hers, the custody will be given to the father.

However, though the law may demonstrate only a partial preference for maternal custody awards, the predominantly Afrikaans-speaking National Party (which holds 70 per cent of the seats in the dominant House in Parliament and has been in power for thirty-seven years) has frequently expressed its views on the ethos in which it sees the law operating. Recent and authoritative utterances of the ruling party were epitomized in a parliamentary debate on the legal disabilities of women, in which the Minister of Justice assured the house (*Hansard*:

18.02.75, col.1002) that 'under Roman-Dutch law [which is the law of South Africa] the woman occupied a special position. Normally, she was the woman in the home. She was the one who had to keep the pot boiling, rear the children and keep the family ties unbroken, while the husband was the person who went out.' Furthermore, as regards African families, there have been repeated assurances from the government that it wishes to encourage stable urban family life — for example, as far back as 1956 Dr Piet Koornhof (who from 1968 to 1984 was Minister for the department which handles most African affairs and is now chairman of the President's Council) declared 'Everything possible must be done towards the building up of a stable, contented African urban population. Any policy which runs counter to this can only be to the detriment of South African social life' (*Cape Times*, 15.09.81). Since then, the government has pointed to a number of its policies as proof of its desire to create a stable urban population: for example, its acceptance of the report of the Riekert Commission of 1979 (which aimed to strengthen the position of established African communities in the 'white designated' urban areas outside the Coloured Labour Preference Area, and to afford them wider opportunities), the introduction of 99-year leasehold; the Black Communities Development Act, No.4 of 1984 (which makes such leasehold registerable and automatically renewable), and the recent announcement that the Coloured Labour Preference Area Policy is to be abolished in the Cape.[5]

For all population groups except Africans, the court for divorce is the Supreme Court, which falls under the Department of Justice. It is staffed by tenured judges drawn from the legal profession. For African divorces, the court utilized may also be the Supreme Court, at least in theory, but in practice is usually the much cheaper African Divorce Court, which until late 1984 fell under the Department of Co-operation and Development (which handles most African affairs) and was staffed by civil servants.[6] Our field work was conducted before the process of transfer began, but even at the time of writing, the personnel and venues of the Southern Divorce Court remain unchanged in practice, despite the official change. Judges are drawn from both the Afrikaans- and English-speaking sections of the white community and do not necessarily support the government's views, but the Department of Co-operation and Development is mainly comprised of Afrikaans government supporters. On the basis of these facts and the quotes above, we hypothesized that the stress on the role of the woman in child-rearing and providing a stable home would result in custody awards in both the Supreme Court and the African Divorce Court — especially the latter — reflecting a strong maternal preference, compared with awards in the United Kingdom and California. Studies of these two jurisdictions were conducted at a comparable legal stage to our study in South Africa, in that they took place between two to four years after the introduction in 1970 in both jurisdictions of no-fault divorce embodying a similar legal criterion for custody allocation.

The Statistical Findings[7]

Both the United Kingdom and Californian studies found that only a small proportion of fathers actually sought to be awarded custody of their children. Practical considerations, sex stereotypes, and legal advice all played a role in this. Only the Californian study provided a figure for the success rate of fathers who did apply — 61.1 per cent. The 1974 figure for England and Wales of fathers obtaining custody of their children on divorce was 5.5 per cent, and the 1975 figure for Scotland was 8.9 per cent (Eekelaar and Clive 1977). The Californian figure in 1972 was 7.7 per cent (Weitzman and Dixon 1979). (The figures for cases where custody of the children of one family was split between the parents came to an average of 2.7 per cent for the 1974 and 1975 samples from England, Wales, and Scotland, and was 2.4 per cent in California.)

In South Africa exactly comparable information to ascertain the success rate of applications is not available. Since it is so expensive to contest a Supreme Court divorce, only 3.8 per cent were contested in Cape Town in 1979, for example. This figure is fairly typical. (While legal aid may be obtained for a divorce case, the maximum qualifying income is very low.) The remaining 96.2 per cent of divorce cases would in the majority of instances have come before the judges at the divorce hearing with a consent paper already signed by the parties, although much bargaining may have gone on behind the scenes beforehand. Possibly a fiercely contested case may even have taken place over interim custody, which would have indicated to the parties how a judge was likely to view their opposing claims at divorce. It is therefore impossible to estimate how many fathers might apply for custody of their children were South African procedural arrangements and costs more like those in the United Kingdom and California. Nor can the success rate of those who do apply in South Africa be compared realistically with the Californian example. While judges are not bound by consent papers, in most cases agreements are accepted as they stand and made part of the divorce order. In our sample of 100 Supreme Court cases, only one case showed the court changing the custody or access arrangements from those agreed on in the consent paper.

Defended cases in the Southern Divorce Court sitting in Cape Town while much cheaper than the Supreme Court, require the use of a lawyer and are still proportionately very expensive, given the incomes of most litigants (Burman 1983).[8] It seems likely that more litigants in this court obtain legal aid than in the Supreme Court, but the files do not always reveal who has been granted legal aid and we cannot assess comparative rates. A small number of consent papers were placed before the Southern Divorce Court in Cape Town (in 7 per cent of our sample of 100 cases), but since attorneys rather than advocates may appear in the Southern Divorce Court, the main expense is incurred as soon as the services of a lawyer are engaged, and an actual courtroom contest is proportionately less expensive than in the Supreme Court. Moreover, as will be discussed below, so many additional factors for African litigants are involved in the allocation of custody that compromise is even more difficult and many more cases are contested in court than in the Supreme Court. However, because less formal procedure is used than in the Supreme Court, the files do not always reflect a father's last-minute attempt to obtain custody, and figures on success rates are therefore not available.

As regards the actual allocation of custody, Table 2 sets out our sample of 100 divorce cases drawn from the Cape Provincial Division of the Supreme Court and 100 cases drawn from the Southern Divorce Court when each was sitting in Cape Town. Table 3 sets out our one-year Cape Provincial Division Supreme Court sample of over 80 per cent of cases where one or both parties were African, or where one or both parties were Asian. The 'not applicable/not known' (NA/NK) figures apply to marriages where there were no minor children or to the rare cases (2 in our sample of 200, both in the Southern Divorce Court) where custody orders were not made at divorce. 'Other' includes cases where custody of the children was split between the parents.

Table 2: Custody Allocation in Divorce Cases: Cape Supreme Court and Southern Divorce Court Samples, 1978 – 1981

Sample Breakdown*	Wife	Husb.	Other	NA/NK	Total	% Orders Husband
Supreme Crt.						
White	35	4	3	25	67	9.5
Coloured	13	1	2	7	23	6.3
African	1	1	—	—	2	50.0
Not known/ Not applic.	5	—	—	3	8	—
Total:	54	6	5	35	100	NA
S. Div. Crt.						
African	42	13	3	42	100	21.7

* No Asians appear in the sample.

Table 3: Custody Allocation in Divorce Cases: Supreme Court Sample of Cases Selected by Population Group, 1981 – 1983

Husb./Wife breakdown*	Wife	Husb.	Other	NA/NK	Total	% Orders Husband
Asian/Asian	3	—	—	3	6	—
Asian/Coloured	6	—	—	1	7	—
African/African	15	1	—	4	20	6.3
African/Coloured	6	5	—	8	19	45.5
Coloured/African	1	—	—	—	1	—

* No coloured husbands with Asian wives appeared in the sample.

As can be seen from the last column of the tables, showing the percentage of husbands who got custody of all the minor children in the family in all cases where there were children, contrary to our expectations, the proportion of fathers obtaining custody of their children generally exceeded those in England and Wales, Scotland, or California. In our sample of 100 Supreme Court cases, 9.2 per cent of fathers with minor children obtained custody (contested or otherwise) of all their minor children, and 45.5 per cent of fathers in African/coloured marriages. Despite the acknowledged importance of age and sex in the allocation of custody, the pleadings and other documents in the case records of a third of father custody cases lacked these details. Of the 20 children involved whose ages were known, six (30 per cent) were below the age of seven. Of the 21 whose sex was known, ten (47.6 per cent) were female. The total number of children involved was thirty, and all the cases where the case records did not reveal age or sex occurred in the African/coloured marriages. In the Southern Divorce Court sample, 21.7 per cent of fathers obtained custody of all their minor children. Of the 32 children involved (all of whose ages were known), ten (31.3 per cent) were below the age of seven. Fifteen (46.9 per cent) were girls, and the court record of one case did not show the sex of the two children. In addition, in four cases (6.2 per cent of cases with minor children) in the Supreme Court and three cases (5 per cent) in the Southern Divorce Court, custody of siblings was split between the parents — an average of 5.6 per cent for both courts. In each court 2 out of 5 females and 1 out of 2 children below the age of seven were awarded to the husband in split custody cases. Information on the ages of two of the children was not shown in these case records.

Apart from the startlingly high figure for paternal custody awards in the African/coloured cases, the Southern Divorce Court figures for paternal custody are particularly remarkable in view of our hypothesis. We therefore first examined the views of the presiding officers in the courts and the lawyers.

The Presiding Officers

Interviews with five of the eighteen judges of the Cape Supreme Court did not reveal a strong maternal preference, except in the case of young children, who were usually defined as those under seven. Judges stressed that even this might not be adhered to in individual cases. One judge, for example, cited a case where the father was awarded custody of two children aged two and a half years and less than a year, because he was stable while 'his wife had gone off with a neighbour's son and was dragging these kids through sleezy flats; there was no security, no anything . . . he [the husband] was a very good father and I said, "Right, the children should be with him", and I did it with pleasure.' Judges also said that they would refuse to accept a consent paper agreement if they thought the child's interests were being sacrificed, though one said that he would call for a social welfare worker's report only if the advocates wanted it, and another acknowledged that provisions in divorce cases were frequently not carefully considered, since the pleadings provided only the bare outline of the case and 'you get in the court and there are a vast number of cases and they are thrust at you, one after the other, without a great deal of time to think about them because of the sheer volume'. (Undefended Supreme Court cases take approximately four to six minutes each, both in Johannesburg (Sinclair 1982) and Cape Town.) The judges interviewed expressed disapproval of splitting custody of siblings between the parents, and said that they would prefer to avoid such an order.

As judges stressed, in the negotiating circumstances that pertain before the divorce case reaches court, lawyers are very influential in deciding who shall obtain the custody of the children. One judge, having expressed the view that boys over seven probably need their father more than their mother, went on to say:

> We are very seldom given this sort of opportunity, except that you sit in the background as a watchbird and the attorneys know that you won't permit anything outrageous. So that's how it works: the attorneys make the law and we just do it; we've got a pruning shear but we've got nothing creative really.

Our sample of 26 lawyers, when interviewed, gave their answers largely in the light of how they would expect the judge to decide. They generally had a strong expectation of a maternal preference, unless the wife had behaved exceptionally badly and was held to be unfit to have custody. However, what they thought would constitute unacceptable behaviour in judicial eyes varied considerably, some believing that 'an immoral life-style' would weigh heavily with the judges, while others thought it would not but that heavy drinking or the use of dagga (marijuana) by the wife would — on which point others disagreed again. The case law in fact indicates that an immoral life-style *per se* would not prevent the wife from obtaining custody (Hahlo 1985: 390-91) and the judges themselves seemed more preoccupied with the stability of the home provided for the children and the quality of the care they would receive, although some expressed strong views on the use of drugs.

Interviews with all the Southern Divorce Court presiding officers (referred to as Chairmen, or where appropriate, Presidents of the Court) revealed a maternal preference in the case of young children, similar to that expressed by the Supreme Court judges, and in addition a belief that girls should stay with their mothers irrespective of age. However, again the presiding officers tended to stress that each case had to be viewed individually, though one insisted that it was up to the parents to make what provision they thought suitable for the children after custody had been awarded, rather than for the judge to investigate in detail what arrangements would be made. The presiding officers expressed disapproval of dividing the custody of siblings if it could be avoided.

As a result of the procedure observed in the Southern Divorce Court, lawyers are less frequently involved in cases there than in the Supreme Court, and the presiding officers therefore bear a much heavier responsibility in deciding on custody allocation. However, our research showed that in the Southern Divorce Court undefended cases take four to six minutes each, although this period includes the time taken by an interpreter to translate everything said in court. Where the father requested custody but the presiding officer thought the children too young to leave the mother, she had not deserted and vanished, and there was no consent paper, a social worker's report was frequently called for. The judicial officers' preference for girls remaining with the mother also occasionally led to a social worker's report being requested. But apart from these cases, the court usually accepted the request of a parent for custody, with only perfunctory enquiries as to child care provisions. Often, when a parent claimed that his or her mother or other relative would care for the child, the judicial officer did not enquire where the relative was living, although, as is explained below, it is particularly important for an African child's future.

In summary, there seems to be no strong legal authority or judicial preference, except in the case of young children and, to some extent, girls, as to how custody should be allocated, and presiding officers of both the Supreme Court and the Southern Divorce Court tended to accept the arrangements put before them in most cases. In so far as a legal and judicial preference does exist, it is against dividing custody of siblings between parents and is mainly in favour of the mother. In addition, many in the influential legal profession would apparently advise their clients that there was a strong judicial preference in favour of mother's custody and that it was a waste of money for most fathers to apply for custody. This impression was corroborated by divorcee fathers interviewed. The reason why such a high proportion of fathers obtained custody in South Africa would not therefore appear to lie with the judiciary or legal profession, but with the attitudes of the litigants themselves, *despite* legal attitudes. We therefore hypothesized that either more fathers were insisting on receiving custody or more mothers were willing to surrender it than in either the United Kingdom or California, or that both factors might operate simultaneously. Given the socio-legal facts of South Africa, we examined each population group separately to see if factors unique to the society might support this hypothesis.

Fathers' Demand for Custody

The Californian study (Weitzman and Dixon 1979: 518) shows that a major deterrent to fathers applying for custody is the practical problems involved in looking after their small children. In South Africa, among whites the use of domestic servants is common, as their wages are very low. They frequently act as nursemaids for children (even where the mother is a full-time housewife) and work long hours, living at their place of work (Cock 1980). With this alternative child care available, much of the practical deterrence to a father seeking custody of his children is removed for those able to afford such service, a category into which a large number of white fathers would fall. This would apply considerably less to other population groups in South Africa.

Although coloured fathers are less likely to be able to afford such service, another factor operating in this sector of the population may lead to a higher number of men requesting custody than would be expected from comparable international statistics. Of the 775 600 coloured population in Cape Town, 16.7 per cent are Muslim. According to Islamic law, the father should retain custody of the children after divorce. There are a number of practical, religious, and political factors which influence the decision whether or not a Muslim couple should also marry in a magistrate's office, including the fact that if they do not and the marriage breaks down, the children are regarded as illegitimate and the mother is the sole guardian. Despite this factor, many Muslims in Cape Town do not have a civil law marriage and therefore do not appear in the divorce and custody figures if the marriage disintegrates. However, those that do are likely to include a higher than average number of fathers requesting custody.

According to interviews with religious leaders and attorneys in Cape Town, the same factors would apply to Muslim and Hindu Asians.

(There are 3 960 Christian Asians in Cape Town according to the 1980 census.) Our actual cases did not confirm this demand for paternal custody, but there are only 17 420 Asians in Cape Town and only three Asian couples with children occurred in our sample, about whose religion we had no information. We were therefore unable to draw any conclusions from these cases.

In the case of Africans, both customary law considerations and the results of apartheid legislation lead to demands for father custody. Among the African population, almost all men give bridewealth (termed *lobola* among the Xhosa, who comprise the vast majority of Cape Town's African population), even where a civil law marriage takes place. In customary law, which continues to govern bridewealth transactions, the giving of *lobola* determines that the children born of the union shall belong to the man's family, and there can be no question of the mother then obtaining custody if the marriage breaks down, except on a short-term basis if the baby is very young. For the same reason, a Xhosa man will not usually pay child maintenance under customary law, except a set amount of one cow in certain circumstances.[9] The attitudes concomitant with *lobola* lead many men to express great indignation when confronted with a civil law which awards the custody of children to the mother and forces the father to pay maintenance for them, especially as African men frequently have an unusually large number of support obligations (Burman 1984) and considerably smaller incomes than the men of any other population group in South Africa. To this must be added the consideration that, despite fixed customary law to the contrary, many custodian mothers who were interviewed expressed great determination that their ex-husbands should not receive any of the *lobola* paid for the daughters of the dissolved marriages when the girls in turn married. *Lobola* payments are often equal to several months' pay — amounts which it would take years to save — and many fathers are reluctant to forfeit or jeopardize them.

An additional and very important factor operates for coloureds, Asians, and, above all, Africans. In South Africa the Group Areas Act, No.41 of 1950, obliges different population groups to live in separate areas. As a result, in the urban area of Cape Town, council housing or its equivalent is in short supply for coloureds, more difficult to come by for Asians, and almost unobtainable for Africans. While it has been officially announced that the Coloured Labour Preference Area policy of the government is to abolished, at the time of writing Africans were not yet allowed to buy any freehold fixed property in the Western Cape and could obtain houses only by renting them from the Western Cape Administration Board (with a very few exceptions).[10] African interviewees told of waiting ten years or more for houses. Houses are registered in the husband's name but, if a marriage breaks down, the wife may be able to get the house transferred to her if she has a divorce certificate showing that custody has been awarded to her. Loss of a house by a man means going to the bottom of the housing list. The policy of influx control prevents any African without urban residence rights from living in an urban area, and a woman from a rural area cannot obtain urban rights unless her husband has a house in which they can live. Thus, if an African man loses custody of his children, and thereby loses his house, should he subsequently marry a woman without urban rights, he will not be able to bring her to live in the urban area until he can get another house. They may not become lodgers. The incentive to contest custody, not for the sake of the children but to retain the house, is therefore strong.

For all these reasons, it is not surprising that every session in the Southern Divorce Court is the scene of bitter custody fights and that our sample showed 21.7 per cent of African fathers obtaining custody.

The group areas policy gives rise to even stronger reasons for paternal custody claims in the case of marriages between different population groups, particularly between Africans and coloureds.[11] Our one-year sample included twenty such marriages, in all but one of which the wife was coloured. In these cases, the couple must live in an African township and their children will be classified as African unless the mother has been able to obtain coloured classification for them, which is very difficult.[12] (Coloured classification carries many economic and other benefits, compared to African classification, and is therefore much sought after.) Should the marriage break up, children classified as African cannot live in a coloured group area. Nor can they attend a school in a coloured area. Thus, if, as is frequently the case, the wife in such marriages is coloured and the children are classified as African, the children must remain with the father. According to the law, their mother, as a coloured divorced woman, cannot obtain any house or lodger's permit in an African area (although the housing officials in practice can, and frequently do, turn a blind eye to the mother's classification if there are children and she wishes to remain in the marital home). The children cannot live with her in her coloured area. Nor are the children who are not white allowed to live with a parent who is a live-in domestic servant in a white area. Lawyers and social workers told of distraught women clients finding themselves trapped by the law. If, as interviews indicated, a frequent pattern is that women in such marriage breakdowns wish to leave the township, it is not surprising that almost half our sample of fathers in this type of marriage obtained custody of their children.

Mothers' Surrender and Custody

Similarly, a variety of factors unique to South Africa may cause a woman to surrender her custody claim more frequently than is the case in the United Kingdom or California. Some affect all population groups.

First, South Africa is a country with a strong Calvinist tradition in some sections of the community, and the concept of no-fault divorce is of only recent introduction. The attitudes and expectations that still exist as a result, and the quite frequently found lawyers' view that adultery would prevent a mother from obtaining custody, probably deter some women from even contesting it.

Second, among the poorer sections of the community, many women cannot afford to support their children on their own. There is no equal pay legislation in South Africa, and the disparity between women's and men's pay exists at all income levels except, to some extent, the professional, with the greatest disparities in Cape Town found between African men's and women's pay. As a result of the Coloured Labour Preference Area policy, most African women with jobs in Cape Town work as domestic servants. Live-in jobs are easier to find but do not permit children to live with their mothers. Live-out jobs frequently involve very long hours. In either case, the problems of obtaining and paying for child care are manifold (Burman and Barry 1984; Cock, Emdon and Klugman 1984). In addition, South Africa's welfare system is both rudimentary and racially graded, providing very little assistance for divorced African mothers, and none where the mother is able-bodied but unemployed. Maintenance payments from husbands, where awarded and actually paid, are usually minimal (Burman and Barry 1984). For such a woman (and for a coloured domestic live-in servant too) without a second household income to shorten her work hours or help pay expensive boarding school fees, the two most common alternatives are equally distasteful. Her children may roam the streets in gangs constantly involved in petty crime — a feature of the African and coloured townships (Hund and Kotu-Rammopo 1983, Pinnock 1984) — or may be sent back to their grandparents or other family in the rural areas. In the latter case they will probably be better supervised and it is cheaper to support them there, but their mother will not see them for long periods and the rural solution frequently involves loss of urban rights for the African children, a problem discussed in more detail below. Both divorce records and interviews produced cases where women were unable to to contest custody because they felt unable to care for and provide for their children in the circumstances they faced.

Third, for African women there is the consideration of preserving their children's rights to urban residence. As there was large-scale malnutrition, an absence of employment opportunities, and a high child mortality rate in many of the rural areas even before the recent disastrous drought (Randall 1983: 529), urban rights are exceptionally valuable. Many women hold urban rights only by virtue of being the wife of a man who qualified for them in the past through birth, ten years' legal residence, or fifteen years' legal employment in an urban area. On divorce they lose these rights and are liable to be endorsed out to a rural area. Should they obtain custody, the children must accompany them. Residence away from the urban area for more than a few months usually results in loss of existing urban rights, even where acquired by virtue of birth in an urban area. Rather than deprive their children of urban rights in this way, some women may choose not to contest custody.

Given all these considerations, it seems likely that the high number of fathers gaining custody of their children is the result both of more fathers requesting it and more women surrendering it. In other words, despite government pronouncements and legal expectations to the contrary, local conditions, legal procedure, attitudes engendered by religious and customary laws, and apartheid policy produce an unusually high proportion of children who are not brought up by their mothers.

The Reality of Custody Allocation in South Africa

Even the above figures of non-maternal custody do not reflect the degree of non-maternal care for many children after divorce. The implications for the children of a custody allocation will depend on what arrangements are made for their care after the divorce, which in turn will depend on the child care and incomes available, as well as family patterns.

As noted above, the Supreme Court and Southern Divorce Court devote very little time to investigating exact arrangements for the children after divorce, and one President of the Southern Divorce Court specifically stated that it was not the court's business to do so. This attitude is no doubt dictated by the Southern Divorce Court's relative helplessness to influence the post-divorce situation of the children. The court is unable to reallocate the crucially important urban house, for example (this is done by an administrative committee), and so is unable to ensure that the mother will in fact obtain it. If she does not, she may be unable to claim the children in practice, even after winning custody, and cases of this type were encountered, especially where the father remarried. As indicated above as well, for many Cape Town children, custody allocation to mothers who are forced to work long hours means that the children receive very little maternal care in practice. One divorced social worker who had herself been a domestic worker described their situation as 'sometimes going to work, leaving not a piece of bread in the house and not knowing who will look after the children after school'.

Much the same may apply if the father is granted custody, though the evidence indicates that more frequently the lack of care is due to interests outside the home rather than extreme economic pressure. A President of the Southern Divorce Court who spoke of the difficulty of distinguishing in court which men wished to obtain custody of their children merely to avoid paying maintenance, described the result of allocation to such fathers:

> If he gets custody, he doesn't pay anything and he doesn't feed them either — he just leaves them to themselves. That's why you find perhaps dozens of them, perhaps thousands of them — I don't know — roaming the streets, looking for food, stealing. They're hungry. And not because they're orphans; they have parents, but . . . they're in the care of the father, who doesn't care.

Non-parental care in either case, if provided at all, is often from busy relatives, friends, or other children. The housing policy, which prevents non-working grandparents without urban rights from joining their children in the towns, deprives many urban families of a common source of child care and discipline in rural settings. Interviewees from all sections of Cape Town's African areas repeatedly stressed that the uncontrollable child is a major problem confronting township parents, and court social workers identified the absence of family control and resulting truancy as the almost invariable early background of children appearing before the juvenile court.

Because of child care difficulties, financial problems, and traditional African extended family patterns, African parents who obtain custody of their children (and to a lesser extent, coloured parents) frequently send their children to live with grandparents or family in either urban or rural areas. Even our small Southern Divorce Court sample showed that, to the Court's knowledge, children in a third of the cases were being reared by grandparents or other family members without the presence of the parents. Moreover, the disruption of family life has led not only to a high divorce rate among the African and coloured population groups, but also to a very high rate of illegitimacy (by any legal definition). As a result, interviews frequently revealed grandparents bringing up the offspring of several of their children; thus, a number of cousins were being reared together. While it was common in traditional Xhosa homesteads for cousins to grow up together, their parents lived in the homesteads too. In contrast, our fieldwork showed that many of the households in which, for example, grandparents and grandchildren resided, did not encompass the young children's parents. African children, particularly, appeared to be moved between parents and various relatives several times as they grew up, as circumstances necessitated. Stories of child neglect, especially where parents failed to send money, were told by divorcees, doctors, and social workers on a number of occasions. Despite its resemblance to the extended family described by legal and ethnographic textbooks early this century, it is a new form of extended family that appears to be taking shape, with children frequently seeing very little of their parents and often placed with poverty-stricken relatives who sometimes provide most inferior care. While there are indications that such a family pattern has been increasing throughout this century, especially since the large-scale urbanization of African women began, court records and interview data all indicate that it now operates on so large a scale as to have a major effect on African family life.

In contrast, in other sections of the community, especially the white, the very high divorce rate at a young age, with remarriage frequently to other divorcees, is producing a complex pattern of children growing up with their full brothers and sisters, and, in addition, one or more sets of half- and/or step-brothers and sisters. Our interview sample, for example, included one woman who had married and divorced twice, producing children in each marriage. Her second husband went on to marry a second time, producing another family. His second wife was a divorcee with a family from her first marriage. As a result of normal weekend and holiday access arrangements, the children of the interviewee's two marriages lived with a total of four families of half-and step-brothers and sisters, as well as spending periods in children's homes. While this was the most extreme case we encountered in our very small sample, it was echoed in various forms by a number of other such cases. The amount of contact between such families may be much increased where the man has custody of his children by an earlier marriage rather than just having them to stay at weekends or for holidays. In the case mentioned above, a daughter of the second marriage went to live with her father and his second wife and families for several years, since her mother's work kept her away from home so much, even though she remained the nominal custodian. As with the African family, marriage break-up is causing extended families to emerge among the whites too, but of a type different from that of Africans. The main feature of the white extended family is that it always includes one biological parent of the children and usually spans only two generations. While it resembles the type of extended family of earlier centuries which was sometimes created by the high mortality rate in relatively young spouses, it is, potentially at least, both more complex in composition and emotionally more fraught. Neither the white nor the black form repeats extended family patterns of the nineteenth century, and both frequently involve a large amount of non-maternal care. Whether either pattern provides a stable background for the children is open to question.

It would therefore seem that, despite the stated aim of the law and enunciated government policy to ensure that the most stable family pattern possible is provided for the children involved in divorce cases, the socio-legal system of South Africa has an autonomous, complex logic of its own. More than in the United Kingdom or California, the law, the judicial officers, and the government interpret maternal custody as generally the most satisfactory way of providing stability for the children of a family in a range of circumstances, yet the courts make more custody allocations to fathers than occurs in either of the overseas countries examined. Many of these awards are of children whose age and sex should, according to the given criteria, lead to them being placed in maternal custody. This is especially so in the case of African families, where the reasons why custody is sought by fathers are clearly frequently dictated by considerations other than the children's best interests. The presiding officers in the South African courts examined were also opposed to split custody, yet again a higher proportion of split custody allocations occurred in our sample than in either of the overseas countries examined. Moreover, even where maternal custody is granted, South African conditions have resulted in economic and legislated circumstances which frequently make maternal care difficult to provide and have led to a pattern of family care in which children live with their mother far less than in families which have not suffered from divorce. Nor is it clear that these family patterns provide stable environments for the children. The evidence available would seem to indicate that quite the reverse is the case.

It is instructive that even as authoritarian a government as the South African, which purports to control so many aspects of life, cannot control the results of the complex forces it has generated through its social engineering. While law in South Africa may well be formulated and enforced by the ruling regime more nakedly than in most countries, its limitations as a manipulative tool are evident. The basic unit desired for urban South African society — a stable nuclear family in which the mother provides child care — is disintegrating, partly as a result of legislation arising from other aspects of government policy. And as nuclear families become increasingly unstable, socio-legal forces are inexorably producing family patterns diametrically opposed to that which the government desires.

Notes

We are indebted to Dr K. Hughes and Mr B. du Plessis for helpful comments on a preliminary draft of this chapter. The research for it was sponsored by the British Academy, Lady Margaret Hall, Oxford, the Nuffield Foundation, the Social Science Research Council, the Anglo-American and De Beer's Chairman's Fund, the Centre for Intergroup Studies, the Harry Oppenheimer Institute for African Studies, and the Research Committee, University of Cape Town.

1. This figure is taken from the 1980 census table of religious affiliation, for which some of the population did not supply details.

2. To qualify as a marriage officer, a religious leader must have reached a prescribed level of education and, in addition, pass a state examination and swear an oath which includes an undertaking not to perform polygamous marriages.

3. This figure excludes those areas of South Africa which in 1980 were classified as independent African national states.

4. An alternative interpretation of the early Dutch legal authorities places a different emphasis on custody and guardianship during the subsistence of the marriage: 'Although the parental power over a legitimate minor child is vested in both parents, the father has the decisive say in the case of a difference of opinion between the parents . . . . Custody is normally an integral incident of the parental power, which power normally includes the control of a minor child's person ("custody"), and administration of his property and the power to represent him in the performance of juristic acts or in civil litigation . . . . However, this incident can be (and in the case of divorce between the child's parents usually is) separated from the remainder of the parental power.' (Erasmus, Van der Merwe and Van Wyk 1983: 161, 131).

5. For a discussion of the government's desired limits to the policy, see Morris (1985).

6. In September 1984 courts which were administered by the Department of Co-operation and Development were officially transferred to the Department of Justice (GN R131 *GG* of 10.08.84 (*Reg. Gaz.* 3729)).

7. The data for this investigation is the result of a small-scale study of the question in Cape Town, with some supplementary interviews in Johannesburg, Grahamstown, and King William's Town. A random sample of 100 divorce cases was drawn from the Cape Provincial Division of the Supreme Court sitting in Cape Town, taking every case after certain arbitrary dates between 1978 and 1981. One hundred divorce cases were drawn in the same way from the Southern (African) Divorce Court. In addition, details were noted of over 80 per cent of all Cape Provincial Division Supreme Court cases over a period of twelve months (1981-82) where one or both divorcees were recorded as African or Asian. As none of these records are open to the public, individual cases may not be identified. Further, over 450 cases were observed in the Southern Divorce Court and several days were also spent observing cases in the office of the Southern Divorce Court clerk. Again, as office cases are not open to the public, individual cases cannot be identified. Lengthy interviews were conducted with over a quarter of the Cape Supreme Court judges and a Transvaal Supreme Court judge, all the presiding officers of the Southern Divorce Court, court officials of all the courts involved, 26 practising attorneys and advocates, 15 social workers, 7 religious leaders, and 30 divorcees, all samples being chosen to give as wide a

range as possible of the different income, religious and 'racial' sections of Cape Town. However, given the sensitive nature of the questions being asked, most interviews were granted on condition that the informants were not cited by name. The Supreme Court is divided into six divisions and the African Divorce Court into three. Each division has certain practices peculiar to it, and some of the customary law cited is peculiar to the Xhosa, who comprise the vast majority of Cape Town's African population. The varied population distribution and economic conditions of the different areas of South Africa make this study to some extent peculiar to Cape Town.

8. The practice of the Divorce Court clerk ceasing to act for the plaintiff where the case is defended is, it seems, unique to Cape Town.

9. In customary law it is payable by a child's guardian who claims custody of the child after it has been brought up or maintained by another, irrespective of the length of time for which it was kept or the actual expenditure incurred in keeping it (Bekker and Coertze 1982: 241). In practice nowadays, the amount paid may be adjusted closer to the actual expense incurred.

10. The Uluntu Utility Company, sponsored by three companies, leases a very limited number of houses on 30-year leasehold in one of the townships, and in addition, at the time of writing, a site-and-service scheme is in the process of being established by the housing authorities. It has been announced that 99-year leasehold is being introduced into the Western Cape for Africans too.

11. In the period during which our research took place, a marriage between a white person and anyone of another population group was invalid under the Prohibition of Mixed Marriages Act, No.55 of 1949. Hence we had no marriages of this kind in the sample. Population groups other than whites were not prohibited from intermarrying, and in 1985 the abolition of the Act made marriages between whites and other population groups legal as well, for the first time in thirty-five years. However, the Group Areas Act and 'racial' classification system (initially legislated under the Population Registration Act, No.30 of 1950) remain in force. Whites who marry someone of another population classification have to move to that person's Group Area.

12. The father's 'race classification' is normally followed for the children but, in terms of the Population Registration Act, the mother may obtain coloured classification for her children if she can show that in appearance and lifestyle they more closely resemble their coloured parent than their African one. What will happen in the case of a white parent in a 'mixed' marriage who wishes to pass on his or her classification to the children of the marriage, particularly those who are light-skinned and educated at multi-racial private schools, remains to be seen.

Beginning Life in an Apartheid Society: Childbirth in South Africa

Helen Zille

Although we all came into the world that way and do not remember how we did it, birth is probably the most momentous of all life's passages. It is also one of the most precarious. A single mistake can make the difference between a 'normal' life and one burdened with disability. Yet childbirth is more than the start of a new life. It is also the entry into a new existence for the mother. It makes no difference that billions of women have lived through the experience. Unlike a space-walk or a heart-transplant, the uniqueness of a first childbirth is never dulled by repetition.

During a first pregnancy, when an expectant mother's attention is focussed on the climax of birth, it is difficult to imagine life after labour. Yet childbirth is merely the short beginning of a lifetime's commitment and responsibility. As Ann Oakley points out (1979: 24), a first childbirth is never just another event in a woman's life. It is 'a turning point, a transition, a life crisis. A first baby turns a woman into a mother, and mothers' lives are incurably affected by their motherhood; in one way or another the child will be a theme forever'.

The aim of this chapter is to reflect the vastly different ways South Africans enter the world and to examine some of the factors responsible for this discrepancy. Although sociological studies of childbirth have been done in other countries, in South Africa the subject is generally approached from a strictly medical perspective. What follows is an attempt to place the available data in a socio-political perspective.[1]

Privileged South Africa

In the enormity of its impact, my own experience of childbirth was entirely unremarkable. Yet it would be difficult to find an example less representative of the majority of South African women. Using my own experience as a starting point, I set out to compare the different ways South African mothers and their babies experience birth. It soon became clear how all the factors that make me 'typical' — a career woman grappling to come to terms with childbirth in an advanced industrial society — make me the rare exception in the South African context.

Here, in brief, is my story. I am married to my child's father and we live together in our own home. Our decision to have a child was a conscious and deliberate one, taken when I was thirty-two years old and had devoted ten uninterrupted years to my career. After two early miscarriages, I had ready access to the best private gynaecological care, which we could comfortably afford through our medical aid scheme. My husband showed an abiding interest in my pregancy and together we read many books on the subject, following the development of our fetus with fascination. I attended ante-natal classes and felt free to discuss the most trivial concern with a gynaecologist who made me an equal partner in his step-by-step monitoring of my pregnancy. We toyed with the idea of a home birth, but eventually decided that an 'elderly primigravida' should have a maternity hospital's back-up services. Nevertheless, we were determined that nature should take its course without any technical assistance. Fourteen hours into labour, we changed our minds. In the end, I had every assistance advanced technology could offer — from epidural anaesthesia to a forceps delivery. Our son emerged unscathed, weighing a healthy 3.75 kg (7 lbs 14 ozs) — the only evidence of the metallic grip that pulled him into the world being two pink pincer marks perfectly positioned on either side of his skull.

The quality of post-natal care did not match that of the labour ward. With several notable exceptions, the nursing sisters seemed like perpetual school prefects — officious and inflexible, with that rare ability to recognize vulnerability at a distance and approach it with a sugar-coated rapier: 'I really don't know how you are ever going to manage at home, my dear.' I failed to get a grip on the hospital routine, and found out about the available facilities by accident, usually after I needed them. Overwhelmed by contradictory advice and ragged from lack of sleep, I consulted my mini-library of child care books for clues as to why my baby cried continually when all the other babies seemed to wake only for their four-hourly feeds. Eventually I found out about what nursing jargon describes as the 'test-weigh' that enabled me to gauge how much milk he was getting and confirm my suspicion that he was grossly underfed. Ignoring warnings that bottle-fed babies reject the breast, I followed each breast feed with a complement feed, using the sterilized bottles of milk that conveniently appeared each day on a trolley in the nursery.

When I went home, we could comfortably afford to buy formula feeds and had the modern conveniences — such as running water and electricity — that made sterilizing his bottles and washing his nappies a relatively painless procedure. And when I began to sink beneath a post-partum depression, I found solace and understanding through books, the best medical care available, and a supportive husband.

Although the quality of medical and marital support I received were probably exceptional, even in the context of the white community, my account fits fairly comfortably within the parameters Ann Oakley describes as she works towards 'a sociology of childbirth' in her book *Women Confined* (1980: 293). She defines her work as 'an elaboration of the way in which women as reproducers are socially defined in one particular historical period — the advanced industrial society of Britain in the latter half of the twentieth century'. Challenging the prevailing 'mistakes and mystiques' of 'male science' that imbue all women with natural childbearing capabilities, she argues that women experience childbirth as a 'life-event', in a similar category to other major watersheds (such as surgery or bereavement) that are normally accompanied by disturbing effects. Drawing on a wide range of interviews with women who have experienced a first childbirth, she describes the vast discrepancy between the idealized 'institution' of motherhood and 'the reality'.

Her analysis strikes a resonant chord in women who are in a similar personal, cultural, political and economic position — the patriarchal world of the advanced industrialized society. Yet, looking beyond these boundaries to the experience of the majority of mothers in South Africa, it becomes clear that many conditions Western feminists regard as pathological often represent the highest form of relative privilege.

Majority South Africa

In South Africa, most women suffer a more broadly based and pervasive form of structural oppression than the patriarchal bias of economically developed capitalist societies. With their traditional social networks damaged after a century of industrialization, many black women are battling against great odds to build new, stable relationship structures in the developing urban economy or in remote rural areas. To a great extent, their positions are defined and controlled by a system known to the world in its shorthand form as apartheid.

As part of its original formulation, apartheid sought to perpetuate white control over the developing economy in 87 per cent of South Africa by dividing the remaining 13 per cent into ten fragmented rural 'homelands' for 67 per cent of the population according to their ethnic affiliations, thus depriving them of any 'right' to political power in the rest of the country. Although the South African government has now undertaken to revise key aspects of apartheid, the rigid implementation of the policy for more than three decades has etched deep scars in South African society that will long outlive the system itself. One of its most devastating effects has been its contribution to the decimation of African social bonds while making urban nuclear family structures extremely difficult to attain. Trudi Thomas (1982: 1), a doctor who has spent much of her working life at a rural clinic in the Ciskei, describes the situation as one of 'social chaos — the word chaos being used advisedly and unemotionally to describe gross disorganization'.

This disorganization lies at the root of the vast discrepancy between the birth (and life) experiences of different categories of South African women. Each individual is radically affected by her own legal position in relation to the central tenets of apartheid: migrant labour, influx control, the urban housing policy, and forced removals. These laws have divided South African women into two main groups: those who are legally permitted to live with their husbands and children in their own homes in the place of their choice, and those who are not. While most white women take these rights for granted, black women are all subject to some combination of these laws which sets the parameters for all their life options.

All blacks are not equally disadvantaged. Indeed, apartheid has created and entrenched marked stratification within black society. Among African women, the peak of the pyramid of relative privilege is occupied by those with legal rights to live in the city with their partners and children. At the bottom are the unemployed single parents in remote rural areas, unmarried or abandoned by their husbands, and without the means or rights to move to the cities in search of work. University of Cape Town economist Charles Simkins (1983: 83) estimates that one in four African women is separated from her husband, primarily through the operation of influx control laws which have kept South Africa's urbanization rate considerably below what would be expected in a country of its economic development. Many of the last remaining bastions of African rural security and self-sufficiency have also been destroyed through the policy of forced removals, by which entire communities were moved off productive and fertile land into already overcrowded 'homelands'. In combination these policies have had a devastating effect on the family bonds of people not classified white.

'The destruction of the family is probably the most fundamental problem which will face any democratic government coming to power in the future. The foundations of our society have crumbled and it will be generations before the damage wrought can be undone,' comments Sheena Duncan (1983: 37), president of the Black Sash, the human rights organization which specializes in assisting victims of influx control laws.

Contrasting Aspects of Two Worlds

To have one's personal life unaffected by this disruption is to be the exception rather than the rule in South Africa. This is the central reason why my experience of childbirth represents a yardstick of extreme privilege that most other South African women cannot hope to achieve. It is possible to dissect my own story, point by point, to show how far removed it is from the general experience of childbirth.

Illegitimacy

Firstly, I am married to my child's father. This cannot be considered commonplace in the major urban African centres where people with first-hand knowledge estimate that between 50 and 60 per cent of children (and an even higher percentage of first children) are illegitimate (Thomas 1982: 19; Duncan 1983: 38; Van der Vliet 1984: 10-11). Official statistics for 1979 put the illegitimacy rate somewhat lower: at 43 per cent for Africans and 52 per cent for coloureds (Department of Statistics 1983; Simkins's chapter in this volume). However, more recent figures are available for Cape Town (excluding the Divisional Council area, with its large squatter settlements). The figures for 1984 show an illegitimacy rate for live births of 10.3 per cent for whites, 40.3 per cent for coloureds, 2.2 per cent for Asians and 64 per cent for Africans (Medical Officer of Health, Cape Town 1984: Table III.13). Although most statistics are based on the conservative, legal definition of marriage, premarital pregnancy is an accepted fact of life outside the confines of white society.

Looking at the matter from a rural perspective, Trudi Thomas describes illegitimacy as 'a self fertilising catastrophe' and concludes that it is the inevitable harvest of the migrant labour system. The situation is particularly serious in the overcrowded rural slums, known as 'closer settlements', where many family units consist only of a grandmother and a large number of children abandoned in her care. 'The younger women leave and disappear into the "illegal" underground in the cities, returning infrequently to leave another illegitimate baby with the grandmother', says Sheena Duncan (1983: 37). These children face the worst fate of all. In purely physical terms, Thomas (1982: 11) reports that 60 per cent of malnourished children are illegitimate. Inevitably, these children are unwanted and resented. 'To his parents, if he is acknowledged at all, [the illegitimate child] is a nuisance, an embarrassment, a liability, a calamity, a mistake that refuses to be erased,' comments Thomas.

Although abortion is illegal in South Africa and its practioners severely punished, privileged women can obtain abortions reasonably easily, discreetly and safely — even if it means flying to London. Underprivileged women have no way to end an unwanted pregnancy other than risking their lives in the hands of unskilled and often unscrupulous practitioners. The Family Planning Association estimates that 200 000 illegal abortions are performed each year.

According to Thomas (1982: 4), infanticide is not an uncommon way for women to get rid of unwanted babies. She describes it as 'a socially accepted but tautly "hushed up" solution'.

> Babies are delivered into lavatories or found and cleared away with the rubbish in the bins in the morning. Women may be left to give birth to unwanted babies without any attendants, and if the infant does not survive despite lusty crying at birth, clearly heard by the neighbours, there

is an end to the matter. Even up till nine months women bowing to social pressures, are driven to kill their offspring probably by smothering them. The more common course is to give the baby to granny who must, in charity, be forgiven if she begins to show resentment.

Maternal age at first childbirth

Another uncommon feature of my first childbirth was my age. Although detailed statistics are not available, doctors who have conducted the most recent research on comparative maternal ages in South Africa conclude that 'no other country has such an alarming increase of young teenage mothers' (De Villiers 1985: 301). They base this conclusion on a ten-year case study of mothers in the hospital at Paarl, near Cape Town, where 30.51 per cent of the 20 590 mothers who gave birth between 1973 and 1983 were teenagers — and 5 per cent of all mothers were aged sixteen or younger. Projecting the figure of 5 per cent onto the country as a whole, the study concludes that there could be about 50 000 young girls aged sixteen and younger who give birth to unplanned babies annually. Worst of all, because of the age factor 'the babies born are often defective at birth, with little chance of holding their own in life because of their subsequent inferior intellectual and somatic development. The demographic consequences are formidable'.

Examining the situation in the 'homelands', Trudi Thomas (1982: 6) says that it is common for young girls to be sexually active by the age of twelve or thirteen. 'The only reason why [many] girls don't become pregnant before fifteen or sixteen is because they are not biologically mature until then'.

Medical care

Yet a further factor that distinguishes my experience from many others was the quality of medical care I received during pregnancy and labour. I could be virtually certain that — barring an undetectable congenital abnormality — my child would survive the passage of birth. Once he was born, I could just as confidently expect that he would not die of the most common causes of infant mortality in South Africa such as gastro-enteritis, tuberculosis, measles, nutritional deficiencies and pneumonia (Wyndham 1984b). Many mothers do not share that peace of mind. As Elin Hammar, chairwoman of Johannesburg's

Family Planning Centre, observes: 'there are thousands of South African mothers whose primary concern is whether their children will survive birth and the first years of life'.[2]

This is clearly reflected in comparative infant mortality statistics, which are among the most reliable indices of the general health of a population, its standard of living and the efficacy of its health services. The socio-economic advantages of urban living are evident from the available data. Despite a dearth of official statistics, the most recent study concludes that Soweto, a black township on the threshold of South Africa's industrial heartland on the Witwatersrand, has an infant mortality rate of 25.5 per 1 000 births compared to 130 per 1 000 in rural Transkei (Herman and Wyndham 1985: 2). The Transkei study (Irwig and Ingle 1984: 608) concludes that almost one in five children was at risk of dying before the age of five. In the Gelukspan area of the Bophuthatswana 'homeland', an epidemiological survey (Graal and Schmeets 1983: 35) puts the infant mortality rate at 34.4 per 1 000 in villages, compared with 65 per 1 000 in 'resettlement camps'.

Although infant mortality rates of Africans and coloureds in urban centres have dropped dramatically in the last decade (and generally compare favourably with the World Health Organization's mortality estimate for Africa of 116 infants per 1 000 live births), they are all considerably higher than the 1983 white South African rate of 12.6 per 1 000 (World Health Organization 1983: 769-73; Irwig and Ingle 1984: 612; Herman and Wyndham 1985: 1).

A high infant mortality rate is generally associated with a large number of deaths after the first month of life, during what is medically referred to as the postneonatal period. These deaths are not usually attributable to factors relating to birth or pregnancy, but to diseases — particularly gastro-enteritis — that have been virtually eradicated in the more privileged sectors of society. As Irwig and Ingle observe, a great many of these deaths are considered preventable. 'Clinical experience and data from Transkei and elsewhere suggest that a major part of the mortality is likely to be associated with diarrhoea' (Irwig and Ingle 1984: 612). Low birth weight babies (below 2 500 g) are particularly vulnerable. A case in point is a review of Tygerberg Hospital's neonatal statistics for 1983, showing that low birth weight deaths accounted for 89.2 per cent of the neonatal mortality (Henning and Beyers 1984: 9).

Dr Harry Stein (1982: 20-24), Chief Paediatrician at Baragwanath Hospital, points out the social correlations between the two commonly-used categories of low birth weight babies: premature infants who are small because they are born before term, and dysmature infants who are small because their growth has been retarded, even though they may reach full term. Among the privileged sector of society, premature babies are at least twice as common as dysmature babies, while 'in the Soweto population the dysmature baby predominates', comments Stein. The incidence of low birth weight babies, he says, parallels the socio-economic development of the community and reflects the quality of antenatal care and maternal nutrition. He singles out two factors that contribute to dysmaturity: smoking and poor nutrition. Challenging the common perception that the fetus is protected irrespective of the mother's nutrition, Stein says dysmaturity occurs in children of women who appear clinically normal, but are found on biochemical examination to suffer from sub-clinical malnutrition. 'We have found that nature cannot protect against chronic malnutrition, even if this is subclinical' (1982: 23).

Comparative studies bear out his observations. The Tygerberg survey quoted above (Henning and Beyers 1984: 8) reported that 14.8 per cent of white babies and 25.3 per cent of black babies were characterized by low birth weight. A study of birth weights in Cape Town during 1982 shows less disturbing figures (Rip and Tibbit 1984: 11). Low birth weight babies accounted for 4.5 per cent of white babies compared with 8.7 per cent of Africans and 16.1 per cent of coloureds. To those who assume that the coloured population of Cape Town enjoys a higher socio-economic standard of living than Africans, it comes as something of a surprise that the coloured babies in the study were twice as likely to have low birth weights as African babies. Although the reasons for this discrepancy have not been adequately examined, Michael Rip, who co-authored the comparative study, said in an interview in autumn 1985 that he believed smoking, alcoholism, and poor nutrition to be more prevalent amongst coloured people.

Despite the lower birth weights characteristic of coloured births, statistics reflect a higher perinatal mortality rate for Africans in the Cape (35.5 per 1 000) than for coloured patients (26.5 per 1 000) (Van Coeverden de Groot and Van der Elst 1983: 48). Explaining these statistics, Dr Herman A. van Coeverden de Groot of Cape Town University's Department of Obstetrics and Gynaecology comments: '[Africans] contribute the largest percentage of unbooked and born before arrival patients and constitute a very high risk group.

Unbooked patients made up 5% of the total but were responsible for 20% of all perinatal and 9% of maternal deaths' (p.8).

An 'unbooked' patient is one who has not been able to benefit from antenatal or obstetric care. This usually means that the patient has paid no more than one visit to a clinic or doctor during pregnancy. Several factors contribute to non-attendance at clinics. For some, the cost is prohibitive. One clinic visit might involve a day's lost earnings or money spent on a childminder to care for older siblings. Transport costs (particularly in rural areas) and a nominal clinic fee can also act as disincentives.

A report compiled by doctors of the Department of Paediatrics and Child Health at the University of the Orange Free State on the situation at Bloemfontein's Pelonomi Hospital states (Wessels, Hoek, and Van Niekerk 1984: 14):

> In 82% of neonatal deaths, the mothers had received no antenatal care whatsoever and presented at the hospital for the first time in labour. Of the mothers who delivered a baby weighing [less than] 1 000 g, only 2 out of a total of 50 mothers had received any form of antenatal care. It was only in babies with a birth weight of [more than] 2 500 g that there was a notable increase in the number of mothers who attended antenatal clinics.

Different levels of obstetric care also contribute to differing mortality rates. While home births are becoming fashionable amongst certain sectors of the white community, they rarely occur without careful screening, the presence of trained medical personnel and the possibility of a quick transfer to hospital in the event of complications. Home births amongst Africans, particularly in rural areas, take place without any such precautions. A survey at Tygerberg Hospital in 1983 (De Jong and Pattinson 1984: 3) found that 85 per cent of all stillbirths occurred prior to admission to hospital. The Pelonomi study (Wessels, Hoek, and Van Niekerk 1984: 15) shows that babies born outside the hospital (mostly at home) accounted for 22.5 per cent of all deaths in the first month of life. Without exception, these babies were found to have one or more (mostly preventable) complications, such as hypothermia, hypoglycemia, hypoxia or infection. At Ga-Rankuwa, in the 'homeland' of Bophuthatswana, home births accounted for only 12.5 per cent of all admissions but contributed to 20 per cent of the deaths during the last six months of 1983 (Hay,

Ellis, and Shipham 1984: 21).

Several studies have referred to the lack of care and facilities available to women giving birth in small rural villages. In a survey of conditions of the poor in Philipstown, Mary-Jane Morifi (1984: 15) comments:

> Looking at the conditions in which the people themselves live, and in which the babies are to be born, one perceives the dangers of letting the people deliver their babies themselves. There is a great danger to the mothers' and babies' lives because there are no provisions for complications in labour, and if the baby is premature, the baby stands [low] chances of surviving. The clinic itself cannot deliver babies because there are no instruments to help the nurse to do so. The responsibility therefore devolves upon the grannies in the location.

Even if African women deliver in medical institutions (as the vast majority in the major urban centres do), they are unlikely to receive the same degree of personalized expert attention as whites routinely take for granted. While the majority of white babies in the major centres are delivered by doctors in private practice, this is hardly ever the case amongst Africans, who usually have to compete for the attention of over-stretched staff in a grossly overcrowded hospital or midwife obstetric unit (MOU) (Arens et al 1978: 319; cf. Henning and Beyers 1984: 13). Indeed, doctors at hospitals for blacks say overcrowding is the biggest problem with which they have to contend.

Hospital segregation is still the norm in South Africa — leading to the under-utilization of some facilities reserved for whites and the hopeless overcrowding of hospitals for blacks. In Cape Town, for example, 8 000 (or a third) of all deliveries in 1983 took place in a mere thirty-three beds in the midwife obstetric units compared with 795 babies born in about three times as many beds at the Mowbray Maternity Hospital, which caters for more privileged patients. (White, coloured and Indian infants are delivered at this hospital, on three floors — one for white private patients, another for coloured and Indian private patients, and a 'mixed' floor for hospital patients.) (Van Coeverden de Groot and Van der Elst 1983: 12, 28.) Professor Dennis A. Davey of Cape Town University's Department of Obstetrics and Gynaecology comments (1983: 12):

> An additional MOU in Guguletu [an African township], also requested a decade ago, is an urgent necessity and would take a great load off the

existing MOUs and maternity hospitals. It is equally distressing that no concrete plans exist for a maternity hospital in Mitchell's Plain, which will soon have a population of over 250 000 (larger than the city of Bloemfontein).

At Baragwanath Hospital and its satellite clinics in Soweto, 30 000 babies are born each year — accounting for about a third of all births in the Transvaal.

Overcrowding has serious implications. Black women rarely stay in hospital more than twenty-four hours after giving birth. The serious shortage of space, time, and equipment forces doctors to set a cut-off limit for the treatment of babies. At Baragwanath for example, children weighing less than 1 000 g are not ventilated[3] — a practice not restricted to South Africa. The level of care needed to save these tiny babies would put too much strain on the available facilities which must be utilized to treat more viable infants. At white maternity units there are no limits to the lengths to which staff will go to save every child.

However, the dedicated doctors at Baragwanath have turned some of the hospital's greatest disadvantages into opportunities to pioneer techniques that have earned the hospital an international reputation. The greatest strides have been made in treating and saving low weight babies on a mass scale. The conventional method of small nurseries containing five or six incubators capable of coping with a maximum of 200 babies a year did not suit Baragwanath, which has to handle over 3 000 low birth weight babies annually. The doctors therefore achieved the same results by heating a whole ward, effectively turning it into a giant incubator, wrapping the babies (sometimes literally in cotton wool) and bringing in the mothers to nurse their own infants. According to Professor Stein (1982: 25):

> The use of the mothers meant that each baby was cared for almost exclusively by one person and this, plus stringent care, prevented the predicted cross infection. The nurse's role was largely supervisory. The system has been very successful and our survival rate for these babies compares favourably with those where more sophisticated techniques are used.

One of the spin-offs of this system has been the positive effects on bonding between mother and child. Professor Marshall Klaus, a world authority on bonding, has cited the Baragwanath Premature Unit as a model for the facilitating of bonding between mothers and low birth weight babies.

Despite such developments, it would be wrong to romanticize the situation at maternity units for black women. Dr Stein readily acknowledges that some mothers of underweight babies worry about being kept in the hospital because it means they have to neglect their responsibilities and their other children at home.[4]

Yet, in my discussions with mothers who had given birth in clinics or hospitals such as Baragwanath, none described the experience as bad or traumatic.[5] Indeed, the responses, even to leading questions about their treatment and experience, elicited no condemnation. Answers on questions about their experience of the hospital ranged from 'all right' to 'very good'. One woman, who had various birth experiences (at home, at a clinic, and at Baragwanath) singled out the latter as the 'best by far'. This woman was amongst the hundreds who come to hospitals like Baragwanath 'illegally' from rural areas, giving a false township address, simply to have their babies in the best available circumstances.

A very different perspective was presented by white medical students who had worked both in white obstetric units and in the maternity wards of African hospitals. One final year student, who asked not to be cited by name, spoke of her comparative experiences at the white obstetric unit at the Johannesburg Hospital and at Natalspruit, a Transvaal hospital for Africans.

> At the Johannesburg hospital there was one woman per delivery room, equipped with everything necessary for resuscitating the baby. At Natalspruit, where there is tremendous pressure on space, there were sometimes eight women delivering in one ward. Gloves are used for examination and that is about the end of sterility.
>
> With that sort of pressure, there is very little personal care and concern. There is no privacy. Some mothers told me it was bad enough going through the experience of birth without having to listen to other people screaming.
>
> When a baby is about to be born, a nurse will shout 'Delivery!' and a trolley with instruments gets wheeled in and two midwives see to the birth. In September, which is the baby-boom month, nine months after December [the month when migrant labourers are home on their annual leave], women deliver on trolleys in the corridor.
>
> It was not uncommon for women to be slapped or shouted at. At first I simply couldn't function in that set-up but in time you learn to cope. (Interview April 1985.)

This student doctor also referred to the lack of doctor-patient communication, attributable to many factors, including language barriers between white doctors and African patients, the work-load on the doctors, and the patients' unwillingness to question or challenge medical authority.

> Patients seldom ask questions, but tend to accept things, even worrying things, far more easily. There is a lack of understanding between doctor and patient. There may be verbalizing but no communication. Patients seldom know what treatment they are being given or what the diagnosis is. Most white mothers would not accept such a situation. (Interview April 1985.)

Preparation for labour

Another major discrepancy between birth experiences is preparedness for labour. A growing number of white women routinely attend antenatal classes and read books and articles discussing all aspects of the process of becoming a mother. Nothing can really prepare one adequately for the birth of a first child, but this sort of exposure is a great advance on the total unpreparedness with which many South African women face childbirth. Although birth-preparation practices differ substantially between groups, none of the predominantly Xhosa-speaking women interviewed in this survey had been prepared for the birth experience by their mothers or other women. 'We do not talk about such matters with our daughters. Our mothers did not talk about them to us,' said one woman, summing up what appeared to be a general aversion to discussing the topic. The women also recoiled from the notion of the child's father being present during birth. 'It is not a time for men to be there. What do they want there?' was a typical response to questions about the father's role in childbirth.

Parental roles

Indeed, the role of the father is another differentiating factor between birth experiences and, in particular, between experiences in the early years of the lives of different children. Few South African women, including whites, have husbands who are exposed and amenable to feminist principles or prepared to share parenting, particularly given such structural constraints as conventional, full-time jobs. Many white women would echo the feelings of one young mother who said of her husband: 'He never accepted the change in my life as a result of having the child. He comes home and expects the house to be in order. He makes no allowances' (Cobb 1984: 136).

While white South African society is generally strongly patriarchal, recent studies (eg. Van der Vliet 1984; Mullins 1983) have shown that African women suffer even more from gender oppression at the hands of their men — to the extent that some now reject marriage as an institution and have 'chosen to stay single as a strategy for survival'. 'I would rather live in one room with my children than have to depend on a man' is the typical remark recorded by anthropologist Virginia van der Vliet (1984) while reseaching the problems African women face in marriage. Van der Vliet found that many women in her study viewed men as necessary for a healthy sex life but regarded them more as an economic liability than an asset and 'a nuisance in general'. Women also resented the traditional male dominance over all spheres of women's lives, including their fertility.

> Given that men are often in favour of a large family, that they may not regard their family as complete until the wife has produced a son, or that they actively discourage, even forbid, the use of contraception in the belief that it might encourage the wife to be unfaithful, women often find themselves having more children than they want or can afford. While many wives resort to practising contraception secretly, other women believe staying single offers a solution to the problem. (Van der Vliet 1984: 6-7.)

Other studies confirm a trend away from marriage. There has been a corresponding increase in female-headed households, or the multi-generation households consisting of 'a married couple with husband-less daughters and their children, the majority of these daughters being unmarried mothers' (Simkins's chapter in this volume).

Rural women suffer particularly. Apart from the fact that remittances from husbands and other male relatives living and working in urban areas can be sporadic and unreliable, customary law demands that men take all major family decisions. Many women who are alone for eleven months of the year find themselves in a highly oppressive and contradictory situation. 'To all intents and purposes it is women who head the household in rural areas, while male authority is only formal and when exercised, often oppressive' comments one study (*Work in Progress* 1983: 41). As the same writer stresses: 'rural doctors quote cases of children dying because the mothers are too scared to allow them to be admitted to hospital without permission from their husbands.'

Post-natal depression

Finally, there is the question of post-natal depression — the 'most common complication of the period following childbirth.' Despite its frequency, it is grossly neglected either because it is unrecognized by doctors or because 'depressed mothers think it is shameful to feel miserable after the "happy event" and they neither seek nor receive help' (Welburn 1980: 37, back cover).

According to Welburn (1980: 38), one of the few studies of the phenomenon shows that 10.8 per cent of women suffer from depression six to eight weeks after delivery with another 6.2 per cent being 'doubtfully depressed'. Almost half the women who suffer from postnatal depression continue to be handicapped for more than a year. The data indicate several contributory causes, ranging from socio-economic and personal factors to hormonal changes. 'It would be comforting to think that there is one major cause of post-natal depression, but unfortunately it is now almost certain that there is not . . . . Just one relatively small stress may be sufficient to set off a vicious cycle of emotional turmoil', says Dr John Cobb (1984: 130) in his book covering the first five years of motherhood.

Symptoms also differ widely, but usually include various combinations of some of the following: listlessness, weariness, tearfulness, an inability to function, hyperactivity, a sense of inadequacy or futility, sleeplessness, desperation, total rejection of the child, neurotic anxiety over the child's well-being, and psychotic fears connected with the child. Post-partum depression is simply a blanket term, covering a wide range of 'causes' and responses. The common condition of depressed mothers is a feeling that they are unable to cope.

> Trapped in a cycle of apparently inexplicable emotions, feeling increasingly isolated from people she loves and trusts, facing an overwhelming present and an uncertain future, things may reach the point where a women starts to wonder if she is going mad. (Cobb 1984: 130.)

The problem of non-detection is particularly severe amongst black women: 'Not so long ago it was generally thought that black women didn't suffer from post-natal depression. We know now how fallacious this is,' says Dr Cliff Allwood, a Johannesburg psychiatrist.[6] Dr S. Rataemane, Registrar in Psychiatry at the Hillbrow Hospital in Johannesburg, says comparative cross-cultural studies show that the causes and symptoms of post-natal depression are the same for all groups but 'the very great majority of depressed black mothers go undetected unless there is severe psychosis involved'. Life-stress situations, says Dr Rataemane, can play catalytic roles in precipitating post-partum depression. 'We find it is more common amongst women who have housing problems or family difficulties. We had one case where a woman went into severe depression after the birth of her child, precipitated by the fact that she failed to get the right stamp in her reference book to stay in Soweto.'[7]

What effect does post-natal depression have on the child? Usually the mother suffers more than her baby, who is likely to escape emotionally and physically unscathed, particularly if the depression is short-lived and attended by good social and medical support. In extreme cases, however, infanticide, gross neglect or physical abuse can accompany post-natal depression. Dr Rataemane cited a case of a woman who killed six babies in the nursery at Baragwanath Hospital: 'it seems clear that she was suffering from a severe psychotic depression'.

Such extreme cases are rare. However, social workers point to an increasing number of abandoned babies, a phenomenon that indicates severe social dislocation.[8] This is particularly so amongst Africans where a relative or friend is almost always prepared to adopt a child permanently or temporarily in an emergency. The increasing incidence of abandoned babies is considered to be a sign that these support networks are breaking under the weight of social and economic pressures.

Abandoned babies are most often left in hospital by unbooked mothers who have no legal right to be in the city. Many of these women have no permanent place to live, and lead a nomadic squatter existence, often further complicated by continual official harassment. Lacking the necessary papers, these women generally battle to get jobs — a struggle that would be severely aggravated by the addition of a new baby. They know their children will be doomed to the same insecurity and rightlessness if, from the start, they are documented as the children of 'illegal' women.

In another category of abandoned babies are those left in public places such as railway stations, where they are certain to be noticed quickly, indicating the mother's concern that the child be found and cared for as soon as possible. Although no follow-up study has been done to establish why mothers abandon their babies, social workers hypothesize that they feel unable to cope with motherhood — a severely depressed perception that may be a highly rational and valid response to structural circumstances.

Conclusion

No two births anywhere are alike, but in South Africa childbirth reflects extremes of privilege and deprivation comparable to anything in the world. Most women fall somewhere between these poles, their numbers increasing towards the poverty end of the social continuum. Children are always an extremely emotive issue as they are the innocent victims of social, political, and economic circumstances that shape their life chances. This is particularly so in South Africa, where superabundance and gross deprivation are entrenched and maintained in a political and economic system.

This descriptive chapter has not sought to answer the all-important question: what can be done? The question has been addressed in other contexts, perhaps most comprehensively by Ann Oakley (1980: 295), who has put forward a 14-point programme to combat the problems most women face in the transition to motherhood. It is, however, impossible and undesirable to embrace a programme drawn up in the context of a different society. South Africa's particular circumstances demand particular responses. While many Western feminists, for example, call for an end to 'unnecessary medical intervention in childbirth' and the 're-domestication of birth', the evidence suggests that most South African pregnancies and childbirths proceed with too little medical supervision.

Nor do these proposals, moulded for another society, take account of the social ravages wrought by apartheid. This must be the starting point in any attempt to tackle the issue of childbirth and motherhood in South Africa. It is easy (and not particularly helpful) to join the chorus demanding the repeal of laws that entrench inequality and destroy social bonds. The real challenge is to find ways to achieve this end and implement programmes now to begin repairing some of the damage done (such as those suggested by Molteno, Kibel and Roberts elsewhere in this volume). Only in this way can we approach the minimal ideal of enabling all South Africa's children at least to start life with an equal chance.

Notes

1. This pilot study utilizes both existing research and hospital reports, in-depth interviews, and discussions in Cape Town and Johannesburg with more than twenty-five women of all groups; ten doctors; two medical students; and interviews and research notes of interviews with social workers.
2. Interview with Ms Elin Hammar, Chairwoman, Family Planning Centre, Johannesburg, 25.03.85.
3. Interview with Professor Harry Stein, Professor of Paediatrics and Chief Paediatrician, Baragwanath Hospital, Johannesburg, 15.03.85.
4. Interview with Professor Harry Stein, 15.03.85.
5. Several African mothers in the survey did not know me well and may have been reluctant to discuss their feelings with a stranger.
6. Telephone discussion with Dr Cliff Allwood, psychiatrist, Johannesburg, March 1985.
7. Interview with Dr S. Rataemane, Registrar in Psychiatry, Hillbrow Hospital, Johannesburg, 29.03.85.
8. The remainder of this section is drawn from research notes made available to me by Dr S. Burman and Ms F. Mphahlele of interviews which they had conducted with Cape Town African social workers between March 1981 and October 1985.

The Development of Racial Orientation in Children: A Review of South African Research

Don Foster

While it is no longer possible to maintain, as earlier was often the case, that racial ideation and attitudinal orientation are the primary determinants of the South African social formation, it is also clear that racist attitudes are not wholly irrelevant in constituting the particular nature of intergroup relations in South Africa. As long as one is circumspect in recognizing the limits of that for which racist ideology can account, the topic is still of interest and value in providing an understanding of society. This chapter offers a comprehensive examination of one aspect of the area of racial ideology — the development of racial attitudes in young children.

Given the potential importance of the subject, it is surprising how little research has been conducted in South Africa. And though there is a small but steadily growing literature, produced mainly over the past twenty years, it has never been comprehensively examined. As these findings are important and interesting in their own right, and as a number of them are not readily accessible, the aim here is to draw this research together for the first time and to consider it in relation to general findings from international work.

A number of central questions may be posed. First, at what age do children acquire an awareness of race, and what processes are involved in the early acquisition of racial categories? Second, in what manner does subsequent development regarding racial orientation occur? Third, do black and white children develop racial attitudes in the same manner and at the same rates? And fourth, are minority group children damaged psychologically by racist social structures?

All of these questions have been examined, but the answers in certain areas are not quite as clear as might be expected. Before examining the South African research, a brief overview of international research findings will be provided. As this literature is substantial and has been adequately reviewed elsewhere (see Aboud and Skerry 1984; Brand, Ruiz, and Padilla 1974; Davey 1983; Katz 1976; Leahy 1983; Milner 1983, 1984; Williams and Morland 1976) only the general outlines will be given here.

Children and Race: International Research Findings

Since the earliest research in the United States (Clark and Clark 1939; Horowitz 1939) it has been recognized that children become aware of racial categories at a very early age. This finding has been supported by a good deal of subsequent research (Goodman 1964; Porter 1971; Vaughan 1964) and although frequently neither parents (Goodman 1964) nor teachers (Davey 1983) believe this to be the case, it is now well established that by age three, many children have acquired the rudiments of a racial awareness. This rudimentary consciousness develops particularly rapidly between ages three and four and is firmly established by six, the usual school-going age (Katz 1976).

It is considerably less clear what processes are involved in this early awareness and recognition of race categories. Direct instruction both from parents and from cultural artefacts such as games, toys, and pictures may obviously be supposed to constitute one major factor; yet although this could hardly be denied, the formal evidence is surprisingly sparse. Even with older, school-aged children, the evidence of a relationship between parental and children's attitudes has not been very clearly established (Bagley 1979; Katz 1976).

A second hypothesis is that racial awareness has its antecedents in non-verbal forms growing out of either fear of the dark or evaluative connotations attached to light and dark colours. In partial support of this view has been the finding that all cultures prefer light to dark colours. The colour-concept is then hypothesized to generalize to light-and dark-skinned people. White stimulus figures, both animal and human, have certainly been preferred by both black and white children (Williams and Morland 1976) but against this hypothesis is the finding that in the same group of children, racial attitudes towards people showed more bias than did attitudes towards the colours black and white (Williams and Robertson 1967; also Bhana and Bhana 1975, discussed below). It must be conceded that not a great deal is known about the processes whereby children gain such early awareness of race. It should be noted furthermore that while most children ultimately acquire some degree of racial awareness, not all develop prejudiced outgroup attitudes. It is not quite clear therefore what relationship exists between early awareness and preference and subsequent development of race attitudes proper. As Katz (1976) has argued, the early stage of awareness should not be equated with the fully developed race attitudes which probably crystallize only around the ages of eleven or twelve.

While it is fairly clear that accurate recognition of racial categories increasingly develops from ages three to about seven, the pattern of subsequent development is less definitively demarcated. Katz (1976) is undoubtedly correct in recognizing a series of interrelated and overlapping steps in this process. Building on a base of simple conceptual differentiation, subsequent processes involve recognizing the irrevocability of cues (the notion that gender and racial characteristics are immutable), a consolidation of the concept of a group, then further perceptual and cognitive elaboration until a functionally interrelated attitudinal cluster is formed. Katz has provided a model of eight separable steps in the process of attitudinal development.

One of the major earlier findings was that development may occur differently for black and white children. Since the Clarks' work (Clark and Clark 1939, 1947), repeated studies have shown that black children prefer and identify with white stimulus figures to a greater extent than white children do with black figures (Asher and Allen 1969; Goodman 1964; Milner 1973; Morland 1966; Porter 1971; Vaughan 1964). This well-established phenomenon of 'misidentification' among young black children has frequently been assumed, but seldom demonstrated, to be the basis for deleterious psychological states such as impaired self-esteem, alienation, or identity-conflicts. Some results supporting such views have been reported however (Bagley 1979; Ward and Braun 1972).

Age-related findings regarding identification have tended to confirm the following patterns. Among whites, ethnocentrism is established early, by about age four, and increases to a peak by about seven following which it either decreases or remains at roughly the same level (Aboud and Skerry 1984; Vaughan 1964). Among black children, the pattern evidenced by earlier studies showed a relatively strong out-group preference and identification at age four which gradually decreased, starting at age six or seven with either further reduction to eventual own-group identification by age eleven or twelve (Clark and Clark 1947; Vaughan 1964) or alternatively no change with age (Davey 1983). No studies have reported an increased misidentification with increasing chronological age among black children (Aboud and Skerry 1984).

A notable change has been observed however in more recent studies of misidentification since the early seventies, in which own-group identification has been the dominant finding among black children (Hraba and Grant 1970; Fox and Jordan 1973; Katz and Zalk 1974; Vaughan 1978). Similar findings of a reduction in black misidentification over historical time have been reported in Britain (Davey 1983; Louden 1981; Milner 1983, 1984). These changes have largely been attributed to historical social shifts, including the growing success of black pride and other minority-group political movements as well as the liberalization of the media in the portrayal of blacks. Such an explanation sees psychological changes in identity and racial attitude development as a reflection of real historical changes. The seventies also saw a considerable increase in research on self-esteem among black children which supported the misidentification results in finding black self-esteem to be generally similar to that of whites (Simmons 1978; Spencer 1984; Yancey, Rigsby and McCarthy 1973).

The historical and social change hypothesis has not been the only one put forward to account for changes in findings. Banks (1976), for example, in a careful reinterpretation of twelve earlier misidentification studies, found that none showed clear statistical preference for whites while most showed choices which did not differ significantly from chance for either black or white. Similar dominantly nonsignificant results were obtained from twenty-one preference studies. In short, Banks claimed that the case for black misidentification had never really been proven. Against this claim it has been quite correctly argued that Banks's case ignored the comparison between black and white children; most white children preferred and identified with white figures, while typically half the black children have preferred and identified with white (Williams and Morland 1979). Therefore considerable and important differences in misidentification do remain.

Other interpretations have criticized the earlier reliance on the forced-choice technique. Most of the early studies used either the doll technique or picture preference, in which children were asked to choose between a white or black doll or between photographic or line-drawing stimuli depicting black and white figures. There is little doubt that criticism of the forced-choice technique *is* warranted on the grounds of doubtful external validity, the lack of an index of intensity and the limited descriptive rather than explanatory nature of studies based on such techniques. There is also no doubt that some of the more recent work using attitude scales or more open-ended responses has found less extreme and dichotomous results than the forced-choice studies (Aboud and Skerry 1984; Lerner and Buehrig 1975). Against this position, however, it must be noted that the reversal of original findings has not been entirely unequivocal. While black own-group preference has in general increased in the most recent post-1977 research, and white ethnocentrism has declined somewhat, whites have still evidenced a stronger own-group bias than blacks (Aboud and Skerry 1984).

In this regard Adam (1978) argued that the seventies produced a metatheoretical position overridden by a wish to 'put to rest' the earlier view of inferiorized, damaged, and alienated blacks and replace it with a view of 'no difference' between black and white (McCarthy and Yancey 1971). As a result there was a counter over-reliance on self-esteem measures which 'psychologized' the issue, removing scale items from the social context and measuring personal self-esteem rather than racial self-esteem. In other words, Adam is critical of the emphasis on demonstrating 'no differences' between black and white, which have the implication of 'no further problem'. The original problem — how racially inferiorized people cope with this stigmatization — still remains, even though the historical context of the problem may have altered in certain ways.

A recent, spendidly comprehensive British study of white, Asian, and West Indian seven to ten year old children from sixteen schools, eight in London and eight in industrial Yorkshire, illustrates the contemporary picture of race attitudes very clearly, and also goes some way to resolving the contradictions of findings and interpretations over the past decade (Davey 1983). Although, in line with some recent research, misidentification had declined and all three groups evinced strong own-group identification in response to photographic stimuli, a very different picture emerged from a preference test. When given a choice, roughly half the West Indian children and 55 per cent of the Asian children indicated that they would prefer to be white, whereas about 90 per cent of white children preferred their own group.

Furthermore, there was little desire by Asian children to be West Indian or vice versa. On three additional tests, white children were consistently and markedly more ethnocentric than either of the minority groups. Regarding friendship patterns, there was a negligible interracial choice, with whites showing the highest degree of in-group preference. This form of own-group preference was firmly established by age seven and did not alter further with age. In keeping with other research findings, this study found a weak trend for girls to be less ethnocentric than boys. Also, in general support of previous research, there was no decisive evidence of direct parental influence on the racial attitudes of children. Neither region nor the ethnic composition of the school seemed to have much impact upon the attitudinal patterns. The study concluded that racial/ethnic characteristics were of primary importance as intergroup differentiating criteria among children in England, and that the social images attached to black and white were sufficiently salient to form a serious impediment to intergroup friendship.

The study is an important one for a number of reasons, not least for showing that an observed reduction in misidentification does not necessarily mean than racism has disappeared nor that there are 'no differences' in the processes of racial attitude development in black and white children. The value of Davey's work lies primarily in the multiple measures utilized with the same children, indicating various dimensions in the development of prejudice, ethnocentrism and inter-group orientation. These results suggest that both the historical change thesis (eg. Milner 1983, 1984) and the biased ideology and measurement thesis (Adam 1978) may be partially correct in account-ing for observed shifts in empirical studies since the seventies. It does now appear, with hindsight, that forms of racial attitude expression have shifted with real historical changes but that white structural dominance still manifests in psychological forms which are structurally similar to those observed in earlier studies (Pettigrew 1978). It is worth noting furthermore that most studies have focussed on either black or white samples, with less work on such minority groups as Chinese or Puerto Ricans. A recent review of some fifteen studies of these minority groups (Aboud and Skerry 1984) indicates that their preference for white out-groups is more pronounced and long-lasting than that found in comparable studies of black children. Thus own-group preference seems to develop later than among either white or black. Perhaps, the reviewers argue, as these groups are relatively less oppressed, there is less support and reduced drive to politicize and establish group pride.

The above sketch of general trends in international, primarily American and British, research on children's development of race attitudes provides us with some basis for comparison. We now turn to an examination of South African research literature.

South African Research: A Review

The bulk of research on racial attitudes, prejudice and related phenomena in South Africa has been conducted with adults, much of it following in the pioneering tradition begun by MacCrone in the 1930s (see Lever 1978; Mann 1971 for reviews). As far as can be ascertained, the first work with children or adolescents was Rakoff's (1949) University of Cape Town thesis. A few important papers appeared during the sixties with a steadier volume of research since the mid-seventies. Much of this research has been unprogrammatic and not particularly innovative, but since it is largely unknown and has never been reviewed, a close examination of it could serve a useful purpose.

The literature will be reviewed under the following sections: first, age-related aspects, including developmental trends; second, blacks' misidentification and ethnocentrism in general; third, related attitudinal aspects and political socialization; fourth, processes involved in the acquisition of race attitudes; and finally, some recent research conducted at the University of Cape Town.

Age-related aspects

It appears that South African children acquire an awareness of race categories at as early an age as children reported in other studies. By the age of three or four the majority (roughly 70 per cent) of children in two studies (Meij 1966; Gregor and McPherson 1966) were able to respond correctly to recognition tasks on the Clarks' doll test, with questions posed such as 'show me the doll that looks like a white / African child'. According to these two studies, accurate awareness increases in a linear fashion with age to nearly 100 per cent at age seven. Gregor and McPherson (1966) found that the sharpest increase in race awareness occurred between the ages of three and four. These two studies were conducted with African children in and around Johannesburg and Pretoria as well as with a small group of white children (Gregor and McPherson 1966). A third doll-choice study was conducted with coloured children from Cape Town and Stellenbosch (De Groot 1978). Recalculated data from these three studies, pooled for all 'race-awareness' questions in each study separately, are graphically represented in Figure 1, as percentages of children who responded correctly.

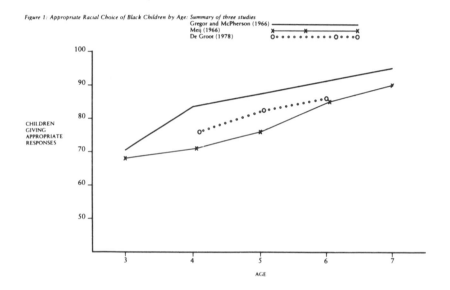

Figure 1: Appropriate Racial Choice of Black Children by Age: Summary of three studies

As may be seen from Figure 1, the studies provide strongly similar pictures of the degree of race awareness of black children as a linear function of age.

A further phenomenon has been uncovered through additional analysis of the three South African doll studies. It seems as though black children have a greater tendency towards accurate recognition of white figures than black figures. In Meij's study, 82 per cent of the total black sample of 425 correctly recognized the white doll as a white child, whereas 77 per cent correctly recognized the African doll. This difference was even stronger for Gregor and McPherson who found the following in their overall sample of 139 Venda children: 97 per cent correctly recognized white, 90 per cent were correct when asked to show a Venda child, but only 79 per cent were correct in response to the African child cues. In the calculation of De Groot's results, 71 per cent replied correctly to the white child request cue, 61 per cent to the African child, and only 52 per cent to the coloured child. This phenomenon of more readily available awareness of the white category seems from results to be age-related. By about six years old, black children seem adept at correctly recognizing the different racial categories to an equal extent, whereas it is the younger children, aged three to four, who recognize white more accurately than black.

The research discussed above was with black children. Systematic age-related data for white children has not been obtained. Gregor and McPherson included a small (n = 30) white sample aged five to seven, and although it was too small to give breakdown by age, over 90 per cent of the total sample were accurate in recognizing both white and African. Beitz (1960, cited in Melamed 1968) reported increases with age of race awareness among white children from ages three to ten.

In comparative studies of six, eight, and ten year old white children, Melamed (1968, 1970) found no further development beyond age six in either cue utilization for racial differentiation or in preference for or attribution of stereotypes. It would seem from this research that by age six white South African children differentiated between groups in response to line drawings of physiognomic cues (which included varied skin colour, hair type, nose and lip shape) primarily in terms of skin colour, as well as showing strong preference for and assigning positive stereotypes predominantly to a caucasoid-featured face. Melamed concluded that 'already at age six a response hierarchy similar to the one existing in the adult world' (1968: 7) had been established; and also that by age six children have 'formed associations with socially significant features other than only skin colour' (1970: 14). By six they were also found to reject stimuli least resembling caucasoid features, suggesting a possible tendency to avoid black people.

In contrast to Melamed's findings, Barling (1981) in a study of 309 white children using the Children's Scale of Social Attitudes (Wilson, Nias, and Insel 1972) found that ethnocentrism increased with age for children aged seven to twelve. However, neither the global conservatism score, nor four other component factors, changed with increasing age. Barling's findings should not be read as contradicting those of Melamed. It does seem from these studies that the basic structures of white children's intergroup attitudes are established at an early age, about six years, but that the degree of in-group favouritism may indicate conformity to racist norms of South African white society. The increasing age awareness of race as a salient social category was further supported by Moodie's (1980) study of 112 upper-middle-class white children aged six to thirteen. Using less structured test materials, such as drawings of self and the 'people of my country' as well as responses to sixteen photographs, Moodie found that awareness of race was well established by age six but mentions of race increased with age and peaked at about ages ten and eleven. Similarly, the ethnocentrism of whites, in terms of the number of positive mentions of their own group and negative mentions of the other group, was shown to increase from age six to age thirteen.

The pattern of age-related racial awareness or attitude developments among blacks after the age of seven is not very clear, but the cross-national study in the 1960s by Lambert and Klineberg (1968), which included a sample of 300 Zulu and Sotho children, divided into hundreds in the age groups six, ten, and fourteen, provides some interesting clues. In response to the open-ended questions 'What are you?' and 'What else are you?', African children aged six and ten referred to themselves primarily in terms of 'race'. By age fourteen the most important self-descriptive category was gender but 'race' remained an important criterion. At the same time, however, these children 'appeared to have a very limited conception of their own group, Zulu or Sotho' (1968: 36). In comparison to children from eleven other countries, the African children were the only group for whom race was the most important self-description; other criteria such as gender, age, religion, language, regional or national groups were by comparison far less salient. In general, it was found cross-nationally that references to physical features declined in importance as children grew older, but the African (and Japanese) children were exceptions. Both samples emphasized the physical traits of their own groups and of foreign groups, indicating salience in their thinking. In the South African context this undoubtedly reflects the very real implications of the centrality of racial categorization and discrimination for black children.

Ethnocentrism and minority group misidentification

As discussed above, a common finding in the literature on children and race is that minority children tend to identify incorrectly in showing *preference* for and *identification* with the dominant social group.

Evidence from South African research, which has been largely ignored by international reviews, is examined here. We might hypothesize that South African society discriminates finely between 'races', and because power and wealth are closely related to these differentiations, the psychological mechanisms of minority mis-identification and preference for the dominant group would be more evident than that which is reported in the international literature. For example, in a study of comparative situations, Morland (1966) found that black children, aged three to six years, in both northern and southern states of America, preferred and identified with whites, but that such processes were accentuated for children from southern states. White children in both regions preferred and identified with their own group.

Results from South African research have consistently shown that black children from an early age prefer white stimulus figures. On the forced-choice dolls test, all three South African studies found a strong, statistically significant preference for the white doll figure among young black children. *Preference* results for all three studies are given in Table 1, expressed in percentages of black children who chose the white doll.

Table 1: Preference for White Stimulus Figure among Black Children: Summary of South African Doll-Choice Studies

Questions	Percentage black children choosing white		
	Gregor and McPherson (n = 139)	Meij (n = 425)	De Groot (n = 196)
Like to play with	77*	—	—
Like the best	76*	77*	67*
Nice doll	83*	72*	50
Nice colour	72*	67*	58*
Looks bad	21*	21*	20*

* p < .05, following Banks's criteria (1976)

The 'white-preference' results appear to be larger and more consis-tent than those reported in the earlier American literature (see Banks 1976 for a summary of data). Close scrutiny of the studies also shows that there is no clear age-related change in preference, spanning ages three to seven. Gregor and McPherson (1966), however, found a significant urban-rural difference among their subjects. Rural African children consistently showed a greater preference for the white doll than did urban children.

The smaller degree of white preference found in De Groot's study conducted in the late seventies, in contrast to the other two sets of results, may perhaps reflect historical changes, as found in other international research. Alternatively, results may reflect a regional difference — Cape and Transvaal — or the slightly different social structural positionings of coloured people compared with African people in South Africa.

Research using other techniques has provided further support for the phenomenon of out-group preference among black children. Bhana and Bhana (1975) found clear evidence for white preference among forty Indian children aged three to six years. Figures, coloured and black, both animal and human pictures, were predominantly seen as lazy, bad, ugly, stupid, and dirty, whereas white figures were viewed positively. Similarly Lambert and Klineberg (1968) found that most of their African sample wanted to be white, although there was a decrease in this tendency with increasing age.

White children, by contrast, have been shown to prefer white-coloured stimuli. Gregor and McPherson (1966) found that the majority of their young white sample evidenced in-group choices. As reported above, Melamed (1970) found the greatest number of positive characteristics attributed by white children to the caucasoid-featured face, and the least number to the negroid-characteristic facial drawing. No change in this biased response was seen from ages six to ten. Press, Burt, and Barling (1979), using Katz and Zalk's (1974) racial preference questionnaire and a behavioural measure in a comparative study of four to five year old black and white children, found further strong evidence that both sets of children showed preference for whites. This supports a notion that white children in South Africa are more ethnocentric than blacks. In another study white children aged about eight and nine were also found to be more ethnocentric than a sample of Indian children (Barling and Fincham 1979).

Identification rather than preference indices have frequently been evaluated as the most critical measures. In the doll test this traditionally has taken the form of a question (usually the last to be asked following preference and awareness questions) such as 'Show me the doll that looks like you'. Responses in the case of the three South African doll studies were quite contradictory, unlike the results for racial awareness and preference, which were generally similar. Considering first only the global sample responses, misidentification results (that is, choice of the white doll by black children) were as follows: De Groot (1978) 64 per cent, Meij (1966) 51 per cent, and Gregor and McPherson (1966) 34 per cent. Following Banks's (1976) criteria, one study shows a significant identification with the white stimulus, one a significant identification with the black stimulus figure, while one shows non-preference. If the raw data of all three studies are pooled, including all children who responded, then from a total of 747 choices by black South African children aged from three to seven, 51 per cent identified with the white stimulus figure. According to Banks's (1976) argument, we cannot conclude that these results, taken overall, show black self-rejection, or white preference. Statistically, these overall results show less than chance choice for either black or white.

White children, in contrast, have evidenced a far stronger own-group identification. In Gregor and McPherson's (1966) study, all white children accurately identified with the white stimulus figure. In this regard it should be recalled that the degree of racial *awareness* shown by white and African children in this study was virtually identical. Therefore the differences in own-group identification between white and African children must be viewed as considerable. In similar vein, results of a behavioural task in which children (age four to five years) were asked to allocate sweets to photographs of black or white figures, 5 per cent of whites gave sweets to the black figure, whereas 50 per cent of black children gave sweets to the white stimulus figure (Press, Burt and Barling 1979), confirming the notion that white children generally appear to be more ethnocentric than black.

Three other factors have been found to relate to incorrect identification among black children. First, Gregor and McPherson found that rural children evidenced own-group identification significantly more (83 per cent) than urban children (51 per cent), despite both sets showing similar race awareness. When the urban sample was further split into those long and recently-established in urban areas, the same trend was evident; the more-established urban group showed greater misidentification than the less urbanized. This result does not contradict that reported above (Gregor and McPherson 1966). Rural African children, despite showing a stronger *preference* for white figures than urban children did, nevertheless *identified* to a far greater extent with the brown doll. This phenomenon, while not fully understood, must in part be due to greater contact with white culture by black urban children.

Second, consistent with other international research (eg. Davey 1983; Vaughan 1964, 1978), increasing age was found to be related to a decrease in misidentification. Figure 2 presents a graphic summary of the three South African doll studies in this respect. It is clear that seven year olds misidentify considerably less than three year olds.

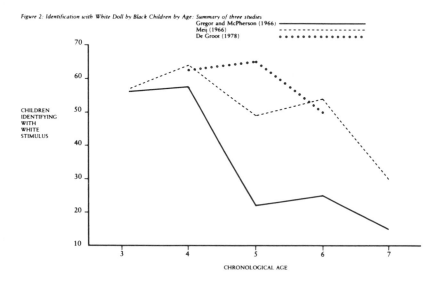

Figure 2: Identification with White Doll by Black Children by Age: Summary of three studies
Gregor and McPherson (1966)
Meij (1966)
De Groot (1978)

Third, both De Groot and Gregor and McPherson found that girls identify more with white figures than do boys. Meij unfortunately did not provide gender differences. While international research on this matter has not been entirely unequivocal (see Brand, Ruiz, and Padilla 1974) the weight of evidence goes in the same direction. The recent British study also found greater out-group identification and less ethnocentrism by girls, of both white and Asian groups (Davey 1983).

Two studies cast some further light on chronological development of minority group identity and ethnocentrism beyond the age of seven. Using MacCrone's (1937) social distance scale, Rakoff (1949) tested well over 500 twelve to fourteen year old adolescents, mainly coloured, from a range of areas in the Cape Peninsula. Taken overall, results showed that coloured adolescents evinced most tolerance towards their own group, followed by a 'Malay' group. However, the third most favoured group was English-speaking whites, and this 1949 sample evidenced little by way of general solidarity with fellow oppressed blacks. A high degree of intolerance was shown towards Indian, African and Chinese, all rated as less acceptable than Afrikaans-speaking white South Africans. In contrast to this relatively favourable rating of whites by these minority group adolescents, the attitudinal colour-bar was strongly evidenced by the small (n = 38) white adolescent sample who rated all white groups as more acceptable than any black group.

In Lambert and Klineberg's (1968) research, most African children aged six to fourteen wanted to be white, when given a choice of a classification other than their own. Most undesirable at all ages were other South African tribal groups — especially those groups generally regarded as most similar to their own. At age fourteen the 'Boers' were rated as the second most undesirable nation. The most common evaluative label at all ages given to undesirables was that of 'aggressive'.

The complex results suggest that while minority group identification with the out-group may decrease beyond the age of seven through to adolescence, a complicated set of contradictions and inconsistencies remain as part of the attitudinal structure. The white out-group, particularly English-speaking, is still favourably regarded, while similarly oppressed other black groups are not well rated. Even the black in-group is not particularly well regarded. For example, in Rakoff's (1949) sample the social distance indices were largely based on negative scores towards out-groups rather than upon particularly positive tolerance scores towards the in-group. In contrast Moodie (1980), in a sample of white children aged six to thirteen, found steady increases in both positive mentions of own group and negative mentions of other groups. Interestingly, this study also found Afrikaans-speaking children to be four times more negative than English-speakers in their response to black groups.

On the available evidence there seems little doubt that white children are in general more ethnocentric than black children, when this concept refers to a cluster of dimensions including positive preference for, and identification with, the in-group as well as negative and derogatory views of the out-group. Although the evidence for chronological trends among whites is rather flimsy, it seems as though this ethnocentric attitude is firmly established by six years of age or earlier and tends to increase with age (Barling 1981), more strongly so for Afrikaans- rather than English-speaking white children (Moodie 1980). On the other hand, black children evinced a more complex pattern. Early misidentification decreases with chronological age and gives way to identification with own group. Judging from Rakoff's data (1949) based on responses from coloured children, the attitudinal structure found among early adolescents is roughly similar to that of adults (Edelstein 1974), in that own group is most highly tolerated while whites are also tolerantly regarded and other black groups are perceived as remote. Similar patterns of contradiction were indicated for African children and adolescents. This complexity of intergroup attitudinal structures is further stressed by the Lambert and Klineberg (1968) data, which suggests that similarity and affectional indices may constitute independent attitude components. The African children in their study were found to express a relatively higher degree of affection both for similar and dissimilar others compared with that shown by groups of other nationalities, such as Japanese, Germans and Americans.

Other attitudinal characteristics and general political socialization

It may be argued that racial attitudes do not exist in a vacuum but are clustered with other, more general, attitudes as well as personality components and deeper value structures. However, for children the clustering may not be as consistent as may be expected for adults. In this respect, Heaven (1978), using a sample of white children aged thirteen, found that the various attitude clusters measured by the Wilson *et al* (1972) scale were less highly correlated than had been shown with adults.

On a global measure of conservative attitudes, Barling and Fincham (1979) found no difference between eight year old Indian and white children, but white children were less conservative on two subscale factors relating to sex and religion. The sample as a whole was more conservative than an adult white South African sample as well as adult samples from the UK and USA. In related studies, Barling (1981, 1982) further found that conservatism did not decrease among white children aged from seven to twelve. In support of these trends Heaven (1978) found white children (mean age thirteen years) to be considerably more conservative than a comparable sample from England.

It would be unrealistic to expect that attitudes and values of black children would be homogeneous, and that indeed is what was found by Geber and Newman (1980) in a study of nearly 1 000 African adolescents from Soweto, aged about seventeen or eighteen years, during the late 1960s. Attitudinal responses were found to cluster into three major groups, labelled for convenience as 'accommodated', 'radical', and 'constrained'. The *'accommodated'* group displayed a conservative set of attitudes, endorsing traditional support of church and tribal affiliations, and acceptance of the wider political system. The group was optimistic about the educational system as a vehicle for solving personal and social needs. The *'radical'* constellation rejected both tribal and political institutions and expressed doubt about the educational system as a solution to personal aspirations. Additional characteristics of this group included a preference for the English language, a high degree of cognitive complexity in responses, and positive views of personal and family relationships but attitudinal resistance towards formal authorities. The *'constrained'* group were characterized by a depressed and resigned set of attitudes. Acceptance of the status quo, both political and tribal, appeared to be based on a belief that there was no choice in the matter. The group displayed a generally low level of personal or social aspiration and, in response to a projective personality test, evidenced high levels of hostility and criminality.

Unfortunately, Geber and Newman gave no evidence of the numbers of adolescents who constituted each of the three attitudinal clusters. Furthermore, considerable doubt should be expressed regarding the authors' claims in their text, written after the 1976 events of Soweto, that these psychological investigations conducted in the late 1960s, however useful they may be in their own right, could have predicted the Soweto uprising (1980: 7). It is highly unlikely that extrapolation from psychological research to large-scale social events is ever warranted without a simultaneous, full analysis of political, economic, and social factors. From their research it is not possible to predict which of the three attitudinal clusters would predominate.

Returning to focus on white children, Moodie's (1980) study revealed some patterns beyond mere racial attitudes. She found an increasing awareness on the part of white children aged six to thirteen on language group identity, specifically English and Afrikaans. In general support of Piaget's theory, there was a substantial shift in children from an egocentric stance to a sociocentric stance. At age six 57 per cent drew pictures of their family in response to a request to 'draw the people of your country'. By thirteen years of age 100 per cent produced pictures either depicting racial groups or public scenes. Concomitantly,

with increasing age there was an increased awareness of and identification with national symbols such as the national flag, animal,
anthem, and well-known South African white personages. Afrikaner
children, however, showed both an earlier and closer identification
(recognition and preference) of national symbols than English-
speakers. The latter seemed to remain at a personal level for a longer
period than Afrikaner children, for whom a national symbol was more
readily provided. The ethnocentric nationalism of Afrikaner children
was also evidenced by the finding that of the thirteen year olds, 47 per
cent of English children drew only black figures whereas none of the
Afrikaner children did so. English-speaking children were also shown
to be considerably more critical of the government at age thirteen than
Afrikaans-speaking: 57 per cent in contrast to 14 per cent. It should be
noted however that when a wider range of symbols, including beauty
and nature, were considered English-speakers showed as strong an identification with South African national identity as Afrikaans-speaking
children. It is rather unfortunate that no data of this sort are yet
available for black children.

Processes in racial attitude acquisition

In South Africa the least work has been done in this area, perhaps the
most important of all aspects of race attitude development. It is widely
assumed in the literature on socialization that direct instruction or
modelling in relation to parents, teachers, peer group, the media or
educational aids constitutes one of the central mechanisms of acquiring
racial attitudes. Although the most obvious factor would appear to be
that of parental influence, the international data supporting this
hypothesis is surprisingly thin (Katz 1976; Kolman 1979).

There seems to be no published South African research of direct
bearing on this matter, but we refer the reader to the recent unpublished study reported in the following section.

There is data to suggest that parental influence upon the general
political socialization of black adolescents is minimal. In one of the
few studies of processes involved in general political socialization,
Kotze and Norval (1983) found that black matric pupils in the
Johannesburg area were more substantially influenced by their peers
in development of political attitudes than by either parents or
teachers. In contrast, white adolescents were more strongly influenced
by their parents. Geber and Newman (1980), in their Soweto high

school sample, similarly found that the influence of the family upon general attitudes and aspirations was considerably less pronounced than the familial influence reported in the British and American literature. They also reported that other family variables such as size, structure, or overcrowding had little impact on attitudes. Dreyer (1980), in a study of Zulu adolescents, in similar vein reported large-scale rejection of parental values and norms. Although these studies provide no direct information on the role of parental influence on development of racial attitudes per se, and they were all conducted with adolescents, they suggest that parents may have a greater role in attitude and value development among whites rather than Africans, and that African and white children may undergo different processes of political socialization.

The educational system as a whole is too complex to treat in any causal fashion, but there is some sound information available on the bias in South African high school textbooks. Auerbach (1965) and Dean, Hartmann, and Katzen (1983) have shown that coverage of South African history texts is largely devoted to the history of white groups at the expense of blacks. Blacks are primarily presented as obstacles to the achievement of white objectives. In a recent comprehensive study, Du Preez (1983) surveyed fifty-three secondary school texts prescribed for both black and white scholars in fields such as history, geography, social studies, and literature. Extracting the underlying values and attitudes, she identified twelve 'master symbols' repeatedly found in these texts. It is beyond the scope of this chapter to discuss all her findings, but, in general, information on events and people in South Africa was found to be depicted in terms of the symbolic system of whites and was supportive of the status quo. For example the three 'master symbols' characteristic of the political order were as follows: legal authority is not questioned; whites are superior, blacks inferior; South Africa rightly belongs to the white Afrikaner.

There seems little doubt that school textbooks are likely to be of some influence in the general process of political socialization and development of racist ideology. The empirical demonstration of such influence is long overdue.

Returning to the question of racist attitude acquisition in early childhood, two partial tests of the colour meaning hypothesis (Williams and Morland 1976) have been provided locally. It may be recalled that the central thrust of this hypothesis is that children, both black and white, first acquire socially embedded meanings related to the light and dark symbols, then generalize the symbolism to racial attitudes. Bhana and Bhana (1975) tested whether contact with African nannies would have any effect upon the attitudes of Indian pre-school children (aged three to six years) towards black and white animal and human figures. They found that contact had some small effect upon the intensity of attitudes (resulting in somewhat more positive views towards black figures) but the effect was limited in that both long and short contact duration subjects expressed a predominantly negative bias towards black figures. In addition, a significant response difference was found between reactions to black animal and black human figures (less positive responses to black human figures), indicating that children were not simply generalizing colour bias from animals to humans, but were evaluating human figures themselves.

In another experiment Elliot and Tyson (1983) modified the colour-concepts of four year old black and white children by use of reinforcement techniques, and found that this modification led to improvements in racial attitudes to blacks. With subsequent testing, these effects were found to be sustained over a two month period. This study, apart from indicating that race attitudes of young children could be modified, provides some measure of support for the Williams-Morland (1976) thesis of a link between colour-concepts and race attitudes. However, as the study by Bhana and Bhana (1975) did not find strong positive support, the general status of the hypothesis should be regarded as tenuous and in need of further research in South Africa. It is also clear that remarkably little is known of the processes involved in acquisition of racial attitudes among South African children.

Some recent research

This section reports briefly on some research on race attitudes in children conducted in the Department of Psychology at the University of Cape Town. While consistent with other South African research in being less than soundly programmatic, the work does constitute an effort to redress some of the lacunae in this area.

Given the lack, even in the international literature, of clear evidence of parental influence (Katz 1976; Kolman 1979), two recent studies provide some interesting data. The first studied the relationship between race attitudes of white parents and their offspring. Attitudes in young children aged six to eight and their parents were compared with those in adolescents aged fifteen to seventeen and their parents. For both samples positive correlations were found between parents and their offspring, but this relationship was far stronger for the young children sample than the adolescent sample. This difference was found to be owing to less negative attitudes towards blacks by adolescents, whereas young children scored as high as their parents. As an interesting aside, mothers' and fathers' race attitudes were found to be strongly positively correlated. This provides useful suggestive evidence that the influence of parents (at least among whites) may be quite strong in the acquisition of race attitudes among young children but that this influence is reduced during adolescence. It suggests in addition that race attitudes of white English-speakers in South Africa may become more positive during middle to late adolescence.

A second study of the attitudinal relationship between parents and their offspring tested the interesting hypothesis that a greater positive self-concept would be evidence by black children whose mothers were aware of Black Consciousness ideas (Lasovsky 1982). Coloured women in the Western Cape were divided into two groups, high and low awareness of Black Consciousness, on the basis of semi-structured interviews. Self-esteem measures were obtained from mothers and their children, whose ages ranged from six to nine years. Findings were that the 'high aware' group of mothers scored higher on the self-esteem measure than the 'low aware' group. The same trend was found for the children, although results in this case were only marginally significant (10 per cent level). This is the first attempt to measure such a relationship in South Africa, and these results point to the priority of identifying relationships between political stance and psychological characteristics.

Two further studies investigated ethnocentrism and race awareness in school-going children. The first studied stereotypes and social distance attitudes of white, English-speaking middle-class children towards each of the four major 'ethnic' groups in South Africa. Children of two age groups, younger (eight and nine years) and older (eleven and twelve years), were asked to evaluate photographic stimuli of African, Indian, coloured, and white children by assigning stereotype labels to each photograph separately. No age-related differences were found. Detailed results are too complex to describe fully here (see Wilson 1983), but two broad trends emerged. First, the eighty white children did not evidence strong ethnocentrism on any measure. The second indication, however, was that white children were highly aware of group distinctions, for when the stereotype *content* was examined more closely, the picture regarding other groups was not quite so neutral. For example the positive attributes granted by boys to all three black out-groups were characterized by labels such as 'brave' and 'strong' but not 'clever' or 'friendly' or 'honest'. Girls, in general less ethnocentric than boys, nevertheless differentiated between the three black groups to a greater extent. For example, the African figure was seen as predominantly 'brave' and 'strong', the coloured figure as 'helpful' and 'friendly' but not particularly clever or strong, and the Indian figure as 'clever' but also 'weak' and 'scared'.

Results of this study, viewed overall, suggest a more subtle form of liberalized racism in which the degree of ethnocentrism and surface prejudice is reduced, but in which the content of assigned characteristics reveals still the presence of category distinctions between black and white groups.

A second recent study used the forced-choice technique (cut-out black, brown and white figures) to compare age and gender effects related to race awareness and identification (Whitehead 1984). While racial awareness among white children was found to increase with chronological age from six to eleven, the most significant finding for our purpose here was that both African and white children evidenced in-group identification and preference responses, thus supporting the trend of international findings of reduced misidentification among blacks in recent years. Ethnocentrism, in terms of in-group preference and dislike of out-groups, was however found to be more pronounced in white children than in black, confirming the established pattern of South African findings. Further evidence of contradictory attitudes of black children towards their own group was found, in that black figures here were seen as less law-abiding than white figures by both black and white children. So, although black misidentification was not present in this study, black children still evidenced mixed feelings towards their own group.

In summary, these recent studies have provided the following additional information. First, parental attitudinal influence appears to play a significant role in younger children's racial attitudes and psychological characteristics, but is reduced in adolescence. Second, prejudice among white English-speaking adolescents seems to decrease with age. Third, Black Consciousness ideology does appear to be positively related to improved self-esteem among minority-group members. Fourth, misidentification among black children is minimal but contradictory views are still held towards the in-group, with positive characteristics attributed to white and negative characteristics to black figures. Finally, white English-speaking children from the Western Cape seem to hold less prejudiced views towards black groups than suggested by previous research, but subtle forms of differential categorization were nevertheless still present.

Conclusion

Research into the development of racial orientation in South Africa has produced patterns which generally support those reported elsewhere. These patterns may be summarized as follows:

(i) In rudimentary forms awareness of race categories is present by age three, although not all children have consistent awareness at this age. Awareness of and preference for social categories subsequently develops rapidly and appears to be firmly founded by age six or seven for majority-group children.

(ii) Intergroup orientations of majority and minority children develop in different ways. Majority-group children develop an early awareness of who they are and the benefits accruing to dominant group membership. In other less racially divided societies there is evidence to show that white ethnocentrism may decrease somewhat in degree through later childhood, whereas in South Africa ethnocentrism may increase in conformity with racist social norms. Afrikaner children appear to be more prejudiced towards blacks than English-speaking children, mirroring the established findings from adult research.

Minority-group children, on the other hand, prefer and identify with white group symbols in early childhood. Misidentification begins early, but then appears to decrease gradually so that by mid- to late childhood most black children show accurate own-group identification, but not necessarily preference. Very little is known of the processes involved in such chronological patternings. However, black and other minority children seem to be affected from an early age by their social position. Despite correction of early misidentification, substantial traces seem to remain in the form of contradictions and internal conflicts, perhaps similar to Fanon's (1968) hypothesized 'white mask neurosis'.

Some South African evidence suggests that by mid- to late adolescence the developmental processes among black children may coalesce into three major attitudinal structures, either radical, accommodatory, or resigned-apathetic-alienated. These three positions denote very different inter-group strategies, and evidence of the past decade clearly shows the radical strategy to be dominant among black youth. One should therefore be wary of simplifying the case by claiming that oppressive social structures invariably produce 'damaged' psychological forms. There can be no doubt that material damage — violence, poverty, inadequate facilities for health, housing, education, and development — is a product of apartheid. The evidence presented in this chapter is more than suggestive of a high degree of subtle psychological forms of damage. It is worth observing, however, that oppressive social forces are also likely to produce the psychological forms and inter-group attitudes necessary for resistance and active striving for change — as amply demonstrated by black youth since Soweto 1976.

(iii) Surprisingly little is known of the processes or mechanisms involved in the development of social attitudes and intergroup orientations. The research reviewed provides only tentative evidence of parental influence (different for black and white children), of the role of school textbooks, and of peer group influence which appeared to be stronger amongst blacks. Relatively little is known of the processes at the earliest ages whereby children acquire preference for black and white symbolic representations.

In all these areas a great deal more work needs to be done, preferably within a broader framework than has presently been attempted. To recast some of the questions in terms of intergroup relations or political socialization would undoubtedly be an improvement. As yet such work is in its infancy in South Africa. However, even such approaches, as traditionally conceived, are somewhat empiricist and ahistorical.

The research findings summarized above should not be regarded uncritically. Viewed overall, mainstream research has allowed available empirical methodology to dictate what questions should be examined instead of a prior focus being given to theoretical analysis. The standard methods are not without problems. Much of the data have been based upon forced-choice methods such as the doll test.

Responses are unfortunately limited so that choice is restricted to ethnocentrism (choice of own group) or misidentification (choice of out-group symbol). As stated earlier, recently employed methods such as open-ended interviews or attitude scales have produced greater variability of responses than the 'either-or' type emerging from forced-choice techniques (Aboud and Skerry 1984; Lerner and Buehrig 1975).

A further problem is the relation between attitudes and behaviour. It is now well established that there is not necessarily a direct relationship between purported internal psychological states on the one hand and concrete action on the other. In the research by Davey (1983) for example, friendship and play patterns were even more ethnocentric than stated attitudes. Few attempts have been made to understand the situational demands, normative constraints, rules and ideological processes that mediate between attitude, intention, and action. In addition, not much attention has been given to children's own understanding of ethnic relations; children therefore continue to be seen exclusively as passive victims of circumstances rather than as active agents.

Numerous questions remain with regard to what the standard measures, such as the doll test, actually mean. Does a black child's preference for a white doll necessarily mean there is a psychological desire to be white or that self-esteem is impaired? No easy answers to such questions are available. According to Katz (1976), neither reliability nor validity data for the forced-choice methods have been presented, and therefore no definitive claims may be made that such techniques measure race attitudes, nor that the same attitude is consistent at different times of measurement. Despite these deficiencies, surprisingly consistent patterns of results have been obtained over a thirty-year period and from a range of geographical locations. Furthermore, the findings are in general accord with expectations drawn from theories of racism of the Black Consciousness or Fanonesque type. For these reasons, neither the methods nor the findings should be treated too lightly, despite their limitations.

Perhaps the most severe criticism to be levelled at standard approaches to the study of race attitude development is that the problem has been decontextualized. The issue of race or ethnicity is artificially removed from the context of social class relations, authoritarian state structures, and ideologies of ethnic relations which in South Africa are together employed to maintain and justify both capitalist and white hegemony. Stated differently, if concrete actions of children were to be studied and observed in the real contexts of classrooms, playgrounds, streets, factories, farms, and homes, it is likely that different questions could be posed and that different patterns would emerge. Issues of 'race relations' might well become secondary. It is quite conceivable that the very focus of study on race and ethnic attitudes in isolation rather than the development of ideas about social class or nationality (both sorely neglected) contributes to the myth of racist ideology.

This is not to suggest that racism is benign or to be ignored. On the contrary, the establishment of ideas about ethnicity among children may well be a powerful device for reducing resistance within a racist state, and we certainly need to know more about how such ideas develop.

We also, however, need to ask how ideas of race relate to those of class, and how these ideas and attitudes are translated into practice. In particular, we need to ask how young people have managed to resist and challenge the deleterious effects of pervasive racist ideology in South Africa. In this regard, the main merit of the present chapter may lie in understanding past methods in order to pose new challenging questions. Our chief need is to explore the ideas and practices required to build a society beyond racism.

Growing Up an Afrikaner

Pieter le Roux

Introduction

There are probably very few societies in the world where people grow up under circumstances as diverse and with perceptions of reality as divergent as in South Africa. In this chapter I relate some experiences of growing up an Afrikaner in the Transvaal.[1]

What follows has many of the shortcomings of a one-sample survey, for most of the insights are based on my own experiences, although reference is at times made to the few studies containing relevant material. On the other hand, it has some of the advantages of participatory observation, for one has an in-depth knowledge of one's own experiences which is never available to the survey researcher. By this I do not wish to imply that an analysis of this type is unproblematic. As Piaget (1976: 43) cautioned, 'the past itself is constantly restructured by the present'. The selection of incidents and the relative emphasis placed on different explanations are bound to be related to the theoretical perceptions of the author.

This chapter has both a theoretical and practical intent. On the theoretical level it questions functionalist explanations of the socialization process according to which the society, or monopoly capitalism, for the sake of its own reproduction, internalizes certain values and norms in the youth. It is argued that this process of indoctrination is far more consciously undertaken, and far more successfully resisted than either the structural functionalists or the Marxist economic reductionists are willing to admit. On the practical level the intention is both to give those unacquainted with Afrikaners some understanding of the factors that form their perception of reality, and to encourage Afrikaners themselves to reflect on what is happening to black youth in the light of their own experiences.

In the section which follows I set the scene by giving a general background to my experience of growing up as an Afrikaner.

Setting the Scene

In 1950, at the age of four, I discovered that not all South Africans spoke Afrikaans. We were living in a semi-detached miners' house on the East Rand and our neighbours came of British mining stock. My mother battled in vain to convince me that a horse was called a horse and not an 'orse, as I insisted. After all, Aubrey, my friend from next door, was English and knew best.

The first African whom I can remember is a man who gained my eternal gratitude by making a fleeting appearance in my life when, at the age of three, I was attacked by a cow who disapproved of my interest in her calf. I do not, however, have any specific memories from that early age of those who helped in our home. Africans were in the background. I remember occasionally buying a penny's 'nicker' balls or some black toffees at the store in the mining compound only half a mile from our house, or watching Africans playing soccer on Sunday afternoons when my parents were sleeping. At that stage there were probably far more Africans within a three to four mile radius of our home than whites, but they were in the compound at night and down the mines during the day. The children with whom I played and with whom I later went to school were white.

The history books tell us that those were the years when the National Party was entrenching itself in government after having gained power with the slogan that they would protect people from the *Swart Gevaar* (Black Danger).[2] Although my parents were ardent Nationalists, I do not remember being warned to stay away from the African compound or having any fear of Africans.

If there was group friction, it was with the English. Particularly after I had started school our battles were with the English children (some erstwhile friends) who lived further down the street and called us *bokslagters*.[3] We branded them *rooinekke* (red necks), a term which might have been applicable to British soldiers during the

Anglo-Boer war, but did not cause much embarrassment to the deeply tanned miners' children.

In spite of our rivalries, we had one hero in common: Hennie Muller, the great Springbok rugby flanker, who lived in one of the corner houses and spent his weekends tinkering with an old car. In 1955 when the British Lions came to play, the Springboks had their final practice on the mine's rugby field, and we were there in a big swarm to look on in pride as local boy Jack van der Schyff invariably succeeded with his goal kicks from all corners of the field. On the Saturday of the test match, however, he missed the crucial final conversion and the Springboks lost 22-23. We never forgave the English neighbour who was the only one to revel in the result.

There is ample evidence, discussed below, that school was intended to indoctrinate. But we did not see it that way. It was simply boring and restrictive. Breaks were fun, though. We would play all sorts of games on our sexually segregated playing fields. Occasionally cries of 'Fight! Fight!' would fill the air, and soon what might have been a minor squabble was turned into a vicious confrontation, often against the wishes of the adversaries. Thus one of my best friends and I, during our third year at school, were so reckless as both to lay claim to the affections of the new girl with beautiful blue-grey eyes. Older children soon forced us to fight it out in what, to their disappointment, turned out to be a bloodless wrestling match.

Caning was common — especially in the higher standards — in all three of the primary schools I attended, and also in high school. In standard three, when we were nine to ten years old, we had a particularly vicious teacher who drew blood when he was angry. He was restrained, after parental complaints to the headmaster. In high school some teachers regularly caned pupils who fared badly in tests and examinations. This meant that there were times when some had two or three canings a week. In mathematics one was caned for every theorem one did not know. The sentences imposed on girl offenders were more lenient: they were usually given 'lines'.

Several teachers in high school were very capable. Our intelligent and attractive English teacher struggled in vain to get us to show some interest in King Lear. Admittedly we were all keen to listen to her recordings of the unexpurgated version, which contained a number of explicit passages left out in the version prescribed, but our English was of such a low standard that we had problems understanding even contemporary texts. Shakespeare, though enthusiastically taught, could not engage children who heard English only once a week when they attended the matinee at the local 'bioscope' (cinema).

Our German teacher was also very able, but again his talents were wasted. He had a far more attentive audience when describing in detail how his mother and elder sisters were confined in a concentration camp (our school was built on the exact site) by the English, than when attempting to explain the subjunctive mood or to captivate us with Goethe and Heinrich Heine.

For many pupils and teachers sport was by far the most important activity. The year our rugby team won the Transvaal Administrator's Cup, the players were hero-worshipped and we wore our school blazer with pride. Excellence in sport was every child's dream, and was recognized and rewarded above academic work. Defeat was not smiled upon, and to lose to the local English high school was unthinkable. It was named after Alfred Milner, whom we held responsible both for the concentration camps and the burning of farms during the Anglo-Boer War.

After school came nine months in the army and four years at the University of Stellenbosch. Army life at that stage was very different from today. Official army parlance still referred to 'guerillas' instead of 'terrorists'. No war was being fought, and live ammunition was issued only on the shooting range. Stellenbosch University was, from the point of view of some of the issues to be raised in the analysis which follows, going through an interesting phase. After many decades of support for the Afrikaanse Studentebond (the ASB — a federation of conservative students), the student body of Stellenbosch disaffiliated from the ASB and, for the first time in years, the Stellenbosch Student Council was taken over by a group which did not have the backing of the Nationalist establishment.

Afrikaner Nationalist Indoctrination

There is no doubt that the Christian National Education to which the Nationalist government committed itself was designed to inculcate very specific values. There was no pretence, to the horror of liberal educators, that education could be neutral. Unashamedly the educational system, the news media and cultural organizations were given the task of promoting a particular perception of reality. A number of studies have drawn attention to the nature of this indoctrination.

Some have focussed on the specific content of the curricula and the books prescribed in the different provinces (eg. Auerbach 1965; Du Preez 1982). It is shown how negative stereotypes of other groups are developed, and how a 'positive' perception of the Afrikaner is promoted. Recently the Main Committee of the Human Sciences Research Council Investigation into Intergroup Relations similarly found that

> Research done by the Work Committee Communication revealed, *inter alia*, that school handbooks and youth literature contain very negative stereotypes. Although there are indications that these stereotypes are also becoming less distinct in general literature, it must be remembered that older books with more negative stereotypes are still used as set books, are read and that films based on them are shown on television. (Main Committee 1985: 81.)

There are other studies concerned with attempts by Nationalist ideologues and in particular the Afrikaner Broederbond to manipulate and control the thinking of Afrikaners on a much broader level. (See, for example, Wilkins and Strydom 1978; Du Toit 1955; Patterson 1957). These clearly show the extent of attempts to determine who is appointed to key posts and to control perceptions of reality. Particularly in the Church, the schools, and the media it became very difficult if not impossible to obtain an important post if one did not have the support of the secret Afrikaner Broederbond. In the official history of the Broederbond, Pelzer, with false modesty, underplays the active role of the Broederbond in influencing key appointments. He, for example, writes that 'the Afrikaner Broederbond found itself in a fortunate position . . . with such men as M C Botha, S H Pelliser and P J Meyer [all senior Broederbonders] for long periods in control of broadcasting' (Pelzer 1979: 103). In fact, as the above-mentioned studies show, it was more than good fortune that the Broederbonders occupied these and most other important posts in education, the media, and the Church.

While it is beyond doubt that the Broederbond intended to mould the minds of the young, at school we had no understanding of this.[4] I do remember our high school librarian being incensed when she got instructions to throw out a lot of books which were declared unsuitable for us, including *Uncle Tom's Cabin*, which I then bought for five cents. I also knew about the problems the father of one of my good friends had over his appointment as principal at a neighbouring school because he was a supporter of the United Party. Only after he had explained that he was merely a *bloedsap* — that is, that his father, who was a strong Smuts supporter,[5] would never forgive him should he vote for the National Party, and that he himself would never do anything to harm the party — was he finally appointed permanent head of the school where he had been a very successful acting headmaster for a long period. However, these were isolated incidents of which most pupils were probably not even aware.

If the planners in education had had their way, virtually all our opinions and behaviour patterns would have been decided from above. Whereas most observers accept that this concerted effort to indoctrinate the youth inevitably succeeded, it would on reflection seem to me as though there was quite strong resistance from a number of the pupils. In the sections which follow it is argued that many of the values that the educational system and cultural organizations were attempting to inculcate were questioned and rejected. By this I do not wish to imply that the indoctrination did not meet with much success. I do, however, contend that the pupils themselves did show a great deal of independence. They were not simply clay in the hands of Big Brother.

Voortrekkers, Volkspele and all that

During my first year at university I was most incensed when an English friend proclaimed that Voortrekkers (the Afrikaner Nationalist answer to the Boy Scout movement) were similar to the Hitler Youth movement. After all, at school I was one of the few in my class who remained a Voortrekker up to the final year. I still think today that my friend was wrong, if only for the reason that the Voortrekker attempt to engender mass support among the children was a dismal failure.

The activities of the Voortrekkers appealed most to younger children. At the age of six a weekend in the mountains was the greatest adventure imaginable. There are pleasant memories of building big campfires, catching frogs in the pools and digging deep furrows around the tents to survive untimely highveld thunderstorms. In high school, however, the Voortrekker movement was not held in high regard. Although most would not express it as crudely as the boy who once taunted us: 'Voortrekkers, Voortrekkers, Draadtrekkers!' (om draad te trek: to masturbate), the movement was too boring to attract many of those it was intended to indoctrinate.

There is no doubt that one of the main functions of the Voortrekkers, apart from keeping us out of the claws of the Scouts, was to instil carefully the Civil Religion, to use Dunbar Moodie's phrase (1975), which proclaimed that the Afrikaner was elected to bring Christianity and western civilization to a barbarous southern Africa. However, institutions do not always function the way they are supposed to. One of our officers undoubtedly had what were left-wing sentiments by western Transvaal standards. He, for example, challenged the article of faith that good Afrikaners should not buy at Indian shops, arguing that if those shops gave better service, they should be entitled to draw a bigger clientele. Although his defiance of official doctrine did not make a marked impression on me at the time, he clearly sowed seeds of doubt. The hierarchy would certainly have disapproved.

One can only speculate on the reasons for the Voortrekkers' failure to become a mass youth movement. Clearly it was never an organization with an appeal to high school youth. The question is whether it would have been more successful had it been more exciting. Personally I doubt the ability of any youth movement to gain mass support if it is not fostered by a totalitarian state or engaged in a liberation struggle — the Voortrekkers borrowed the rhetoric, though none of the substance, of the latter. The young people I knew were far too independent to acquiesce willingly in the dominance of any one movement when it did not directly serve their interests.

Probably the most artificial cultural creation ever to see the light of day was *volkspele* (folk dances). Gustav Preller selected the less erotic movements from European folk dances, coordinated these with Afrikaans songs, and hey presto — we had our own folk dances! We were neither aware of, nor interested in, the history of *volkspele*. At our school no dancing whatsoever was permitted, and hence *volkspele* evenings could be very well attended indeed, but only if we were allowed to do *volkspele* our way.

Evenings under the leadership of the science teacher, who actually toured Europe with a *volkspele* group and insisted on the dances being performed very correctly, were boycotted by most pupils. However, one of the other teachers, who drank a brandy or two before he started, was very popular, for he permitted us to hold the girls far closer in the *tiekiedraai* (a whirling dance movement) than the rules allowed, and showed no concern when some couples disappeared for a while during interval. *Volkspele* themselves never had a chance of becoming popular at a time when listening to the Lourenço Marques hit parade was all the rage.

Among the other cultural activities encouraged by the school was the annual eisteddfod, but most pupils, except those who sang in choirs, flatly refused to participate. This, however, may have been a reflection of anti-intellectualism rather than rebellion against official culture.

The *volksfeeste* (folk festivals) — Republic Day, Kruger Day, and Day of the Covenant — interspersed with National Party *stryddae* (fêtes), attracted fewer participants every year. Endless speeches and the nostalgia for great battles and great heroes of years gone by did not appeal to most pupils. Once the Afrikaner Nationalists had risen to power the rallying cries of yesteryear lost their potency. It was easier to unite against English imperialism when the English actually had some power.

From the preceding it is clear that in the cultural sphere the efforts of the Afrikaner Broederbond, if they are to be judged by my own experience, met with mixed results. Cultural activities drawn up in the confines of Broederbond meetings did not appeal to most young people. Even when an organization controls most informal sources of entertainment outside school hours, it is not necessarily able to shape the entire cultural experience of a new generation.

The Church

Although I was more susceptible to attempts at cultural indoctrination than most of my contemporaries, I was sceptical of the Church from an early age. It is thus with some hesitation that I write about the rebellion of the youth against this powerful institution, as I may give too much weight to a personal experience.

The Church was undoubtedly powerful. But its power was also strongly resented. At school we knew that the minister, who was chairman of the school committee, strongly opposed dancing. Even at the matriculation farewell we could dance only after he, the guest of honour, had left. This was widely resented. But to prohibit dancing at school was a mild exercise of power when compared with other sanctions the Church saw fit to impose. It could be relentless towards those who did not heed its moral injunctions. I know of the ruthlessness with which a minister, when an unmarried girl in a neighbouring congregation fell pregnant, persecuted and punished not only the girl, but in effect the whole family. Ironically, the same minister was found in a most compromising position not many months later. He was subsequently convicted under the Immorality Act, and had to resign from the Church.

Youth probably always resents those who prescribe rules to which they themselves do not adhere. The story of the undisciplined disciplinarian does not, however, justify a condemnation of the Church as such. The average minister was both less destructive in disciplining those of the flock who misbehaved, and less tempted to throw overboard both the sexual and racial taboos of our society. Far more typical of what alienated the youth was the sermon in which our minister, his hair gleaming with Brylcream, prophesied hell and damnation for women who used make-up. Similarly, women who smoked were condemned by ministers who called down God's wrath with nicotine-stained fingers.

The racial bigotry of the Dutch Reformed Church is captured by the joke about the Pretoria policeman who demanded that an African he had caught kneeling in a place of worship should explain what he was doing. On being informed that he was polishing the floors, the policemen let the African go, remarking, 'Oh, that's OK, I thought you were praying'. The Afrikaans radio announcer who was suspended after he had told this joke on his morning programme had the admiration of a number of my matric classmates because of his willingness to challenge the Church (but not because of any sympathy with his implicit political critique). In the Western Transvaal there were not many who questioned the political stance of the Church. It was the pettiness of the prescriptions with regard to personal behaviour against which many of us reacted. The Church was often regarded with more than a mild degree of irritation.

Puritan values

'Puritans in Africa' is how Afrikaners are described in the title of a book by a well-known Afrikaans writer, W.A. de Klerk. He claims that this puritanism is reflected in the Afrikaner's 'attempt to remake a society in the total vision of a socio-political ideal'. Apartheid is thus seen to be 'yet another of the many secular manifestations with their roots in the protestant ethic' (De Klerk 1975: xiii).

> Calvinism undoubtedly has had a significant impact on Afrikaner behaviour in many spheres. The primary blame for apartheid should,

however, be placed on a desire to retain and extend economic and political power rather than on any version of Calvinism. Protestant puritanism is primarily concerned with sexual morality and a work ethic. The question is how important an impact this puritanism had on those who were growing up as Afrikaners.

As far as sexual behaviour is concerned there is every reason to doubt the ability of schools and the Church to have a determining influence. In many instances behaviour deviated from the prescribed norms, following to some extent patterns of revolt by the younger generation all over the Western world. Already in primary school a classmate proudly passed around a pen with a peephole featuring a lady who rapidly lost her costume whenever the pen was turned upside down. Later a married teacher at a neighbouring school was suspended after what was by all accounts a passionate relationship with a pupil fifteen years her junior, and there were strong rumours among pupils about a similar, although more discreet, affair in our school. In the higher standards sex was as popular a topic of conversation as rugby, and in the boys' hostel there was a regular competition to establish who was the best endowed — the winner enjoying much status also among the girls 'in the know'. It was well-established who the 'easy' girls were, and stories of conquest were freely told. Though in the army there was pressure on those who could not relate true stories of conquests to invent them, the young men[6] who claimed that one had not eaten sweets yet if one had not tasted chocolates probably were the connoisseurs they claimed to be.

From the preceding it does not follow that Calvinist teachings had no impact whatsoever on sexual morality. It is most likely that, in comparison with English-speaking South Africans and the youth of some other western societies, a significantly larger proportion of both Afrikaner boys and girls did commit themselves to strict standards. In this respect survey results are of limited value, for in a society in which puritan norms apply respondents may be unwilling to admit to unacceptable sexual activity, whereas in other societies there may be pressures to pretend to be sexually experienced. Illegitimacy rates were often rumoured to be higher at Stellenbosch University than at the University of Cape Town, but even if there were reliable statistics to support these rumours — which I doubt — it may merely be an indication that birth control was less widely practised or abortions less readily available among Afrikaans girls. From the point of view of this analysis it is, however, sufficient to note that a significant proportion of Afrikaner youth rejected puritan sexual values in spite of (or perhaps, in reaction to) their Christian National Education and the strong position of the Church. The dominant norms do not determine the social behaviour of all.

Puritan values are not merely concerned with sexual behaviour, of course.

> The insistence on the value of time, the condemnation and abhorrence of pleasure and diversion — all those censorious prohibitions and internalized inhibitions that we denote as puritanism with a small p . . . constituted in effect an imposition of the criterion of efficiency on every activity. (Landes 1972: 24).

We thus also need to consider to what extent schools and the Church succeeded in imbuing the children with the puritan work ethic.

During the 1930s as many as a third of all Afrikaners were considered to be 'poor whites'. A Canadian sociologist, who accepted Weber's theory that the Protestant ethic enables one to succeed economically, tried to explain Afrikaner poverty by arguing that, since the Afrikaner considered himself to be of the elect by virtue of being white, there was no need to prove this in the economic sphere (Stokes 1975). A supporter of the original Weberian thesis could counter that the majority of the 'poor whites' did not belong to any of the Calvinist churches, but were either without any church connection or members of the evangelical churches. To this another critic might retort that the Afrikaners who were not economically successful escaped puritan moral sanctions by leaving the Calvinist church.[7] From the historical evidence it is thus not at all clear whether the protestant ethic did or did not play an important role in motivating the Afrikaner to be more successful in the economic sphere.

On the basis of my own experience it is difficult to judge to what extent the attempts to implant a puritan work ethic had a significant impact. Clearly, hard work was extolled by parents, Church, and schools, but at the same time many did not practise what they preached. These daily and weekly doses of moralizing must have had some influence, and for some it may even have been very important later in their lives. There were many, however, who consciously refused to take the medicine. Working hard at school was not generally admired. Success in sports had much higher status than academic success.

Political indoctrination

One of the cornerstones of Christian National Education[8] was a commitment to a political philosophy which laid great stress on separateness. In the early years the battle was one for separate Afrikaner schools. In their book on the Afrikaner Broederbond, Wilkins and Strydom reveal how M.C. Botha had planned a school boycott by Afrikaans children in the 1940s in order to enforce their demand for separate Afrikaans schools rather than the parallel medium the United Party government favoured. The strike, which was aborted when it became public, was to last long enough 'to bring the Government to its senses' (Wilkins and Strydom 1978: 256). The fear was that, if 50 per cent of all teaching was in English, the Afrikaners who gained a proficiency in a world language would be tempted to anglicize. (Ironically, the same M.C. Botha was Minister of Bantu Education and Development in 1976 when African schoolchildren staged a widespread school boycott, sparked off by government insistence that the medium of instruction in African high schools in some of the subjects be Afrikaans.)

By the time I reached school the English threat had, in the Transvaal at least, been averted. Although the Afrikaner remained on his guard against the English, the Afrikaner Broederbond was at this time concentrating its efforts on promoting apartheid — that is, separateness between black and white — in the belief that continued support for the Afrikaner government and the long term survival of the Afrikaner depended on the acceptance of this philosophy.

Whereas attempts to prescribe loyalty to cultural organizations and the Church and a commitment to puritan values were at best partially successful, Nationalist political propaganda was very effective. One of the most pervasive features of the political scene during the 1950s, 1960s, and 1970s is what Adam and Giliomee (1979) called the ethnic mobilization of the Afrikaner. By the time I left school virtually all Afrikaners supported the National Party. How can this success be explained?

Recent studies concerning political socialization by Kotze (1985) and Kotze and Norval (1983) show that Afrikaans youth experience a greater degree of political socialization within the family than English youth. In both groups the family is found to be a more important agent of political socialization than schools and the peer group.[9] However, whereas 65 per cent of the Afrikaners in the study claimed that their fathers had a great interest in politics, only 33 per cent of the English pupils claimed that this was the case. With respect to mothers, these percentages were 30 and 12 respectively. It is hardly surprising that whereas only 8 per cent of the Afrikaans respondents claimed to have no interest whatsoever in politics, more than a quarter of the English respondents made a similar claim.

Politics was important in my family and, as seems to be the case with many young Afrikaners today, this was probably where the most important political socialization took place. I remember the excitement of the 1953 election when as a kindergarten child I got up early in the morning to listen to the results with my parents. (Later, at university, I compared notes with an English friend whose father was a prominent opposition politician during these times: he had no memory whatsoever of this election, although he was one year older than I.) Five years later, by 1958, I was quite an expert, knowing which were the marginal seats. A strong feeling against the English imperialists, who seemed to be all those who spoke of England as their home, motivated my parents' loyalty to the National Party. Both their families were from the the Cape Province and did not directly experience the civilian horrors, on the Boer side, of the Anglo-Boer War. Though a great-uncle who joined the Cape rebels and fought against the English in the western Transvaal was summarily executed when he was caught, the bloody shirt was never waved at home. My parents' strong feelings were based on a collection of small and, at times, seemingly insignificant anecdotes demonstrating British arrogance. People forgive atrocities committed in the heat of war far more readily than what they regard as subtle and persistent signs that their language and culture, and they themselves in fact, are regarded as inferior.

By the preceding I do not wish to imply that the historic conflict with English imperialism was unimportant for the development of the Afrikaner's political consciousness. In particular, the history of the British concentration camps during the Anglo-Boer War was recounted time and again. Twenty-six thousand women and children died, about a tenth of the total Afrikaner population in the two states that were at war with England. But the historic wrongs would in my opinion not have been sufficient to keep the fires of resentment burning had English people not repeatedly rekindled the flames by often unconscious revelations of feelings of superiority.

During and after the Second World War there was an understandable English reaction against the Afrikaner Nationalists, who openly supported Germany. Once the National Party took over, Afrikaner Nationalists were rapidly promoted over the heads of many English-speaking South Africans, and this gave further cause for strong resentment of all Afrikaners. However, whatever the motives, Afrikaners saw all English resentment of them and their culture as proof of an English superiority complex.

This anti-English feeling was instilled in us as children from a relatively early age. Sheila Patterson (1957: 231) relates how during the 1953 election the Afrikaans children who were officially called upon to make sacrifices for South Africa, did not confine themselves to the relatively innocent task of

> acting as guards of honour at meetings, distributing pamphlets and tracking down lost voters . . . . Large groups of them attended political meetings, where their usual practice was to sit in blocks and to heckle the speaker, or even prevent him from getting a hearing at all.

Patterson was particularly shocked by the degree of indoctrination of the youth when she, while

> being driven through a predominantly Afrikaans working-class area in Johannesburg in a car with a United Party label on the windscreen . . . was stoned by a group of very young children . . . [with] Nationalist sympathies.

Although I personally have no memories of breaking up meetings or stoning cars, there is no doubt that these incidents reflected the strength of the resentment felt against the English. South Africa in the 1980s offers intriguing parallels.

It is interesting to note that the first Afrikaner establishment which succeeded in overcoming this anti-English bias was the student body at the University of Stellenbosch, which in the late 1960s disaffiliated from the extremely conservative Afrikaanse Studente Bond. One of the reasons for this move, which caused as much resentment in the Afrikaner hierarchy as the more recent attempt by Stellenbosch students to visit the African National Congress Youth League, was the unsuitability of links with an exclusively Afrikaans organization, especially one with very conservative political views, when between ten and fifteen per cent of the students were English-speaking. The Afrikaans students at Stellenbosch felt less strongly anti-English than those at other universities for two reasons. First, at Stellenbosch a fair number of Afrikaans students had close English friends (there being proportionately more English students at Stellenbosch than at other Afrikaans universities) and, by a process of self-selection, these English students generally did not have strong anti-Afrikaans feelings. Second, judged on the basis of the school-leaving examination results of new admissions, the average Afrikaans student at Stellenbosch was academically far stronger than the average student at other Afrikaans universities. It is possible that they consequently had more self-confidence and were thus less likely to suspect other groups of feeling superior. Where there were indeed cases of English arrogance, they were more likely to be amused than affronted by such chauvinism.

The 1950s were the years of the African National Congress's defiance campaigns and the Freedom Charter, but of those I have no memory whatsoever. Until 1960 I believed that politics had to do with the Afrikaner asserting control over the political and economic spheres from which the English had excluded him. There was little or no awareness among any of us of how the blacks were progressively being excluded from these spheres, or if there were, there was little concern. The removal of those classified as coloureds from the common voters' roll did give rise to protest in some Afrikaans quarters, but it took the Sharpeville shootings in 1960 to make me aware that Africans were not acquiescing in Verwoerd's grand apartheid philosophy. I remember that when I was fifteen a visit to the Rand Easter Agricultural Show was cancelled because it was considered to be unsafe. What that meant to us, however, was that Africans were predisposed to riotous behaviour. We had no sense of the anger of black South Africans at the long-standing denial of their economic and political rights.

Young Afrikaners of the 1950s and early 1960s grew up in an atmosphere of pervasive and unquestioned racism. Racial stereotypes which we acquired at home were mostly reinforced at school. Our history books (Du Preez 1982), our literature (Gerwel 1983; Tötemeyer 1984), and the attitudes of teachers, preachers, parents, and friends left us in no doubt that Africans were very different from whites and had to be treated as a separate, inferior group. From this it does not follow that extreme, racist behaviour was condoned. On the contrary, many parents and teachers would punish rude behaviour to Africans. However, beliefs of racial superiority were fostered by most. There were a few exceptions, such as the Voortrekker officer I referred to above, and a history teacher who, because of his somewhat more sympathetic attitude towards Africans, was rumoured to be a communist. Among us pupils, however, this was never an issue on which to revolt against the official dogma. With regard to racial dogma we were very compliant indeed.

It is self-revealing to re-read an English essay I wrote in the June examinations of my final year at school in 1963 and then submitted to our school yearbook. I argued against the removal of African women to the 'homeland' — a position which might seem to be enlightened for that time — but justified my position by contending:

> Ultimately the time will come when domestic servants will be able to find better work in other spheres due to the development of the Border Industries. Why should we then try to obtain by revolution that which will eventually come by evolution. (Le Roux 1963: 73.)

The philosophy of separate development was swallowed as readily as good *koeksisters*.

According to Tötemeyer's 1984 study of youth literature, the theme of black-white conflict (black barbarian and white pioneer) was very prevalent in the earlier Afrikaans texts. There was a slight respite in the 1950s and early 1960s, before this theme re-emerged with a vengeance in the stories of the border war in which the African was often portrayed as a terrorist or communist. It may be that this is reflective of a general cycle of Afrikaner evolution. Up to the late 1940s the National Party, for political purposes, exploited the fear of the poorer whites of being ploughed under by the 'uncivilized' Africans, but during the first decade of a Nationalist government apartheid measures such as job reservation, the Group Areas Act, and the strict enforcement of the Urban Areas Act (the pass laws) created a false sense of security. However, when in the 1960s the possibility of a prolonged military conflict emerged, it became important to condition the youth to regard Africans as potential terrorists and communists.

Self-reflection by the youth

Although, as I have shown, some values that Christian National Education attempted to instil in us were often questioned and rejected, the political indoctrination went virtually unchallenged. How can this 'success' be explained?

Adopting a Giddensian perception of social transformation (Giddens

1979), I would argue that the pupils consciously and subconsciously reflected upon the normative prescriptions and perceptions of reality which confronted them. Those which they found to be of limited or no relevance to their own situation they rejected; those which seemed to serve their interests and/or conformed to their perception of reality they accepted.

The partial rejection by many of the Church's authority is not surprising. In an increasingly secularized world, there was less acceptance of the belief that the Church leaders had special access to God. On the other hand, there was an increasing awareness of how the Church and particularly the ministers had an interest in maintaining the traditional order. Thus, when the congregation was exhorted to contribute, and to contribute liberally, to the cause of the Church, we as children were thoroughly aware that the possibility of increases in the minister's salary and improvements in his other perks were dependent on the success of such financial appeals. Because of these and other considerations discussed above, the youth's increasing scepticism is understandable.

That some of the puritan values would be questioned is to be expected once one accepts that individual children actually reflect on what has been prescribed to them, and do not, as the structural functionalists would have us believe, automatically internalize the norms of society. This is not to deny that morality in the sexual sphere and commitment to a work ethic were in some respects clearly in the interests of the pupils. Indeed, I have not argued that a significant group rejected all morality. However, the specific versions of sexual morality and of the work ethic we pupils often encountered were very strict. Much of the enjoyment of life had to be repressed without there being any obvious advantages to abiding by these rules. This many of the pupils realized. Hence their 'deviant' behaviour.

The lack of interest in cultural organizations and official culture was not surprising. These types of organizations, the Broederbond included, might have made sense in the early decades of this century when there was a real danger that the English imperialists might succeed in their attempt to destroy the Afrikaans language and culture. Whereas there was considerable concern in Broederbond circles that increasing apathy about cultural organizations was an indication that Afrikaans was again becoming vulnerable to English imperialism, I believe that Afrikaans pupils were starting to feel secure enough in themselves and their language no longer to need these rather artificial structures. They saw no function for what the Broederbond still claimed was essential.

In contrast to the other types of indoctrination, political indoctrination did strike a very responsive chord. This is not surprising. The anti-English propaganda had a factual basis. Historically it is true that the British committed the atrocities of which they were accused; more importantly, most of us at one time or another experienced a version of English arrogance towards Afrikaners. At that stage, when the average Afrikaner was still much poorer than most English speakers, and when a far greater percentage of the latter were well-qualified, the Afrikaner was likely to suffer from the resentments generated by a feeling of inferiority, irrespective of how considerate the English might have been. As Giddens (1981: 193-95) has argued in general terms and Adam and Giliomee (1979: 52) with specific reference to the Afrikaner, nationalist feelings have psychological roots in the need for ontological security. Although O'Meara (1983: 8) criticizes Adam and Giliomee by arguing that 'they rely finally on an extreme form of idealism', he blatantly misquotes Adam as having excluded material factors.[10] It is thus not at all surprising that indoctrination in this sphere seemed to work well.

By the preceding I do not wish to imply that it actually is in the Afrikaner's long term self-interest to perpetuate anti-English feelings. As they have moved economically and culturally closer to each other (after a first trip overseas Afrikaners often admit with surprise that they were more at home in England than in any of the countries from which their ancestors emigrated), the divisions have been artificially perpetuated by the system of separate schooling. Only those Afrikaners who get preferential treatment in the civil service still benefit from this anti-English sentiment, but at an increasing cost for Afrikanerdom as a whole. Many of the most capable English South Africans, who could have made significant contributions to the efficiency of our sluggish civil service, now have strong anti-Afrikaner Nationalist feelings, nurtured by this exclusion from the corridors of power.[11]

Whereas most English South Africans would naturally have acquired Afrikaans as a second language if South Africa had had parallel-medium schools, the separate school system has artificially perpetuated anti-Afrikaans feelings, and vice versa. There is a strong resentment among many English against having to learn Afrikaans as a second language when they could have acquired a 'more useful' language such as French or German. One of the characteristics which still reflects the imperialist attitude of times gone by is the belief that one can, as a small minority group, be part of a country and yet refuse to learn any of the other languages. However, Afrikaner Nationalists have been extremely short-sighted in insisting that Afrikaans should be the second language the English speaker has to learn. There should be a free choice. For example, in Natal Zulu or an Indian language should be options, in the Cape Xhosa, and in the Transvaal Sotho. If a true proficiency in the second language is required, most English speakers are likely to choose the linguistically closer Afrikaans, but with far less resentment than when it is forced upon them. And the more Afrikaans and English pupils opt for one of the indigenous languages, the better South Africa's long term interests will be served.

If anti-English feelings took root, racist indoctrination — to judge by the attitudes of virtually all my classmates — was even more successful. It would be wrong, though, to conclude that this was a major focus of the schools and Church. Far more effort went into inculcating puritan values, and if my memory serves me correctly, into making us aware of the wrongs and injustices which the English had committed, than into developing any argument that blacks were inferior or that blacks should be kept apart. Indeed, as far as the conviction of black inferiority is concerned, this was so much part of the average child's perception of reality that the school and Church merely had to reinforce it. Indoctrination only found an unreceptive audience to the extent that it attempted to modify more extreme forms of racism. For example, many children would insist on speaking about 'kaffirs' in spite of being encouraged to use the official term 'Bantu'.

Racist ideology went unchallenged because we never heard dissenting voices: it seemed to be rational, and it seemed to serve the interests of all of us. Whereas at least some parents would differ quite strongly from the official dogma with regard to church and party political issues, and whereas puritan morality was often not accepted by all, not a single parent or teacher (not even the history teacher accused of being a communist) believed in a non-racial society. The facts seemed to be clear. Blacks seemed less able than whites, and as most people with domestic servants would tell one, they were not as hardworking either. We believed it to be obvious that they did not maintain the same standards of cleanliness as whites, and did not take as good care of their homes or children. Furthermore, we all 'knew' that in those countries where blacks were getting independence, chaos immediately set in. We or our parents also directly experienced some of the benefits of the discriminatory measures. Job reservation, both in the private and public sector, the Group Areas Act, the lack of black trade union rights, and many other apartheid measures directly served our interests. The moral defence that blacks could exercise all these rights in their own areas seemed to be quite acceptable. The success with which a racist perception of social reality was established and maintained is thus hardly surprising.

Today even some of the most dogmatic Afrikaner Nationalists realize that these perceptions of reality were simply wrong. Some would even admit that the conclusion that blacks were inferior was fallacious, and that although many apartheid measures were in the short term interest of the Afrikaner, they have created circumstances under which the very existence of the Afrikaner is threatened. However, given the world occupied by the average Afrikaans pupil of the 1950s and the 1960s, the success of racist indoctrination was to be expected. It was in harmony with the world as the pupils experienced it and conformed with their perception of their self interest.

Conclusion

In the preceding sections I have rejected the functionalist argument which assumes that, since norms automatically fulfil an integrative function, the internalization of dominant norms by young people is unproblematic. The young, instead, reflect on the norms prescribed and the accepted perceptions of reality, and reject those which do not seem to make sense in terms of their own experience.

Factors which coloured perceptions of reality

I have argued that the political indoctrination of Afrikaner youth was successful because it was possible to present the Nationalist picture of reality as plausible, for at least two reasons.

First, one should not underestimate the effect of geographical and social apartheid. Merely by the separation of Afrikaans and English youth, the National Party government succeeded in perpetuating differences and reproducing political tensions which would otherwise have disappeared because of the rapid economic advance of the Afrikaners and the decreasing inclination among English speakers to remain loyal to a disintegrating empire. Group Areas, the pass laws, and other measures taken to separate black from white physically also served to perpetuate stereotypical perceptions of those groups with whom one could not be in daily social intercourse. As Giddens (1979: 202) has correctly pointed out, social theorists have hitherto not been sufficiently aware of the importance of the spatial attributes of social conduct. The racial separation of people has not only had physical consequences: separate social worlds have been created.

A second major reason was the control the Nationalists could exert over the media. We have already noted how the directors of the South African Broadcasting Corporation have been Afrikaner Broeder-bonders for many years. For their understanding of what is happening in the wider world beyond South Africa's borders, most Afrikaners were dependent on media controlled by dogmatic Nationalists. Ever since the 1950s much has been published in other countries which has undermined traditional racial prejudice. From these new trends Afrikaners have been carefully insulated.

Political power was the key to the successful indoctrination of the Afrikaner. It was also its goal. Clearly the economic power and the economic interest of the capitalists led to some of them having a strong influence on the media, and in particular the English media. The perception of reality the Afrikaans media so successfully projected was primarily in the interest of the Afrikaans politicians and the Afrikaner Broederbond, which also represented the interests of Afrikaner capitalists. It ensured virtually unanimous Afrikaner support for the National Party.

Failure to indoctrinate black youth

Today many Nationalists are themselves most perturbed by the consequences of the policy they adopted. The very measures that were supposed to ensure that the Afrikaner Nationalist would retain control in the centuries ahead have in fact had unintended consequences. Probably the most crucial of the mistakes the National Party and Broederbond made was to believe that if they controlled the school curricula and the media, they would be as successful in the political indoctrination of African youth as they were in the case of Afrikaner youth. As I have attempted to show in this chapter, even young Afrikaners could not be indoctrinated to accept what clearly was not in their interests. There simply was no possibility that young blacks, who daily had to face the consequences of the apartheid policy, would accept the myth that it brought justice to all.

The atrocities of the Anglo-Boer War fade into insignificance in comparison with what has for nearly forty years been done in the name of apartheid ideology. And the subtle sneer a superior Englishman might direct at an Afrikaner Nationalist contains no malice whatsoever when compared to the naked arrogance and complete insensitivity so many whites show to black South Africans. It is thus not surprising that so many black 'hearts and minds' are irrevocably committed to the struggle for liberation. Any Afrikaner able to reflect on his own past must realize that this was inevitable. The National Party could never hope to control black political socialization in a manner comparable with its indoctrination of the Afrikaner. It is not sufficient to hold the reins of power. One must also be able to present a picture of reality which is plausible. There are circumstances in which the young can be fooled, but these do not pertain today. Young blacks are bound to reflect and act upon the reality confronting them.

Changing realities facing Afrikaners

Afrikaners who were at school during the 1950s and 1960s are now moving into positions of responsibility and power in a very different world from that which, as schoolchildren, they were led to expect. Although the initiative in social transformation has now passed to blacks, and in particular to young blacks, the outcome will depend on how whites in positions of power react as they realize that the future which they desired cannot be achieved.

It is possible that the conviction that 'blacks cannot govern a country' has become so deeply ingrained in the thinking of the vast majority of my generation that they will resist the development of democratic structures with all means at their disposal, even though they no longer believe that an alternative can work. The caning at school we discussed above, the initiation ceremonies at many Afrikaans university and college residences, and the brutalizing impact of military service can all contribute to the acceptance of violence as the only means of social control.

There is, however, nothing inevitable about the choices that will be made. Much depends on how pressure will be exerted, and on the alternatives available to escalating violence. Violence and a destructive conflict is an option which might very well be chosen. However, the old vision which gave a moral justification to holding onto power tenaciously has collapsed, and it would not be surprising if many are rational enough to call off resistance once they realize that in the end change is unavoidable. Young people today should be less susceptible to political indoctrination than we were in our time; it is no longer likely that they will accept a totally skewed picture of reality. On the other hand, they are particularly vulnerable to the anti-rational effects of the military conflict. The old world is collapsing, but it is not at all clear how the majority of Afrikaners will adjust to the new.

Notes

1. I should like to express my sincere thanks to both of the editors for encouraging me to write this paper, and for their editorial advice and support.
2. By this I do not wish to imply that the success of the National Party could primarily be ascribed to its apartheid slogans. In the case of my parents, for example, ethnic mobilization as Afrikaners also played a very important role.
3. Goat slaughterers. This probably referred to the fact that some of the poorer Afrikaners on the plots kept goats.
4. It was only when I got to university, and read Du Toit's unpublished dissertation (1955), that I began to understand what was happening behind the scenes.
5. General J.C. Smuts, who was a Boer general and later became Prime Minister and member of the British War Cabinet, had the very loyal support of a significant proportion of Afrikaners, particularly in the Western Transvaal, and they and their children continued to vote for the United Party after his death.
6. It was the same men who during smoke breaks obtained their dagga (marijuana) from the ice-cream delivery man who came into the military camp every day.
7. This argument has the same logic as the traditional criticism of the Weberian thesis that '[i]t was not Protestantism that promoted capitalism, but the reverse: pushful, hard-working, successful businessmen sought moral sanction for their way of life and their gains and found it in Protestantism.' (Landes 1972: 23.)
8. Christian National Education is based on fundamentalist Calvinist tenets and on the belief that the Afrikaner and the other ethnic groups should be taught in separate schools. The principles of CNE are embodied in the Educational Advisory Council Act, No.86 of 1962 and the National Education Policy Act, No.39 of 1967.

9. According to Kotze (1985), amongst urban African youth the order is reversed, peer groups being the most important and parents playing a very insignificant role.

10. O'Meara's inaccurate quote from Adam and Giliomee states that 'psychological security *rather* [instead of *more*!] than the material benefits attached to it must be seen as the secret appeal of nationalism everywhere'.

11. This anti-Afrikaans feeling has been reported in numerous surveys on social distance. Charlton (1975: 45) summarizes her discussion of earlier surveys as follows: 'Afrikaners are clearly seen as being less cultured, less educated people on a lower stratum of society'.

The Open Ghetto: Growing Up Jewish in South Africa[1]

Sally Frankental and Milton Shain

This chapter describes growing up Jewish in South Africa, focussing on the family, educational institutions, and the relationship of young Jews with the wider social environment. Special attention is given to the attempt to reconcile a specifically Jewish identity with membership in the wider society. The chapter deals with the period after 1961, the year in which South Africa left the British Commonwealth and became a republic.

The post-1960s generation was born into a society in which racial categorization, institutionalized separation, and black subordination are the norm. Legislation has ensured the insularity of whites.[2] Within the privileged white minority there is a further division, that between Afrikaans and English speakers. The 117 963 Jews — 2.6 per cent of the entire white population, according to the 1980 census (Dubb 1985: 66) — generally identify with the English-speaking community. These Jews are, in the main, descendants of Lithuanian immigrants, most of whom arrived in South Africa between 1890 and 1930.[3] They entered a community dominated by an Anglo-German establishment. The East European immigrants readily adopted the Anglo-Jewish style, rapidly discarding their distinctive garb, mannerisms and mores. They did not, however, dilute their Jewish identity and indeed helped to establish a wide range of communal institutions and organizations designed specifically to safeguard that identity. Most importantly, the East Europeans brought with them a Zionist fervour which continues to mark the South African Jewish community to this day.

Both Anglo-German and East European Jews had great respect for

Britain, its liberal institutions and its reputation for justice and fair play. This showed in their support for British-oriented parties, first the Unionists and later the United Party.[4] The latter's attractiveness was enhanced by Smuts's association with the Zionist movement and, more importantly, by the serious manifestations of anti-semitism from right-wing Afrikaners in the 1930s and 1940s. These anti-semitic movements, partly a response to the influx of German Jews in the early 1930s, left Jews with a profound sense of vulnerability and fear of Afrikaner hegemony in South Africa. Their fears were exacerbated when right-wing Afrikaners opposed South Africa's entry into World War II, even going so far as to harass Jewish and other volunteers.[5] Jewish identification with the English was thus reinforced. Indeed, concern about Afrikaner extremism was so marked that on the eve of the 1948 general election the South African Jewish Board of Deputies — the representative body of South African Jewry — saw fit to recommend explicitly that Jews should not support the National Party. This was a notable departure from earlier Board policy which had made it quite clear that the Board represented Jews only in so far as specifically Jewish matters were concerned and did not prescribe general political affiliation.[6] That decision had been left to individual Jews as citizens of the country. The Nationalists, however, won the 1948 election and within thirteen years had achieved their two primary goals: a policy of (racial) separate development and the severing of formal links with the Commonwealth. In these years, Jewish fears regarding anti-semitism were alleviated because of the new government's overriding concern with institutionalizing apartheid. Jews, however, now had to reconcile Jewish teachings of social justice with a blatantly discriminatory social system.

By 1961, virtually the entire Jewish population was urbanized, with the overwhelming majority resident in the four metropolitan areas of Johannesburg, Cape Town, Durban and Pretoria. The Jewish population was relatively well-educated. According to Arkin (1985), by 1970 56 per cent of all Jews had matriculated in comparison with 23 per cent of the total white population. In addition, 10 per cent of all Jews held university degrees in 1970 compared with 4 per cent of the total white population. Jews showed consistent upward mobility with the proportion of administrative and professional workers in the labour force increasing from 12 per cent in 1936 to 40 per cent in 1960. By 1970, Jews were still over-represented (in relation to their numbers in the population) in the commercial and financial sectors.

Indeed, by then, 94 per cent of Jewish males were concentrated in the four sectors of manufacturing, commerce, finance and services. Jews were employed almost exclusively in the private sector, with 28 per cent of economically active Jews being employers. As Arkin (1985: 29) succinctly summarizes, 'the Jewish labour force is wholly urbanized, highly educated and centred in the major metropolitan areas'.[7]

The prevailing ethos of the legitimacy of cultural pluralism in South Africa has aided in both the creation and maintenance of Jewish identity. It has facilitated the development of a particularly cohesive social entity as evidenced in the strong network of communal and welfare organizations, surburban residential clustering (increasingly up-market), intensive social and personal interaction with other Jews and even, in some cases, a distinctive manner of speech. In religious terms the community could be defined as nominally orthodox or, as Hellig (1984: 102) puts it, as 'non-observant orthodox'. That is to say, the overwhelming majority are affiliated to orthodox synagogues although this bears no necessary relation to their religious practice.

Jews are bound more by an ethnic than a religious consciousness. (This phenomenon is not uncommon in other modern Western societies but, as noted above, is accentuated in South Africa, where ethnic consciousness is all-pervasive.) South African Jewish ethnic identity is reinforced by a strong Zionist commitment, haunting memories of the Holocaust, and recollections of overt local hostility towards the Jews in the 1930s and 1940s. However, notwithstanding their strong Jewish identification, South African Jewry cannot be described as a ghetto community. For the most part they interact with the wider society in the same way as do other identifiable segments of the urban population. Jewish South Africans, like other white South Africans, are deeply concerned with their own survival — individual and collective — in South Africa. Most are as strongly rooted in the country as any other segment of the white population and so have a vested interest in the outcome of the struggle for political control that is currently being waged. Jewish South Africans therefore engage in the dilemmas and problematics of South African society. These dilemmas are at times acute, given historical memories of discrimination, persecution, and the emphasis on social justice which is stressed in Jewish teachings. In Shimoni's words (1980: 272) the Jews are a 'community with a conscience'.

The modern Jewish condition in South Africa, then, is one of seeking a balance between perpetuating the Jewish tradition on the one hand and integrating into the wider community on the other. This process is common to all Jews in modern secular societies. The South African reality, however, fraught as it is with social and political problems, necessitates a far more complicated balancing act. This is evident in the socialization process that confronts the Jewish child.

Family and Home

The Jewish child in South Africa is born into a family and home not unlike that of other middle-class children in white South Africa. The relatively small nuclear family will usually reside independently in a comfortable house or apartment in a comparatively affluent suburb. Large, well-tended grounds and even swimming-pools and tennis courts are not uncommon. In short, the Jewish child enjoys, at least in the material sense, privilege and opportunity. However, it must be said that a significant proportion live in far less luxurious circumstances.

The young child will, if possible, be surrounded by the 'right' books for his age, the latest educational toys (often expensive), and the constant ministrations of a black nanny. But mother has not abrogated her nurturing role — indeed, she will advise, guide, instruct, and monitor, usually with enormous concern and care. The child of this generation has the advantage of a literate mother, often university-educated and usually not working. An increasingly common pattern is for skilled mothers to take up their careers once the youngest child enters school.

Parent-child relationships in the Jewish home are generally informal and relatively non-authoritarian. Conversation is often lively and argumentative and is usually characterized by a palpable sense of mutual concern, warmth, and engagement. Informality, however, does not indicate lack of guidance, direction, and even pressure; the child's behaviour is closely observed.

Parents of the generation under consideration will very often be professionals with similar aspirations for their children. Indeed, their own socialization will have emphasized the value of a quality education.[8] The Jewish child is subtly, and sometimes not so subtly, made aware of the limited range of occupational options considered suitable. Poor scholastic performance is often followed by extra tuition but emotional development is also of major concern. Ambition and achievement encompass more than merely scholastic performance. If possible, most children will be offered a range of extra-mural lessons such as music, dance, and elocution. These activities are considered enjoyable and enriching experiences for the child but are by no means enforced. Non-working mothers are available to ferry children, often in lift-clubs. Being ferried is, indeed, normative for the suburban child and certainly not perceived as a privilege. Jewish parents, then, especially mothers, are constantly engaged with their children's intellectual, emotional, and social development. The 'Yiddishe Mama' (Jewish mother) stereotype, portrayed in popular fiction and film as an over-protective, over-anxious figure always offering yet another culinary delight, is not without a kernel of truth and certainly survives in South Africa.

To a greater or lesser extent the South African Jewish home embodies a distinctive Jewish dimension. From the earliest years children will observe a range of religious rituals and become familiar with many Jewish artefacts such as Sabbath candlesticks and *mezuzot*.[9] In a *kosher* home (one where Jewish dietary laws are observed) the separation of crockery and cutlery along with other *kashrut*-related distinctions[10] is mandatory and is therefore taken for granted by the child. Friday night (the Sabbath eve) is a special evening. In a religiously oriented home it is customary for children to attend the Friday night service together with their parents. It is usual for family members, even the not-so-religious, to be together for Friday night dinner, and often the extended family will gather for this purpose. Frequently three or more generations are present. How different the richly-laden table and moderate climate must be for the grandparents who remember the poverty and the struggle to celebrate the Sabbath in the harsh winters of eastern Europe.[11] For many children these occasions are pleasurable, with the presence of doting grandparents and lots of good food. For others, these evenings are burdensome, the generation gap and enforced sociability overriding the warmth and enjoyment. Moreover, the Friday night dinner can generate friction in the household. The formality interferes with television viewing and those parents who stress the family togetherness of the evening are often faced with irate teenagers denied the pleasures of the suburban discothèque. But the Sabbath tradition survives — even the secular Jewish youth movements schedule Friday night meetings for late in the evening, to accommodate the dinner period.

The festivals add a further dimension to the child's specifically

Jewish experience in the home. Once again these are synagogue and family occasions characterized by ritual, customary foods, and *bonhomie*. These family get-togethers can be important socializing experiences for the child. For example, talk of emigration, distant relatives and friends, and calls from well-wishers from abroad teach children that the world is a small place, that family ties are important, and that emigration is a possibility and not to be feared.[12] Family conversations range widely and children can and do participate. A provocative sermon may trigger passionate arguments later at the dinner table. When these are political in nature, the child is introduced to the complexity of the wider social reality. For parents of the 1960s and 1970s, the essential evil of apartheid was its inhumanity. Not only did it deny basic human rights; it also undermined the country's economic interests. Blame was laid squarely at the door of the National Party. The sensitive child listening to such discussions may well have been confused by his parents' liberal pronouncements, given the second-class status in the household of the well-loved maid or gardener. Confusion often turned to confrontation as the growing adolescent challenged adult acquiescence in 'the system'. The Jewish home was and is seldom without debate.

Education

Although many Jewish children in South Africa attend state schools, an ever-increasing majority attend Jewish day schools.[13] The Jewish day school in South Africa merges Jewish and general (state) curricula, and attempts to cater for all Jewish children — reform and orthodox — within a self-styled 'national-traditional' framework. That is to say, emphasis is placed on broad Jewish tradition and Jewish peoplehood (including Zionism) rather than on a narrowly religious education.

In 1955, 6 824 pupils attended these Jewish day schools. This figure had increased to 10 793 by 1983 (Mink 1984: 129). The increase during the 1960s and 1970s was a response to several factors: the introduction of Christian National Education[14] into state schools provoked anxiety in many parents; the recognition of high standards of tuition and the fine matriculation results of the day schools; and this parental generation's concern that it was inadequately equipped to impart Jewish tradition to its offspring. As the first South African-born generation,[15] they had entered an open society and in the process had moved away from traditional Jewish learning. This is a familiar pattern for Jews in Western societies in the twentieth century.

On a daily basis the pupil at the Jewish day school encounters the same mix of general subjects and experiences as does any other white pupil in South Africa. Lessons in such subjects as both official languages, mathematics, and history characterize the school day, as do playtime, sport, debates, and other extra-curricular activities. But in addition, the Jewish school curriculum includes prayer (not always compulsory), Hebrew and Bible studies, Jewish history, and sometimes the study of Jewish source texts.

Some pupils, usually those whose efforts are reinforced by the home environment, maximize the opportunities available for Jewish learning; all pupils will be exposed to a wide range of Jewish experiences. For example, important historical and religious events in the Jewish calendar are celebrated every year. Toddlers will participate in a fancy-dress pageant to commemorate Queen Esther's heroism in saving the Jews from wicked Hamman. In more sombre vein, *Yom Hashoa* remembers the genocide of six million European Jews during World War II, and, in joyous celebration, Israel's Day of Independence is marked. Indeed, all religious and national events in the Jewish calendar, minor and major, are marked and the appropriate laws and customs taught and observed.

The outsider entering the Jewish day school may sense the character of the school through such visible items as Israel/Jewish oriented posters and calendars, skullcaps, the synagogue, and the library holdings. The observer may be struck by the relative informality of the institution, expressed in casual teacher-pupil relations, a lively classroom atmosphere, and the generally non-authoritarian ideology. This is not to be confused with a *laissez-faire* policy but rather reflects the child-centred norm of the home. The non-authoritarian ethos may also be seen as a reflection of the broadly liberal predilections of the community as a whole, which in the school framework manifest in substantial concern with current affairs (South African and Jewish) and a range of charitable undertakings. Student societies exist to explore South African current affairs, usually in the liberal paradigm; other societies' aims have a specific Jewish or Zionist content. The charitable undertakings might include assisting with the distribution of meals-on-wheels to the Jewish elderly, or raising funds for deprived black communities. Such endeavours are often linked to the Jewish value of *tzedakah* (charity). For example, during the Festival of

Weeks, which commemorates the giving of the Law and the harvest of the first fruits, children bring fruit to school, participate in a religious ceremony, and distribute the fruit to the needy.

Included within the experiences provided by the schools are intensive Zionist and religious programmes such as Counterpoint (a week-end religious seminar for high school pupils which incorporates the Sabbath) and a one-term educational programme in Israel. Scholastic ability and social attributes are criteria in the selection of candidates for the latter programme. Only a minority are chosen to participate but on their return their experiences are shared both formally and informally with their co-pupils.

Ironically, the Jewish school experience has caused many children to become educators of their own parents in matters Jewish. Children often remind parents of the important religious occasions and encourage a positive identification with and implementation of Jewish traditional practice. In more extreme form, children demand strict religious practice from non-observant parents. This can lead to conflict in the home.

Straddling two distinct educational streams — the general (state) and the Jewish — the child is constantly confronted with the reality of simultaneous membership in two cultural mileux. This is not to suggest dual loyalty but, given the Jews' minority status within the minority white population, it inevitably raises existential issues. To a greater or lesser degree, these tend to be expressed in later adolescence.

Jewish children not attending Jewish day schools or other private schools must attend the appropriate state school within their residential zone. Because of residential clustering, this usually means that a significant proportion of the pupils at certain schools is Jewish. Even though no studies have examined the social relationships in these schools, there are indications that Jewish children retain a strong sense of Jewish identity. In recent years, for example, active student Jewish associations have emerged at several schools and many of these pupils belong to Jewish youth-movements and attend summer camps.

In several important respects the atmosphere in state schools is not unlike that described for the Jewish day school. The pupils will also be exposed to a liberal critique of their own society, their peers will be middle-class and English-speaking (because of residential clustering and school zoning), and sport serves an important integrative function. For children not residing in predominantly Jewish suburbs, being one of very few Jewish pupils may be an alienating experience. This could heighten Jewish identity. Certainly this will be the case if the child is taunted with anti-semitic comments. However, even the presence of a substantial number of Jewish pupils does not preclude reminders of their 'difference'. Jokes that often incorporate stereotypes flavour the adolescent interchange. Jews are absent *en bloc*on Jewish festivals, though in some cases only for the New Year and Day of Atonement. During Israeli crises (for example the Lebanese war) some response is sought from Jewish children, and this too serves to reinforce ethnic awareness, positively or negatively.

Most government schools permit separate Jewish religious instruction during regular scripture lessons. This is provided for the Cape Province through the Cape Council of the Board of Deputies and for the rest of the country through the office of the Chief Rabbi in Johannesburg. Relative to the very full programme at the Jewish day schools this curriculum is limited. Nevertheless, the very process of separating Jewish children and providing a special programme for them, together with the informal processes described above, must engender a clear Jewish awareness on the part of the children. Even without special programmes, Jewish children need not attend scripture lessons — an exemption that has been in operation for many years. However, notwithstanding the special provisions made for Jewish children, the potential for their complete assimilation into the dominant community is much greater in government schools.

Some parents object to the very notion of a separatist Jewish day school and yet wish their children to acquire more detailed Jewish knowledge than the religious instruction programmes can provide. This is especially true in the pre-*Barmitzvah*[16] years. Such children are catered for through a network of afternoon schools under the auspices of the Boards of Jewish Education and/or individual congregations. For these children the imposition of additional tuition and the acquisition of reading and writing in a third language after regular school hours disrupts sporting and other extra-curricular activities and is often extremely irksome. This kind of tuition is usually seen as preparation for the essential *rite de passage* of the *Barmitzvah* and thereafter formal Jewish education frequently ends. Small wonder that one South African rabbi referred to the *Barmitzvah* as a '*shul*-leaving certificate'.[17] Despite this rabbi's cynicism, the *Barmitzvah* remains a major event in the child's life. Lavish parties are frequently given, expensive clothes purchased, and tears of pride and joy shed. The young person supposedly on the threshold of adulthood, while enjoying the centre stage, often experiences great apprehension and tension on this solemn and momentous occasion.

Each of the three formal Jewish education frameworks outlined above — the day schools, religious instruction in the state schools, and the afternoon schools — contributes, in varying degrees, both cognitively and affectively to the child's identity. That identity, forged in the home, is thus perpetuated and given substance.

Social Interaction

While the family and school are inevitable socializing frameworks in all industrial societies, simultaneously and alongside these the child confronts a world which includes the neighbourhood, places of entertainment, sporting arenas, and other places where the wider society is encountered. These are additional contexts in which social relationships develop. Of course, all these are influenced by the general cultural milieu and informed by the media. The South African Jewish experience is not self-contained and divorced from the larger society.

The early immigrant communities tended to cluster, residentially and socially, but their offspring took advantage of the open society and entered it enthusiastically. They did not, however, reject their Jewish identity and have devoted much energy to raising well-integrated Jewish South Africans. However, the extent to which the Jewish child identifies and interacts with Jews or others varies with individual responses to the total environment. Consistent influence in one direction must affect the child's response. A strong religious emphasis, for example, will inevitably leave its mark.

From the child's first forays beyond the parental home, contact is made with children who may not be Jewish. This may take the form of a walk in the park with nanny or a drive with mother to play with children in another suburb. Of course the younger child is unaware of an 'us-them' distinction but sooner or later he or she will become aware (or be made conscious) that some children are Jewish and some are not. This differentiation need not have judgemental connotations but, by and large, unless parents consciously wish to assimilate, the distinction will gradually be internalized. Being self-consciously Jewish does add a dimension to youthful behaviour which in most respects is not significantly different from that of other white, middle-class children. The child's tastes and preferences, interests and concerns are no less the product of the media and parental pressure than are those of non-Jewish children. Young boys will have pictures of sports heroes on the well-decorated walls of their rooms, while young girls will have their favourite pop-idols adorning theirs.

Jews inculcate gender distinctions no less than do other groups. South Africa's sporting culture makes its impact early in the developmental cycle. The primary school boy will soon ask for a pair of soccer boots, and if he enjoys school sport, is more than likely to join a local club with his parents' enthusiastic support. Indeed, parents will enjoy boasting of their offspring's prowess on the sporting fields. Young girls also participate in school sport although the 'dedication' of their male counterparts is not generally emulated. The girls' enthusiasm is most likely to be directed towards such pastimes as ballet or modern dance. This pattern continues throughout high school. The importance of sport in South African Jewish life is reflected in the coverage given to it in the local Jewish press. The hundred metre sprinter is at least as important as the winner of a Bible quiz. Sporting and other extra-curricular activities, along with the school and neighbourhood, provide a range of frameworks in which friendships are formed.

Because the Jewish day schools draw their pupils from many suburbs, friendship patterns are less neighbourhood-related than is the case of children attending zoned state schools. Of course, the opportunity for state-school children to establish friendships with non-Jews is greater. This can be seen, for instance, in the choice of after-school playmates and even in the guest lists for birthday parties. Parties are important events in the young child's social calendar and, it might be noted, have become increasingly sophisticated as the socio-economic status of the parents has improved. Much attention is given to choosing invitations, venues, and form. Of late, birthday parties have emerged as one example of the inherent tension between specifically Jewish norms and the norms of the dominant society. This tension was evident in a recent conflict between parents and educators over the common practice of Saturday morning birthday celebrations at the movies. The Jewish day school principals explicitly requested that this practice cease but the request met with both resentment and resistance.

Vacations, like birthday parties, also reflect increasing sophistication and rising socio-economic status. Most Jewish families enjoy at least an annual vacation away from home and frequent holiday weekends are not uncommon. For the more affluent, overseas holidays have become popular and Israel is usually included in the itinerary. Sometimes the vacation abroad is a *barmitzvah* gift.

In adolescence, social horizons expand. Discotheques, ice-cream parlours, even restaurants (and in coastal areas, the beach) have become popular meeting places and the arenas for the beginnings of relationships with the opposite sex. Fashion now assumes great importance — young Jewish adolescents are clearly willing participants in the consumer society.

By the age of sixteen many, if not most, adolescents are organizing their own social calendars independently and some even arrange their vacations with peers rather than with family. But pleasure is not the only concern of the Jewish adolescent. This is the age when questions about identity, values, justice and 'the future' are posed. Is there a God? Why kill helpless animals to make fur coats? Why don't we live in Israel? Why must I marry a Jew? Why is there so much suffering in the world? How can any Jew support oppression and discrimination? Where was God during the Holocaust? Do the Palestinians have a case? Can one live in an apartheid society and not be contaminated? Can I alleviate black suffering? Will I survive as a white in South Africa? Such questions are raised and debated both formally and informally at school and at home, where these very issues are often a source of great conflict and may expose generational differences.

Another important framework in which these questions are explored is that of the Jewish youth movements. Today approximately one in three children over the age of ten belongs to one of the four Jewish movements in South Africa: *Betar, Bnei Akiva, Habonim,* and *Maginim.*[18] Each of these is dedicated to 'the education of the youth in Zionism and Judaism . . .' (Katz 1980: 645). All the movements deal with the kinds of questions elaborated above, giving different emphases according to their respective ideologies and adapting the topics to suit the stages of the child's cognitive development. For the pre-adolescent, ideology takes second place to the social function of the movement. Affiliation for the most part is more a product of friendships and organizational effectiveness in the different residential areas than a reflection of ideological adherence. Annual summer camps provide the educational and social highlight of the movements and attract much larger numbers than the weekly meetings.

Notwithstanding greater interaction with and integration into the wider society, the developing Jewish adolescent clearly maintains a strong sense of ethnic identity. However, as horizons broaden and choices widen, the tension between Jewishness and integration mounts.

On Leaving School

Since 1960 the male South African Jewish school-leaver, like other white South African males, has been obliged to serve in the South African Defence Force. In the late 1960s the period of service was approximately one year but was subsequently extended, first to eighteen months and thereafter to two years. Because of the option of deferring national service until completion of studies, young men have to make serious choices at the time of leaving school. Since the mid-1970s increasing numbers of students have chosen to study further prior to army service. This reflects both the extended period of service and the change in the nature of South Africa's geo-political position.

Religious needs are recognized and catered for in the army. The Jewish national serviceman is thus usually able to enjoy *kosher* food and Sabbath privileges. The army also releases Jewish servicemen for important religious festivals. For the young soldier far from home, it is heart-warming to attend a synagogue service and be invited to the homes of other Jews for a Sabbath meal. In these ways ethnic consciousness is reinforced even in a national defence force.

The female Jewish school-leaver does not face the military experience. She is thus immediately free to pursue the career of her choice. A significant number do not go to university but instead enter the labour market, often having completed diploma courses of various kinds. It is rare for a young Jewish woman to enter the labour market completely untrained. As in any modern city, in the cities of South Africa the young Jewish working woman participates in the urban whirl, experimenting with her new-found independence and the give and take of human relationships. Although many young women continue residing with their parents until marriage, it has become increasingly acceptable to live away from home. However even for those who' move away, the Jewish dimension of their identity is perpetuated through ethnic association and the maintenance of strong family bonds. The latter are facilitated by the fact that most Jewish South Africans have kin in all the major centres.

Some Jewish girls will virtually act out a fascinating stereotype which has been named and articulated in recent years. This is the 'kugel' phenomenon, a caricature of a young woman with 'the latest' in everything and a single-minded determination to find the 'right' husband, the 'perfect' home in the best area and to raise 'perfect' children. Clearly, the 'kugel' is a product of urban affluence associated with the *nouveau riche*, to be found in many countries and not restricted to Jews. The word, however, has become a code reference for young Jews (and increasingly for non-Jews) in South Africa, with the user aspiring sometimes to the status, but more often rejecting association with the category. As the author of a humorous work about 'kugels' noted: 'everyone professes to know them. Nobody admits to being one' (Klevansky 1982: back cover).

Although most male Jewish school-leavers enter tertiary education (in the main, universities), significant numbers do not. These young men will often enter family businesses or frequently become trainee managers with one of the larger companies. Like their female counterparts they too will enjoy their growing independence and a relatively affluent urban lifestyle. Independence, however, comes later for most South African Jewish school-leavers, who continue to university. While all South African universities have dormitory facilities, the majority of students are day students. Most Jewish students continue to live with their families although in recent years increasing numbers leave home at this time.

Irrespective of faculty choice, all Jewish students (at English-speaking South African universities)[19] are confronted with a university 'culture' which is both liberal and universalistic in ethos. Ethnic parochialism is implicitly challenged in an environment which 'places a positive value on inter-group mixing and on playing down ethnicity' (Dubb 1972: 60). Jews respond to the challenge by joining the full range of university activities, while nevertheless maintaining the strong Jewish social networks established earlier. Only a small minority, however, is regularly active in specifically Jewish organizations on campus.

In the 1960s Jews participated fully and actively, both individually and collectively, in all aspects of campus life. They were prominent in student politics[20] and their overt Jewishness co-existed within the liberal climate of university politics. Zionism, embodied in the State of Israel, continued to capture the imagination of Jews and Gentiles alike. Israel's socialist orientation and involvement in the upliftment of black Africa was compatible with the political world view of many

Jewish South African students. Indeed, Israel provided the fulcrum of their Jewish identity.

This comfortable compatibility on the campus was increasingly eroded from the 1970s. As the South African student leadership was drawn more and more towards a radical critique of politics in general and South African politics in particular, the legitimacy of ethnicity came increasingly under fire. The challenge to campus Jews, at least at an intellectual level, became explicit rather than implicit. The Jewish student who identified proudly with both his heritage and modern Israel and who was painfully aware of the incompatibility between Judaism and apartheid, now grappled with this conflict in an environment increasingly hostile to Israel and ethnic particularism. In the popular radical mind Israel had become an oppressor and therefore the Palestinian Liberation Organization was believed to have as much legitimacy as the African National Congress. The 1975 United Nations resolution equating Zionism with racism only confirmed this view. For the politically active Jewish student, the need to reconcile Jewish-Zionist loyalties with the radical critique of South African society assumed existential proportions.

The Unknown Future

Jewish children of the 1960s have now reached adulthood. They have been a segment of the privileged white minority insulated from the black majority and socialized with all the prejudices that growing up in a divided society implies. Their liberal upbringing has not enabled them to transcend the rigid barriers that separate all South Africans. They, like other whites, live in a world divorced from the realities of black anger, anguish, and frustration. In 1985 this reality was brought vividly into the daily consciousness of whites through the popular media. Every social encounter today contemplates and debates the country's unknown future.

Until now, South African Jews have not had to resort to camouflaging their Jewishness in order to participate fully in South African society. Jews have frequently been outspoken critics of apartheid precisely because of their knowledge and understanding of Jewish social ethics.[21] Indeed, the Jews for Justice[22] movement was initiated by young Jews as a specifically Jewish response to the South African crisis of 1985. Will such responses be welcome in a non-racial, united South

Africa, a South Africa without enforced ethnic or class differentiation? What implications will such a society have for a Jewish corporate identity? Will past Jewish mobility and economic success be cause for friction? Undoubtedly the 'new South Africa' will present new challenges to those socializing agencies that until now have managed to balance a proud Jewish identity with full membership and participation in the country of their birth. These challenges await the future.

Notes

1. Any attempt to describe the process of growing up Jewish in South Africa inevitably involves some degree of generalization. The authors have tried to minimize this by drawing on research which, although not specifically designed to examine childhood, has some bearing on the topic. The authors wish to thank Gillian Mitchell and Deena Strauss for their assistance in the preparation of this chapter and Sandra Burman and Mary Simons for their helpful comments on earlier drafts.
2. See Introduction, p.5.
3. Many of these immigrants settled in the rural areas where they often established close relationships with the predominantly Afrikaans-speaking local communities. In many cases their children's first language was Afrikaans. For the history of early Jewish settlement see Abrahams (1955), Herrman (1935), Saron and Hotz (eds) (1955), Shain (1983).
4. A small section of the Jewish population held socialist views. Several Jews rose to prominence in the trade union movement and in the Labour Party. For details see Shimoni (1980: 87-89).
5. Some 10 000 Jews served in the South African forces, ten per cent of the total Jewish population. Jewish soldiers constituted 4.9 per cent of the army, Jews 4.45 per cent of the white population. (*South African Jews in World War II* 1950: 14).
6. See Shimoni (1980: 76). Recently the Board has taken a far more overtly political stance. At its 33rd national biennial congress in 1985, the Board adopted several resolutions pertaining to the changing political process in South Africa. The congress rejected apartheid and recorded its 'support and commitment to justice, equal opportunity and removal of all provisions in the laws of South Africa which discriminate on the grounds of colour and race . . .' (Goldberg 1985: 16).
7. It should be noted that despite this profile of an upwardly mobile and educated population, Jews have never constituted a significant political force. Their small number, the 'English' control of commerce, and the

constituency-based parliamentary system within a Westminister framework, have precluded their access to real power.

8. In some cases children were even sent to church schools to obtain a good education.

9. *Mezuzah* (s), *mezuzot* (pl). In Jewish religious terminology, *mezuzah* is the designation for the parchment scroll, in a metal or wooden box, attached to the doorposts of dwellings. The scroll contains two portions of the Pentateuch, Deuteronomy 6: 4-9 and Deuteronomy 11: 13-21.

10. Distinctions based on Jewish dietary laws.

11. For a vivid description of Jewish life in eastern Europe, see Zborowksi and Herzog (1962).

12. The Sharpeville shootings of 1960, the Soweto uprisings of 1976, and no doubt the current unrest, have all contributed towards emigration. There are no recent statistics for Jewish emigration. The 1974 South African Jewish Population Study showed that 18.7 per cent of the 'children' of all ages of the 29 665 households included in the survey, did not live in South Africa (Della Pergola 1977: 6). The Kaplan Centre at the University of Cape Town has recently begun research in this field and preliminary investigation suggests an increase in the rate of emigration since the 1970s. In addition, Israel and several cities abroad are known to contain sizeable South African Jewish 'pockets' — for example, Toronto, Canada, and Houston, USA.

13. There is no figure available for the total number of Jewish children attending state schools. However, Jewish children in state schools in the Transvaal and in Cape Town receive Jewish religious instruction during regular school hours (personal communication, Office of the Chief Rabbi, Johannesburg and the Religious Instruction Department of the Board of Deputies, Cape Town). It is estimated that approximately ninety per cent of Jewish state high school children receive this supplementary education. It is also estimated that the overwhelming majority of Jewish pre-school children attend Jewish pre-primary school (personal communication, Jewish Pre-Primary School Association, Cape Town).

14. See introduction, p.15.

15. In 1970, 20 110 (75 per cent) of the 26 810 Jews aged between 35 and 54 were locally born (Dubb, Della Pergola and Tal 1978: 7).

16. *Barmitzvah* — name given to the male Jewish initiation rite undergone at age 13; the female equivalent is the *batmitzvah*. The ceremony for males includes reading specific portions of the Bible before a congregation in the synagogue, a practice reserved for those defined as adults.

17. *Shul* — colloquial name for 'synagogue'.

18. *Betar*: acronym of *Brit* Yosef Trumpeldor — the Union of Joseph Trumpeldor. Associated with the Zionist Revisionist Organization of Ze'ev Jabotinsky. There were groups in Johannesburg and Cape Town

by about 1930.

Habonim: Hebrew — The Builders. Socialist oriented Zionist Scout Movement introduced into South Africa in 1931 by Norman Lourie.

Bnei Akiva: Hebrew — Sons of Akiva. Religious Zionist Movement established in Johannesburg in 1936.

Maginim: Hebrew — Shields. The youngest and smallest movement, associated with the Progressive Jewish (Reform) Movement. Established in the late 1960s.

19. A small proportion of Jewish students attends Afrikaans universities. For an estimate of student numbers, see Frankental (1984).

20. Jews have been prominent in radical opposition movements (including the African National Congress) disproportionately to their numbers in the population. See Shimoni (1980: 227-28).

21. See Shimoni (1980: chapter 9, *passim*).

22. This organization was launched in Cape Town in October 1985 (*Weekly Mail* 4-10.10.85) and in Johannesburg with the name Jews for Social Justice, in November (*Star* 28.11.85). Broadly, the movement calls for the abolition of apartheid and the establishment of a non-racial, democratic, and just society.

Children of the Sugar Company: Tradition and Change in an Indian Community

Gina Buijs

This is a study of a group of South African Indian children growing up with their families, extended kin groups, friends, and school mates. Their lives differ, however, from those of many other South African children in that in the background looms 'the Company', for the setting is one of the largest sugar estates in southern Africa. The focus of the study is the effect of the interaction of community tradition, government action, and company policy on the children's life styles, expectations, and opportunities.

Greenfields

In 1985 the Indian population of South Africa numbered some 900 000, most of whom lived in the urban areas of Natal and, to a lesser extent, the Transvaal. Comparatively few now live on sugar estates such as the one I shall call Greenfields.[1] Nevertheless, the first Indians to arrive in Natal were brought to the colony 125 years ago to work as indentured labourers on sugar plantations, and the industry owes its present success in no small measure to the efforts of generations of Indian workers.

The sugar industry in Natal is now dominated by those large concerns which over the years have absorbed the smaller, once autonomous companies, one of which in 1882 established the sugar estate on which the Greenfields sugar mill was built. Greenfields is situated some distance from Durban on the Natal South Coast and fifteen kilometres from the nearest town, which has a majority of Indian inhabitants. Originally the mill workers, as opposed to the field workers, were Mauritian creoles, but by 1930 they had been replaced by Indians (Thompson 1952). Africans had largely taken over as field labourers, although a few Indians were employed in supervisory positions in the fields. In more recent times the trend has been for Africans to replace Indians in the mill too. Africans predominate in the unskilled sector, where no whites are employed, while only whites occupy management positions, although one or two Indians and Africans are being trained to take over lower management positions. At the time of writing there were over 700 Africans employed in the mill, 230 Indians, 30 coloureds, and 77 whites.

Officially the company has a non-discriminatory housing policy but in practice housing is a major problem. Fifty per cent of the African employees are contract workers from the Transkei. Although most are married, they are all housed as single men in company hostels near the mill. There is very limited accommodation for married couples in the hostels, and this is usually reserved for occasions when wives in need of medical attention visit their husbands in order to obtain such aid. The rest of the African workers live with their families in nearby areas of KwaZulu and receive a living-out allowance, which is calculated at twenty per cent of their basic salary. This allowance is paid to all employees who buy or rent accommodation off the estate. Most coloured families (except for five living in houses on the estate which were previously occupied by white families) live twelve kilometres from the mill at the site of the company garage, where most of their menfolk work. As a result of South Africa's Group Areas legislation, the two nearest towns where Indians can rent or own homes are both about fifteen kilometres from Greenfields. There is no convenient bus service, so a car is necessary and transport costs are high compared with those for Africans, who live only approximately six kilometres away and can walk or cycle to work.

In consequence, although Indians no longer form the largest percentage of workers in the mill, they do form the largest residential group in the company village which has grown up around the mill. Altogether they constitute some two thousand people. Most of them live in the Greenfields 'barracks', rows of one- or two-roomed dwellings which originally housed the indentured Indian workers. Two-thirds of the Indians employed by the mill live in the main Greenfields barracks, most of the rest being housed in barracks in Upper and

Lower Greenfields, some five kilometres away.

Until recently the housing available to Indians in Greenfields, which is entirely provided by the company, was of a markedly inferior quality to the spacious homes occupied by white employees. The barracks homes of Indians are built of bricks and corrugated iron, with from four to ten dwellings in each row. Each dwelling consists of one, two, or very occasionally three, rooms, measuring about four metres square, with no ceiling and a concrete floor. There is no electricity, so water has to be heated in the tiny kitchen on a coal stove. Washing facilities and lavatories are communal. About ten years ago the mill management decided to build some modern, three-bedroomed homes for senior Indian (but not African) employees. These new houses are some way from the mill and form a separate area called 'New Delhi'. Workers who live in New Delhi include clerks and skilled artisans. The old barracks community has now been broken up, with workers who live in New Delhi forming an incipient middle class with distinctive aspirations and consumer patterns. Wives and children in New Delhi are socially and physically separated from their old neighbours in the barracks, who do not have access to shiny new electric stoves, or, nowadays, colour television sets. There is a feeling in the new village that the barracks are 'primitive' and a 'slum area'. Those who are left behind in the barracks are anxious to obtain better housing and the Personnel Officer is often petitioned by wives to allocate houses in New Delhi to their husbands ahead of others. A few senior Indian employees and their families have been accommodated in the village in houses previously occupied by white families. While management has said that the old barracks will be renovated and bathrooms and electricity installed, only a few barracks rows have been modernized in this way. Living space in the barracks is at a premium, with the average occupancy per dwelling being 5.8 persons in 1978. In an effort to alleviate the overcrowding, management has decreed that male children over the age of twenty-one and not employed by the company may not live with their parents in company housing. This edict (which does not apply to whites) has caused a great deal of ill-feeling, particularly in view of the current recession and high levels of unemployment, and is largely circumvented.

While New Delhi and Upper and Lower Greenfields are quite isolated, the main Greenfields barracks are close to the mill and separated from the houses of the white employees only by steep contours: the whites on top of the hills, the Indians on the slopes or near the bed of the Greenfields river. Despite the existence of these contours, the actual distance between Indian and white housing is only a couple of hundred metres and the two sets of housing are clearly visible to each other. However, this proximity does not mean that Indian and white residents mix outside the workplace. Separate facilities, following the apartheid plan, exist for each group. There are two separate primary schools in the village — one for whites and one for Indians; two separate recreation clubs, each with its own swimming pool and tennis courts; and separate places of worship, including separate churches. While the one small, privately-owned supermarket in Greenfields caters for all, its stocks are limited and most housewives, both Indian and white, prefer to patronize larger shops in bigger towns nearby. Under these arrangements, Indian children in Greenfields almost never have occasion to meet their young white neighbours.

It might be expected that this isolated community would successfully inculcate in its children very similar patterns of belief and behaviour to those observed by their parents. However, the lifestyles, expectations, and opportunities of the Indian children of Greenfields proved on examination to be very different from those of their parents. In the sections which follow aspects of these differences are described and the mechanisms which have led to them are discussed.

Education

As shown by my 1975 survey, children form a high proportion of the Indian community in Greenfields, as they do in the Indian community as a whole in South Africa. In Greenfields 630 people or 53.7 per cent of the Indian community were under the age of nineteen in 1975. Just under a quarter of the community, 24.5 per cent, were in the six to twelve year age bracket and attending primary school, and a lower proportion, 11.7 per cent, were under the age of six years. However, the birth rate is falling: in 1976 the number of live births on the estate was a third lower than five years previously. This latter figure is in line with the general decline in the number of births among Indians in South Africa, though it may also be at least partially attributable to a birth control drive begun by the company management in 1972. The white nursing sister in charge of the clinic at the mill, which provides antenatal care for Indian wives, said that nowadays Indian women in Greenfields want a family of only three or four children, whereas in the past eight or nine live children was considered the norm.

With forty-two per cent of the barracks population of school-going age, the Indian primary school plays an important role in the community. The present government school was founded in 1945, superseding several small, informal schools for Indian children run by Christian missionaries. In 1952 permanent school buildings were completed and government teachers appointed. However, by 1970 the original buildings were insufficient for the growing number of pupils and 'platoon' or shift classes had to be held. In 1976 the Greenfields Primary School had an enrolment of over 600 children. By 1980 more buildings had been added and platoon classes finally abolished. This improvement over the past forty years on earlier provision of Indian schooling should, nonetheless, be viewed in the wider context of Greenfields. The white primary school in Greenfields has rarely had an enrolment of more than 100 children and classes are small, which makes individual attention for every child possible. Despite the geographical proximity of the two schools, neither children nor staff mix, facilities are not shared, and sports competitions are not held between the two schools.

However, despite the overcrowded conditions of the primary school, since 1971 there has been a large increase in the number of village children who continue their education beyond the primary school level of standard five. In 1971 the results of a census of the school-going population showed no appreciable difference in the number of boys and girls attending primary school, but at the standard five level the number of girls dropped by 50 per cent. A major reason was that at this age most girls enter puberty and orthodox parents kept their daughters at home, afraid that they would be 'spoilt' (that is, become pregnant) if they attended a co-educational school. This conservative attitude of Indian fathers changed quite rapidly, however, as educational and job opportunities arose, such as teaching and nursing, and the average age at which many girls married rose as a result. By 1976 fathers were more willing to let their daughters have at least a few years of high school education. Approximately 120 children from Greenfields attended the Indian high school in a nearby town in 1976, and of these a third were girls.

Although school books and tuition are free, parents still have to provide their children with expensive school uniforms, bus fares, and other incidentals. Yet less than ten years later the attitude of most Indian parents in Greenfields (and elsewhere) towards education for their children has changed radically, especially in relation to girls. Money spent in educating daughters is now seen as an investment, as daughters will be better able to look after their aged parents in due course. Some form of tertiary or post-school training is considered essential by parents and children to ensure employment in a depressed job market. University is the goal of those who do best at school, while others aim at teacher training or technical colleges. In this context it should be noted that of the more than six thousand students at the University of Durban-Westville in 1984, a majority were in the Arts Faculty and half of these were women.[2]

Aspirations of Greenfields school-leavers are typically 'white collar' — clerical work for those with standard eight or matriculation (school leaving certificate) and teaching or other professional careers for bright students. Few intend to follow their fathers into the mill. Their aspirations and achievements may be compared with those of their parents. Table 1 details the levels of education of household heads in the barracks in 1975, as shown by my survey. The 21.9 per cent of household heads who had no formal education at all are mostly pensioners or older men and women who grew up on neighbouring farms or in Greenfields before schooling was available. The largest percentage, 27.9 per cent, comprises men who have completed primary education at standard six level, while only 2 per cent of household heads had completed a high school education.

Table 1: Approximate Levels of Education of Household Heads in the Greenfields Barracks, 1975

Standard reached	Don't know	Nil	1	2	3	4	5	6	7	8	9	10
No. of household heads	3	41	12	9	13	18	30	56	4	7	1	4
Percentage	1.5	21.9	6.0	4.5	6.5	9.0	14.9	27.9	2.0	3.5	0.5	2.0

Within two generations educational opportunities for young people in Greenfields have improved to such an extent that they are now able to look forward to well-paid salaried jobs in commerce or service industries, while their fathers hoped only for unskilled or semi-skilled wage employment and their mothers for an early marriage and childbearing. Nowadays women often combine motherhood and a career, and granny looks after the children. Young husbands are proud of their wives' educational and professional achievements, which enhance their own status.

Religion

Besides the demographic preponderance of children and young people, another characteristic of the barracks inhabitants which resembles that of the Indian population of South Africa in general is that they are predominantly Tamil or Telegu, that is, South Indian in origin. In 1975 Tamil was spoken as the main vernacular language by at least some of the members of 83.1 per cent of the households in the village, and Hindi was spoken in only 11.9 per cent of the homes. In the remainder, English was the only language used. There were no Muslims or Gujerati-speaking Hindu families in Greenfields. It is important to note, however, that even in those homes where a vernacular language was spoken, children and teenagers used English as a rule in daily conversation. Knowledge of the vernacular is quickly dying out among young people and most Indian children today claim not to be able to speak a vernacular language. However, enough knowledge is retained to follow the conversation of older people and to enjoy imported films from India in Tamil or Hindi.

Although English is widely used in the barracks, the general knowledge of Tamil is an indicator of the continuing importance of Hinduism as a religious force among barracks residents. Of the 202 households in the barracks, 152 or 75.2 per cent gave Hinduism as the religion of household members in 1975. Numerous Hindu rites and ceremonies, many of which concern infants and children, commemorate stages in the life cycles of residents. Of the remaining households, 46 or 22.8 per cent gave Christianity as their religion. This percentage is somewhat higher than the average for Indians in general at that time, but it does seem that membership of Christian churches has grown considerably in the last decade among South African Indians of South Indian descent especially. Indian Christian families in Greenfields are all members of one particular church, the South African General Mission, which is part of the Evangelical Church of Southern Africa. This church, which became established in Greenfields over forty years ago, caters exclusively for Indians but has several visiting white pastors and missionaries, most of whom are from Britain or the United States. Although some Tamil hymns are sung in church for the benefit of older members, the Christian community in Greenfields barracks uses English predominantly in its church services and encourages the adoption of a modern 'western' outlook by its members (Buijs 1981); in other words, the church encourages young people to gain higher educational qualifications and to achieve higher social status.

In the past religious education also played an important formal educational role in the lives of girls in particular. In addition to the government-run primary and high schools which barracks children attended, there was for many years a small school attached to the Hindu temple in the barracks which gave lessons in Tamil and taught Hindu religious precepts and hymns. Classes were held for primary school children in the afternoons when government school instruction was over. Pupils were mostly small girls; mothers complained that their sons were naughty and refused to attend. The female emphasis in the Tamil school attendance was paralleled in other aspects of day-to-day Hindu ritual and observance, a much greater part being played by women and girls than by men. By 1985 the Tamil school had ceased to exist (the former teacher having married), although instruction was given intermittently to children in some Hindu homes. The expense of bringing another teacher in from the nearest town may have deterred the village from replacing the teacher, who had given her services free and had not been employed elsewhere. However, it is also noticeable that the influence of the Hindu temple and Hindu village ritual has become less important over the last decade to village residents, as levels of secular education have increased. Village Hinduism was largely based on folk religious practices which centred on healing and beliefs in local deities (Buijs 1980). These beliefs appear superstitious and 'primitive' to educated South African Indians today. Since most of the indentured were of low caste, they were denied access to the Vedas or sacred scriptures of Hinduism, and knowledge of these writings is limited among their descendants. Hinduism as commonly practised today in South Africa thus has little intellectual attraction for most Indians of indentured stock. While caste was important in India, it has little or no place in the lives of the majority of South African Indians. Young people, especially, think of caste as a system of discrimination in many ways similar to apartheid and one which is irrelevant in the modern world. Although until recently caste was an important factor in marriage negotiations (Buijs 1978), today considerations of class, education, and financial position are paramount.

Christianity in the 1980s has become a much more appealing alternative to Hinduism as far as the young people in Greenfields are concerned. Since 1974 there has been a resident Indian pastor whose influence and status in the community have increased greatly in the last decade as the popularity of Hinduism has declined. Pastor James is a licensed marriage officer and is often consulted about secular as well as spiritual problems by Hindus as well as Christians. He has recently returned from a study trip to the United States. Because Pastor James and his church recognize that there is a preponderance of young people in the community, youth activities are emphasized. There is an active Sunday School, a Junior Club, and a Youth Group, as well as a Ladies Prayer Group. Inter-district rallies are held every three months and week-long evangelical campaigns yearly. Although all these are attended exclusively by Indians, some white ministers may preach. Moreover, unlike attendance at the temple school, both boys and girls come to the youth services, and on Saturday afternoons a programme of outdoor games is held in the church grounds. These activities give young people a chance to meet members of the opposite sex outside the home environment in a context of which their parents approve — unlike, for instance, the cinema or a football match. Several Christian women commented that they had met their future husbands at a 'campaign'. The Christian church in Greenfields thus does afford a degree of social interaction normally forbidden in orthodox Hindu homes, where village women and girls lead circumscribed social lives and expect to find friendship and companionship among female relatives only. The church in Greenfields is thus associated by youngsters with 'western' or white patterns of social interaction as observed on television or in films, and thus with progress. It is effecting a marked change in social relations between the sexes and in the religious affiliations of the rising generation.

Kinship and Expectations

In the time of indenture Indian men outnumbered women by about three to one, and the disproportion continued until the end of the last century, making normal marriage patterns impossible. However, by the second decade of the twentieth century considerable efforts had been made to re-establish the pattern of joint or extended families common in India. Fatima Meer comments (1969: 64) that there is no word in any Indian language which corresponds to the English word 'family'. The nearest is *kutum* for North Indians and *kuduma* or *kudumbom* for South Indians. She writes, 'these terms define a kinship system of several nuclear families arranged hierarchically by male seniority'. The ideal of the joint family is that the different generations should actually live together under one roof, sharing a common kitchen and living area; that is, that they should be co-residential and commensal, if not co-parcenary (sharing property and goods in common) as joint families in India usually are. While some 8 per cent of barracks households were joint in this sense in 1975, there was no evidence of complete pooling of wages or of joint ownership of fixed property outside the village. (Within the village, the company owned all Indian housing.)[3] In practice, the cramped dwellings usually available to Indians in South Africa today often make it impossible for several nuclear families to live together, at least for any length of time. It may be helpful to view both nuclear and joint families in terms of stages in a developmental cycle. Thus, in Greenfields when an Indian youth married he remained with his wife in his natal home until the birth of his second child, when he usually applied for a separate dwelling, often next door to his parents. Pressure for a man to move out of his natal home by the time his second child is born may also come from younger sons, hoping to marry themselves and bring their brides to live there. A last stage of this developmental cycle from nuclear to joint family may be an extended family, by which I mean the presence in a family of a couple, their unmarried children, and one or more senior relatives. A joint family in which one of the senior couple dies automatically becomes an extended family so defined, and seventy-six houses in the barracks (42 per cent of the total number of households) were extended in this sense. Although extended families are therefore much more common than joint ones, the idealized concept of joint family or *kutum* in this restricted sense does influence Indian attitudes and sentiments to a considerable degree and is especially important in childhood.

Moving from joint or extended family to the wider kin group, the average *kutum* may number anything from fifty to over a hundred members. These members are expected to attend informal social occasions (such as children's birthday parties) and their attendance at formal ones is obligatory. Fatima Meer (1969: 66) defines the *kutum* as 'a restricted kinship group tracing descent through a male head, in which the classificatory principle defines relations between members'. As members of an immediate family, 'members of a *kutum* are [felt to be] in a similar relation to each other, . . . and this is reflected in the fact that aunts, uncles, and cousins are not only addressed in common terms but the associated sentiment and role expectations are also extended to them in decreasing order of intensity, depending on the closeness of blood ties'. Meer characterized the *kutum* as 'an intimate *collective conscience* which socialises and controls; binds and integrates members into a closely watched system of social interaction'.

The closest associations are those formed in the nuclear family, such as the relationship between siblings. These may be broken down into a set of dyads, that is, brother to brother, brother to sister, and sister to sister. Norms and stereotypes of behaviour were implicit rather than explicit in what informants said about their kin and in the way such kin behaved. Nonetheless, it was possible to get an impression of how informants felt kin *should* behave and contrast this with actual behaviour. Hilda Kuper has written of Indian South Africans that 'seniority regulates the relationship between siblings of the same sex and particular deference is shown the eldest brother; between brothers mutual help is the ideal with responsibility placed on the oldest for assisting in the education and marriage of the younger' (Kuper 1960: 130). Kuper's comments reflect the feelings of informants that this is how the relationship between brothers should be even today. It was noticeable in the village that in the senior generations elder brothers were still accorded respect by their juniors, who accepted interference in their affairs. Muniamma's father, for instance, who was the eldest of seven brothers, all of whom lived in Greenfields at one time, was able to convene meetings of his brothers to discuss family affairs such as weddings and funerals, and his brothers came to ask his advice. However, some of the younger generation seem to feel no such obligation to consult elder brothers. Ram, Maniamma's younger brother, was something of a scallywag with a history of frequent job changing and a broken engagement. Ram appeared to avoid the company of his elder brother, Hamilton. He rarely attended family gatherings, which Hamilton made a point of doing, and spent most of his spare time lounging under a large fig tree in the open area of the barracks with other youths. Hamilton appeared to have little influence over his younger brother and could not persuade him to mend his ways. The authority which elder brothers may have been able to wield over younger ones in the past appears to have eroded today as a result of the financial independence many younger brothers attain, often because they have been able to obtain a better education than their elder brothers. Nevertheless, elder brothers and their wives are still expected to perform services for younger siblings. Mrs Jacob, for example, looked after one of her husband's younger brother's children daily because both he and his wife worked, yet there was no question of any payment or gift to the Jacobs in return, although this brother could well have afforded a recompense. On the other hand, Mr Jacob expected his brothers to visit him at Christmas; he did not expect, as the eldest, to have to go to their homes.

Moving from the relationship between brothers to that between brothers and their sisters, female informants were usually very close to their brothers, both older and younger. Informants implied that an older brother was owed respect and obedience by his sisters, but sisters were not obliged to obey or respect a younger brother, with whom the relationship was a more informal, almost joking one. My observations of behaviour between brothers and sisters appeared to conform by and large to informants' stereotypes. Hamilton, Muniamma's elder brother, had lived and worked for many years in Durban, but he kept in close touch with his younger sisters in Greenfields. He and his young wife attended every rite of passage of his sisters' children, gave them gifts, and took photographs of the proceedings. When Hamilton's spinster sisters married, he spent several hundred rands on elaborate saris and kists to hold their trousseaux. In return he expected his sisters to help him and his family. One night at 11.00 p.m. Hamilton arrived in the barracks with news that his wife was ill and the doctor had told her to stay in bed. There and then he took two of his unmarried sisters back with him to his home in Durban. The sisters remained at their brother's home for two weeks, doing the housework and shopping for their sister-in-law, caring for her children and accompanying her on visits to the doctor. There appeared to be no question of any possible refusal of help on the sisters' part; the illness of their elder brother's wife put them under immediate obligation to help.

Such obligations are reciprocal, and a brother's solicitude goes beyond contributing to the expense of a wedding. He is also taught from an early age to protect and look after his sister and, before her marriage, it is he who accompanies her to films or soccer matches which her parents do not attend. Mrs Raj encouraged her sons to chaperone her daughters on visits to kin or friends in Durban. The girls would almost certainly not have been allowed out of the home without their brothers. In several instances informants recalled meeting their future husbands through their brothers; 'he is my brother's best friend', said one girl. Brothers often give their sisters small, spontaneous gifts of clothes, jewellery, or cash, quite apart from expected gifts at rites of passage ceremonies. Mrs David gave one of her unmarried brothers his midday meal for which he did not pay her, although she was badly off and in debt, but he did give her part of his winnings from the races on one occasion. Thus there often appears to be a sense of duty or obligation involved in the relationship between brother and sister.

This sense of duty or responsibility tends to make relationships between elder brothers and younger sisters more inhibited and formal than between sister and sister. Muniamma and her sisters were all extremely attached to one another. The sisters paid one another daily visits and often stayed to meals at each other's homes. Seniority was still acknowledged among them and since Betty was the eldest, her younger sisters often helped her with her housework and family chores, but in return she did much of the cooking and supervision of the arrangements for kin ceremonies. Mrs Jacob was also very attached to her eldest sister, Mariamma, who since the death of their mother had become a substitute parent to the other sisters. Mariamma and her children were frequent visitors to the Jacob family and often gave Mrs Jacob gifts. Mrs Jacob said she was very fond of her eldest sister: 'she is like a mother to me'. Although Mrs Jacob had become a convert to Christianity when she married, this did not appear to have changed her relationship to her Hindu sisters in any way. She attended the large Hindu naming ceremony of one of Mariamma's grandchildren and was asked by another sister to choose the name of the last of her five children, which she considered a special honour. Such warm relationships between siblings have a very visible foundation in childhood. As children, older girls spend much time caring for younger siblings as nannies, and this surrogate-mother relationship continues in later life.

Sisters show considerable interest in one another's children, exchanging information on child care and comparing rates of growth. Women who have lost children in childbirth have been known to 'give away' subsequent infants to siblings to nurse in the belief that the evil spirits thought to be responsible for the previous death would be misled into regarding the child as another woman's. Nalini and her twin brother were given away in this manner to one of her mother's sisters shortly after birth and they lived with her until they were weaned. This aunt was henceforth regarded in a special manner by the twins as a 'mother'. She took a particular interest in them and Nalini said that at her wedding she was obliged to wear a sari given to her by this mother's sister rather than one given by her parents, as an acknowledgement of the relationship. Another instance of the 'loan' of children was to be found in Mrs Samuel's home. She had one of the daughters of her favourite sister boarding with her on a permanent basis. The girl returned to her natal home in the school holidays, when her place in the Samuel household was taken by one of her sisters since Mrs Samuel's sister had eight children living in crowded conditions in Durban. Apart from such loans, there were also cases of outright adoption of siblings' children. Informants related that it was acceptable for a childless woman to 'beg' a son or daughter from a sibling with many children. One of Mr Samuel's married sisters was childless and when his younger brother's wife gave birth to their third daughter, the child was adopted by the childless couple and registered in the husband's name. Although the fact of the adoption was known in the *kutum*, the girl was always referred to as her adoptive parents' daughter.

Unmarried aunts were expected to give their sisters' children small cash presents when the nieces and nephews visited them and on their birthdays. Junie, a single girl, commented,

> I send my nieces cards and when they come here I give them what I have . . . money. They don't want coins or silver, it has to be notes. I give them R1 each. Most of them expect it . . . . My mother made a habit of it and when she died I was expected to carry it on.

Despite the ideal of harmony symbolized in the gift-giving, jealousy and back-biting does occur among sisters, although informants were unwilling to admit this or acknowledge that quarrels occurred between them and their sisters. It was only after I had spent many months doing fieldwork in the village that Junie told me how her mother had left her a number of good saris when she died but her widowed sister had helped herself to them. When Junie had complained she was told by another sister that she should not mind because her widowed sister had very few clothes. I was unable to observe any actual quarrels between sisters, and my impressions gathered from personal observation were that sisters did indeed fulfil the role of 'best friends' and that even as children they tried to avoid open breaches among themselves.

Quite apart from the importance of sibling relationships, a Greenfields resident is also involved in a continually developing relationship with his or her own parents, and this relationship has four possible dyads: father-son, father-daughter, mother-son, and mother-daughter. Informants implied that sons should always be obedient and respectful to their fathers, often quoting Hindu scriptures to this effect, but there was little evidence in the case histories of my informants of father-son relationships conforming to this norm. Boys tended to be independent of their father's jurisdiction at an early age, when they roamed freely around the barracks. Until a boy reaches school-going age, his father takes little part in disciplining him and his paternal grandmother is often the one to administer slaps and scolds. Nor, as will be discussed below in greater detail, do fathers appear to be able to assert control later.

Maintaining control over daughters is less of a problem. While a girl's mother is alive she is the main disciplinarian and the father reinforces her decisions, but if the mother dies early before the marriage of her daughter, then the father must take on a dual role. Junie's mother had died the year before interviews began and Junie was left alone to housekeep for her widowed father. Junie was lonely without female companionship (her other siblings were married or working away from home), although she continued a small business selling snuff and betel nut to old women in the barracks, as her mother had done from home. Junie's overtures of friendship to other single girls in the barracks were rejected and she tended to be the target of gossip and criticism, since she had no female companions to chaperone her. Her elderly father was a strict disciplinarian and although Junie loved him she was also afraid of his anger. At one time she had a clandestine boyfriend who telephoned her occasionally at the call box in the barracks. She admitted that her father would have been very cross if he had known about the calls or the boyfriend. 'He used to say that place [the call box] was no good for a young girl because the boys hang around there'. Telephone calls from young men outside the family, especially ones considered to be wastrels and therefore unsuitable as potential marriage partners (as Junie's boyfriend was), could only lessen a girl's chances of marrying elsewhere if the relationship became known, even if nothing except the telephone conversations took place between the couple. The emphasis in this instance was on fatherly protection of a daughter's reputation, and a similar attitude was displayed by Muniamma's widower father towards her and her two unmarried sisters. He insisted that they remain indoors when they were at home and did not allow them to sit outside the house and chat to passers-by. Women or girls who are seen chatting to neighbours or friends in the barracks may be accused of fomenting trouble between husbands and wives or else of acting as go-betweens for lovers. Nor would Muniamma's father allow his daughter to attend the mixed sports evenings organized by the Social and Cultural Club and Muniamma said that most parents would not let their daughters go. 'They are afraid that they will misbehave,' she said. Muniamma's father was very reserved in his behaviour towards his daughters; he rarely spoke to them directly and they served him his food in a different room from theirs. At the same time he was very fond of them and personally chose and paid for new saris and trousseaux at their weddings. His daughters stressed his kindness to them and their children and he often joined in childish games with his grandchildren. Nowadays fathers often have a more relaxed relationship with their daughters, though they still frown on their fraternizing with boys unless suitably chaperoned.

While the relationship between father and daughter is often a formal, rather inhibited one, that between mother and son is usually much closer. The first-born in every Indian family should preferably be a male and there is great rejoicing when a son arrives, although mothers also welcome daughters. Mothers are especially proud of their sons and from an early age they are allowed considerably more freedom than girls. Boyish escapades (such as wreaking havoc in other people's vegetable gardens) are looked upon by mothers with indulgence and the offender can usually tell that mother's scolding carries no real threat of punishment. Indian mothers in Greenfields tend to spoil their sons whereas this happens to daughters only if they are the youngest of the family. Boys are often given more pocket money than their sisters and always more freedom to roam around the village with companions, a freedom denied to girls. Mothers can be heard to complain with pride, 'He is so naughty!'

As sons grow older their mother remains a stable influence in their lives, through her presence in the home, although she has little disciplinary authority over her sons. Traditionally, when the time came for sons to marry it was the mother or her sister who went to look for a bride — in other words, a girl who would be acceptable to the family as well as the boy. Mrs Virasami commented, 'You know our Indian custom, it is not the boy who comes [with an offer of marriage] but his mother'. The developing parent-child relationship is obviously affected by what happens after marriage but these changes are beyond the scope of this chapter.

While the keynote of the relationship between mother and son may be said to be 'indulgence', the same is not true of the behaviour of mothers towards their daughters. From an early age mothers instruct their daughters in household supervision and chores. The ability to cook well is considered especially important in Indian homes, and girls are given instruction in socially acceptable behaviour in and outside the home. Until they marry, girls in Greenfields spend most of their time, except when at school and work, with their mother. Free time is necessarily limited and in the past few girls were allowed to work after they left school unless there was a pressing financial need. Even today a clerical job or three years at a university is often seen as a stepping stone to a good marriage, as much by the girls themselves as by their parents. Friendship with other girls the same age in Greenfields is often discouraged, unless two sets of parents are themselves close friends. Here the village may well be more conservative than urban areas, but even there parents would enquire closely about the background and family of their daughters' girlfriends before approving of their friendship. Although children of immediate neighbours are allowed to visit one another unhindered (a quasi-kin relationship being established), an unmarried girl in Greenfields should always be accompanied by a sister or younger brother if she ventures any further afield, even to visit kin living elsewhere in the barracks. In such circumstances daughters are likely to become attached to their mothers, who in turn rely on their daughters for companionship and support, particularly in illness or childbirth. Because of this close attachment, a girl's marriage is often a wrench to both mother and daughter. The blow is softened by the frequent visits of the young bride to her natal home, where she is treated as an honoured guest, and by the mother's pride in her daughter's new married status and in her son-in-law.

The birth of grandchildren brings mother and daughter together once more, as a daughter expects to spend the months immediately preceding and following the birth of at least her first child at her mother's home. Moreover, it is her mother who pays for all the expenses connected with the birth: for the child's layette, the traditional midwife or, nowadays, hospital fees. Mrs David was particularly attached to her mother, for she was the only girl in a family of seven boys. She commented that she had gone to her mother's home for the birth of her first four children, but that when the fifth arrived the eldest was already at school and it was not easy to go away. At her mother's house, Mrs David said, her mother had taken care of her and she had stayed in bed, but in her own home she had to get up two days after giving birth because there was too much to do. As daughters become mothers themselves and their children grow up, contact with the mother may become less frequent and the mother may be seen less often than in the early days of marriage, unless she lives near. Nevertheless, daughters always remember their mothers with affection and a mother's death is a particularly sad occasion. At one stage during Muniamma's wedding tears were rolling down her cheeks and one of the guests whispered to me 'she is remembering her mother' (who had died three years previously). One of Muniamma's sisters remarked about the infant of another sister, 'this is the only one that [our] mother has not bathed, all the others she did', it being the traditional task of the mother's mother to bathe a newborn grandchild.

It can therefore be seen that within the Indian community of Greenfields, separated from the rest of the population for all social purposes, females form a group further encapsulated within the capsule. A combination of apartheid and company policy may isolate Indians within Greenfields, but it is traditional norms which insulate unmarried girls in particular from the rest of the community except their kin groups. Those norms even formalize, to some extent, their relationships with the senior male members of their families. Yet even within their enclosed world, changes are taking place, if more slowly than in other spheres. The effects of the educational and religious changes discussed above, with the lifestyles they bring for girls as well as boys, cannot be totally ignored by the *kutum*. And as the boys' education and expectations change, it is likely, though not inevitable, that major changes will take place in relations between boys and girls outside the family, with girls foregoing much of the security offered by the tightly-knit, controlling family in return for greater freedom.

Economic Opportunities in a Changing World

The rapidly rising educational level of Greenfields children does not, however, guarantee an improved future for them. Since competition for the still limited opportunities for higher education is keen because professional training is considered important, many less able boys become 'drop-outs' at the high school stage and live at home at their parents' expense. Instead of throwing these sons out of the house to fend for themselves, fathers frequently go to considerable lengths to try to obtain employment for them with the company at Greenfields, often calling daily at the offices to see if any vacancies have occurred and campaigning on their behalf with the Labour Officer. These sons, however, frequently do not appear to show their fathers any overt gratitude in return. Teenage boys and youths in their twenties often form gangs of age mates with whom they spend as much time as possible, avoiding their homes and their fathers' company. Fathers know that their sons are liable to be led astray in this way, for drinking liquor and smoking are features of gang activities, but they seem to lack the authority to forbid their sons to do these things and are extremely reluctant to have recourse to the only sanction available to them — that of evicting their sons from the house.

Mr Virasami was horrified when his son was caught shoplifting at the local supermarket, but his reaction was more one of shame at the fact that the affair was generally known in the barracks than at the wrongdoing itself. The boy was prosecuted in the local magistrate's court and sentenced to six cuts. Mrs Virasami said she knew her son had been in the wrong but felt that he had been led astray by others in his gang who had also stolen from the shop but had not been caught. The affair soon died down, but the next year Mr Virasami took his son away from the local school and sent him to one in Durban, where he boarded with a cousin. While Mr Virasami was able to send his son away and thus remove him from the company of other youths in Greenfields, most parents do not have this option and have to try to find other solutions to the problem. One way in which gangs do eventually break up is when the leader marries. Marriage removes a youth from the company of single men, and, although his companions may jeer at him, he is unlikely to spend much time with them again. Fathers, therefore, are often keen to arrange suitable matches for their errant sons, or at least to establish an engagement.

While not all young men become petty criminals, even some who leave school with matriculation certificates fail to find employment and this can have a devastating effect on morale. Krish matriculated at the end of 1983 but has been unemployed ever since in spite of applying for numerous jobs and attending interviews. Krish and his younger brother are the only children of a widow who married a widower late in life. When her husband died, she returned to Greenfields to look after her aged mother and because she had nowhere else to go. With the death last year of her old mother, she and her two sons face eviction from their barracks home since none of them is employed by the company and housing is supposed to be allocated only to company employees. Krish, like his mother, is nervous and consequently has been unable to make a good impression on prospective employers. He is now a withdrawn and pathetic figure. He wanders about looking for odd jobs in the barracks and depends on the charity of neighbours for food for himself, his mother and brother. A number of Greenfields youths find themselves in a similar position to Krish. Having worked hard for years to obtain a matriculation certificate, they find that it is not the passport to the secure white-collar job for which they had hoped. Unemployment is especially disappointing for boys who have been brought up by their parents to aspire to professional careers and regard manual labour of the sort that their fathers have done all their lives as beneath them.

Kevin said that he wants to read for a Bachelor of Commerce degree when he leaves school and then he wants to be an accountant. He lives with his parents and three siblings in a two-roomed barracks dwelling with no electricity. His father is a plant operator. Kevin said he is excused from most household chores on the grounds that he must study for at least two hours each night. Instead, his younger brother, aged fifteen, and his sister, aged thirteen, do most of the household tasks such as chopping wood and cleaning. A common complaint from youngsters I spoke to was that the poor standard of housing for Indians in Greenfields prevented barracks children from achieving better results at school and that the scholastic achievements of barracks children compared unfavourably with those from the nearby town, where Indian homes have electric light and other amenities. Nevertheless, it is possible for barracks children to excel despite a deprived home background. Michael is the illegitimate son of Chiuamma. Chiuamma's relationship with Michael's father is a long-standing one but cannot be legalized as he is married. Despite the stigma attached to an unmarried mother and her child in the barracks, Chiuamma insisted on keeping her child. She has always been extremely ambitious for her son and she encouraged him to enter Medical School when he matriculated. He qualified as a doctor and keeps in close touch with his mother, often telephoning her. Last year he paid for her to go on holiday to the Far East. Michael's father has always taken a keen interest in the boy and has been supportive. Michael was able to finance his studies with a company bursary, since his mother works for the company as a tea lady.

However, whether the Indian boys of Greenfields join the ranks of the professionals, the semi-skilled, the artisans, or the unemployed, what is clear is that they are discarding the pattern of life established by their fathers and grandfathers. It is estimated by company sources that 95 per cent of the present Indian mill workforce had fathers who were previously employed in the mill. (The remaining 5 per cent come from Durban and are usually highly qualified in skills for which the local population is not trained.) However, most of the Indian workers, according to the Personnel Officer, are aged forty years or more, and their children do not expect or want jobs in the mill to the same extent as their fathers did. Youngsters who receive bursaries for university or technikon courses are obliged to work for the company for only four years on completion of their degree or diploma, and all four of the Indians in management positions are 'outsiders' whose fathers were not employed in the mill. Among youngsters with matriculation who cannot continue with tertiary education, the most popular careers, according to the Welfare Officer, are the police force and the navy. Boys with matriculation are not prepared to work in the clothing and textile factories, as do less educated girls. For these girls too, however, the roles of their mothers are no longer providing models for many spheres of their lives.

Conclusion

Unexpectedly, perhaps, to grow up in Greenfields is not to live in an insulated world with ready-made and acceptable models of behaviour unaffected by social and economic change. Rather, for many of the children today, to grow up in this setting is to move in one generation from a world of poor labourers to one where aspirations, and often reality, are of white-collar or professional work. For girls, the move may be from the strict enclosure of family supervision to work in the larger community or university. They may still be chaperoned to some extent, but with wider horizons unfolding before them a series of situations for which their mother's behaviour can provide no model. While the kinship network remains ostensibly intact, the strains on it are new and must, inevitably, transform its relationships to some extent, even before job mobility stretches it in many directions geographically. The economic recession is likely further to reduce the small number of sons of the Indian community in the mill following in their fathers' footsteps. If present patterns continue, it is the company's own combination of housing and welfare policy, inter-acting with the other changes transforming the Greenfields Indian community, that may well make this the last generation of Indians to grow up in Greenfields as 'children of the company'.

Notes

1. I have changed the name of the estate to give informants anonymity. Personal names have also been changed. My material is based partly on research carried out for an MA thesis in Social Anthropology between 1974 and 1978, but also on continued social interaction before and since those dates with the Indian people of Greenfields. I lived in Green-fields from 1972 to 1983. I interviewed a member of each household in the barracks (202 in all) as part of a general census of the population in 1974 and also conducted in-depth interviews with selected informants later. I was invited to attend numerous ceremonies connected with rites of passage, such as naming ceremonies, weddings, and funerals, and also participated on an informal basis in the lives of barracks residents and their children.
2. This university was originally established exclusively for Indians.
3. See Jithoo (1978) for a discussion of the definition of joint and extended families in South Africa, and Shah (1964, 1974) for India.

The Children of the 'Surplus People': A Case Study of Elukhanyweni[1]

Ina Roux

In 1977-78, four hundred families were moved by the South African government from a number of small reserves in the Lower Tsitsikama forest near Humansdorp in the Cape. The move was a consequence of the government's policy of separate development, under which scattered African settlements were appropriated and their inhabitants moved to the newly created bantustans or 'black homelands' as part of the government's attempt to consolidate African settlement in these designated areas, away from white lands. The move in this case followed more than two years of opposition from the people, who formed groups, held meetings with officials, and even took legal action to prevent the removal. Judgement, however, went in favour of the state, and over a period of two months from December 1977, police, Eastern Cape Administration Board Officials, and troops supervised their removal at gunpoint. Once evicted, the people were transported in convoys — buses for women and children, open trucks for men and furniture (Platzky and Walker 1985). After a slow 300 kilometre journey, they arrived at Elukhanyweni to begin a very different life.

During 1982 I interviewed a number of adults in Elukhanyweni. What struck me most, apart from the poverty and the bleakness of the landscape, was the pervading silence. Where there are children and dogs all in close proximity one expects laughter, barking and whining, shouts, arguments. Yet the children and the dogs in these areas seemed to be hidden by the same blank, exhausted silence. The occasional twosome or threesome huddled together, but their voices drifted in the dust and were scarcely recognizable as the voices of children. Girls of five or six, walking to and from the shop, could tell the exact price of every item they had ever bought or considered buying. Adolescents (as adolescents everywhere in the world do) walked together or stood around in groups, but they seemed to look past one another at the houses and the sand. They, too, spoke little. The dominant impression was of a culture without children, or rather, children as we know them, firmly rooted in childhood; and of children without a culture.

Three years later, early in 1985, I returned to the area to study this phenomenon. My aim was to establish, first, whether or not the extreme dislocation experienced by people in these areas had resulted in a breakdown of cultural cohesion; and second, whether, if there had been a breakdown, a new complex of consciously approved and accepted behaviour patterns could be seen to be in the process of formulation. In other words, the aspects of culture which interested me were not only shared beliefs and values, but the ways in which these and other influences caused members of the society to interact with each other to produce distinctive patterns of behaviour and organization within the sub-groups of the society. To examine these questions in depth requires both historical work and lengthy participant observation, together with interviews. Financial and legal constraints, as well as lack of time, made such research impossible, and what follows is in the nature of a pilot study rather than any attempt at a definitive statement.

Methodology

Every third house in a street chosen at random was selected for interviews, and a Xhosa interviewer and I interviewed thirty adults aged between forty-two and seventy-six. The interviews were semi-structured in that certain topics were covered, including religion, social organizations, marriage, the family, and social and racial hierarchies. A questionnaire was compiled from themes that emerged during the interviews and was administered at every fourth house in a street chosen at random. Thirty adults, aged between forty and eighty, completed the questionnaire. People were asked not to discuss the questionnaire among themselves, but it was not possible to check whether or not discussions in fact occurred. Thirty-seven young people, aged between thirteen and eighteen, were interviewed with a semi-structured questionnaire different from that administered to the adults. A questionnaire requiring only yes/no responses was drawn from the answers received, and distributed at an athletics gathering. Twenty-seven were filled in and returned. Twenty-four of the respondents were aged between fifteen and nineteen. It was explicitly stated that no names were required, only age and school standard.

Elukhanyweni

Elukhanyweni has proved a bitter disappointment to the adults moved there. They had for generations lived on reserves in the Tsitsikama area where most households had approximately four morgen of arable land and access to a grazing area of some thirty morgen. From this land they derived a substantial portion of their family food requirements as subsistence households, and supplemented it with working on white farms, on Department of Forestry plantations in the area, and as weekly and monthly migrant labourers in the manufacturing, construction, and service sectors of the economy in Humansdorp and Port Elizabeth. At Elukhanyweni they have access to very little agricultural land — at most two or three small garden plots — and can no longer obtain enough food from their land for some degree of independence from the consumer market (Surplus People Project 1983: 251, 262). Half the adult males aged twenty to sixty-four and 35 per cent of the adult females migrate to obtain work and prevent their families from starving. The effect on family life and child rearing has been marked (Surplus People Project 1983: 261).

More than this, the move which deprived them of their land deprived them of the agricultural base of their society. For more than a century agriculture was central to their lives, moulding their everyday existence: their personal activities, interpersonal relationships, and expectations for the future. The land therefore symbolized for them an entire way of life. The Surplus People Project Report described the people's attitude to their original reserves:

> To this land the Tsitsikama people were intensely attached. In their memories the land, the fields, are permanent. They dwell on it, everyone, obsessively. In their recollections, a refrain of sorts, 'one had fields'. For them 'without fields there is starvation' (1983: 250).

It was in this atmosphere of deadening despair and poverty that the children of Elukhanyweni were growing up when I visited the area in 1982. For the adults, the situation had not changed when I returned in 1985. A very high proportion of children were still being reared by their grandparents, and women still formed a large majority of the adult population. Nor did Elukhanyweni look different. The roads were still muddy, the houses drab, and the corrugated iron latrines still dotted the landscape like a series of grotesque exclamation marks. But the children were different. This time gum-chewing youngsters coolly squinted at my car, disco music blared from the shops, children noisily built and broke up sagas of make-believe. The boys had plans, ambitions. They explained that they were going to leave this place soon. They were going to become teachers, broadcasters, clerks, policemen, lawyers. No, not farmers. Yes, they were going to live well. Soon, soon, they would be leaving to fulfil their dreams. They offered their dreams gladly: dreams of affluence. The girls were nowhere to be seen at first. They were found huddled together in pokey rooms, nursing babies, bent over stoves, brooms, a younger brother or sister. Some, the exceptions, those in standards nine and ten (the last two years of schooling), were confident about the future: they were going to be teachers or nurses and have their own houses. But the majority of girls aged fifteen or sixteen were only in standard four of five, or were pregnant, or suckling babies, or looking after ill grandparents. They too volunteered their dreams — if more hesitantly — of becoming teachers or nurses. When pressed, they admitted that this was unlikely and that they would probably marry or become domestic servants. Grandmothers would look after their children.

It was a grandmother who encapsulated for us the way in which the move from the old reserves had led to the changes we observed in the youth:

> Things were good when I was a child. They were good and right and we knew how things were done. I learned many things, but the most important thing I learned, was to love and respect all grown-ups because they were all my parents and they would help me if I needed help and love me when I needed love. And I learned to love God. We went to church because we wanted to. And to Sunday School and we had concerts and we sang in the church choir.
>
> But these children now. They are not me. They are different. I don't know them. Perhaps they love us but they don't respect what we know. They are left loose here, and we cannot help them. We had faith but our

children, oh, our children go but they don't believe. Even the little ones. They already say: 'Your people lied to you'. Now, my people were not clever. They followed Moses, and they did not ask things and they did not fight the Lord.

But we are wrong too. What can we teach our children? Because the Lord had left us. First we wanted to belong to God, we were in God. But now we can forget God because he isn't here.

What can we teach our children? My father told me: 'This land is yours. We bought this land with our life. We fought for this land'.[2] And we knew: our children will inherit this land, and our daughters, yes, our daughters too will have their piece of earth. But what can I tell my sons, and see [what has become of] my daughters. They already have daughters who have sons, and the sons don't have fathers and they don't have names and they will never, never have land. No, indeed, God has left us. Now all I can tell my children is: 'Your ancestors had land, and they lived in God'. But they tell me: 'This is where we live now, and we have education and we will live better'. Oh, they dream dreams, our children. They dream the dreams we never had because we could look at our land, and touch it, and we knew, there it was, there, and it was ours. But the children, they don't look at the future like we did. We saw the future, we knew: here I will live, like this, in this house or that one, and I will have children and they will live here or there. This here is the future. But our children say: 'I will become a teacher, I will become a lawyer'. How? Without money, without land. How will they become these things? And we can give them nothing. And they want nothing from us because we are useless.[3]

This description of the dissolution of a way of life, and the values inherent in it, brings into focus what the youth have lost with the land: a feeling of certainty about their future, the supportive family network based on family ownership of land, and the faith of their elders in a Christian God. In addition, the authority of the older generations had derived from the body of survival skills and knowledge they possessed and were able to hand on to the succeeding generations. With the change in environment from essentially subsistence farming to that of the resettlement area, many of these skills became relatively unimportant or obsolete. Parents and grandparents, with very little formal education or knowledge of the economic structures with which they were confronted, lost much of their usefulness as guides. More than this, many also lost their confidence in their role as mentors, and their insecurity could not be communicated to the youth, already deprived of so many of the sources of security their elders had enjoyed. As our interviews showed, many of the formal structures which gave coherence to the communities in their original settlements had either ceased to exist or no longer held the same importance for everyone at Elukhanyweni, so that they were to a large extent faced with the need to develop new skills, new forms of behaviour, new ways of organizing themselves, and new supportive values — in other words, a partially new culture. But these changes began to occur within the rather battered framework of the original values and social institutions by which the society had been living when the disruptive changes took place. Indeed, with the destruction of so many sources of security, it was to be expected that the uprooted generations would try to preserve all that they could of the old way of life, even where certain institutions no longer had a practical *raison d'etre*. As Beals points out (1967: x), when cultural patterns lose their practical and therefore symbolic value as a result of an environmental shift, 'new cultural material must be found and used to modify the cultural tradition without destroying its essential unity'. It was the beginning of this intricate process, which was particularly conspicuous among the youth, that we found ourselves studying. In doing so, we focussed on three sources of social values and organization: religion, the family, and the peer group.

Religion

The choice of religion as a structuring and identifying cultural force was determined by the interviews with the older generations. With three exceptions, all the adults interviewed cited the church as the centre of cultural activity in the Tsitsikama. A recurring theme in their descriptions of their childhood was the sense of loss they now felt by comparison: loss of the secure religious environment with its rigid and explicit rules of conduct and its supportive network of sanctioning principles of interaction. The church, as the older generations saw it, consciously articulated the spiritual guidelines according to which they organized their social activities and their understanding of proper behaviour towards others in their community. All social activities centred around the church. Sunday School, church-organized sports activities, concerts, and picnics structured the children's participation in the social activities of the communities. Women belonged to the women's organizations offered by the church, and men aspired to the positions of deacon and elder, positions of respect and high status. It was generally accepted that the Christian philosophy accorded to each and every person a God-given position in the world and clearly delineated acceptable as opposed to improper behaviour.

> We just knew. This is right, this is wrong, this you do, but this you must not do. We knew this because God told Moses and he wrote it all down and they read his writing to us in church.

> My mother told me: you must do things this way otherwise you go to Hell, and I did not want to go to Hell.

> When I was a child, I knew what was proper and I did things right. But now I am old and I don't know any more because then God was with us but now he isn't here any more and I don't know why.

At first sight it appears curious that the older generations express such a sense of loss, since their church is still very much with them. The Moravian Brotherhood established the mission station of Clarkson in the Tsitsikama area in the nineteenth century, and this is the church to which the older generations belong. After the forced removal of Clarkson's congregants, a Moravian church was established at Elukhanyweni and the original membership has been maintained. However, the older generations are adamant that it is not as important as it was in the Tsitsikama. A loss of faith appears to be one reason for this: a substantial number of people expressed doubt in a loving God and many maintained that God had left them. A second reason, which emerged in approximately 80 per cent of interviews, was that adults felt that their children and grandchildren did not belong to the church in the way that they themselves had belonged and still did, to some extent. They felt that the family was not linked to the church any more and had thus lost its roots. This was corroborated by the opinions young people expressed towards religion. About 90 per cent of those interviewed felt that the church did not play any significant role in their lives. All those in the fifteen to nineteen age group felt that, although they might go to church services and Sunday School, it meant very little to them. Typical statements included:

> I go to church because it upsets my grandparents if I don't go but it does not mean much to me.

> I don't know what they say in church. I don't understand what they say.

> I don't go to church because Sundays I am tired on account of dancing all Saturday night.

> The church can teach me nothing. We learn in school the things we must know.

Much research in the history of South African churches makes it clear that religion may become a politically revolutionary vehicle and is not necessarily politically conservative (eg. Hanekom 1975; West 1975; Sundkler 1976). However, in the light of the above quotations and figures, it seems unlikely that the church will serve as a focus around which the young people of Elukhanyweni will organize themselves.

The Family

Almost more than the absence of an active community life centred around the church, the older generations mourned the loss of the close kinship network in which they had grown up. They talked longingly of a time when responsibility for a child did not rest with the parents alone but with all the adults in the wider family group, and of a time when a child showed respect and love to all adult relatives, not only to his or her parents. Almost all the adults to whom I spoke confirmed this notion of a community of related grown-ups of several generations, who assumed responsibility for every child in the wider family. They said that the extended kinship network gave greater support than the nuclear family. Probably, they romanticized their past but it is clear that it provided much emotional and material security which is no longer available in the resettlement area. Women and their children born out of wedlock would have been catered for within the wider family structure, for example. In contrast, it was frequently said to us that, 'now, in this place, there are only grandparents to look after a girl and her child'.

Both the young and the older generations were very aware of the difference in outlook between the two groups. Among the older there was incomprehension and distrust of the youth; while the youth expressed pity and some contempt. They repeatedly talked of the weakness of the adults, in which the youth stressed adults' idleness and lack of education:

> They just sit around the whole day; there is nothing for them to do.

They don't understand us; they want to help us but they can't because they don't know the things we know.

The old people are weak now. They have no authority over us because they are idle now.

We still respect them but only because they are old.

We still love our parents and grandparents but only because they are our family. They can do nothing for us because they are weak and they have nothing to give us.

It is not that we don't have respect for our elders, but they can't help us; they are weak and they don't know us.

One story told us by a young boy vividly illustrates the dilemma for both adults and youth:

One night, when it was full moon, my grandmother pointed at the moon and said, 'There Adam and Eve are sitting. I wonder when God will stop punishing them'. I asked her what she meant. She then told me that because Adam and Eve disobeyed God's word, he banished them to the moon. And when I said it was all nonsense, she became so angry that she hit me over the head with her shoe. She said that I would be punished for mocking God. I love her but how can I talk to her? She knows nothing.

The older generations understandably resented the young people's pity, dismissive attitudes to the past, and lack of respect for their knowledge and values. As a result, relations between the two groups often seemed strained, finding expression in bitter, disillusioned outbursts from the adults as well as the youth.

I just want to go back; I want to leave; I don't know these children. These children aren't for me; I just want to go; I want to put my things on my head and walk back to where I know the children.

Since the young no longer seek their identity within the framework of a kinship network, patterns of behaviour towards people not part of the immediate family have changed. Young people are attempting to distance themselves as a group different from and superior to the old, since they view the skills which made survival possible for their forebears as irrelevant. There is not much, they feel, that their parents and grandparents can teach them.

They have to survive in a new environment. For the elders, resettlement meant a rupture with everything familiar and loved: the world has become alien and barren and they cannot accept it. The youth have no choice. This is their world: the small houses, the mud roads, the shifting sands, the little gardens which have replaced their ancestors' lands. Somehow they must build a new identity, even if that means ignoring the litany of grief of the older generations and thus incurring the cost of being thrown on their own pitifully small resources. Under these circumstances, the family is not likely to be an important source of the new values and organizational framework needed by the young to meet their situation now.

The Peer Group

Margaret Mead (1978), in discussing the reactions of a society to being wrenched from its familiar and sanctioned environment, suggests that a new style of cultural transmission inevitably evolves. She argues that, when a major social disruption occurs in a society which had until then been characterized by the unquestioning acceptance of the values of older generations, the peer group tends to replace the older generations as the source and transmitter of values. Yet despite our evidence of rejection of parental values, there is as yet very little evidence in Elukhanyweni of the type of youth organizations in which peer group values are often formulated and through which pressures for conformity are applied. There are no gangs and no youth clubs affiliated to either the church or the school. Nor are there any sports clubs. As indicated above, a 'smart' style of behaviour, imitative of 'disco-culture' is developing on the streets and the other places where children meet their peers. When asked to name their heroes, they listed the Reverend Ndlovu, a priest who popularized church music, and Brenda Fassie, a disco singer. Disco music seemed to be a passion they all shared but no youth-created, *institutionally* based leaders of their new-found disco-culture have yet emerged locally. However, given the change in the bearing of the youth and the street atmosphere of Elukhanyweni over the period between my two visits, it may be conjectured that such institutions will eventually come into existence. Whether they take the form of youth clubs or gangs remains to be seen. As discussed by Schärf, Powell and Thomas elsewhere in this volume, gangs in particular have been found to provide refuges for youths who reject parental values and need alternative sources of norms.

The Way Forward?

Margaret Mead suggests that, implicit in the search for a new system of values and behavioural patterns, there is a commitment to a specific cause, a new lifestyle, a different ideology. It seems that such commitment to an ideal, and the common working together of a group towards the aims of that shared ideal, are frequently the most important ingredients in the creation of new cultural patterns. Such an ideal seems to have played a major role in the emergence of the politically oriented youth culture so prominent in black urban areas. As school boycotts and widespread parental dismay at them clearly demonstrate, peer group pressure plays the dominant role in transmitting the new cultural patterns. Possibly the subtleties of political organization and actions are not always fully appreciated by the youth leaders, but they have created their own forms of action, different from those followed by political activists of the previous generation during, for example, the Defiance Campaign of the early fifties.

The youth of Elukhanyweni, however, appear to be unaware of the political views and aspirations of black urban youth.[4] At a time when Mandela's refusal to accept the South African President's conditional offer of freedom was discussed in most households in the country, young people in Elukhanyweni hardly knew who the man was. About 80 per cent of the total group who answered the questions recognized the name, and they all linked it to political imprisonment, but none was able to connect it to a specific organization or a specific time in the political history of the country. Only two girls knew that Mandela was still in prison and the length of the imprisonment; none of the group knew who Tambo and Sisulu were.[5] Only five of them could link names such as AZAPO, COSAS, and the UDF[6] to political organizations that were currently active in South Africa. Discussions about school boycotts in all cases elicited the response that education was important and therefore not to be rejected under any circumstances. Approximately 80 per cent had heard of the boycotts taking place at the time, but none could describe the issues involved.

Indeed, if there is a shared commitment to an ideal among the youth in Elukhanyweni, it is a commitment to education. During the interviews the young people repeatedly stated that only education could help them to live a different life from that of their parents. It was during the discussions on education that they told us of their plans for the future, and those of their friends, brothers, sisters, and neighbours. They were going to be lawyers, broadcasters, doctors, teachers, nurses, businessmen. And they were going to be rich. All those interviewed or who completed questionnaires saw the future in terms of high status occupations and affluence. But this vision of affluence had been created in a cultural vacuum. It encompassed visions of abundant food, furniture, and clothes, but the dream could neither locate this place of abundance, nor could it envisage how the life of plenty would be lived, surrounded by whom, under what kind of social regime. Nevertheless, they were adamant that their lives were going to be different from that of their parents. They offered dreams of their own houses, cars, and travel to other countries. When pressed on how they were going to achieve these ambitions, the formula was always education.

Young blacks in the urban areas have realized and articulated the fact that education may be a tool of oppression rather than the gateway to opportunity. The essence of their justification for the school boycotts is that the inferior black education they receive effectively excludes them from positions where they can have any part in the power structure and policy-making decisions of the country. But the young people in resettlement areas, isolated from mainstream political activities, forcibly wrenched from their land, betrayed by the impotence and despair of their parents and grandparents, still see education as the only means of escape.

It seems improbable, however, that this recipe for their future can retain credibility for long among the youth of Elukhanyweni. Only 4.1 per cent of black pupils reach standard eight, the minimum qualification for most further educational opportunities, and only 1.6 per cent reach standard ten (Cooper *et al* 1985: 660). These figures are likely to be above those achieved in Elukhanyweni, where poverty is all-pervasive. In such circumstances, it usually requires a total commitment from the whole family to put a child through school. A uniform, tie, jersey, shoes and socks, are all compulsory and cost, at the time of my research, R64. Books cost between R36 and R60 each year. This meant a total outlay of at least R100 per annum per child in an environment where the average monthly cash income for a family of 7.1 members amounted to R213.93, including income from migrants (Surplus People Project 1983: 273). The difficulty for

Elukyhanyweni children of reaching matriculation in such circumstances may delay the realization for some years that matriculation does not guarantee the golden future expected. Eventually, however, unless the current economic situation improves substantially and major changes are effected in the laws excluding blacks from urban areas, it will become evident to all that the probable prospect for matriculants from Elukhanyweni is low-paid work in the poverty-stricken Ciskei, or migrant labour.

Conclusion

The young people of Elukhanyweni are growing up in a situation where the guidelines for living which were used by their grandparents and parents are no longer applicable in major spheres of their lives. They are having to build a new world but have neither the tools nor the necessary support from their elders. Many, with migrant worker parents, live with their grandparents, who circle within a world of grief and memories. Money is very scarce. They are isolated from the centres of political activity. Newspapers and television are absent, radios in short supply. It is hardly surprising that, growing up in a society which was uprooted so recently and which is suffering from so many disadvantages, they have not yet found a realistic formula for dealing with their new world. However, as they become disillusioned with their present 'solution' of trusting to education to improve their lot, they will look elsewhere. Those who have found that even matriculation is not the magic panacea will return — on visits at least — and increasingly news of the outside world and its ideas will filter through. It seems probable that the youth culture and politics of the children of Soweto, East London, and Cape Town will come to play a major part in the new world that the children of Elukhanyweni are shaping for themselves.

Notes

1. This study was financed by the Ivan Greenstein Research Fund, through the Institute of Social and Economic Research, Rhodes University.
2. During the sixth frontier war of 1835 the Mfengu, a group of refugees from earlier wars connected with the expansion of the Zulu state,

assisted the British against the Xhosa. In return the British granted the Mfengu land rights in parts of the Eastern Cape.

3. The interview was conducted in Afrikaans, as many of the people originally from the Humansdorp district speak a fluent and idiomatic Afrikaans. The rest of the quotes, save two, were originally in Xhosa.

4. There are obvious methodological problems about the trustworthiness of information gathered through interviews on political parties, especially illegal ones. To minimize these as far as possible in the time available, the Xhosa interviewer took time to get to know the youth a little, and interviewees were not asked to express any opinions about the organizations and leaders referred to, but merely to identify them and their aims.

5. Nelson Mandela was a key strategist of the African National Congress in the 1950s and, from 1961, leader of its new National Action Council and military wing, Umkhonto we Sizwe (Spear of the Nation). As a result of its activities in 1963 he was one of the defendants in a major sabotage trial (known as the Rivonia trial) and was sentenced to life imprisonment. He has become a famous symbol of black resistance. Oliver Tambo is the present president of the banned African National Congress. Walter Sisulu was the secretary-general of the African National Congress at the time of the Rivonia trial and was sentenced to life imprisonment at the same time as Mandela for his part in the Rivonia conspiracy.

6. Important black and non-racial political organizations in the Eastern Cape and nationally, viz. the Azanian People's Organization, the Congress of South African Students, and the United Democratic Front.

Strollers — Street Children of Cape Town

Wilfried Schärf, Marlene Powell and
Edgar Thomas[1]

Die Kaap is lekker. A stroller is someone who don't sleep by his house —
he sleeps in the street. He don't eat by his house — he eats by the bins. A
stroller is someone who thinks he is free. Do what his mind says. It's a
nice name for us.[2]

Introduction

Strollers are children who have run away from home and school while
still under sixteen years of age, the minimum legal school-leaving age.
They live on the streets and eke out an existence by a variety of means.
In greater Cape Town there were in May 1985 an estimated three hundred strollers, approximately thirty of whom were girls.[3]

Our information relating to strollers' family and school experience
consists largely of the assertions and attitudes of the children
themselves. For data on both parents' and teachers' perceptions of
strollers we have drawn on previous research done by members of the
Community Arts Project (CAP) for an exhibition. Although we have
spoken to social workers and house-parents involved in the shelters
for the children,[4] and have gained considerable insight from them, this
chapter concerns itself mainly with the way in which the strollers
themselves make sense of their world. We explore not only their
physical groupings and methods of survival, but also what it means to
them to be on the streets.

Several factors militated against a complete understanding of their world of meaning and their values. As adults we were identified with those whom the strollers had rejected in the two key areas of their lives — family and school. Their method of coping with adults, particularly punitively-inclined adults, was escape. In order to overcome their suspicions and fears, our approaches to them were staged very gradually. Initially we were given front stories, but as our research progressed we were accorded a certain amount of trust by the strollers. Moreover, we were able to check information by internal corroboration and by comparing the accounts and perceptions of other strollers in the same group.

In some cases our skin colour also constituted a barrier.[5] Furthermore, there was initially no reason why the strollers should differentiate in favour of us as researchers and tell us the truth, particularly about their home and school experiences. A large part of their financial survival depends, as will be explained below, on presenting adults with a story about home and school in a way that elicits pity and donations. Deeper probing was often resisted by the strollers, either because it aroused feelings of guilt about having left home, or because, as some of them indicated, it was a very painful topic to talk about. Some of them therefore avoided the more painful areas of their lives when talking to us.

Despite all these difficulties, we gained a considerable body of data from the children. Once they were willing to allow our conversations to be tape recorded, they usually insisted that we bought them 'dite' (food) first, and after talking for a while their concentration often lagged. They then wandered off, begged for a little money from passing pedestrians and headed for a café, where they played video games. Thereafter, they were often willing to talk once more. And so, by degrees, we were able to piece their stories together, some of which were more credible than others.

The opening quote touches on four of the themes which this paper explores: *first*, the escape from the conventional process of socialization under the influence of the family and school ('who don't sleep by his house'); *second*, the notion of freedom ('A stroller is someone who thinks he is free'); *third*, the trend towards individualism ('do what his mind says'); and *fourth*, the reliance on an alternative pattern of both socializing and basic provisioning ('he sleeps in the streets . . . he eats by the bins').

As we explore these aspects of their lives, we highlight both the individual motivational thrust and the underlying structural dynamics which influence the strollers' existence. We consider it important not merely to analyze the actions and motivations of the children in terms of individual pathologies or inadequacies, but to acknowledge the role that ideology and history have played in their lives. Indeed, to confine an analysis to individual, or even social pathology would fall into the same trap that La Hausse (1982: 66) criticizes:

> The perception of the ruling classes of the conditions under which the working class lives in the city gives rise to a myth of social pathology turning the harshness of economic inequality back upon its victims as moral condemnation. Squalid housing, crime, ignorance and poverty come to be seen as a mutually reinforcing set of circumstances independent of the economic relationships which cause them.

To confine oneself to the social pathology argument ignores the fact that the material conditions in which certain classes find themselves at particular times are partly attributable to the policies of the ruling classes relating to social reproduction. In addition, they are influenced by the ability and willingness of the ruled class or classes to fight for a better deal. Poverty, for example, is influenced by the wage level, the unemployment rate, the level of skilling and schooling, the criminalization of informal sector activity, and the lack of access to other income opportunities in a particular region. Housing problems, to cite another example, are inextricably interwoven with the state's low-cost housing policies and the affordability of, and legal access to, the existing housing stock. Alcoholism, too, cannot be seen in isolation from the state's policy regarding the production of intoxicants, and the institutional encouragement of high drinking levels for a whole segment of the Western Cape's rural labour force. It is no mere oversight that the tot system (whereby farm labourers are 'paid' a portion of their wages in alcohol) is allowed to continue. It performs a valuable function for a part of the ruling class (Schärf 1984: 149-206). Thus, in our view, an explanation of strolling needs to use a model that incorporates both individual and structural factors.

The Escape from the Usual Process of Socialization

By running away from both home and school, strollers have abandoned the conventional sources of emotional and economic security. They have also escaped from the customary sources of guidance and moral inculcation. In most cases they supplant these conventional structures with an alternative 'family and school' — their peer group, their strolling companions. In choosing or drifting into the strolling existence, the children are exceptional, for most youngsters on the Cape Flats have utilized other forms of generating an income and obtaining emotional support.

First, there is the street gang. Most disaffected youngsters who refuse to take up formal employment or cannot find it and have dropped out of school, join gangs. These form tightly knit units which partially replace the emotional support of the family circle. They also supply the children with some money through protection rackets, trading in stolen and illicit goods, and stealing (Pinnock 1982: 15-16). In this situation, however, the child tends to retain his or her home as a base for sleeping and eating when possible (Schärf 1984: 127-28).

Second, children might seek employment, even though they are under the legal age for paid work. Moerat (1983: 6) has demonstrated that many of the five hundred newsvendors in Cape Town are under sixteen. Some children become packers, cleaners, and delivery boys or girls for corner shops in the African and coloured townships (our observations). Then, in the informal sector, among woodcutters and hawkers, rag-bone-and-scrap collectors, among sellers of spices, flowers, and beverages are hundreds of children whose formal schooling is over despite their age (Glover, Schärf *et al* 1981). Most of these children retain fairly strong ties with their families, and many still live at home. As is customary on the Cape Flats, they hand over either all or a large portion of their earnings to the family and are given pocket money in return (Moerat 1983: 5-6).

Third, as in the case of the children being examined here, they might take the more drastic step of becoming strollers, thereby undertaking sole responsibility for their own maintenance and general wellbeing. There is very little overlap between gangs and strollers. In reality members of gangs tend to frown on strollers and vice versa. Out of the the three hundred strollers in Cape Town, only twenty belong to a quasi-gang — the Young Scorpion Kids.[6] The strong rejection of family is evident in both gang members and strollers as both transplant their emotional and economic dependence from family to peer group. There remain, however, several fundamental differences between gang members and strollers.

First, whereas gang members retain contact with their families, exploiting them for certain requirements like shelter, strollers have found themselves unable to do so.

Second, gangs subvert and exploit the mechanisms of capitalist society.[7] They share with the conventional members of the society the aims of accumulating wealth and power; their deviation lies in the rejection of the class position of their families within society (Schärf 1984: 87-111; Pinnock 1982: 347; Hall *et al* 1976: 30-35). Consequently they devise illegal and rapid ways of gaining access to the benefits enjoyed by members of the privileged class. Strollers, on the other hand, step out of the class position of their families and partially suspend the aims and values of that sector of society. They are concerned with immediate consumption and not with the circulation or accumulation of goods, money or power.

Third, gang members seek a group identity based on complete loyalty and a high degree of control. There are intense rivalries and conflicts between gangs. Strollers, on the other hand, manage to retain a degree of individualism, clubbing together in loose groups only for mutual support, not domination. Thus the actions of strollers are not simply the result of a failure to cope with social structures. These alternative courses of action embody many of the strollers' own values, as will become evident below.

Fourth, while many of the gangs are obsessed with nurturing, and posturing with, the symbols of manhood (success with women, fighting prowess, and shrewd business acumen), strollers do not seem to manifest such a 'macho drive'.

All these differences highlight very particular methods of coping with conflict and authority. In the case of gangs a predominantly aggressive confrontational approach is favoured, whereas strollers tend to shy away from conflict and authority. This becomes apparent as we trace both their family and school experiences.

Family Composition and Emotional Support

An important similarity that emerges from our interviews in comparison with gang research is that strollers seem to come from the same types of family as the children who become gangsters, at least as far as family composition is concerned. Eighteen of the thirty-one strollers claimed to have suffered fundamental nuclear family upheaval at some stage of their early childhood. Two of the children reported that they were orphans, one stroller was part of a single-parent family, and four claimed that they lived with relatives while offering no explanation about their parental situation. A further eleven strollers said that they had lost one of their natural parents through death, desertion, or divorce, and had not established a successful relationship with their step-parents. Most of them claimed that the hostility of the step-parent had been an important factor in their decision to leave home. The proportion of children whose families have suffered some sort of upheaval is very similar to the number of gangsters found in the same situation in a 1984 study of Elsies River (Schärf 1984: 127-28). One of the strollers talked about his family situation:

> I had a stepfather, a nightwatchman, and I didn't like him. Every evening when I get home he gives me dirty looks. [*Elke aand as ek daa ko gie hy ve my vuil kyke.*] So I said to my ma, 'If he doesn't leave the house, I'll rather go so then I know there's peace at home'. Every evening we face each other with sour looks . . . . so I just buggered off.[8]

Of course, irregular or altered family structure does not necessarily create a situation in which the child wants to run away. It is the quality of the relationship, and of the care and loving guidance which the children receive, that is of crucial importance — whether they live with their natural parents or not. Many of the strollers who lived with their natural parents ran away because, they said, their parents had been too erratic and punitive. Very often either or both parents drank heavily.

> We [children] were just hit and kicked without reason, and I don't like that any more. My ma and pa fight nearly every night, then we also get hidings. I love my parents because I miss them, but I don't dig hidings any more. My dad invites his friends over and they smoke dagga and when they've left he kicks the door open and fights with us. Then he says to me, 'Come here, you son of a bitch'. Then I and my mother run out of the house and once we slept at other people's place.

Not all family disputes, however, end up with only the children leaving home. One of the girls, aged fifteen, has been on the streets for three years and strolls with her mother, who, on separating from her husband, could not find affordable accommodation close to the city. As former inhabitants of District Six, they refused to move to the Cape Flats but found accommodation in the back yard of a family living in the *Bo-Kaap* (Schotse Kloof). The girl told us:

> My mother and my brothers are strollers so they weren't surprised when
> I began strolling too. My mother and I stroll, and at night we sleep at
> the same spot. We don't have a house to go back to 'coz in Dorp Street I
> and my brothers sleep in people's yard in a shed and that's not what you
> can call a house.

In some cases we found children on the streets who did not
necessarily associate continuous conflict with their parents, but feared
that they would be punished for some transgression were they to
return home. For example, a girl strolling in Athlone, whose parents
live in Graaff-Reinet, was sent to Cape Town at the age of fourteen as
char and nursemaid to a middle-class Cape Flats family. She said that
she did not enjoy working for them ('Hulle het kak met my gewerk')
and so started strolling. Although she had been on the road for two
months, she claimed that her parents did not know that she had left
her employment. Nor did she know how to face them if they found
out and confronted her. It was something, she said, she would prefer
not to think about.

In other cases, African children ended up on the streets as a result of
the double disaster of parental separation and the loss of their house.
Two brothers, aged fourteen and twelve and living with their mother,
said that they had lost their house because, according to the law
governing Africans in Cape Town, the head of the household had to
be male.[9] They lived temporarily in a shed in a Guguletu backyard,
but were evicted from there as well. Their mother found some accommodation with friends, and the two brothers took to the road. Their
mother then remarried, and one of the boys returned home, worked as
a newsvendor, and contributed his earnings to the family. His relationship with his stepfather was not satisfactory, so he took to strolling
once again. By the time we interviewed him, he had been on the road
for eighteen months. One of the strollers, whose mother had died
when he was still an infant, was put into foster-care by his father. His
father took ill and died when the child was ten. The child did not
enjoy living with the foster-parents:

> . . . those people also drank a lot and I didn't like that. They fought so
> much at home. So I thought [to myself] I can't stay here, so I ran away
> from there [Elsies River] and came here [the city] to stroll.

There are, thus, a variety of circumstances relating to the parent-child, or rather adult-child relationship, which induce or occasion these children to run away. Initially we had theorized that it involved a very conscious rejection of the parents or family, but on closer scrutiny of the strollers' stories, most cases entailed escape in the sense of not facing up to or trying to solve their problems. In addition to these personal and personality traits, some broader, structural factors need to be taken into account.

It is clear from some of the above examples that the children who faced nuclear family upheavals had a limited support structure to soften their hardships. Some of them could not be accommodated with relatives but went to foster-parents. It could be argued that low-income families that live as extended family units are more likely to be able to serve as support groups in difficult times. This not only refers to financial and material support in times of unemployment, illness, separation, desertion, or even death, but also to psychological and emotional support. Furthermore, the extended family can mitigate the harshness of particular character deficiencies or idiosyncrasies of individual members. Moral guidance and a feeling of belonging is more likely to be generated in an environment where there are several concerned adults present. Pinnock (1982: 175-216) advanced this argument persuasively to explain the massive increase in street-gang membership when extended families were destroyed by Group Areas removals in the Western Cape. We suggest that the destruction of the extended family has also had an influence on the lives of those children at risk of becoming strollers.

Escape from School

In the great majority of cases, the thirty-one strollers not only experienced problems at home, but also had difficulties at school. Only four of them said that they had enjoyed their school experience. Significantly, they were the only ones who seem to have coped academically and passed all the annual examinations while they were there. When they left school at the ages of 12, 11, 11, and 14 they had passed standards two, three, two, and three respectively.[10] All the other children had experienced the humiliation of failing one year at least once. Fifteen said that they had failed two years, two strollers had failed three times, and three failed four years before dropping out of school entirely. On average their level of achievement at school was standard three, and they had achieved that by the average age of thirteen. Although these averages are informative, they conceal the whole range of different circumstances and levels of achievement. In tabulated form the spread over the twelve years of South African schooling becomes apparent:

Table 1: Strollers' Level of Schooling

Level of school passed	Number of strollers	Level of school passed	Number of strollers
Sub A	0	Std 5	6
Sub B	2	Std 6	0
Std 1	1	Std 7	0
Std 2	6	Std 8	1
Std 3	10	Std 9	0
Std 4	5	Std 10	0

During the interviews most of the strollers were very reluctant to speak about their school experiences, either because they felt guilty about having run away or because it was a painful area in their lives which they preferred not to talk about. This is also the subject on which they are questioned most frequently by pedestrians, policemen, social workers, shop assistants, and magistrates. We were frequently brushed off with one-liners such as 'school wasn't fun' or 'school became tough for me', or 'I didn't like going to school'. Repeated probing to gain better insights was to no avail in these cases. Some were prepared to talk and that revealed a little more.

> Well, I didn't want to go to school anymore, so my mother took me [forcefully] to the police station for them to give me a hiding. They did, and I ran away. I didn't enjoy school, I don't like school. The teacher, he wants to boss one around and use one as a messenger boy. [Die meneer daar binne wil 'n mens kom vetel en 'n mens vir posboytjies vat].

In many cases a disciplinary transgression was the catalyst which, through mishandling, resulted in a child fleeing from that environment. In some instances it was the collusion of the family and the school to discipline the children which inclined them to run away from both:

One morning I was stoned [literally 'smoked myself drunk' — on marijuana], and my friends, once we went to school and got into a fight at school in the classroom. So the teacher tried to stop us but we kept fighting. So they took us to the headmaster. We just ran out of the office and of the school. The next day my mother took me to school [forcibly] but they had expelled me.

Several strollers maintained that they were beaten at school and that they left school on account of that. The practice of caning students was confirmed by a number of former teachers:

One of the things I couldn't stand, were teachers beating children. That is another reason why they sometimes dropped out. They were experiencing the same type of life at home. At high school, the children know what their rights are regarding corporal punishment, whereas at primary school they think it's the teacher's right. Imagine coming to school and being beaten up and then going home and being beaten up again. You have to leave one or the other. So you leave school first. That is less difficult. (Former Primary School teacher, Retreat 'Another Street'.)

Children of working-class families on the Cape Flats arrive at school to face several problems. First, they have very seldom been fortunate enough to gain any pre-school care and education (Short 1984). Second, the state has not provided sufficient schools and facilities to accommodate them adequately (Pinnock 1980: 14; 1982: 350). Consequently the educational facilities are overcrowded and the environment for both work and play can be stifling rather than stimulating. Interviews with both principals and teachers confirm that schools frequently operate with more than twice as many pupils as intended.

Schools were very overcrowded in the 70s to the very early 80s — from 1974 onwards. I remember schools were overcrowded especially in 1974 and 1975. Our school was initially opened to cater for children from the immediate area, which was mostly shanties and most families were quite large, with eight or nine children. We also had children from Vrygrond [squatter area] coming to our school. It was actually built to cater for about 600 pupils, but then they had more than 1 000. I think at one time they had 1 300 pupils. (Primary School Principal, Retreat 'Another Street'.)

Third, conditions, especially the need to conduct double shifts, place great stress on teachers, who frequently resort to punitive methods to obtain discipline in the classroom. Shifts start at 8 a.m. and 2 p.m. and last for five hours. Fourth, high staff-student ratios result in very little individual guidance to help disadvantaged children ('Another Street').

Consequently, children are also educationally disadvantaged throughout their schooling, and for many of them school becomes a frightening and alienating experience. Particularly at risk are those children who have experienced emotional trauma and family disruption. In our observations of the strollers' responses to school and home, a common theme that surfaced was the inability to cope with conflict situations. In drifting out of school and away from home, the strollers distance themselves from the norms and values of the dominant society. Their response is essentially evasive, non-structured, and is not strategic in the long-term. Among the alternative values they choose for themselves, the two most important are the notions of unfettered freedom and individualism.

The Notion of Freedom

Many of the strollers have experienced control through harsh disciplinary means: they perceive adults as being punitive and authoritarian. By taking control of their own lives strollers imitate that which they see to be the status of adults. This perceived freedom from overt control is for strollers possibly the most important attribute of their adopted way of life.

The newly found freedom expresses itself as freedom from institutions, freedom of movement, freedom to choose activities and daily rhythms, and freedom from commitments. Their way of life is, however, not without its own constraints, such as those imposed by police activities, client relationships, and the physical constraints of the environment in which they choose to exist.

At the very least, strollers consider themselves freer than their contemporaries who have remained in formal socialization structures. They also consider themselves much freer than those children who work but hand over their earnings to their families. Central to their sense of freedom is a concept of fluid opportunism in which commitments to authority structures and authority figures are minimal. Strollers adopt different survival patterns as and when necessity or whim dictates.

They handle conflict most often by escaping from the situation. The escape can take a variety of forms. One of these is physical: they are fairly constantly on the move, keeping a very keen eye open for the police, who continually harass them. The children are vulnerable to arrest, as the definition of 'a child in need of care' is very broad and any such child may be arrested by the police pending an investigation. The definition is so wide that a stroller need not have committed any crime, but is simply, in the opinion of the policeman, without visible physical means of support.[11] Not every encounter with the police results in formal legal processing. Police use a variety of methods to keep the children out of the city. One is simply dumping them in the townships, combined with a threat of more serious action should the strollers return to the city centre. Another is partial processing through the legal channels: once arrested, the strollers are taken to state social workers who give them the alternative of returning home or facing a Children's Court enquiry, with a possible institutional placement as a consequence. Most strollers choose the former option, then run away from home and are back on the streets within a few days.[12] Strollers can also be arrested for one of the many public nuisance offences such as begging, spitting, being drunk or dirty, swearing, shouting and the like.[13] There is, too, the danger of being arrested for common law crime: for example, theft and shoplifting.

The more experienced strollers have equipped themselves and their fellows with a variety of both verbal and physical escape routes from almost any given situation. These entail, among other possibilities, developing the ability to distort the truth to meet the requirements of the most immediate threats. Adults attempting to ascertain the circumstances of strollers leaving home are frequently told exaggerated or patently untrue tales designed to provoke sympathy and elicit donations. The 'truth', by degrees, becomes a commodity 'sold', in a number of versions, to persons who are either a threat to the strollers, or potential buyers of their stories. Strollers' behaviour is extremely manipulative of adults. Manipulation becomes a survival skill of considerable importance in enabling them to remain full-time strollers and therefore free of the need to 'sink' into some form of semi-fixed employment such as newsvending.

Their sense of freedom and lack of commitment results in a relatively high level of physical mobility. This mobility is a response to particular pressures (such as the need to avoid police), opportunism (the need to be close to potential clients), and problems in personal relationships between strollers. Such problems arise whenever too many strollers try to survive off the same 'turf'. Usually disputes centre around encroachment into areas already regarded (by strollers) as the domain of a particular group.

Of the three hundred strollers, about forty survive in the Athlone-Gatesville (coloured) shopping areas, while up to forty of them live along seven kilometres of the (white) suburban Main Road in prosperous areas such as Mowbray, Rondebosch, Newlands, Claremont, and Wynberg. But by far the largest concentration of boys and girls is found in the central city area, occasionally moving around the mountain some four kilometres to the nearby seafront suburbs of Sea Point and further to Camps Bay. The population is never constant nor is it static. For example, strollers, whose usual 'beat' is Rondebosch, moved to the city centre:

> The cops picked us up in Rondebosch and took us to Mowbray station. There they buggered [beat] us up thoroughly. They wanted to take me home, but let us go at the station in Langa [a black township of Cape Town]. So we ran back this way, then we breezed over to Sea Point.

Holidays and market days pull strollers towards Sea Point and the city centre but the opening of Parliament finds them in Athlone evading the heightened police activity around their normal haunts. Those children apprehended by the police are either admitted to Bonnytoun (a place of detention for coloured children) or are sent to social workers in Bellville and are referred by them, through the Children's Courts, to various institutions or houses.[14]

One of the most consistently enthusiastic responses we elicited from the strollers was in answer to the question about what is so good about being on the streets. A typical statement was:

> On the streets it's easier [than at home] 'coz I'm my own boss. No-one can tell me what to do, and I can do what I like.

Similar statements from other strollers included references to freedom from going to school and the freedom to make and spend money as they liked. Closely related to their love of freedom is their inclination towards individualism.

The Trend Towards Individualism

Strollers primarily follow their own needs and motivations inasmuch as they attempt to minimize the extent to which they defer to authority. Yet at the same time the individualism is tempered by the realization that they are vulnerable and lonely on their own. It is, therefore, a contradictory notion which sometimes has to be temporarily abandoned when satisfaction of their needs requires unselfishness and cooperation with other strollers.

Their rejected families are supplanted by an extraordinarily supportive companionship system. Most strollers move around in groups of between four and six children. They continually reinforce each other in their survival activities, in their joys and fears, and in the majority of cases they share their earnings equally among themselves. The method of sharing depends on the dynamics of each group. Of the six groupings encountered in May 1985, three regularly pooled their money and each person was allocated his or her share. Each stroller could then spend the money as he or she chose. Two other groups gave all their earnings to the recognized group leader, who decided for the group how the money was to be spent. The amount of money spent on food under this arrangement for each stroller was, in principle, equal. The sixth group worked on a system of individual earning and spending.

Support is also offered in cases of illness. In Athlone, for example, a group of children negotiated with the cinema manager for the use of a room in the building so that an ailing stroller could lie and recover while the rest of the group tended to her. Some members of the group helped the manager with odd jobs to pay for the use of the room. In another incident a stroller who was knocked down by a car while he was 'immune' from danger (intoxicated from sniffing paint thinners and feeling very confident) was carried several hundred yards by his fellows to the nearest all-night café. The owner then summoned an ambulance for him.

The supportive framework (as in a family) extends from illness, economic requirements and shelter to the realm of enjoyment. Strollers spend their money on food and cigarettes, on playing video games at corner cafés or gaming rooms, watching movies, and getting 'high' on a variety of intoxicants. They seldom indulge in the intoxicants commonly consumed by adults, or even adult vagrants, such as liquor, dagga (marijuana), or 'blue train' (methylated spirits). Their favourite 'highs' are derived from sniffing glue, paint thinners, and sometimes benzine. In winter they tell us that they usually sniff petrol late at night to keep them 'glowing' through the cold and wet.

In one respect only is the loose and informal companionship arrangement replaced by a rigid social convention. Individual whims and actions may not threaten the existence of other strollers. 'Pimping' (telling) on fellow strollers is therefore taboo and brutally punished. For example, a newcomer to the streets, who had been strolling for only three weeks, 'pimped' on the rest of his group to the police about a housebreaking incident. He was very severely beaten by the group and ended up in hospital. According to the rest of the group, this hiding was simply part of teaching him the skills of the road — to protect his fellow strollers above all other allegiances.

As the inner city covers a relatively small area, most strollers know each other, at least by sight. Individuals are not necessarily bound to any single group but can, and do, change their friendship groups as frequently as they desire. Disagreements and personal animosities are seldom resolved through physical fights. It seems as if the overall mood is amiable enough for those who cannot agree simply to part company. A dissenting stroller will join another strolling group in which he or she may have acquaintances, or even friends. Again, their solution to clashes to with other strollers, as to most problems encountered, is to run away.

Alternative Patterns of Survival and Socialization

Having escaped from survival and socialization patterns which were painful and onerous, the strollers attempt to live a life commensurate with their needs. Food, warmth, safety, companionship, fun and intoxicants are the main requirements of this lifestyle. Strollers develop a whole range of survival skills by which they procure their needs.

Operating procedure is determined by the area in which they are working and the most likely means of getting money from adults in that area. The most common skill is begging (aanklop). The smallest or most pitiful-looking urchins, who can loosen the heart- and pursestrings of the city's pedestrians, specialize in begging. Quite frequently they construct a story of woe and desolation for additional effect. If there is a young girl among them, she may do the begging on behalf of the group.

Living on the streets does not automatically imply that the girls are promiscuous. A mother who strolls with her two daughters has a secret sleeping place where a 'girls-only' group of six sleep. The mother also keeps a watchful eye on the girls all day long. Several of the girls interviewed said they would rather starve than prostitute themselves. They survive mainly by begging on the streets, and pool the proceeds. After deducting enough to purchase the evening meal, the mother hands out a little money to each of the children to spend as they wish.

After dark, when the city is relatively deserted, begging takes on a different form and name. The strollers move into the nearest suburbs (mainly to Greenpoint, Three Anchor Bay, Sea Point, and the Gardens/Vredehoek area) for what they call 'bomming' (perhaps a derivative of 'bumming' — pronounced the Afrikaans way). This is simply door to door begging, which differs from 'aanklop' in that they frequently beg for clothing as well as food or money. As soon as they have obtained enough for their immediate needs, the begging or 'bomming' stops and they move to a place where they can enjoy themselves by 'cooling off' ('afkoel').

A typical sequence of many such events we have observed took the following course: a group of four boys and a girl whose ages were eleven, thirteen, fourteen, fourteen, and sixteen. drifted from city centre to Green Point and, as they walked along, begged from pedestrians. Their success rate varied but the girl managed to procure the highest number of donations. The story she told them ('die kaart wat ek geskiet het', translatable as 'the line I spun them') was that she was hungry and cold and wanted to go home. When asked where she lived, she replied with her parents but that they did not have enough food for the family so she was obliged to come to town to beg for food. If the potential donor ventured further than that and wanted to know why she was not at school, her reply was that her parents did not have enough money for her uniform. Usually that elicited a donation. The boys, on the other hand, faced more intensive questioning and had a lower success rate. On average one in eight pedestrians stopped and listened to them, and of those an average of one in six donated some money to them. By the time they reached the residential areas they had collected R3.80 between them. There they chose a street of houses, split up, and told their stories. Within an hour they had collected some old clothing, some left-over food, some bread, and another R8.32. With this they headed for the shops and bought some bread and cool-drinks. They scrounged around the dustbins for some 'pinies' (plastic fruit-juice containers), soaked a piece of rag in some paint thinners which they had brought with them in a bottle, and after eating, sniffed away at their 'pinies'. Within a short while they became giggly, and joked and jostled around, sniffing as they went. Two of the boys drifted off to sit down and sniff at their 'pinies', while the others continued to frolic and giggle. The two who had isolated themselves became more serious and stared with fairly glazed eyes down at the top of the low wooden fencing poles in front of them. One described what he saw:

> Every time I take a long sniff [of my 'pinie'], such a long drag, Mister, then they come out [the year-rings of the poles telescope out], see Mister. So, the other day S and I were alone here, so the poles dropped, they dropped, see Mister. But, umm, now, I don't know what's going on with them, they're wasting my [sniffing] breath, see Mister. [Maar, mm, nou, ek witie wat gat aan saam met hulle, hulle mors my asem, sien Meneer.] Now they don't want to come out again, I talk [through my 'pinie'] to them, to them, but they don' wanna come out.

His companion had a slightly different experience, which he described as it happened:

> . . . look at the magic that the poles, that I'm gonna do. They weren't like this yet, then the poles were, nearly like, like ordinary poles, see Mister. Jaaa, so I say to them, 'look at the magic', when I looked again they were all like they're now, like this one [moving telescopically], sooo, like soooo . . . . So I told S, they're a . . . all, [coughs] they're all robots these things, they are controoollled, these things . . . .
>
> *Researcher:* Where are they controlled from?
>
> They're standing over there [the controllers], see Mister [points to a building across the road].

A skill closely related to begging is 'parking' — that is, directing motorists to vacant spaces in parking lots. Here territoriality is a limiting factor as there are only two parking lots in central Cape Town that lend themselves to this form of income generation.[15] In the suburbs close to the big shopping complexes there is great scope for 'parking' and approximately sixty strollers operate there. In rare cases where parking lots adjoin accessible water supplies, some of the strollers attempt to earn money by washing cars. From time to time, as their whims dictate, some strollers also resort to pushing trolleys for shoppers at supermarkets, and various other odd jobs.

The most lucrative skill which the children acquire exposes them to a pattern of behaviour that is both unusual in terms of their upbringing and deviant from mainstream moral values. All but four of the twenty-eight male strollers indicated that they had derived part of their income from prostitution at some stage of their strolling careers. In June 1984, when we started gathering information about strollers, there was a lot more talk among the boys about catching 'bunnies' (white men) and 'sugarmummies' (white women) than occurred a year later. This is partially attributable to the international AIDS scare, which started filtering through to South Africa in April 1985, when it received considerable media coverage. Between February and May 1985 seven of the twenty-eight boys still said they earned most of their money from prostitution with males, while three claimed that female clients were their major source of income.

Each of these survival techniques involves the strollers in some communication with adults. Both the strollers and the adults enter the communication with a particular image of one another. This, on the part of the adults, may be a preconceived notion as to what these children should be or should become. When children beg, the most common stance taken by adults is either one of pity, mingled with disapproval and embarrassment (our observations), or outright hostility. When the adults show pity, it is often combined with recommendations that the strollers change their ways, reform their habits, and revert to conventional socialization patterns. The message, which the strollers reject, is similar to the one that they used to receive from most adults, certainly from their teachers, if not also from their parents. In order to elicit donations from adults, the strollers feign obedience and agreement, often phrasing the begging plea as if it were the first step in a process of voluntary rehabilitation ('I need money for train fare to my [distant] home').

Although strollers become adept at ignoring the image of them which adults hold, it is unlikely that they can ignore such attitudes altogether. Strollers, like others, form images of themselves in relation to the rest of society and it is probable that a residue of the adult images communicated to them will become embedded in their own images of themselves. As Dallos and Sapsford (1981: 448) have argued:

. . . the 'self' develops as a process not only as the person's experience of
the actions of others but also of the person's experience of the other's
experience of them.

The adults' attitudes towards strollers are usually conditioned by
the images which state agencies use to portray strollers. In the vast
majority of cases, the police adopt a punitive attitude, attempting by
means of threats of violence or actual violence to chase the children
out of the city.[16] The magistrates, social workers and staff at the cor-
rective institutions, in the opinion of most strollers, reiterate the image
of the children as deviant and unworthy of approval. The only adult
group which generates partially approving images of the strollers are
the clients who purchase their sexual services. The need to perform
effectively to the clients' satisfaction imbues the strollers with a sense
of manhood which they perceive to be both flattering and edifying.
This is particularly significant in view of the fact that virtually the only
approval given to strollers comes in a very problematic area of their
lives — their sexuality. Many of the strollers we have interviewed expressed ambivalence about prostituting themselves to males.

One noticeable contradiction in the strollers' images of themselves is
that their expectations of the future coincide with conventional
working-class expectations. With only three exceptions, all strollers
interviewed intended to raise families in the conventional manner and
hoped to occupy houses. All of the twenty-eight were adamant that
their children should not become strollers. When asked how they
intended to prevent that from happening, they either proposed the use
of violent discipline or material comforts. They had no realistic plans
for achieving their ambitions. The types of jobs they wished to hold as
adults were usually out of their reach, considering their low level of
education. Only eight of the thirty-one strollers mentioned unskilled
employment as their goal. The others wished to be traffic police,
bricklayers, signwriters, lorry drivers, and, most frequently,
policemen. The five girls expressed hopes of becoming nurses, factory
workers, and one wanted to be a magistrate. While the wish to
become a policeman or a magistrate initially seems contradictory, it
should be borne in mind that these are the people with power with
whom they most frequently come into contact. They were also fairly
unrealistic in assessing their prospects of fitting into hierarchies, considering that they had manifested a low ability to cope with authority
thus far in their lives.

Thus, despite the fact that strollers appropriate important values and practices to themselves by constructing their own world of meaning in a predominantly hostile environment, they also carry with them some of the values and norms inherited from their earlier phase of socialization. If they so wish, these values and norms can be revived.

Conclusion

We have attempted to demonstrate that the move towards becoming strollers is the product of a complex overlap of structural and personal factors. All of Cape Town's strollers come from the structurally disadvantaged African and coloured communities, particularly from the poorer sections of these communities. It is a glaring demonstration of the considerable material and educational inequalities in South Africa that no white strollers are to be found in the whole of Cape Town.

Part of the explanation may well be that the African and coloured communities are by law confined to low-cost housing settlements with insufficient public and recreational amenities in most cases. They are also subjected to inferior education where poorly equipped schools are staffed by predominantly poorly qualified teachers, who have to cope with exceedingly high teacher-pupil ratios. It is not at all surprising that under such circumstances teachers resort to punitive measures, including violence, to retain control of their classes.

We have also endeavoured to convey that the move into strolling was not necessarily a sudden one. It was more usually the culmination of a series of problematic processes for the children. Notable among these was a poor relationship to the male parent or step-parent. That relationship too, as in the case of schooling, was characterized by a punitive approach to the children, which frequently included violence. It needs also to be remembered that the strollers are children who, in most cases, had considerable difficulties in coping with the learning process and had, more often than not, failed at least one if not several years at school. Thus some particularly traumatic event which contained a punitive element from both parents and school may have constituted the final push into the strolling lifestyle. Strollers broke or drifted away from, or as some of them saw it, were pushed out of, the two primary institutions of conventional socialization.

Once on the streets their lives were restructured by their survival needs and their leisure pursuits. Moving in loose-knit, mutually supportive groups that are characterized by an egalitarian ethic, the strollers attempt to win for themselves that which their previous lifestyle had denied them: freedom, money, and pleasure. Yet this mode of survival, while creating for them a value system unique to their world and satisfying many of their needs and short-term aspirations, brings them into conflict with the dominant culture. The adult world and the enforcers of its norms — the police — tolerate strollers only when it suits their own needs. When this is not the case, the strollers are again subjected to punitive and often violent treatment by the state and its correctional and welfare institutions. The children thus live through the strolling phase of their lives with contradictory images of themselves. One image, their own, is of hedonistic enjoyment and shrewd manipulation. The other image is of themselves as unwanted deviants. From our observations these contradictions are sustained in the minds of the children throughout their strolling phase.

It is important to emphasize that strolling apparently constitutes only a phase in the lives of the children. This is one of the most surprising discoveries of our research, as we had often assumed that the adult vagrants on the streets of Cape Town were older versions of the strollers. But in reality we found hardly any strollers in their mid-twenties. Whether they had joined the labour force, been imprisoned, died of ill-health as a result of their lifestyle and habits, or established a niche for themselves in the informal sector, is not clear at this stage of our investigation. As far as we could ascertain, hardly any of the numerous adult vagrants in the Cape used to be strollers when they were young.[17] However, while strolling may be only a phase, it is a fairly long phase for some.[18]

This discovery poses the dominant culture with two alternatives. Given that the children have conventional expectations for the future and that strolling is only a phase, the first possibility is to allow them to live through the phase. The difficulty with this approach is that it undermines the effects of conventional socialization in preparing children for their role in the labour force. Yet it can be argued, on the basis of the present pattern of employment, that these children would in any case probably have been candidates for the reserve labour force, and in all likelihood would have ended up in the informal sector anyhow.

The second approach, the common one, is interventionist in nature. The children are forcibly removed from the streets and subjected to 'placements' which vary in degree from welfarist to punitive. The purported aim in terms of the dominant ideology is 'rehabilitation'. This approach emphasizes the symptoms of the problem rather than its causes. The individual 'pathologies' of the children are supposedly addressed while leaving the conditions which generated their situation untouched.

Until both structural and personal factors are tackled in a meaningful manner, our society will continue to generate a disturbingly large population of children who cannot cope with existing modes of socialization. Further, the educational crisis of 1985 and the State of Emergency in Cape Town drastically increased the strolling population. By December 1985 a count of strollers indicated a 100 per cent increase in their numbers since May, bringing the figure to some six hundred. At the time of writing it seems probable that, until the grievances underlying the recurrent educational crises in African and coloured schools are resolved, there will be further periodic surges in the number of children living and sleeping on the streets of Cape Town.

Notes

1. The authors gratefully acknowledge the contributions of Christine Glover, Mike Maughan-Brown, Professor van Zyl Smit, and Associate Professor Davis to this chapter. Their ideas, comments, and constructive criticism have been extremely helpful to us.
2. The only work on strollers in Cape Town to date is a documented photographic exhibition entitled 'Another Street'. It was researched and presented by three photographers who belong to the Community Arts Project (CAP): Jenny Altschuler, Costa Christie, and Pam Warne. It was exhibited at St George's Cathedral in Cape Town during 1984, at UCT during 1985, and it has also been exhibited in Johannesburg. It includes interviews with parents, teachers, social workers, police, detectives, newspaper van drivers and, of course, strollers.
3. We intend, as part of an extensive research project, to interview one hundred strollers, and have thus far completed thirty-one in-depth interviews. Some details about the strollers' school achievements are contained in Table 1. Uncompleted interviews with a further fourteen strollers are still in progress and we have begun our pre-interview contacts with, and observations of, another seventeen. All interviews with the children were conducted in their daily haunts — the streets, their sleeping places, and their favourite sniffing hideouts. The interviews were done at various times of day and night, during the week and over weekends, in an attempt to explore their entire range of activities,

movements and moods. In most cases we first followed and observed the small groups of children without communicating with them. Thereafter pre-interview contact was established in order to minimize suspicion. The duration of this phase varied from a few days to two weeks, depending on the circumstances and mood of each strolling group. As soon as they indicated their willingness to talk to us, three or four and sometimes six separate interview sessions were held. Each session lasted between 30 minutes and two hours, depending on the stroller's ability to concentrate, the degree of extraneous interruptions, and the level of police harassment. The children spoke whatever language they knew best, and every attempt has been made not to inhibit their special strolling-slang. All interviews were taped and then transferred onto a 120-question interview schedule. From the outset we were aware that typed questionnaires would intimidate these children, whose experience of the official side of life had been, in most cases, an unhappy one. Key areas of the 120-question schedule were memorized by the interviewers, and administered in a flexible manner, depending on the child's particular response. Edgar Thomas, who had been a house-father at one of the stroller-shelters for a year, did most of the interviewing.

4. Jane Keen of Child Life, has been a central figure in establishing and running the two existing shelters in Cape Town, The Homestead and The Activity Centre. House-fathers John Fortune and Desmond Lombard taught us a lot about the boys (there are no shelters for girls). Edgar Thomas, needless to say, enriched our understanding considerably and steered us away from many blind alleys.

5. We object in principle to the use of racial categories, but as the law treats different communities in different ways. their responses are likely to differ. Influx control and the Coloured Labour Preference Area Policy have had a distinct influence on the number of strollers in greater Cape Town. African youths who are not in any recognizable employment (usually newsvending) in the inner city are policed more strenuously than coloured children (our observations). Whereas in 1984 the racial composition of the strolling population was 60 per cent African and 40 per cent coloured, a change occurred in 1985 so that 70 per cent are now coloured and 30 per cent African.

6. The reason for this otherwise uncharacteristic overlap of gangsterdom and strollerhood is that their leader did time in a reformatory, where he followed the near inevitable path of joining one of the three gangs that 'rule' those institutions (Pinnock 1982: 220-62; Berkowitz 1984; Chisholm 1985). After being 'reformed' he chose to survive off the streets in Cape Town and soon gathered around him a number of strollers whom he impressed with his man-talk and bravado, the mystique

of gang existence, the cosiness of belonging, and the sense of gang/male power. But despite the rhetoric and ritual of the Young Scorpion Kids, they do not indulge in survival strategies characteristic of Cape Town's street gangs. Whereas the gangs usually market illegal goods (such as liquor, drugs, stolen articles), or specialize in protection or housebreaking, the 'Y$K's' (sic) survive predominantly from begging, a little shoplifting, and bag-snatching. Occasionally they will also do a stint of 'broking' (selling) newspapers or exploiting the hospitality of charitable institutions which provide shelter, food, and care. In their case the gang-name is little more than a label for their support group, which has some quasi-gang characteristics such as a clearly identified leader and a lot of rhetoric and jargon.

7. We are not, of course, suggesting that gangs are a feature only of capitalist systems. They potentially exist in every economic system in which black market activities are likely to occur.

8. All quotes by strollers were originally in Afrikaans.

9. This was the reason given by the boys. The information is, however, inaccurate, as Administration Board practice changed some years ago, enabling a woman to have the house registered in her name in the event of death or divorce, subject to certain conditions. Among these conditions are that the wife gets custody of the children and that, by the time the issue is decided, the husband does not have dependants legally living with him, such as a new wife.

10. Education for coloured children became compulsory only in 1981 in response to scholars' demands for equal education during the 1980 schools boycott. Compulsory education has been introduced for Africans only in schools where school committees have requested it. Under 'normal circumstances' children are meant to start school when aged six, except for African children, who are supposed to begin school at the age of seven. In the South African schooling system Standard 3 represents the fifth year of schooling.

11. Section 1(1) of the Children's Act, No. 33 of 1960 (as amended) defines 'a child in need of care'. Among many other attributes he or she is a child who:

   (a)   has been abandoned or is without visible means of support; or . . .

   (e)   is an habitual truant; or . . .

   (g)(i) begs . . . .

This Act is to be replaced by the Child Care Act, No. 74 of 1983. At the time of writing it was not yet in operation. The latter Act, at least in form, purports to shift the emphasis of the enquiry away from what the child is, or is doing, and emphasizes what its parents or responsible adults have done, or failed to do, for or to the child (Section 14). The definition of 'a child in need of care' falls away in terms of the 1983 Act.

In reality however, the Children's Court would first need to inquire what the child is, or is doing — that is, what the child has turned out to be — before it can investigate what actions or neglect on the part of the responsible adults contributed to such a state of affairs (McLachlan 1983: 2-4).

12. Interview with social worker (Department of the Interior, Own Affairs) and our own observations.

13. A useful summary of the main public nuisance offences in Cape Town is contained in the Annexure of the 1974 NICRO publication, *Vagrancy: A Limited Study of Vagrants in the Metropolitan Area of Cape Town.*

14. Information obtained from an interview with a social worker at the Department of Internal Affairs, Wynberg, through whom all coloured strollers picked up by the police are 'processed'.

15. Many of the municipal or free enterprise parking lots employ attendants who do not tolerate strollers interfering in their work space.

16. Most of the strollers interviewed have related incidents of police violence against them at some stage of their careers. This takes the form, according to their accounts, of assaults, by means of fists, batons, hose-pipes, leather straps from batons, belts, and boots. Some claim to have had their paint thinners thrown into their faces, while another group told of being locked in a police van and being sprayed with teargas. Two groups claimed to have been teargassed in their sleeping places by the police, and then forcefully prevented from escaping ('Another Street' and our interviews). One of the strollers told us about his 'aeroplane' experience at the police station:

> Sometimes they let us fly the 'aeroplanes'. There's a long table and they grab you by the scruff of your neck then they say: 'Onto the table, like that' [so oppie tafel], [gesticulates lying on belly]. Then there's a wall, and they throw you hard, and you sail [along the table]. Now, you can't protect yourself and hold onto anything. And when you've crashed [into the wall] you can end up being unconscious.

There are, however, exceptions to the rule. One police officer, who knew about the night-shelters, established a habit of contacting the house-parents, in the case of children living there, once they had been brought into the police station on charges of loitering or other petty crimes. By May 1985, however, only thirty of the over three hundred strollers in Cape Town could be accommodated in the shelters.

17. Interview with Brian Francis (April 1985), social worker with many years' experience in running night shelters and workshops for adult vagrants. Most adult vagrants leave home in their mid-thirties to early forties as a result of relationship breakdown compounded by financial difficulties, and often accompanied by job loss and drinking problems.

(This is confirmed by a random sample of adult vagrants we interviewed on the street.)

18. The time the children have spent on the street ranged from two weeks to twelve years. Of thirty-one children, nine had lived as strollers for less than six months, four had done so for between six months and a year, twelve had been strollers for between one and three years, one for four years, one for five, three for six years, and one for twelve years (our interviews).

Children's Use of Language in District Six

Kay McCormick

Mr A. If you want to become middle-class you speak English. You bring up your kids in English.

Mr N. I've got another friend who's just as much anti-South African government as I am but he likes the Afrikaans language. I can't agree with him there because I find whenever I speak it it reminds me of something bad and that's going to stay with me. Some- thing drastic would have to happen to make me change my mind.

Interviewer. So you don't like the Afrikaans language?

Mr N. No, but I have to speak it here because everybody else speaks it and I would feel sort of — how can I put it — people would think I'm some sort of show off if I speak English *now* and all the years I've been speaking Afrikaans. It's only with particular friends that I speak English. But I would prefer to speak English.

Interviewer. In this neighbourhood what would happen if a person suddenly started speaking *suiwer* [pure] English or Afrikaans?

Mr E. For one thing I think the person himself will feel quite awkward. People would look at him strange, you know. They'd straight away identify that there is something wrong with the person's speech and he will automatically try to rectify it and try to join in. I think that is why people mix their language also, you know.

In the Cape Town neighbourhood from which these speakers come many children face conflicting demands in the development of their language loyalty and skills. South Africa's two official languages, English and Afrikaans, have different symbolic values for this speech community and are seen to have different pragmatic advantages.[1] The school system demands competence in the standard dialects of both languages but there is community pressure on residents not to use them in informal interaction.[2]

This study is part of a larger sociolinguistic project which I began in 1981. The chief focus of the project is the analysis of certain linguistic features of language and dialect switching in District Six, Cape Town.[3] The analysis is set in the context of an account of the speakers' shared attitudes towards the two languages. The material for this chapter forms part of that context and deals with the relationship between language preferences exercised by and on behalf of children and factors which shape the positions of residents in their community and in the wider South African society. These factors include: the demands of good neighbourly relations, social class position and aspirations, stereotyping of linguistic or ethnic groups, actual and desired level of education, response to laws defining population groups and the related restrictions.[4]

The Speech Community

Factors which make the District Six speech community particularly suitable for a study of the kind I have undertaken are its size — there are 220 homes; its relatively long history of English-Afrikaans bilingualism which, as far as I can reconstruct it, goes back about a hundred years; and the fact that it is fairly clearly defined geographically, largely as a result of the implementation of the Group Areas Act, No. 41 of 1950.[5] And lastly, as will become clear later, there are strong social ties within the community which tend to strengthen the sociolinguistic norms for language use (Milroy 1980).

The people whose language I am studying live in District Six, an area which was formerly called 'Kanaladorp'.[6] Its earliest appearance on city maps is 1818. It is adjacent to the central business district and near many factories. Most of District Six has now been depopulated but before removals began it was a densely populated area. By the middle of this century approximately 33 000 people lived there. In addition to the houses and flats there were numerous shops, a cinema, three mosques, four synagogues, sixteen churches, seventeen schools, a training college, and four community centres. It was a very cosmopolitan area. However, in terms of the Population Registration

Act proclaimed in 1950 and its 1967 amendment, the majority of District Six residents found themselves classified as belonging to the group known as 'coloured', a group that has been described as 'the most heterogeneous component of the South African Population' (Theron Commission 1976: 463).[7]

Classified as 'coloured', most residents lost the right to live in District Six because in 1966 the greater part of it was proclaimed a 'white' area, under the provisions of the Group Areas Act. Over the next seventeen years approximately 31 000 people were evicted and sent to live in areas designated for coloureds, many of which were a long distance away (Centre for Intergroup Studies 1980: 2). Almost all the buildings, apart from the mosques and consecrated churches, were demolished. A small area, separated from the rest by a freeway, was declared an industrial area with no explicit race classification restrictions as to who could live in the houses that were scattered among factories and warehouses. These are the homes of the community whose language I am studying.

The neighbourhood community is a fairly cohesive one. Many families have lived there for four generations, attending the same schools, often working in the same factories, and sharing leisure time. A great deal of socializing takes place on streets and pavements but there is also a well-used community centre. The two largest religious groups are Christians of the Anglican denomination, and Muslims. Within those groups religious faith and the activities centred on the churches and mosques provide further bonds. (For a detailed account of bonds and divisions in District Six, see Ridd 1981.)

It is clear from my interviews that the people who live in this area have, and value, a sense of being a community. The value they put upon it affects children's language use. As I shall show in this chapter, children who at school acquire a language or dialect with higher prestige than the one spoken at home are under pressure to continue using the local vernacular in general neighbourhood interaction.

The people whose speech I have recorded speak English and Afrikaans, but vary in the extent to which they are fluent in both languages. Informal daily discourse is characterized by a high degree of code-switching, both situational and conversational. Situational code-switching refers to language or dialect alternation that is governed by change of topic, participants or situation. Conversational code-switching refers to alternation that occurs within a single conversation — often within a single sentence — even when topic, participants, and situation remain constant. Code-switching may or may not be a result of conscious choice. Some speakers switch in order to achieve a particular effect in discourse, others do so at points in conversation where they feel that they need to draw on vocabulary in the other language. Some people who are able to speak standard English and standard Afrikaans habitually code-switch in informal interaction with neighbours. Non-standard Afrikaans and code-switching, which I shall subsume under the term 'vernacular', constitute the norm in informal discourse. The use of either of the standard dialects would be seen as a deliberate choice that signalled distance.

Research Method

The study focusses on linguistic features of conversation in which code-switching occurs. People tend to avoid code-switching in formal discourse. For this reason, though some samples of formal speech are necessary for comparative purposes, my prime need was for recordings of informal speech obtained in various ways from a variety of speakers. For this kind of linguistic analysis a very large sample of speakers is not required, particularly if the speech community is cohesive (Milroy 1980). The chance of obtaining natural speech is increased if people are interviewed in the presence of close friends or family members, or if the interviewer is a member of the speech community. This consideration affected the way in which interviews were conducted, as I hoped to gain from them not only information but also samples of informal speech.

Interviews were my chief source of information concerning the way speakers saw their own linguistic repertoire and their preference for one language or dialect rather than another for particular purposes. In order to discover productive lines of enquiry I conducted a pilot study over a period of eighteen months among people who came from similar speech communities.[8]

The District Six interviews were conducted in people's homes. Sometimes other family members and neighbours came in during an interview and participated by challenging or confirming what the interviewee was saying. The disadvantage of this was that it was not always possible to ensure that the person being interviewed responded to all of the questions himself or herself, but the advantages were that more opinions were expressed and the language was very informal.

The interview was not rigidly structured as to sequence of questions or amount of time spent on each. People were encouraged to elaborate on topics that interested them. As a result they often moved on to new topics. When that happened, the interviewer kept a record of which questions had been touched on and, towards the end of the interview, returned to those that had not.

These interviews were conducted by six people, including myself. The other five had all either lived in the area or been to school there and were able to code-switch with ease. Interviews were conducted in whichever language(s) the interviewee chose. Seventeen per cent of the houses have been covered by interviews to date.

There are aspects of linguistic behaviour of which speakers are often unaware. In order to capture some of these I relied on observation, both my own and that of one of the interviewers who lived in the area. The observation covered community functions such as bazaars, concerts, and meetings. I also participated in and observed classroom and playground activities at the local nursery school over a period of almost four years from April 1981 to November 1984. For the first seven months I spent one morning each week with the children, and thereafter I visited the school approximately once every five weeks. Between March and December 1984 I paid twenty visits to the dual-medium primary school, where I observed English and Afrikaans oral lessons in nine classes. In addition I interviewed seven teachers about pupils' linguistic and academic difficulties and strengths which might be attributable in part to the kind of code-switching that is prevalent in the neighbourhood.

In order to check generalizations that some primary school children had made about the linguistic homogeneity of friendship groups, I drew up diagrams of friendship networks. Each child was asked whom he or she played with after school or on weekends. If I did not know the children mentioned, I asked whether they were in the English or Afrikaans 'stream' (children are 'streamed' into a linguistic group and instruction in all subjects is given in that language), or whether they were at the local Muslim primary school (where the medium of instruction is Afrikaans). After each child had given all the names of friends who came to mind, I went through a list of children whom I knew the child would have known at nursery school and who lived nearby, and asked whether he or she played with any of them. On the basis of the information offered and elicited in this way, the friendship networks were plotted.

Images and Values Associated with Language by Adults in District Six

Before moving on to the section of the paper dealing with language choices for children, I wish to provide a context for them by summarizing what District Six adults said about the images and values commonly associated with English and Afrikaans. The associations that adults form influence children's preferences and the choices made for them by their parents. Linguistic choice may convey complex information about the speaker's actual or desired position on a number of parameters such as regional background, social class, and political or religious affiliation.

The people interviewed were always quick to assert that the Afrikaans they use is different from *suiwer* (pure / standard) Afrikaans. The local dialect of Afrikaans is referred to pejoratively as 'broken Afrikaans', 'not proper Afrikaans', '*kombuistaal*' (kitchen language). People have mixed feelings about it. They think that outside the speech community it evokes stereotypes of fecklessness, laziness, lack of education, and poverty. Within the community, however, it is the language of intimacy.[9] It is described as 'warm', whereas English is seen as 'cold' and 'intellectual'. *Kombuistaal* has many loan-words from English and other languages, thus facilitating code-switching, a practice about which people feel ambivalent. On the one hand they think it is bad to mix languages, but on the other hand, not to mix them is seen as a sign of distancing oneself from the local community.

In this speech community standard Afrikaans has different connotations. Several people indicated that if they were to hear a coloured person speaking standard Afrikaans they would make one of two assumptions: either that this was an unsophisticated country person, or that he or she was pro-government. The first assumption is based on the knowledge that Afrikaans is the language of most rural coloured people.[10] The second rests on the link between Afrikaner nationalism and institutionalized apartheid. Standard Afrikaans is often called 'the language of the oppressor'. A few people commented wryly or angrily on the process by which the language their ancestors had helped to develop had been appropriated by whites. Only two of the fourteen people who classified themselves as Afrikaans-speaking professed undivided, uncomplicated love of Afrikaans. For all the others and for the English-speaking subjects, Afrikaans was tainted by its association with the enforcement of apartheid legislation.[11]

Interviews showed that people had a very strong sense that there are two dialects of Afrikaans spoken locally but there was no suggestion that the same holds true for English. The English language is associated with city life, good education, good work opportunities, middle-class life-style and access to the world outside South Africa. (For an account of similar perceptions of English, see Ridd 1981: 197.) Not all of the associations with English are positive, however. A few people who revealed some awareness of class oppression had a somewhat tarnished image of English because they saw it as connected with middle-class power and privilege. It is often adopted by people aspiring to middle-class status.

There was also a time when English was adopted by people hoping to gain the rights and status that went with being classified as white. Between 1950 and 1967 official classification as white depended, *inter alia*, on acceptance by whites as white. During that period presenting oneself as English was part of 'trying for white' (Ridd 1981: 226). In 1967, however, the Population Registration Act, No.30 of 1950 was amended to make racial classification of the father the determining criterion. Today's District Six children would, therefore, have had little direct experience of English as a weapon in the race classification battle, though parents remember that use quite clearly. The interview sheet did not contain a question on this topic, but in some interviews there were unsolicited comments on the connection between speaking English and being seen as white. One woman reported that when her family moved to District Six in the 1950s, she and her brothers and sisters were teased by the other children for seeming to be posing:

Ms B.   We came from an English-speaking home. When we first came here the children used to laugh and say in Afrikaans, 'Huh! *Wat dink hulle hulle's wit? Waar kom hulle vandaan?'* [What do they think they are? White? Where do they come from?] You know, things like that.

Int.   Why? Because you spoke English?

Ms B.   Because we spoke English.

A mother who had brought up her older children in Afrikaans said that the youngest one would be brought up in English. When asked why, she made no mention of the father's home language, but said simply, '*his* father is white'.

The confident use of English is seen as a challenge to whites who are thought to stereotype coloureds as uneducated, unsophisticated, and working class:

> *Mr N.*   I feel so good if a white man can't speak English and I as a black man come to them and speak English and I feel more superior to them because they regard us — anybody who speaks English — as superior to them. That is definite.

> *Ms S.*   If I speak to a coloured I speak Afrikaans. And if I come across a native [African] and he can speak Afrikaans I speak to him in Afrikaans. If I come across a white I like to speak English because most of them don't like it.

It is felt that those whites who 'don't like it' take it as a sign that coloureds are leaving their 'proper place' in society if they speak English, because English is seen as a marker of upward social mobility.

Language Choices for Children

The linguistic milieu provided by the neighbourhood at large does not encourage children to think of themselves as 'English' or 'Afrikaans'. People had difficulty answering the question, 'Would you describe this as an English-speaking or Afrikaans-speaking neighbourhood?' One reason is that the dominant language of the older residents is Afrikaans while that of the younger ones is English.[12] Another reason is that local social norms seem to rule out the speaking of both *suiwer* Afrikaans and pure English in day-to-day encounters:

> *Mr M.*   *Van kleins af praat ons Engels in die huis maar wanneer ons meer buite gaan gebruik ons meer Afrikaans met vriende.* [From the time we were small we spoke English at home but when we spent more time outside the home we spoke more Afrikaans with friends.]

> *Ms T.*   I sort of notice among your own clique you don't speak Afrikaans straight or English straight . . . . I think basically people use it [mixing] for convenience you know. And it is true if you speak Afrikaans — complete Afrikaans, *suiwer* Afrikaans — people won't understand you but if you use an English word inbetween — an Afrikaans word in an English context — they almost seem to understand you better.

It is clear from these comments that code-switching contributes to the maintenance of good neighbourly relations. There is little social division along language lines among adults.

All the people interviewed who had young children or who planned to have children in the near future stated that English was the preferred language for bringing up children. Even people who said that they usually spoke Afrikaans to each other and that they were not very competent in English, concurred. Typical explanations follow:

Ms W.   *Ek het niks* against *Afrikaans nie. Kyk, ek wil nie hê dat my kinders moet wees soos ek nie. Ek wil hê dat hulle beter is as ek. Reg?* [I have nothing against Afrikaans. Look, I don't want my children to be like me. I want them to be better than me. Right?]

Ms D.   *Ek sal die kinders in Engels opbring. Afrikaans is baie swaar. Engels is baie meer gemaklik.* [I'll bring the children up in English. Afrikaans is very difficult. English is much easier.]

Mr P.   *By* university *sal hulle beter Engelse woorde dan Afrikaanse woorde verstaan.* [At university they would understand English words better than Afrikaans ones.]

Mr M.   English, they must talk English. English is a nice language, man. English is *sommer* [simply] grand, a medium of exchange better than Afrikaans.

Ms W.   *Afrikaans is 'n taal, is 'n huistaal by ons maar Engels is — ek dink Engels tel meerder. As jy nie Engels kan praat dan kry jy nie maklik werk nie. Engels is 'n beter taal as Afrikaans.* [Afrikaans is a language, a home language for us, but English is — I think English counts more. If you can't speak English it's not easy to get work. I think English is a better language than Afrikaans.]

People consider that a good command of English will give their children access to better educational and job opportunities.[13] They also see it as essential if their children are to be able to assert themselves in a society that is discriminatory on both class and racial lines. Tensions may arise if children do not share their parents' belief that it is better to speak English. One parent, for example, whose own background was Afrikaans, married an English speaker and brought her children up in English. She speaks of how heart-broken she is now when one of her sons, who is working in the post office, comes home and speaks Afrikaans to the family. She clearly feels that he is throwing away his chance of better things.[14]

It is important to distinguish between parents' desire for children to become competent in English in addition to being competent in Afrikaans, and the desire that they should become anglicized and drop Afrikaans and the vernacular. The adoption of English to the exclusion of Afrikaans at home is a course taken by some people who have middle-class aspirations, whereas people who do not necessarily want to move away from the area and from their working-class roots often willingly retain Afrikaans alongside English in their homes.

Since many parents are not in a position to foster skill in English themselves, they look to the schools to do so. It is commonly regarded as insufficient merely to have the children taught English as a second language, and English-medium instruction is preferred. This is not simply because of the increased exposure to English that English-medium instruction provides. It also arises out of the history of schooling in the area: the schools in District Six were predominantly English in the nineteenth and the earlier part of the present century, and English came to be regarded as 'the language of education', a phrase which was used frequently in interviews. At primary school level parental preference is not, in terms of the law, the deciding factor. The law decrees that the language of the home shall be the medium of instruction. For secondary schooling that restriction falls away. Interviews revealed that it was common for children passing through nursery school, primary school and high school in District Six to have had experience of both languages as medium of instruction.

Children at School

At the local nursery school both Afrikaans- and English-speaking children are accepted but, because of its history, the nursery school is seen as English. It is part of a community centre which was founded by English-speaking people, some of whom were British. Ridd (1981: 213) comments that its English connection has given it prestige: 'Even parents who speak little English themselves are keen for their children to be looked after by "Coloured" teachers who speak English well and are conscious of the English tradition in education'.

Few children entering the nursery school are completely monolingual. On average each year a third of the children are Afrikaans-dominant, a third English-dominant, and the rest equally competent in both languages. It is interesting that there is no question about home language on the enrolment form. Through contact with parents and children the teachers come to know which language each child is most familiar with, but that knowledge is not taken into account in placing children in one of the three classes. They are placed according to age. Language dominance is not seen as a highly significant factor at this level of education, and it is assumed that each child will pick up enough of the other language to cope with classroom and playground interaction. My observations over a period of four years suggest that they do exactly this. Although teachers speak more English than Afrikaans, they all use both languages in the classroom. The children clearly take it for granted that they can use whichever language they wish. The following summary of a recording of general classroom talk shows typical alternations.

Two children were quarrelling in Afrikaans about their fathers' work. (The fathers are fruit and vegetable vendors.) A child intervened in English and the teacher redirected the comment to the group as a whole in English and then, in both languages, invited responses from the other children. She asked, among other things, whether they knew a short traditional vendor's song which was in Afrikaans. One of the quarrelling children was encouraged to sing it. After an interlude of physical exercise conducted in English, a child started telling a story in English about how he had been bitten by a spider. He used the word 'bleed' instead of 'blood': '. . . and then the bleed come out'. The teacher supplied the orthodox phrase but did so without drawing attention to the correction: 'Oh! So the blood came out!' Several children started talking at once about spiders, some in English, some in Afrikaans. The teacher picked up some threads in Afrikaans but the next child to hold the floor on the topic did so in English. He was shy and she encouraged him in English. She was then distracted by an upheaval in one corner of the room and asked one of the children in Afrikaans what was happening. And so it continued with neither teacher nor pupils seeming to be at all self-conscious about language choice.

In the nursery school environment, language difference does not constitute a barrier between children. That they are aware of one another's language dominance is shown in the way that the fully bilingual children switch languages to suit less fluent children. The following exchange, which took place in the staff-room during recess, illustrates this.

Two children aged three-and-a-half had drifted in to see what we were doing and to talk to us. Joyce had very little English whereas Terence came from a home where both languages were spoken. The teacher wanted to give me an example of Terence's bilingualism without drawing attention to our interest in his language ability. She whispered to him:

> Terence, ask Joyce who cut her hair.
> T. *Joyce, wie het jou hare gesny?* [Who cut your hair?].
> J. *My ma.* [Pronunciation indicates that this is Afrikaans.]
> T. She say [sic] her mommy cut her hair.

At the nursery school language is not a group marker but at the dual-medium primary school it is, both in the classroom and in the playground. Separating children according to language in the classroom is state policy. The English-medium classes for all age levels are larger than the Afrikaans-medium ones. Teachers say that this is not a reflection of the dominant home language in the area, but of parental belief that prospects are better for children who are educated in English. (Ridd in 1981 reported the same pattern: ch.4.) A teacher who had worked in District Six for thirty-seven years put it this way:

> I do feel that parents *still* think that the children are at a disadvantage if they go into the Afrikaans-medium classes. It was so when they were at school.

The headmaster reported that parents invariably put their children in the English stream if the children are equally competent in both languages. The numbers in the English stream are further increased by children from Afrikaans-dominant homes, whose parents insist that the children are English-speaking. The children are drilled at home to maintain the appearance of being so.

There are problems for those children who have to try to function in an unfamiliar language in a new environment. The difficulties seem greatest in the first two years. Some children find it difficult to follow instructions and will not ask questions for fear of showing that their English is inadequate. For example, in her first week at school a child wet her pants and when gently asked why by the teacher, she burst into tears and said, in Afrikaans, that she had not known how to ask in English for permission to go to the toilet. A less anxious child in the same class coped with his difficulty by asking in the vernacular mixture, 'Teacher, *kan ek gaan* [may I go] pee?'

There are academic difficulties too. Some children have to learn new skills and ideas through the medium of a language in which they are not yet competent. If a child is defeated by the difficulty and is not thought ready to proceed to the next class at the end of the year, parents are advised to let him or her repeat the year in the Afrikaans class.

At school some children have to acquire not only a second language but also a second dialect, namely the standard dialect. All children are expected to develop competence in the standard dialects of both official languages. They have to remember to keep the two languages separate in formal school discourse, while the vernacular which they hear constantly out of school draws on both languages. Learning another dialect of a language can be difficult. When a familiar vocabulary is being used it is not easy to remember to suppress one set of phonological, morphological, or syntactic rules in favour of another, less ingrained set.[15] So, even where there is continuity between home language and the medium of instruction, there may be problems arising from dialect differences.

Where code-switching is the habitual practice and where there is a great deal of lexical borrowing, loan-words are often altered in order to fit the language into which they are being inserted. Pronunciation may be modified and features such as number and tense markers may be those of the recipient language, as in '*gejoin*', the modified version of 'joined'. The result is that speakers do not always know when they are using a loan-word. This process is called relexification. Relexified words either fill a gap or supplant an existing word in the language. Where existing words have been successfully supplanted, speakers may be surprised to learn that a word in common usage in language A actually belongs to language B. Children face the problem that they have to learn that some of the words that they have used as part of one language may now be used only in the other language at school, but outside school their former usage will prevail. In the classroom, if correction of deviance from the standard dialect is not handled with great tact, it can give the children a very negative image of themselves and their homes. It may also render children self-protectively mute (Creber 1972; Trudgill 1975).

In the dual-medium primary school the practice is to work towards command of standard English and Afrikaans without altogether outlawing vernacular forms from the classroom. In oral lessons there is a strong emphasis on dramatic improvisation. In the scenes created by the children, the vernacular is accepted if it is appropriate to the character who is speaking. Children develop a sense that one dialect is suitable for one kind of situation and another for a different situation. By the fifth year in school (if not earlier) most students are able to move reasonably comfortably between the vernacular and the standard dialects. The following account of an Afrikaans oral lesson in a Standard Four class[16] shows the participants' sense of the appropriate language for different situations.

Two short scenes were improvised. One dealt with four gamblers playing dice on the pavement outside the home of a very upright woman who told them to move away. When they did not, she called the police, who arrived and hauled the gamblers off. The gamblers' speech was a mixture of English and Afrikaans, spiced with a number of words unfamiliar to me and very amusing to the audience. The speech of the woman and her friend was standard Afrikaans but with a different accent from that used by the standard-Afrikaans-speaking, probably white policeman. The next play was a trial scene. A woman was being tried for the murder of her baby. The language used by all the characters was strictly standard Afrikaans. The register was very formal.[17] Once or twice the girl playing the public prosecutor darted across to the teacher to ask him the Afrikaans equivalent for words she knew only in English. There was a very strong sense that in this kind of scene language mixing would not do.

The school's annual variety concert featured four plays scripted by the children. Two of them were set in the neighbourhood. One was a serious play, the other was a skit. Both plays used standard English, standard Afrikaans and the vernacular as indicators of relative social status among characters, and of constraint or familiarity in relationships.

Separation by language in the classroom affects relationships in the playground. It hinders easy socialization between the English- and Afrikaans-medium classes. This happens even though children from the two language streams may well have grown up together and continue to associate with one another out of school hours. Six months into one academic year I was talking to two small groups of children at the primary school, asking how they were enjoying school. (I had known them at nursery school from the time that they were three or four years old.) The first group had been at primary school for six months, the second for eighteen. Both groups mentioned in passing that there was hostility between the two language streams:

> T. Amanda's got two teeth out and then the children shout at her '*entjie bek!*' ['cigarette mouth'].
> G. They rude here in this school. *Sommer* [just/simply] call the children names. Make us mad. Afrikaans children!

Following the second group's lively account of practical joking and getting into trouble, I entered the conversation, asking,

> *Int.* Do you fight with other children sometimes at school?
> F. Yes, the boys fight — only the boys fight with the Afrikaanses and the girls.
> *Int.* Why do you fight with the Afrikaanses?
> F. They first start with us, the big boys.
> *Int.* How do they start?
> H. They spoil the game that we're playing.
> F. They first start and then they cry first!
> *Int.* So don't you play with the children in the Afrikaans class?
> R. No, I just play with one.
> *Int.* Is that only in your class — I mean do the big classes, the English and the Afrikaans classes, play with each other?
> H. The English don't want to play with the Afrikaans and the Afrikaans don't want to play with the English.

Three months later, curious to see whether the hostility persisted out of school hours, I worked out the friendship networks of those children and also of all the others at the primary school whom I had known at the nursery school. There were twenty-two children in all, and they came from eight classes: the English and Afrikaans classes of the first four years of school. It emerged that, out of school hours, *all* of them played with children from both the English and the Afrikaans classes. A boy who had been most emphatic about English and Afrikaans children not playing with one another, named as a playmate someone from the Afrikaans Sub B class and added, 'He's my best friend.'

I have not yet done any observation or interviews at the high schools serving the area, but during interviews conducted at people's homes each person was asked about high school experiences with a bearing on language preferences. The time span covered by their memories is considerable as I have drawn on the responses of people aged between fifteen and sixty-three. (Those older than that had had little or no secondary schooling.) There were many reports of rivalry between English and Afrikaans classes. The accounts suggest that the rivalry is not part of a clash between groups who see themselves as being on an equal footing, as the following three interview extracts indicate.

> *Ms K.* There was always friction. The Afrikaans children used to be a bit wild, you know. The English never really wanted to associate with the Afrikaans children.

> *Ms L.* They — the Afrikaans children — would always think that, you know, because you're in an English class, you want to be 'that Miss So-and-So'.

> *Int.*   Why do you think there is rivalry?
> *Mr N.* Status.
> *Int.*   Do you think English has got higher status?
> *Mr N.* Yes. And also you find the Afrikaans-speaking classes, you find more delinquents in the Afrikaans classes than the English class. The English is more 'stiff'. The parents is well-off and things like that and, um, the children maintain that at school too. And that's where the division comes from.

In interviews people expressed the feeling that English-medium classes had been favoured by school authorities in a variety of ways. They said, for example, that prefects were always English, English classes were always the 'A' or 'top' classes, and they felt that teachers preferred working with them. Better teachers were said to have been assigned to English-medium classes.

Responses to the questions, 'Did you ever change language medium at school?' and if not, 'Did you ever want to change medium?' showed that more than half of those who did not start school in English either changed or wanted to change language medium at some point. Most of the changes took place on entry to high school. Accounting for their wish to be in English classes, subjects said that, as they found formal English easier to understand than formal Afrikaans, they had assumed that they would have fewer difficulties with English technical terms and with text-books. For that reason, too, they saw English as giving easier access to secondary and tertiary education. Moreover, they said that they had believed that work opportunities would be better if their schooling was in English.

Conclusion

In making language choices adults and children respond to political, social, and economic forces which may pull in different directions. It would be very problematic for people in District Six to identify themselves as English-speaking only, or Afrikaans-speaking only. Within the community they would lay themselves open to the kinds of suspicions I mentioned earlier, of snobbishness in the case of English, and of government support in the case of standard Afrikaans. If they spoke only *kombuistaal* they would be seen as having been inadequately exposed to city life. In the wider South African society, however, fluency in the standard dialect of at least one of the official languages is necessary for progress in social, intellectual, and material spheres. Children need to learn the standard dialects of the two official languages but they also have to learn when it is appropriate to use them and when it is not.

Learning when it is appropriate to use a particular register, dialect, or language is part of the language acquisition process for any child. What is particularly challenging for these children is that the constraints governing language use in informal neighbourhood interaction prevent them from using such interaction for the consolidation of skills in the standard dialects which they are acquiring at school. Not only do children have little occasion to practise the standard dialects among friends outside school hours, but when they are with neighbours and friends they continue to hear and use non-standard lexical and syntactic features which they have to remember to eliminate at other times when they need to use the standard dialects. The bonds and divisions that exist on a social level thus create academic hurdles for children, but interviews with teachers and observations in classrooms suggest that, for many children, they are not insurmountable.

It would seem that the schools have an important role to play in enabling children to meet the linguistic demands of the neighbourhood and of the world beyond it. Neither the nursery school nor the dual-medium primary school puts pressure on children to abandon the vernacular in informal interaction. Exposure to the standard dialects comes initially through the teachers' language and through stories, rhymes, and songs. At the nursery school there is no systematic attempt to teach the children to use the standard dialects. This occurs in the primary school. In classes devoted to the development of oral skills there is a great deal of encouragement for children to improvise dialogues in dramatized scenes. These classes provide not only opportunity and stimulus for using standard English and Afrikaans, but also an environment for putting knowledge of sociolinguistic norms into practice: characters have to speak in a way that is appropriate to their fictional background and situation. If these two factors call for the vernacular, it is used. This constitutes an unstated validation of its place in the community's linguistic repertoire. The kind of school language policy that allows for the use of standard and non-standard dialects enables children to develop skill in the standard dialects of the official languages while retaining the vernacular, and thus to meet the somewhat conflicting demands of the neighbourhood and the world beyond it.

Notes

The author wishes to thank the University of Cape Town and the Human Sciences Research Council for grants which funded the research.

1. A speech community is defined in *A First Dictionary of Linguistics and Phonetics* (Crystal 1980) as 'any regionally or socially definable human group identified by a shared linguistic system'. The people who constitute this particular speech community could also be said to be a community in the sense used by Dell Hymes and quoted and endorsed by Lesley Milroy (1980: 15): 'For our purposes it appears most useful to reserve the notion of community for a local unit, characterized for its members by common locality and primary interaction'.

2. 'Dialects are subdivisions of languages . . . . Any language with a reasonably large number of speakers will develop dialects, especially if there are geographical barriers separating people from each other. One dialect may predominate as the official or STANDARD form of the language, and this is the variety which may come to be written down' (Crystal 1980).

3. These features are: patterns in the use of loan-words, the transfer of morphological rules, and syntactic features of conversation in which language switching occurs.

4. See Ross (1979) for an analysis of patterns in the relationships of

minority groups to dominant languages in cases where ethnicity is an element in political mobilization. His analysis provides an interesting framework for examining attitudes of people classified as 'white' and 'coloured' towards English and Afrikaans (the home languages of the majority in both groups), and towards one another.

There are two other studies dealing with attitudes to English and Afrikaans in Cape Town. In his survey of coloured people's attitudes towards English and Afrikaans, P. Scheffer (1983) drew primarily on subjects resident in the Cape Peninsula. It is not clear which suburbs were tapped but the analysis of the responses indicates that the opinions of both middle- and working-class people were obtained. The other study, by the anthropologist Rosemary Ridd (1981), devotes a section of one chapter to language attitudes. She worked with coloured and white middle- and working-class people who lived in District Six or in one of two adjacent suburbs. In the main, Scheffer's and Ridd's findings about prevailing attitudes to the two official languages and about linguistic aspects of inter-group relations agree with those that I present in this paper.

5. There is as yet no comprehensive history of District Six. My estimate of the time-span covered by English-Afrikaans bilingualism is based on the dates of establishment of the first English-medium mission schools in the area. For further information concerning the Group Areas Act see the introduction to this volume.

6. 'Kanala' is an Indonesian word meaning 'please'. It is still in use among Cape Town's Muslims. In interviews it was suggested that the older name survived alongside the drier, official name because it indicates the spirit of give-and-take which is a valued characteristic of the area.

7. For further details concerning the Population Registration Act, see the introduction to this volume.

8. During that period I tried to tap the opinions of a wide variety of Capetonians who code-switched so that I could see what they associated with the two official languages and with code-switching. The people interviewed for the pilot stage of the research were told what the focus of the main study was to be and were asked about situations, status factors and allegiances which commonly affect language choice. In addition to their responses I drew on material from essays I had set for sixty university students who came from areas where code-switching was common. The essays required that students reflect on their own attitudes to standard and non-standard dialects of English and Afrikaans, and to code-switching. The patterns that emerged from the essays and interviews were clear enough to suggest productive lines of enquiry for the District Six interviews.

9. See Ryan (1979) for an analysis of the ambivalence of speakers towards

their own, low-prestige dialects.

10. This commonly held impression is validated by Scheffer (1983: xiv): 'The findings show that most of the Coloureds in the rural areas (outside the Peninsula) are unilingual, i.e. Afrikaans speaking' (Scheffer's translation).

11. Speaking of *kombuistaal*, Ridd (1981: 194) says that, 'Although the Dialect is derided, it is preferred to the "suive taal" [sic] ("pure language") of the Afrikaner which District Six people associate with their oppression as non-Whites.' In the 1970s the Black Consciousness movement tried to make people aware that Afrikaans was not just the language of white Afrikaners. In District Six I saw little evidence of Black Consciousness presence, however.

12. In cases of bilingualism where the speaker is not equally fluent in both languages, one language is said to be dominant and the other subordinate (Lyons 1981: 282).

13. Both Ridd and Scheffer report similar attitudes. (Ridd 1981: 194-99; Scheffer 1983: xiv.)

14. Marsden and Jackson (1962) reported similar tensions in some homes in their longitudinal study of working-class children attending a Huddersfield grammar school where the prevalent dialect was a middle-class one. Some parents wanted children to use the higher status dialect at home but not all children felt comfortable doing so.

15. Phonological rules cover the sound system of a language or dialect. Morphological rules deal with the structure of words. Syntactic rules are those which govern the way in which words are combined to form sentences (Crystal 1980).

16. Standard Four children would be roughly twelve years old. The first two years in the primary school are called 'Sub A' and 'Sub B'. Children in those classes are usually six to eight years old. The remaining classes in the primary school are called 'Standards'. Standard One is the class next in sequence after Sub B, and Standard Five is the last class in the primary school. High school classes are Standards Six to Ten.

17. Register is 'a variety of language defined according to its use in social situations' (Crystal 1980).

Calling Kin in Crossroads

Pamela Reynolds

Kinship terminology, an area of study that is beloved by anthropologists and that has attracted the interest of the development psychologists, is here examined in relation to its use and understanding among seven-year-old Xhosa children in the squatter settlement of Crossroads. The settlement lies on the Cape Flats twenty kilometres from the centre of Cape Town. From August 1979 to January 1981 I worked with fourteen children and compiled an ethnographic report of one year of childhood. Emphasis was placed on the relationship between society and children's cognitive development. This chapter, an extract from the whole, explores the possibility of combining anthropological and psychological techniques in the study of individual cognitive process in cultural context.

The analysis of kin terms used by children affords us a clue not only to children's handling of the world about them but also to the interface between the child's world and adult conventions. Kin terminology is a conventional guide to the ways children can divide up that part of the adult world closest to them, revealing both the categories and the processes involved in demarcating what might otherwise be seen as an amorphous world of grown-ups. This chapter examines the value of certain methods used as comparative tools. All too often, methods to test theories of the cognitive, social, and psychological development of children are pioneered in the West. The methods are tested and validated among children in the West, then frequently applied in other settings, and comparisons are drawn between the children of different populations. Not surprisingly, the children in the population about whom the theory was first conceived and in relation to whom methods to test the theory were originated and validated, achieve better than do the children of other populations. South Africans are familiar with the many dubious and invidious theories, including those of racial and cultural deficit, which have been promulgated to explain these results.

If a researcher is interested in describing the cognitive development of children in a non-Western society there are few tests that can be safely adopted. In order to begin to establish an ethnography of childhood we need, first, to examine closely the assumptions that underlie imported methodologies so as not to compound the errors of earlier researchers and, second, we need to build a theoretical base and methodological structure according to which South African children's development can be described.

The tests examined here are to do with children's use and understanding of kinship terminology. Yet a host of problems fly from Pandora's Box as individual attitudes, capabilities and experiences, social conditions, and cultural norms are considered in relation to each test item. We ought not to presume to measure children without establishing whether or not the tests used can be translated across continents, cultural settings, languages groupings, and classes.

According to Van Warmelo (1935), the Cape Nguni include those groups which have been in the Transkei and Eastern Cape for centuries (Xhosa, Thembu, Mpondo, Mpondomise, and Bomvana), Mfengu, and other recent immigrants (Bhaca, Xesibe, and Ntlangwini). The following observations about kinship are taken from Hammond-Tooke (1969: 86-87). The social structure of the Cape Nguni groups is similar in broad outline. Its main features are ideally polygynous families, patrilineal descent groups, and the apparent absence of any form of preferential marriage or formal age-regiment system.

Homesteads show a great variety of structure, from nuclear to compound and extended forms, and a feature (since the 1960s) is the high percentage of widows as homestead heads. Marriage is patrilocal with a strong tendency to settlement in the neighbourhood of the father's homestead (formerly actually *in* the homestead) and effects a transfer of both rights *in uxorem* and *in genetricem* to the groom's group.[1]

Cape Nguni kinship terminologies are broadly similar, being of the bifurcate merging type: that is, the terms for 'father' and 'mother' are also applied respectively to father's brother and mother's sister. Parallel cousins[2] are thus equated with own siblings except that, among the Xhosa, the term *kanina* is used between men only for children of the mother's sister. Separate terms are used for mother's brother (*malume*) and father's sister (*dadebobawo*) and all cross-cousins[3] are referred to as *mza* or *mzala*. Spouses of father's brother and mother's sister are called 'mother' and 'father' respectively: spouses of father's sister are called 'father' (*bawo, bobawo*) and the wife of the mother's brother is termed *malumekazi* or 'mother'. Emphasis on relative age is strongly marked. Father's elder brothers are distinguished terminologically from father's younger brothers, elder brothers from younger brothers, and elder sisters from younger sisters (between siblings of opposite sex). Generally speaking all kin of the first ascending generation are classed either as 'father' or 'mother's brother' and all females as 'mother'. Cousins are either assimilated with siblings or distinguished as 'cross-cousin'. Both paternal and maternal grandfathers are termed *bawomkulu* and both grandmothers *makhulu* except among the Mpondo, who do not make sex differentiation and call all grandfathers and grandmothers *makhulu*. There is a terminological confusion between father's elder brother and father's father (both *bawomkhulu*). In the first descending generation the term 'son' and 'daughter' are applied to children of parallel cousins and, apparently, those of cross-cousins (these relationships have not been recorded in literature). Thus all children in the first descending generation are classified as own children. Great-grandparents are all classified as *khokho* (male) or *gogo* (female) and the reciprocal (grandchild) is the non-sex-denoting *mzukulwana*. The system reflects the lack of discreteness of the nuclear family in Cape Nguni social structure. Among all the Cape Nguni the family is embedded in a wider kinship group, the lineage, and, ultimately, the clan.

Research Methodology

The paper focusses on children's kinship concepts. The material comes from a variety of interviews and exercises conducted with the thirteen sample children over a year (the other child in the sample was not present for these tests). The interviews include two replications of studies done by J Piaget (1928), R LeVine and D Price-Williams (1974). Piaget's purpose in analyzing children's kinship concepts was to use them in describing their grasp of the logic of relations. Through such studies, he claimed to have supported his theory of 'childish realism, i.e. the inability to grasp the relativity of notions or ideas [which] is one of the principal obstacles to the development of childish reasoning' (Piaget 1928: 96). Piaget (1928: 97) interpreted the difficulties that children have in handling the logic of relations as due to the egocentrism of child thought. LeVine and Price-Williams adapted Piaget's approach to suit a non-Western sample of children. They, too, aimed to describe an aspect of cognitive development.

My interest in replicating the two interviews was two-fold: one was to test the sample children's ability to handle relational kinship terms and the other was to use the interview schedules as tools with which to elicit the children's knowledge and application of kinship terms. Besides replicating the two interviews, I recorded at various times the lists given to me by the children of whom they thought were members of their families and of their households. I also noted their use of kinship terms during observation sessions and informal interaction. Finally, I devised an exercise using puppets to test the children's use of kin terms of address. The two replications will be reported on first.

Jean Piaget's Test

Piaget (1928) reported research that he carried out on a set of relational concepts including the two kin terms *brother* and *sister* (*frère* and *soeur*). In this study, he asked 240 French-speaking Swiss children aged four to twelve years a number of questions about brothers and sisters. The children's answers suggested to Piaget that there were three stages in the development of what he called the concept of a term like *brother*.

Stage One consisted of the most primitive definitions, e.g. a brother was simply a boy; a sister, a girl. In addition, children at this stage of definition often maintained that adults could not be brothers or sisters.

Stage Two definitions were relational in nature in that the child would maintain that there had to be more than one child with the same parents. The relationship was not reciprocal, however, because the term *brother* was applied exclusively to only one of the siblings involved. In addition, the restriction excluding adults rarely continued to operate at this stage.

Stage Three definitions were both relational and reciprocal in that the title *brother* (or *sister*) was now allowed to apply to all siblings. In other words, the child understood that in order to *be* a brother, you had to *have* a brother or sister. Most of Piaget's subjects reached Stage Three by about the age of nine or ten.

In addition to Piaget's original study of *brother* and *sister*, there have been two replications of this work with English-speaking children by Danziger (1957) and Elkind (1962).

The questions that Piaget asked each child were:

1. How many brothers have you? And how many sisters? (Let us suppose that the child has a brother A and a sister B.) And how many brothers has A? And how many sisters? And how many brothers has B? And how many sisters?

2. How many brothers are there in the family? How many sisters? How many brothers and sisters altogether?

3. There are three brothers in a family: Auguste, Alfred, and Raymond. How many brothers has Auguste? And Alfred? And Raymond?

4. Are you a brother (or a sister)? What is a brother (or sister, according to the sex of the child)?

5. Ernest has three brothers: Paul, Henry, and Charles. How many brothers has Paul? And Henry? And Charles?

6. How many brothers are there in this family?

Piaget's analysis of the answers is focussed on the child's growing capacity to take the role of the other person and understand that a term like 'brother' is not a static attribute of a person (like 'boy') but a relation between two people, and in particular, a symmetrical relation such that if X is Y's brother, Y is also X's brother. Like the Hausa terms (studied by LeVine and Price-Williams), but unlike the English and French terms for brother, the Xhosa term is not symmetrical and therefore cannot be used to indicate the child's development of the capacity to understand the logical concept of symmetrical relations. The term for elder brother is *umkhuluwe* and for younger brother, *umninawe* (Hunter 1936: 29). The same linguistic term is used for elder and younger sisters. According to Hunter (1936: 34), either *udade wethu* or *umnt'akwethu* may be used for both younger and older sisters.

Despite the problems inherent in replicating Piaget's study in a society in which the kin terms for brother are asymmetrical, I decided to administer the test to see how the children would handle the logic of relations and to ascertain whether or not they used the traditional asymmetrical terms for older brother and sister, and for younger brother and sister, or whether they used the terms current in Crossroads that had been adopted from the Afrikaans, that is *bhuti* for brother and *sisi* for sister.[4] Besides, I was interested in seeing how the children handled the test format.

The test revealed that children aged seven and eight in Crossroads use the terms *ubhuti* and *usisi* (the words used in the test) as reference and address[5] to older brothers and sisters only. The rule seemed to be more firmly entrenched for the former than the latter term. Besides, they are used about or to siblings somewhat older than themselves and there seems to be no firm rule as to how much older a brother or sister should be before he or she is deserving of the form of reference or address under consideration. *Bhuti* and *sisi* are terms of respect that recognize the hierarchical ordering of relationships within the family.

For the first question, one could not replace the question, 'How many brothers have you?' with two questions asking, 'How many older brothers have you?' and 'How many younger brothers?' as one might assume to be possible given the traditional asymmetrical terms, because the children would have denied (and they did deny) that they had any of the latter. Younger brothers and sisters are simply called 'child of the house' (*umtwanabendlu*) or 'child of my mother'.

The test was thus rendered more difficult. For example, question 1 asks how many brothers has one of the subject's brothers (in the following, the same applies to sisters). In order to reply the child must either include or exclude himself as a brother of his brother depending on his age relative to that brother. The question is a more searching test of a child's ability to take another's point of view (decentre) than Piaget's original one.

Question 3 is also made more difficult. The question sets an abstract problem: 'There are three brothers in a family. Sipho, Geza, and Malusi. How many brothers has Sipho? And Geza? and Malusi?' According to the children's use of the term brother, there ought, in that family, to be another child to whom all three are brothers. Some handled the problem by disregarding their usual use of the term and some tried to assign seniority and gave answers accordingly. Questions 5 and 6 presented similar difficulties.

Question 4 asks, 'Are you are a brother?' Most children replied by taking into account their position in the family. Question 4 also asks, 'What is a brother?' and the definitions offered largely concentrated on relative sibling position, not on links established via parentage. For example, a girl defined a sister by describing her own position in the family. 'I am a sister to the young ones. An old girl.' Others used the phrase 'child of the house' assuming it to be an adequate definition of brotherhood or sisterhood.

Apart from the above, anticipated, problem that was peculiar to the social context and age of the children tested, the questions seem to demand a use of number that assumes a conceptual grasp or confidence beyond that possessed by some of the children. If that is so then the test's applicability across cultures is limited. The test demands that the child pay attention without the help of activity or material aids through eighteen questions. It is probable that some societies demand and train children to concentrate on intense verbal exchanges more than do others. Therefore, inattention in certain circumstances could be due to an absence of cultural emphasis on its value under such conditions.

The questions were more difficult for those children with large families, especially if some members lived elsewhere. For example, Saliswa's mother's son, aged eighteen, was living with them in Crossroads. He was one of the three children (one boy and two girls) born of Mrs Qasana's husband whom she had left ten years previously. Saliswa, one of the five children born of her mother's current partner, counted the boy as a brother, yet when she was asked how many sisters he had, she replied, 'Two. I don't know their names but they belong to my mother.' Some children were puzzled as to whether or not to include older siblings born of only one parent.

Another source of confusion was the fact that the terms *bhuti* and *sisi* are sometimes used across a broad spectrum that includes cousins and clan members. For example, Togu mentioned as his brother a boy whom I knew was not his brother and when asked who he was, he said,

> He is a boy. His clan is also N-. Our relationship is from the Transkei. I call him brother.

As a result children other than brothers, as defined in the context of Piaget's test, were sometimes included. As LeVine and Price-Williams (1974) found among the Hausa, children are often encouraged to address (and categorize) certain persons in the homestead with kin terms that indicate a desired social relationship rather than in accordance with accepted definitions of consanguinity and affinity. This occurs among a wide variety of peoples.

According to Piaget's scoring method, no child in the Crossroads sample succeeded on the test. As I knew the children's families well, I could judge whether or not they were using terms for brother and sister in strict accord with their own usage. Scoring thus, Lungiswa obtained full marks, Tozama one less, Zuziwe three less and Peliswe four less. The scores are shown in Table 1.

Table 1: Results on Piaget's Kinship Test

	Lun.	Toz.	Zuz.	Pel.	Tog.	Nuk.	Sal.	Hin.	Yam.	Ged.	Nom.	Gwa.	Ceb.
Scores according to Piaget's definitions	12	10	11	10	8	7	4	7	5	5	3	2	2
Additional marks awarded for use of kin terms in accord with children's definitions	6	7	4	4	4	5	7	2	1	0	1	2	1
Total out of 18	18	17	15	14	12	12	11	9	6	5	4	4	3

The next interview to be discussed is an adaptation of Piaget's test, using a naturalistic approach among a non-Western group of children.

The LeVine/Price-Williams Test

The authors' claim aim was to explore the ways in which individuals, particularly children, use cultural categories to conceptualize their experience. Like Piaget, they selected kinship and family as means through which to explore the topic. LeVine and Price-Williams (1974: 26) claim that:

> Kinship involves the child's social environment and is extremely familiar to him. Like other semantic domains, it entails representation of environmental features that can be assessed independently by the

investigator, and — perhaps more than most domains — its conceptual units are readily identifiable. Furthermore, we assumed on theoretical grounds the special importance of kinship concepts in the child's psychosocial development as an indicator of his interpersonal experience at each stage in the process of socialization.

They set out to devise an approach applicable to the study of children's concepts in a society where kin terms are not symmetrical and a nuclear family system is not the norm. Their specific aims were to discover the extent to which children's verbal reports concerning kin relations in their homes would reveal developmental trends in accord with (a) relational thinking, (b) informational accuracy, and (c) the salience for the child of compound residents in certain relationships to him. The procedure that LeVine and Price-Williams adopted was to administer a single set of questions individually to fifty-three Hausa children aged four to eleven in rural Nigeria. The authors' description follows (LeVine and Price-Williams 1974: 39):

> In the interview, which was entirely taped, the child was first asked who lived in his compound. He would give several names spontaneously. When he stopped, the interviewer asked him, 'Who else?' A distinction was made between the spontaneous list and the elicited list. These lists are of great interest in themselves, not only in terms of how accurate the child is in reporting the membership of his compound, but in terms of which person he omits (if anyone) and which he mentions early and which later. Next, the interviewer went down the list the child had given and asked, 'who is' each person on it; the child could identify the person in any way he chose . . .
>
> The interviewer then went down the list again, this time asking about each person for whom a kin term had not been given already, 'How is he related to you?' If a child had not spontaneously identified the person with a kin term but knew the term applied, he could use it now . . . . The interviewer reviewed the list a final time asking for pairs of adjacent persons, 'How is this one related to that one?' Here the purpose was to tap the child's capacity to view kin relations from a decentred perspective, taking the role of the other relative.
>
> In the final part of the interview, the child was asked to define three kin terms, including ones he had used (if any) and including a general term for 'grandparent'.

The authors conclude that the technique yielded results that suggest that further work along these lines should be encouraged and that the interview produced data that made theoretical and ethnographic sense. The exercise also served to confirm Piaget's major findings.

The set of questions is not ideal for a situation such as the one in Crossroads. In essence, it requires the child to list the members of the household, give each a kin term, describe the relationships of adjacent pairs and define three kin terms. An immediate problem in a squatter camp in South Africa is the shifting nature of household compositions. It is hard for anyone to keep up with changes in membership and even more difficult to keep track of relationships. A new member could be a relative of either the family head or his wife, or a member of their clan, or a neighbour from their country home — a home-man, or simply a lodger. At intervals during the year, I checked household membership and frequently found changes in persons and in number. For instance, seven households had the following number of members at different times:

> Malawu's in March, 13 and in May, 15
> Togu's in March, 11 and in November, 19 (a new house)
> Nukwa's in March, 13 and in August, 6 (a new house)
> Nomvula's in March, 16 and in May, 21
> Zuziwe's in March, 14 and in June, 18
> Gedja's in May, 9 and in November, 12
> Tozama's in March, 12 (composed of 3 adults and 9 children) and in
>   May, 12 (composed of 4 adults and 8 children).

Different marital patterns exacerbated possible confusion: one man, Mr Ketshe, admitted to having two wives and children by each; five parents had had children by someone other than the child's other parent; nine families had at least one child living away from home; one child's father had died and his father's brother was head of the household; three others lived without their fathers and one of them without either her father or mother. Not many of the above complications occurred in accord with established norms that could be explained to a child.

The composition of the household was rendered more difficult for the child to grasp by the nature of work patterns. Some found it difficult to say whether someone was a member of the household or not, because he or she seemed to be away most of the time. Gedja, for example, did not include her grandmother in the list, 'because', she said, 'she is working'. Yet she did include her mother, who was away at work all week and only returned for the weekends.

In attempting to clarify the relationship to the family of someone listed, I sometimes found that I was asking the child to discuss delicate issues that were either not common knowledge or not discussed openly before children. This was particularly true of parentage. Lungiswa, for example, claimed that her youngest brother was the child of a different father from the rest of the children while her mother denied this. I was wary of enquiring too closely from certain children as to whom an 'uncle' (*malume*) was, as mother's current man friend was often introduced as such to the child.

Administering the Interview

In administering the interview I came upon certain problems inherent in its format and acknowledged by the authors. The test varied in difficulty according to the size of the household in which the child lived. With a large household, one could easily confuse or tire the child. I was not sure whether one ought to prompt the child when eliciting household membership. If one did not, the rest of the test would be less searching. For example, Hintsa did not name any children under either question 1 or 2 which asked for a list of members of the household.

Questions 1 and 2 (who lives in your house?) yielded fairly accurate lists of occupants; though, as was to be expected, those from larger households forgot more members than did those from smaller. The following is a table showing the number in each household and the figure beneath the name represents the number listed by that child.

Table 2: Household Membership

	Yam.	Tog.	Zuz.	Nom.	Sal.	Toz.	Ged.	Hin.	Lun.	Pel.	Ceb.	Nuk.	Gwa.
Child's March 1980 list	4	5	8	10	1 (3)	8	8	3	1 (7)	5	3 (6)	2	6
Child's Nov. 1980 list	6	7	13	14	14	11	13	9	8	7	8	9	7
No. in household: *My Nov. 1980 count*	24	19	17	16	14	12	12	9	8	7	7	6	6

* Ego included in each count. Note that 9 children did not include themselves.

Bracketed numbers show totals of those listed after prompting.

It should be noted how many more members per household were named by the children in November than in March. Given that many psychological tests are administered only once to each subject, the disparity is noteworthy. Had the children 'learned' by November how to respond to my questions on the basis of their experience in March? Or had their familiarity with me and my interests rendered them less shy and thus more willing or able to provide full answers, or indeed, to be more observant of their surroundings in relation to my interests? The methodological question is: how much impact do test experiences or familiarity of content have on children's performances?

Togu had six people living in his room: his parents, his younger brother, his father's brother's son, and his mother's sister. The last named came only at weekends. He listed his mother, brother, his father's brother's son and three others from the wider household. Children within a household, even adults on occasion, occupy different rooms for varying amounts of time and even sleep in various rooms. I give the example to illustrate the imponderables that can skew even the list of occupants of a single room.

None of the houses to which the children in the sample belonged were occupied only by members of the nuclear family. In Saliswa's house there were members of the nuclear and extended family, and of her father's clan, lodgers, and a patient of her mother's (her mother is a traditional healer).

Nine of the children listed their mothers in question 1, which asked for a list of members of their households. Two others included her in response to question 2, which asked who else lived in the house. Yameka, who lived with her mother's brother and his wife, listed the latter (her mother's brother's wife) under question 1. Nukwa did not list his mother but included her sister as *mama* and his father's brother as *tata* in his initial response.

Five children included father in the list under question 1 ('the spontaneous list') and two under question 2 ('the elicited list'). Of those without fathers living in the household, Nukwa, as mentioned above, listed his father's brother and Yameka named her mother's brother, both in response to question 1; Gedja did not name her father but later in the interview she referred to her grandfather (mother's father) as *tata*; nor did Lungiswa list her father but named two uncles, one her mother's brother and another, whom I did not know, as *malume* in response to question 1. Neither Togu nor Nomvula listed their fathers and the latter child referred to her mother as *mamkaZukiswa*, that is, her sister's mother. The term is a traditional form of polite address. Saliswa named her parents by their respective clan names.

Wilson and Mafeje (1963: 87-89) found that the extended use of kinship terms indicating seniority was changing in town speech. *uMama* in 1963 was restricted to the speaker's own mother, though in the country it was still being used in address to mother's sister, and also mother's contemporaries. Traditionally *ma*, rather than *mama*, was used in this extended way, but *ma* was also the formal address to mother. Similarly, *bawo* was traditionally used by a man to his father, formally, and to no one else. However, in town girls were using *tata*, the equivalent of the more familiar 'daddy', rather than 'father', and *tata* instead of *bawo* was being used in the extended sense, by both men and women, for father's brothers and senior men.

There were incidents among the boys and girls of Crossroads in which the extended use of *mama* could be heard. This happened often in Cebo's home, where his mother and her elder sister shared a house: the children of both women called them both *mama*. However, there were indications that in other Crossroads homes the term was used in a more restricted sense. The Crossroads children used *utata* much more often in speaking about or to their fathers than *ubawo*. They used *utatomkhulu* rather than *ubawomkhulu* for grandfather.

From an analysis of the persons omitted from the children's census reports, LeVine and Price-Williams (1974: 38) found that 38 per cent of girls omitted their fathers and concluded that 'This undoubtedly reflects the great social distance between the sexes in Hausa compounds, which is in fact weaker between boys and their secluded, home-bound mothers than between girls and their remote and mobile fathers. Thus boys and girls, although living in the "same" compound, may conceptualize their domestic environments differently based on sex-differentiated patterns of interactive experience.' In the Crossroads sample, if substitute figures for mothers or fathers are taken into account, every child listed a 'mother' and ten of the thirteen listed a 'father' in response to either question 1 or 2. That is to say, three children did not name their fathers or father substitutes. One was a girl who lives with her mother and her mother's parents. The other two, a boy and a girl, live with their fathers. Besides, one boy did not name his mother although he named her sister who is married to his guardian (his father's brother) and lives in Crossroads. Curiously enough, the two children who lived with their fathers yet did not name them, both demonstrated particularly close relationships with their fathers and their attachment emerged in other exercises conducted during the year. The boy who did not name his mother, yet lives with her and his younger brother, was close to her and emotionally dependent upon her.

The sample is too small to venture conclusions along the lines drawn by LeVine and Price-Williams. However, one might legitimately wonder whether the authors are justified in assuming the special importance of kinship concepts in the child's psychosocial development as an indicator of his or her interpersonal experience at each stage in the process of socialization. It might be that children play more complex games in revealing and concealing the nature of their relationships. One must be cautious in assigning qualitative value such as salience to data gathered in interviews.

Questions 3 and 4 will be dealt with together. The former asks the child who each of the persons is whom he or she has named, and the next question asks how that person is related to the child (that is, for each name not given a kin term in response to question 3). The most striking feature of these answers was that the children related people through a parent, usually the mother, rather than themselves. The usual kinship diagram looks something like this:

Siblings are tied together, as it were, and then linked to the parents. A diagram that better represents these children's scheme might look like this:

in which the children define their relationship to each other through their mother and to the father through their mother. Lungiswa, for example, defined a mother thus:

> You call someone a mother if you are a child to her.

And a father thus:

> You don't call his name [*hlonipha*][6] because he is your mother's husband.

No child used the words for son or daughter. More often the phrase 'child of the house' (*umtwanabendlu*) was used. Saliswa called her elder sister 'an old child of my house', and Togu described his younger brother as being, 'from the same house'. The word used for house was *indlu*. In traditional Xhosa households a number of such units made up an *umzi*, homestead, at the head of which would be the senior male relative. *Indlu* was used by these children to refer to the children of one mother much as would be done in traditional *umzi* in which each married woman would have her own house and property.

Kinship terms for grandchild, cousin, niece or nephew were not used although the opportunity arose. Only Lungiswa and Peliswe used the word for husband and only the latter used the word for wife. The following ten terms were used by more than one child during the test:

umama	—	mother
utata	—	father
usisi	—	sister
ubhuti	—	brother
utatomkhulu	—	grandfather
umakhulu	—	grandmother
umyeni	—	husband
umalume	—	mother's brother
udadebobawo	—	father's sister
umakazi	—	mother's sister

Terms such as 'father of ......', 'mother of ......' were often used.

Question 5 asks of adjacent pairs of persons in the lists given earlier, 'How is this one related to that one?' Six children did not give acceptable replies but two did, although even here each gave only a one-way definition. For example, Yameka said of the relationship between her mother's brother and his child, 'She is his baby'. Gwali said of his mother and brother, 'My mother is Loyiso's mother'. He denied that there was a relationship between his father and his brother. Five children each gave three adequate definitions of the relationship between two family members.

Finally, question 6 asked for the definition of three kin terms, ones used by the child and a general word for grandparents. Only two children, Lungiswa and Tozama gave meaningful definitions. Tozama's were:

> [Mother.] I don't know. A person is a mother because she has children.
> [Grandmother.] A person who has got grandchildren. Mama says 'mama' to grandmother.
> [Brother.] It is an older boy of the house. At his home there are girls.

Gedja's definition of mother as, 'She is the mother of everybody in the house' is telling for its suggestion that the position entails a position of social status and not simply kinship. Gedja calls her mother either by her English name, Jane, or *sisi*. Gedja knew her relationship to Jane and her grandmother whom she sometimes called *mama*, yet she did not always define it accurately. She could not define her relationship to her mother's sisters and brothers, some of whom were younger than her, except to say that they were all the children of grandmother.

Wilson and Mafeje (1963: 89) recorded the same use of the terms *umama* and *usisi* in Langa among families of migrants, and among town families who send their children to the country to be brought up by grandparents. The grandmother, they note, who has charge of the children, may be called *mama*, and the real mother, who only sees them from time to time, *sisi*. They observe that the substitutes are a direct reflection of change in everyday behaviour. It is of interest, in Gedja's case, that both she and her mother were born in Cape Town and that both live with Gedja's grandparents in the city.

Playing with Puppets

The two tests so far described have two features in common. They each test reference kin terms and none of them uses material or activity. To examine the use of terms of address and to provide concrete aids,

I devised a test using the family of puppets with which the children and I had played during the year. There were five puppets: an old man — Bhololo; his wife, an old woman — Nosipho; their daughter — Thandeka; and her son — Zolani, and daughter — Nopinki. The father was away working on the docks of a small port. They were, of course, African. The children named them. I used them to discuss aspects of the children's experience indirectly. The following was the format used with each child. We took out the puppets, handled them, and reminded each other of their names and kinship. I then said that we were going to play a game in which each puppet in turn was to call each of the others but was not allowed to use their names. It was practice for *hlonipha* (ritual avoidance). One puppet would be placed on the child's hand and Mary (my assistant) and I would have the others on our hands. The child might have the mother. I would say, 'Thandeka wishes to call the family to come and have supper. Zolani and Nopinki are playing on the road, Nosipho is washing in the yard and Bhololo is buying vegetables from a hawker. Thandeka is not allowed to use their names. How does she call Zolani?'

The children seemed relaxed and they enjoyed the game although Nomvula and Hintsa gave up after three puppets had called the others.

There were a limited number of address forms that could be used. A point was given for each correct address form used in the twenty calls (see Table 3).

Table 3: Use of Kin Terms of Address

					Scores on puppet calls (Total Possible — 20)							
Pel.	Toz.	Lun.	Yam.	Tog.	Ceb.	Nuk.	Sal.	Gwa.	Ged.	Zuz.	Hin.	Nom.
20	18	15	12	12	8	7	7	7	7	7	6	3

Peliswe got full marks and Tozame two less; five children got over half marks. Fifty per cent of all possible points were scored, whereas on Piaget's test, only 36 per cent were scored. Although the range of possible kin terms was limited, just as many were used as in the LeVine and Price-Williams interview, where the possible range was far greater. Given the complicating factors in family life for children living in a South African urban squatter camp, I suggest that variations of the use of puppets could prune away some extraneous foliage from family trees and allow a more accurate measure of children's use and understanding of kinship terms to be made. If a list of members of the household is desirable, it could be elicited by using objects such as models.

In writing up his study of kinship, Piaget (1928: 92) remarks on the fact that children handle relational problems on the plane of action long before they do so on the verbal plane. This is because the child has not yet become 'quite definitely and consciously' aware of the distinction between membership (we are three brothers) and relation (I have two brothers). He, therefore, warns against using material objects, at least for the problems set in his interview. However, although the puppets represent concrete forms and their membership as a family is given as well as their reference kin identities from the point of view of the mother puppet, the subject still has to work out relations within a fairly complex network and so demonstrate an ability to handle the symbolic system. For example, while the subject is told that the puppet called Nosipho is the mother of the children's mother, it is not stated what kin term the grandmother should use to call her grandchild(ren). Further, while Nosipho and Bhololo are known to be Thandeka's parents, the subject is not told what kin terms they use to address each other.

The 1928 study carried one of Piaget's strongest statements on his view of childish egocentrism. He stated that until the age of seven or eight the child always takes his own point of view as something absolute and remains ignorant of the habits of relativity and comparison and that his field of consciousness is still restricted. For example, Piaget (1928: 89) says the child 'has always considered his brothers and sisters from his own point of view, calling them brothers and sisters, counting the family only as a whole. But the thought of their individual viewpoints has never crossed his mind . . . .' It is this last comment that the play with puppets questions.

There is no ego involved in the puppet kinship play, but it is interesting to see that when either of the puppets representing the children, Nopinki and Zolani, were asked to call, the success rate was high, as shown in Table 4.

The table shows how many children called the other puppets using the correct kin term when pretending to be each puppet in turn. For example, when the children were holding Nopinki, five of these called all the others and eight called three of the four others correctly. Six of

Table 4: *Puppet Play and the Use of Kin Terms:*
The number of children who called family members correctly using kin terms when holding each puppet in turn

Puppets' names	Kin Identity	Number of Possible Terms				
		4	3	2	1	0
Nopinki	Daughter	5	8			
Zolani	Son	4	8			1
Thandeka	Mother	5	2		2	6
Nosipho	Grandmother	2		1	2	8
Bhololo	Grandfather	2		1	3	6

the eight failed to call Nopinki's brother, Zolani, correctly. When holding Zolani seven of the eight failed to call his sister, Nopinki, correctly. This fits in with the particular use of terms for brother and sister noted earlier. I had not defined which puppet child was older than the other, preferring to allow each child to decide for himself or herself during early play sessions.

A child holding Nopinki or Zolani (the puppet son or daughter), would use the correct kin term more often in calling the others than when an adult puppet was held. Perhaps a fairer description of Piaget's notion of egocentricity in childhood would be the term child-centricity. Child-centricity eliminates some of the secondary meanings that have been loaded onto the term egocentricity. After all, how many adults successfully perceive the world from the point of view of the child? In concluding their study on the acquisition of English kin terms, Haviland and Clark (1974: 46) suggest that a child should have less difficulty in taking the viewpoint of another child than in taking that of an adult. They add that 'it is clearly a factor that should be explored further'. The above study lends support to their suggestion.

The puppet test does not demand a firm conception of number as does the Piagetian test.

Discussion

In preparation for a task that involved estimating the relative size of his or her family, each child gave me a list of family members. The lists highlighted the number of variables that had to be taken into account.

A child may have had to decide whether or not:

a) to include members of the nuclear family, whether or not they lived in the same house or area (ie. parents and/or siblings);
b) to include members of the wider family, whether or not they lived in the same house or area;
c) to include members of either parent's clan;
d) to include a parent's 'husband'/'wife' if other than the child's parent, and/or their offspring;
e) to exclude other household members.

Seven children listed every member of the nuclear family while six did not, as some members lived away from the Crossroads home. Eight children named at least one member outside the nuclear family. With four children (Togu, Nukwa, Saliswa, and Nomvula) it was difficult to establish for certain whether or not they were clear as to who belonged to the nuclear family. It took questioning using a tape recorder, an exercise with clay figures, a life history interview, and kinship interviews to establish that each did know who was a member of the immediate family group. On some occasions Togu and Nukwa each denied having a brother (the latter denied having any kin on one occasion); Nomvula usually insisted on including her father's brother's daughters as her sisters; and Saliswa was sometimes confused as to exactly which parent begat which child in her large, complex family. The point to be made is that a child's conception of family membership is not easily traced when family composition alters in the face of change. However, comments such as the one made by Seagrim and Lendon (1980: 200) about the cognitive concepts of Aborigine children are questionable in the light of the above findings. Their comment was made as part of their explanation of how the 'Aboriginal mode' affects their (lack of) quantitative thinking. Their first reason for the absence of such thinking is that '. . . the Aboriginal infant is brought up in a society in which the notions associated with personal ownership are largely lacking: his care-takers are numerous and largely interchangeable and even the kinship terms used to designate each equivalent person (mother and mother's sister) are the same . . .' The authors link non-ownership of possessions to the number of child care-takers and the equivalence of kin terms. Yet they do not record from the child's point of view just how interchangeable the care-takers are nor how equivalent in value. They fail to plumb the depths of the fiction.

Before concluding, the following conversations recorded during observations of children at home will be offered as illustrations of points made earlier in the chapter. One such point was that, within families, emphasis is placed on seniority among brothers and sisters and the respect due from those younger. Van Warmelo (1931) observed that brothers everywhere scrupulously observe the prerogatives of primogeniture. To lack respect towards an elder brother is a great offence and easily leads to blows. The same applied to the relations of sisters among themselves.

Observation on 11 November 1980 at 5.20 p.m. outside Tozama's home:

Tozama: I have seen Makhosi kicking my ball. What can I do to find it?
Friend: It is easy for you to ask him to give you the ball for it doesn't belong to him. It belongs to you, so he must return it to you.
Tozama: Hey, Makhosi, kindly give me that ball as I want to play with it.
Makhosi (her brother aged 18): I am not your size. You must not call me like that. I am older than you, you must have 'respect' for me. ['Respect' was said in English.]
Tozama: What's that? What's 'respect'? Tell me, brother, I want to know that English word you said to me.
Makhosi: I mean having no manners, a child who is naughty like you is a child who has no 'respect', no manners. Do you hear what I say?
Tozama: Yes, I do understand your explanation of the word.

In the same family on the evening of the following day, a second conversation was recorded.

Tozama's mother upbraids her sister, aged fourteen, for losing a bottle of Permanganate of Potash which she needs to mix in medicine required by people for the journey to Transkei at Christmas. The girl, Nomvuyo, is asked by the *makoti* (her brother's new bride) to wash dishes but she plaintively says that she has to find the Permanganate of Potash although she is not at all certain that her mother gave it to her to keep. Tozama interrupts her plaint saying,

Oh no, Nomvuyo, stop talking nonsense about Mama.
Nomvuyo (angrily): What, Tozama, what do you say? I'll hit you if you are naughty. You must not be naughty. You must know that you are a child. I am older than you.

The following record some instances in which the term *brother* was used: the first came from Cebo's home and reflects the way in which Cebo uses *brother* to address or refer to his cousin (his mother's sister's son, aged fourteen). At 8.30 p.m. on 10 November 1980, Cebo had eaten and his aunt (mother's sister) was dishing up for her son, Mxolisi.

> *Cebo:* I am also going to eat again with Mxolisi. He is my brother, I must eat with him.
> *Mother:* When you eat your own food, he is not your brother, you do not think of him; but when he is having his own food, he is your brother.
> *Cebo laughs.*

At 6.00 p.m. on the next day, Cebo's mother asked Mxolisi, her sister's son, 'Where is my brother, Mxolisi?' meaning his father, her sister's husband.

And on the following day, Cebo's father returned from work at 7.30 p.m. He asked his wife if he could have a fire tin in his bedroom and she said that it was a waste to have one there as well as in the sitting-room where everyone was gathered. Father said, in a hurt tone, 'But I am wet.'

> *Mother:* Oh, I didn't know that you are wet. Please forgive me then. Let me make a fire for you, *my daddy.*
> *Mother's sister:* Here. Take my fire.
> *Father:* Thank you *my swaer*,[7] *my wife* was a bit rude to me though she can see that I am a little wet.
> *Mother:* Cebo, go and take the heater from *my sister's* room.
> *Cebo:* Mama, mama, it is heavy for me to carry.
> *Mother:* Mxolisi, help him please *my dear son.* Hurry up. Here is a cup of coffee for you *daddy.*
> *Father:* Thank you, *mama.*
> *Mxolisi:* Here is a chair for you to sit on, *daddy.*

In the above, kin terms are frequently used and not always in strict accord with nuclear ties. For example, Mother calls her sister's son, 'my dear son' and he calls his mother's sister's husband 'father'.

One example will suffice to suggest the wide use to which the term 'mother' can be put:

In Zuziwe's home at 8.00 p.m. on 27 October 1980, the lodger,

Mimi, is preparing a bottle for Zuziwe's three-year-old brother, Sonwaba. Mimi teases him lightly because he addresses her, using her name:

> *Sonwaba:* Make a bottle for me, Mimi.
> *Mimi:* Who is Mimi?
> *Sonwaba:* My mother is Mimi.

Many examples could be given. They support one of the conclusions of this chapter — that the use to which kinship terms are put by children is not easily ascertained through the medium of formal interviews. Attention must be paid both to their use of the terms in address and reference and to the context.

Conclusion

One of the features of a changing society is the change in kinship terminology. Among the Xhosa, as Hunter (1936) and Wilson and Mafeje (1963) observed, change is not recent. English and Afrikaans words have been extensively assimilated. This study confirms the changes that were recorded by the last two authors in Langa: that is, changes in the use of terms for father's sister, mother's sister, mother's brother's wife, a man's elder brother, a woman's brother, and different, less extended, uses of mother and father. However, terms that were replacing them in Crossroads were different from those in Langa. *Umakazi* was used not *uanti*; *tata* or *umalume* not *ompie*; *sisi* not *usister wam*; and *tata* rather than *bawo*; *usisi* and *ubhuti* were used in the same extended way in Crossroads as in Langa. The use of *umakhulu* had remained the same. Three points must be emphasized. Seventeen years separated the publication of the research on Langa and my fieldwork; second, the class composition of the Crossroads population differed from that of Langa — the latter having a larger group with more years of schooling and another of migrants without their families; and third, my informants were children. The effective time gap may be longer than seventeen years inasmuch as the Langa informants were adults and the Crossroads informants children. Nevertheless, the trends in the use of terms were similar and the issues they raise worthy of closer study. That change in kinship terms was occurring and that their use possibly varied according to class, age, and urban status should caution researchers against drawing hasty conclusions based on set interviews amongst sample groups. Change affects family composition and traditional attitudes towards kin ties and responsibilities. These must all be taken into account in the study of kinship terminology.

The abstract nature of the interview technique and its reliance (in Piaget's version) on number conception make it difficult to administer to some child populations. The complexity of household membership in Crossroads made the gathering of a census through children a task more difficult than the one LeVine and Price-Williams faced with Hausa children.[8] Similarly, lists of family members were difficult to obtain from children because of family dispersal and changing patterns of work, residence and marriage.[9]

It seemed to me that children aged seven or eight were aware of the implications behind the use of kinship terms. They understood the emotional nuances that choice among possible terms might imply. Sometimes I suspected, on the basis of the use of kin terms, that a child did not know his or her exact relationship to a care-taker but other incidents demonstrated that this was not so. Inferences about emotional salience and the child's understanding of the kinship system cannot reliably be drawn from single tests based on the use of kin terms.

Notes

1. Rights *in uxorem* refer to the husband's right to require his wife both to sleep with him and to cook and work for him. Rights *in genetricem* refer to a husband's rights to the children which his wife bears. The distinction is crucial: in some societies, for example, these rights over the children belong not to the husband but the children's mother's brother.
2. Parallel cousins — offspring of father's brother or mother's sister.
3. Cross-cousins — offspring of father's sister or mother's brother.
4. On the origins of the two terms: *bhuti* came from *boetie* and *sisi* is short for *usisiomdala* (older sister) or *usisiomcinci* (younger sister), so my Crossroads informants said. *Sisi* may be derived from the Afrikaans *sussie*.
5. In the vocative case there is no prefix.
6. *Ukuhlonipha* — to show respect, often expressed in avoidance.
7. In Afrikaans, *swaer* means brother-in-law and is often used in addressing a friend, similar to the English 'mate'.

8. See Murray (1976: 54) for a discussion of the criteria by which the household should be defined.

9. Spiegel (1980: 1) gives references to the writings of historians and anthropologists within an emerging body of work that deals with 'the manner in which ordinary people caught up in the rigours of the migrant labour system, have come to cope with the pressure on them and their families'.

First Steps
Paul Alberts

I shall never be disillusioned. Always
I shall be happy at the heart
of things.
       And all their crusted words,
hurled like missiles from foreign soil
shattered across the pages of common lives
scorching choking lungs and minds
of children, I shall suck
again and again and blow
curling images
in a black sky.

(Donald Parenzee 1985: 58)

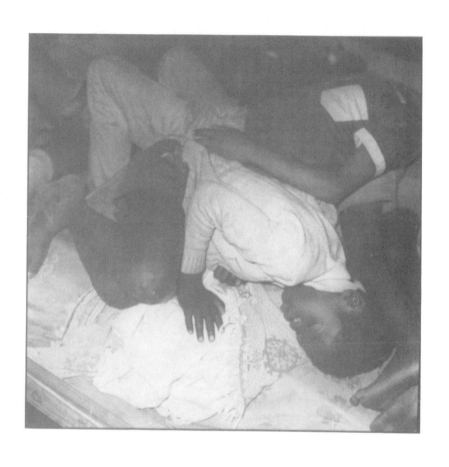

Newspaper sellers awaiting morning newspapers, Mitchells Plain, 1982

Father and daughter, Johannesburg, 1982

Father and son, Athlone, Cape Town, 1978

Nanny and child, Sun City, Bophuthatswana, 1980

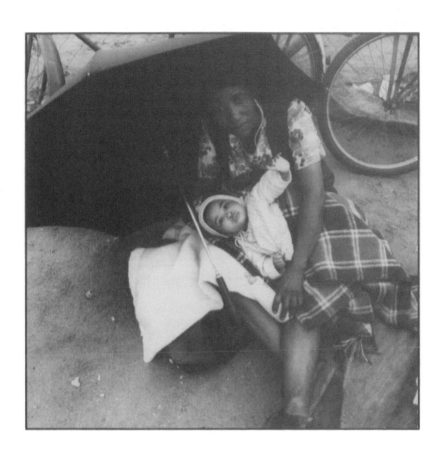

Mother and baby, Taung, Bophuthatswana, 1982

Top: Churchgoers, District Six, Cape Town, 1974
Bottom: Passover meal, Hout Bay, Cape Town, 1986

Top: Nyanga bush squatters fasting in St George's Cathedral, Cape Town, 1982
Bottom: Mosque, Athlone, Cape Town, 1978

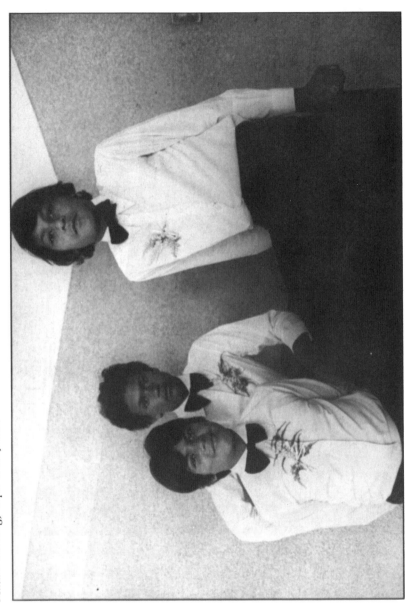

Muslim wedding, Cape Town, 1978

Britstown, Karoo, 1976

Top: High school, Kimberley, 1985
Bottom: Band players, Kew Town, Cape Town, 1978

Top: Chess club, Pace College, Soweto, 1985
Bottom: Inkatha Youth Brigade, Ulundi, 1985

School children dancing, primary school, Die Stadt, Mafikeng, Bophuthatswana, 1982

The audience, primary school, Die Stadt, Mafikeng, Bophuthatswana, 1982

Newspaper seller, Cape Town, 1982

Top: Herdboy, Lesotho, 1978
Bottom: Schoolgirls, Die Stadt, Mafikeng, Bophuthatswana, 1981

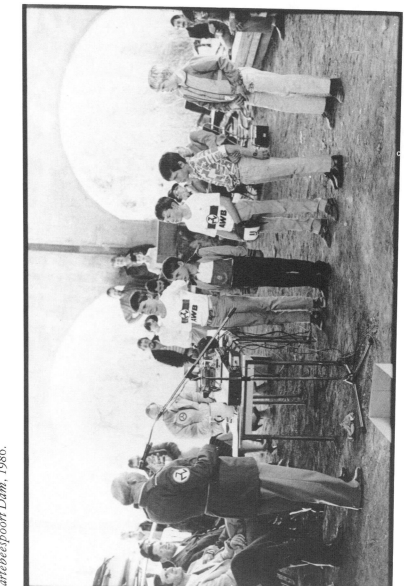

Afrikaner Weerstandbeweging (AWB) Congress, induction of children into the organization at Hartebeespoort Dam, 1986.

Children in Turmoil: The Effects of the Unrest on Township Children

Frank Chikane

This is a report from the heat of the townships of how South Africa appears in 1986 to children and their parents there. It is not so much an academic analysis as a description based largely on the writer's experience as a mediator in recent events in Soweto.

Overview

Thousands of children took to the streets in 1976 in protest against the 'Bantu Education' provided for African pupils. The protest spread to other parts of the country and marked a new era in resistance to apartheid. Township children were jailed, shot and killed. Some served long prison sentences; others lost valuable years of schooling. As a result many were forced into the lowest paid, unskilled jobs while others joined the growing ranks of unemployed youth in South Africa.

A new generation of young militants has emerged. They are the youth who have committed themselves to the struggle for a democratic future. Based on their political experience in 1976, they became the activists of the youth congresses which mushroomed in every corner of the country. These are the young people who continued the battle on the school grounds and joined the ranks of the Congress of South African Students (COSAS), which is now banned. Thousands of school children were mobilized and their demands for equal education and the right to organize at schools were echoed across the country. Young men and women, through their experiences of life under apartheid, through police harassment and violence, came to the conclusion that there was only one option open to them, and that was to take up arms. They are the children of the Soweto of 1976, who swelled the ranks of Umkhonto we Sizwe, the military wing of the African National Congress. They are the children who have been captured and sentenced to long prison terms. It is these children of Soweto who have been executed — Johannes Shabangu, David Moise, Bobby Tsotsobe, and others — for armed attacks on the state.

In the 1980s the struggle against apartheid has escalated and reached the proportions of civil war. The Botha government, faced with a deep economic crisis coupled with the determination of the people to be free, declared a State of Emergency on 21 July 1985. This was a desperate act and an admission that its so-called reform initiatives had failed. The local authorities for Africans set up by the government were rejected by the African people as entrenching apartheid. These local authorities have been the object of much anger in the community and were viciously attacked as apartheid institutions. In the coloured and Indian elections in August 1984 more than eighty per cent of the people showed their rejection of the tricameral parliamentary system. The people's demands were for a non-racial and democratic South Africa, universal franchise, and for a united country free of 'independent' homelands and the Group Areas Act.

Throughout the campaigns of the 1980s, particularly against the local authorities and the tricameral parliamentary system, children participated alongside their parents. They boycotted classes in protest, while others joined their parents on the picket lines, calling on residents not to vote in 'puppet' elections. Widespread school boycotts took place and many children died in unrest at this time. When the State of Emergency was declared, the government paid children the dubious compliment of taking them seriously. It banned COSAS, an organization of school children. Up to 8 000 people, including more than 2 000 children under the age of sixteen, had been detained under the emergency provisions by the end of 1985 (*Sowetan* 13.12.85). Many detainees were members of COSAS and the youth congresses which were affiliates of the United Democratic Front (Detainees' Parents Support Committee Report, November 1985). In reply to questions in parliament recently, the Minister of Law and Order, Louis le Grange, said that the detentions were primarily of a preventive nature.

The effects of detention on these children and their families will be felt for years to come. A boy aged eight was charged with intimidation and refused bail. When he was visited by his family, 'the boy was frantic and crying'. When he appeared in court the next day, he was crying and had a huge bruise on his forehead but could not say how it had been sustained (*Weekly Mail* 7.12.85). There have been other reported incidents of children receiving psychiatric treatment as a result of detention, and McLachlan's chapter in this volume spells out many of the implications.

Detention has been only one form of state violence against children. The presence of the South African Defence Force in the townships has exposed children to a new wave of brutality. Many children have been physically injured and treated by township doctors for the adverse effects of rubber bullets, teargas, and baton charges. There have also been allegations of rape and abuse of children (South African Catholic Bishops' Conference Report 1984).

A group of concerned social workers convened a conference in October 1985 to highlight the brutalization of children. A press release issued by the Concerned Social Workers Conference at that time (25-26.10.85) stated the following:

> A child welfare Social Worker and the Detainees' Parents Support Committee have records of children who have been reported missing. Parents are frantic about the whereabouts of their children. Other forms of violence include the whipping of children by the Defence Force in an attempt to force them out of their homes and into classrooms. The information that we have is still sparse. It relies mainly on testimonies from parents, children and professionals working with such persons. Parents are reluctant to expose their children by reporting them as missing, injured or detained for fear of recrimination from authorities. The result has been that many cases are unreported.
>
> We are concerned about the effects of children's exposure to and experience of violence in the townships. We believe that such exposure can never be conducive to the physical, mental, moral, spiritual and social development of children.

At a meeting of doctors, social workers, psychologists, and psychiatrists on 14 September 1985, the following resolution was passed:

> We express our deeply felt horror and revulsion at the State's assault on children and call upon the Government to release all the detained

children immediately into the custody of their parents or guardians and an immediate end to the security forces' harassment and detention of children. Children are particularly susceptible to the development of long-term adverse effects of these brutalising experiences — such as anxiety disorders, adjustment and behaviour disorder and even psychotic episodes.

Parents themselves have suffered deeply because of their concern for their children. Many frantically contacted friends and organizations in the townships, seeking assistance. The mother of Fanie Guduka, an eleven-year-old who spent 57 days in prison, described the pain: 'I am taking tranquilizers for tension. Since Fanie was in prison I have had pains in my heart. I have also spent a lot of money buying fresh food and fruit for him while he was in prison' (*Sunday Star* 26.01.86).

An editorial in the *Star* (17.09.85), in referring to Fanie's case, condemned the imprisonment of children.

The case of an 11 year old child who was kept in prison for 57 days is at last before the courts . . . . He allegedly threw stones . . . . It took a Supreme Court ruling to get him out of jail . . . . He was kept in police cells to protect society from his influence and to ensure he did not flee justice . . . . What sort of madness is this? . . . Human rights lawyer Mr. Nicholas .Haysom said that South Africa departed significantly from international standards in its imprisonment of children. International Codes, he said, embody an almost peremptory requirement that children should not be held in the same prison as adults. While South African law complies with this and stipulates that children should not be kept in jail at all unless no other institution existed these rules are honoured more in the breach than the observance.

The pressure has resulted in the Minister of Justice, Kobie Coetsee, taking some action in this regard. He announced that a separate prison would be made available at Leeukop Prison by April 1986 for detained and sentenced juveniles.

The facts speak for themselves. The State of Emergency provided security forces with a licence to commit indiscriminate acts of violence against children. South Africa is a signatory to the United Nations charter on the rights of children, yet the South African government has unashamedly violated these terms. Whereas the causes of child abuse were usually sought in the intra-psychic conflicts of parents who may themselves have been abused as children, today South Africa is faced with a new phenomenon of state abuse of children. The African child in the townships is being faced with state repressive machinery instead of being shielded from it. One would have expected the state to have given the protection of children top priority, but the opposite is the case. It was for this reason that the Conference of Concerned Social Workers adopted a resolution 'to promote the rights of the child'. The experiences and exposure of township children to violence will undoubtedly result in the maiming of children in every sphere of their development. Furthermore, all the signs are that the violence will breed yet more violence. The present conflict in South Africa has set in motion the same cycle as that of 1976. Today the 'Young Lions', as they are called in the townships, are the products of that era. They are the marshalls dressed in khaki at mass funerals, leading the singing, directing the crowds, and saluting their fallen comrades with the pledge that 'your struggle will be taken forward'. Another generation is growing up in the townships. What will their future be? The answers are to be seen in the freedom slogans written on the walls. The people know it and the government knows it.

This overview has briefly traced the current unrest in the townships and its major effects on children since 1976. It is evident that children under apartheid are affected in many other ways too, but the most notable results at present have been the great increase in the politicization of this generation of children and their growing militance. From their ranks will come the new generation of young militants with whom parents, teachers, and no doubt the government will be dealing. The section which follows stresses some salient features in the background against which such township children grow up. Then, since the politicization of young people has taken place in the classrooms and school grounds, the writer will trace the nature of the education crisis in the townships, the relationship between parents, pupils, and teachers, and attempts to unite in action. It is through these struggles that children have directly encountered the police. The final section deals with the 'war' in South Africa and its effects on the township child.

The Township Child — Struggling Against the Odds

As many chapters in this volume demonstrate in greater detail, to be born into an apartheid society is to be born on a battlefield. The fight is for human dignity and even survival. For the African child the battle begins from the day it is conceived. The poor diet and nutrition of many mothers cannot feed the fetus adequately. Their stresses and strains in living under apartheid also affect the fetus. Inadequate medical care and long working hours with little rest from helping to meet the needs of the family have consequences for the quality of life of that new-born baby, as Zille graphically shows above.

Malnutrition is a major killer of black children in South Africa. A 1979 survey on infant mortality (*Rand Daily Mail* 13.10.80) demonstrated that mortality rates for both African and coloured children aged one to four years were thirteen times higher than for whites: that the majority of deaths occurred in children under five years of age; and that those below the age of one year were six times higher among African and coloured children than among whites. The chapter on child health in this volume has other appalling figures. There is widespread poverty which makes it impossible in many cases to obtain enough of the right food for adequate nutrition. The emergence of Operation Hunger and the Churches' Hunger Fund are an indication of the state of poverty in this country of plenty.

The townships offer limited recreation and day-care facilities. Working mothers, due to financial circumstances, are frequently forced to go back to work when their children are less than three months old. This can seriously affect the physical and emotional health of the mother and child, since adequate care for the child thereafter is often difficult to obtain. As can be seen in the chapter by Cock *et al* on day-care facilities in Soweto, for example, the six crèches run by the West Rand Administration Board (the only crèches to receive a significant state subsidy) catered for a mere 720 children out of a total of 192 000 pre-school children in the township.

The lack of housing in African townships has resulted in over-crowding, ill-health, and insecurity. Squatting has increased, and there are problems related to poor sanitation and water supply. The government's housing policy is designed to curb its expenditure on housing and pass to township dwellers the responsibility to provide their own homes through self-help schemes. 'Another reason for this cut-back is the fact that the Department of Community Development does not want to be seen as the landlord of the working classes; it does not want to be the target of township protests. Instead, the government wants to shift the responsibility for housing onto the private business sector' (Lipschitz 1985: 25).

At school children are subjected to a form of education which prepares them for life under apartheid. The teacher-pupil ratio in 1983 was 1:43. This means that there was one teacher for every 43 African children in comparison with one teacher for every 18 white children (Christie 1985: 115). Over the period 1975-76, for every R1 spent on an African child, R14.07 was spent on a white child (Christie 1985: 100). As Nasson shows above, the schools are poorly equipped and overcrowded, the teachers underqualified. Consequently, the school drop-out rate for African children is very high. Many do not have more than four years of schooling (Christie 1985: 106).

Since the African child is so educationally disadvantaged, he or she is frequently forced to take on the most unskilled work. Although it is illegal in South Africa to employ any child under the age of sixteen, many African children are obliged to work in order to survive. Children are illegally employed as newspaper-vendors, in factories, and as domestic servants. With the disintegration of many family units because of the migrant labour system and other factors discussed by Burman and Fuchs above in the chapter on family break-up, some African children are homeless and have to find the means to support themselves. The chapter on street children demonstrates an urban solution. In farming areas, while not homeless, black children are often expected to work alongside their parents, for pitiful wages or food rations. Unemployment among black youth is very high. 'Studies done in Soweto have shown that unemployment has risen by 5.5 per cent per annum during the [current] recession' (Bachmayer 1985: 20).

These are some of the realities of life under apartheid for African children. It is a life often filled with insecurity and with little hope for a better future. It is certainly a battle for survival as children and their parents find themselves in the whirlpool of vicious apartheid laws such as influx control, the migrant labour system, and forced removals of the kind described by Roux above. It is a system which breaks up family life and forces every sixteen year old to apply for a passbook. Around this age many African children begin to engage in a series of hide-and-seek games with the police for not carrying a pass. Nor is this generally the first encounter of the township child with the police. In their short lives they may have been exposed to pass raids or even to prison while strapped to their mother's backs. A township child often experiences the cruelty of the system at an early age. They learn survival skills while very young and are generally quite resilient. But for many the world is a harsh one of empty bellies, of disintegrated families, and of violence in many different forms. Theirs is indeed a struggle against the odds.

Education Crisis: Parent-Student-Teacher Alliance

It is important to make the connection between the school children's revolt which started in 1976 and the conditions under which these children grew up and developed. Although the spark that set off the explosion of 1976 was the question of Afrikaans as a medium of instruction in the schools, children's demands shifted very quickly to a rejection of the whole system of education for Africans and of apartheid.

Active support for their demands in 1976 was not forthcoming from parents. Except for isolated instances of support such as that from the Soweto Parents Association, the children were organizing their own struggle with their own leadership, irrespective of the wishes of their elders. The passivity of parents was seen by their offspring as resulting from experience in the 1960s of the oppression of the system. The 1960 declaration of the State of Emergency, the banning of the African National Congress and the Pan African Congress, detentions, torture, and long-term imprisonment all contributed to this state of affairs. In short, because of the repressive nature of the apartheid regime in the early sixties, the children saw the black masses as almost completely silenced and made to live in fear for almost two decades. The failure of parents to struggle with their children and to provide leadership widened the generation gap. The more radical children almost lost confidence in their parents. They felt that their parents were prisoners of fear and death. It took much effort on the part of progressive groups and organizations during the first part of the 1980s to address this crisis of confidence. They knew that this could be achieved only by inducing adults to become actively involved in resisting the apartheid regime.

A major event which began to restore the confidence of the children was the launching of the United Democratic Front in 1983. For the first time in many years parents, who were the residents in the communities and the workers on the factory floor, joined hands with the radical children to denounce apartheid. Together they campaigned against high rents and the hated Community Council system. They were detained, tortured, and teargassed together while fighting for a common cause. This time the work stay-aways of 1984 and 1985 were called by community organizations and trade unions. Chris Dlamini, the then President of the Federation of South African Trade Unions (FOSATU), argued that workers also had to deal with the education crisis which affected their children. He said that the workers were the ones who paid for the education of their children and were therefore obliged to enter this struggle with their children. Children, in turn, supported the unions. A case in point was the support of COSAS for a major boycott of Simba-Quix products, called in September 1984 by the FOSATU-affiliated Sweet, Food and Allied Workers' Union over the dismissal of 422 Africans, which was ultimately successful. Such actions gave meaning to the COSAS slogan of 'Student-Worker Action' and resulted in better communication between students and workers.

As opposition to the educational system intensified, more concerned parents began to support the school children. In September 1985 the Soweto Parents Crisis Committee (SPCC) was formed. In other parts of the country parent-student-teacher committees came into existence (the term 'student' in fact denoting school children). These alliances resulted from a growing awareness that parents must participate in their children's education. There was a realization that the government used education to promote its own ideology, to control the masses, and to produce cheap labour. Parents and teachers also became aware that to change the education system, the political system that controlled education must be changed too.

At the end of 1985 the SPCC convened a national consultative conference in Johannesburg from 28-29 December to address the education crisis. All over the country thousands of children were boycotting classes. They and their parents were calling for the withdrawal of the troops from the townships, the lifting of the State of Emergency, the release of student and other leaders from detention, and the postponement of the final annual examinations. After lengthy deliberations, the national conference of parents, teachers, and students resolved that the children would return to school for the time being and that the Botha regime would be given three months to meet their demands. At the time of writing, the three months have not yet elapsed. What was clear from the conference, however, was that the children's confidence in their parents and teachers had been restored. A relationship based on respect for the ideas and concerns of the children has been forged. In this regard the Reverend Tsele, Publicity Officer of the SPCC, said that 'the most difficult task of the SPCC has been to manage the tension between conservative parents and radical students. It should be noted that these students have been fighting apartheid all by themselves. At times they think that the moderate ideas of their parents will detract them from their goals. The task of the SPCC has been to build an understanding between parents and children. This understanding must be a political one.' (*Sowetan* 13.02.1985.)

Township children have, however, been active not only in student organizations. They have participated in youth organizations, in political organizations, and in church youth groups. These groups have played an important role in the development and training of youth leadership.

The War in South Africa — Its Effects on the Township Child

As the resistance to oppression and exploitation intensified, state repression increased to alarming proportions. The revolt in the Vaal Triangle in 1984 resulted in a bloody confrontation between the people and the police. In the early hours of 23 October some 7 000 police and troops besieged the Vaal townships, conducting house-to-house searches to stamp out the resistance and to restore 'law and order' (Cooper *et al* 1985: 75). As more and more black townships revolted against the regime, the South African Defence Force moved in and occupied the townships. There have been allegations of rape, torture, assaults, and brutal killings by the security forces in the townships. In the Western Cape, the ambushing of three youths on Thornton Road, Athlone, caused national and international outrage. But the state action did not stop the consumer boycotts, particularly in the Eastern Cape. The people demanded an end to the emergency and the withdrawal of troops from the townships. In the minds of the people in the townships there is a war between them and the apartheid army, which is perceived as an enemy army. They see it as defending the white minority government, elected by whites only, for white interests alone. It is seen as an army protecting white privileges at the expense of black lives.

This description of the war situation in South Africa depicts the conditions under which the township child is growing up. They have affected children more than many people realize. The world of the township child is extremely violent. It is a world made up of teargas, bullets, whippings, detention, and death on the streets. It is an experience of military operations and night raids, of roadblocks and body searches. It is a world where parents and friends get carried away in the night to be interrogated. It is a world were people simply disappear, where parents are assassinated and homes are petrol bombed. Such is the environment of the township child today.

Children these days spend their time thinking and planning how to outwit the security forces and to take defensive action. For instance, to fight the effects of teargas, they organize cloths and water. When there are mass funerals, buckets of water are put along the route of the funeral procession in case of a teargas attack. They have learnt how to set up barricades and how to keep the security forces out. Life in the townships seems to have changed irrevocably. A township resident said: 'When my two-year-old daughter sees a military vehicle passing, she looks for a stone.' Nursery school children are no exception. They too have learned the language of *siyanyova* (we will destroy), which is the popular slogan used by the youths when attacking what they call 'targets', meaning the buildings, vehicles, and individuals regarded as symbols of the apartheid regime and its forces.

The exposure of children to outrages in the townships has resulted in adaptive behaviour patterns. They are learning a different set of survival skills. Their songs tell of the world as they perceive it, a violent world, a war situation. They move in groups in the townships: a commander in charge, his 'armed forces' around him. Their ammunition is stones, sticks, and probably petrol bombs. They have different values. No longer are the local football players or the Bruce Lees of the movies their heroes. They know now only of the Mandelas and the Sisulus. And there are those who are joining the ranks of Umkhonto we Sizwe to fight the system. The youth in the churches and church groups are also adapting to this new reality. This is manifested in their songs, prayers, and various forms of expression of the faith. There are indeed some children in the townships who are not as radical or even politically conscious as the majority of their contemporaries, but the pervasive atmosphere of violence and confrontation tends eventually to plunge all into active participation. They find themselves either confronting the system or running away from teargas and bullets.

Whilst many young children are channelling their energies politically, there are those whose exposure and experiences of brutalization will harm their social, physical, spiritual, moral, and mental development forever. The school boycotts, for instance, are affecting children's education, with many having lost two to four years of schooling between 1976 and 1986. A gap is being created between those children who are continuing with their education in private schools or in one of the 'homelands', and those children who are involved in school boycotts as an expression of their struggle against apartheid. Tensions are already developing, with students in Soweto and elsewhere demanding that those who have continued their education rejoin them in the townships to advance the struggle. A further result of the education crisis is that fewer students have qualified for university entrance in the last two or three years. South Africa, even in a post-apartheid era, will have to contend with the problems generated by the large number of children who have not gone through secondary education. Any form of planning for the future has to take this into consideration.

But the most tragic reflection of the war situation in which South Africa finds itself is that it faces the years to come with children who have been socialized to find violence completely acceptable and human life cheap. Moreover, this growing generation will increasingly in future be prepared to make sacrifices, even to die, for what they perceive to be the noble goals of justice and peace. They are more determined than ever before to be free — free, no matter what the cost.

Children in Prison

Fiona McLachlan

Introduction

They arrested me because I stole some clothes. I think I was taken to court about a week after my arrest, when I pleaded guilty. I then spent thirteen months in the police cells waiting for the court to finish with my case. I don't remember a trial with witnesses and I don't remember being told anything about bail. No-one told me why it took so long. I saw a social worker once. There were only juveniles in my cell. We were not assaulted by the police. The only food we received was porridge and bread. My mother brought food for me but they never let me see her.

There was a lot of fighting in the cells. There were many gangsters and they tried to force me to join a gang. They told me not to be a 'baby' or a 'sissy'. When you are first put in the cell, they make you lie down on the cement floor and then they kick your head against the cement. They make you blow out your cheeks and then *klap* [slap] them so hard that your mouth bleeds. They took my food and the 'boss' stole my clothes. I also saw boys being raped in the cells. I was fourteen years old at the time.

My son is fifteen years old and he was detained for fourteen days in the prison. He was fine when they took him but ever since he was released he has been very strange. He is not a child anymore, he is like a beast. He doesn't know where he is, and he keeps wandering off muttering 'let them kill me, they must finish me off'. I don't know what they did to him in there.

When I was about fifteen I spent three months in police cells. Adults and juveniles were mixed up together. At first I was beaten up by the other cell-mates but I knew some of the boys in the cell so I was not assaulted again. The police assaulted me to make me make a statement. They punched me with their fists and pulled a bag over my head and suffocated me while my hands were tied behind my back. There was a lot of fighting amongst the cell-mates. We were given blankets full of lice and we were never taken outside for exercise. We were given raw *pap* [porridge] and soup. My grandmother brought food for me but I never saw her.

I have been arrested many times. The first time I was about twelve years old. I really hate the police. They have always assaulted me. I have been punched in my stomach and ribs and beaten with batons. Children are badly treated by the police. I have been put in cells with adults and children have a bad time, especially the young ones that cannot fight back. Drugs are one of the main problems in prison.

These extracts from interviews with children are common descriptions of life in prison and police cells.[1] Since conditions in police cells are just as inappropriate as those of prisons for the custody of children, police cells are also included in this chapter. Unfortunately reference is made to different racial groups as the writer contends that there is a correlation between a child's race, the reasons for his or her imprisonment, and the conditions of such imprisonment.

It appears that many people of different occupations and persuasions whose work in some way involves children are unaware of the fact that not only does the law permit the imprisonment of children, but also that thousands of children actually experience prison life. It is vital that people who deal with the child and/or the family concerned become aware of the circumstances under which children may be imprisoned. Notwithstanding the argument in favour of abolishing imprisonment for children altogether, it is submitted that even in the present system described below there should and could be a great deal more support for the young prisoner and his or her family, who frequently are ignorant of the few legal rights that exist for the child accused or child prisoner.

A slight indication of the number of children who go to prison is provided by the following figures: on 17 July 1983 there were 1 970 children in prison while on 19 March 1984 there were 974 children in gaol.[2] These figures do not include those children held in police cells.

During the course of 1984, 3 568 children accompanied their mothers to prison (*Hansard* 18.03.85: 671).

Legal Background

In terms of the common law, a child younger than seven years old cannot be held responsible for his or her criminal conduct. Children between the ages of seven and fourteen are presumed not to be criminally responsible and this presumption must be rebutted by the state in order to convict the child accused.[3] It is therefore theoretically possible for a child above the age of seven years old to be imprisoned. In addition, the Children's Act, No. 33 of 1960, includes a police cell in the definition of 'a place of safety', so that a child may be placed in a police cell without having committed any alleged criminal offence at all (Section 1).

The new Child Care Act, No. 74 of 1983, which has been enacted but is not yet in force, does not specifically include a police cell in the definition of a 'place of safety'. This Act instead provides that a 'place of safety' includes any place suitable for the reception of a child, into which the owner, occupier, or person in charge thereof is willing to receive a child (Section 1 (xxviii)). Once this legislation is in force, the use of police cells as 'places of safety' suitable for the reception of children should be challenged in the courts.

Children held in prisons fall into one of four categories: *unconvicted prisoners*, who are either awaiting trial or are held as detainees; *sentenced prisoners*, who have been convicted and sentenced to imprisonment or are awaiting transferral to a reformatory; *transferrals* from a reformatory to a prison; and children who have been *admitted to prison with their mothers*, who are either awaiting-trial or sentenced prisoners.

Children may also be held in police cells for one of the above four reasons. Since police cells are far more numerous than prisons, and more readily available as lock-ups for children temporarily held, the writer estimates that far more children are held in the former than in the latter. As described above, the Children's Act permits the temporary placement of a child in a police cell as a 'place of safety'. However, in practice it appears that children may spend months in police cells awaiting the outcome of a court case and/or their transfer to an alternative institution.

The Role of Apartheid Legislation

Prior to a discussion of the laws and court procedures concerning the imprisonment of children, the link between the effects of apartheid legislation and policies and those children that are arrested and imprisoned should be considered. There are many laws and policies that affect only black children, particularly African children, and it is therefore not surprising that the vast majority of children in prison are black. Examples of such racist laws and policies are discussed in detail in other chapters of this book and include the following.

(a) The Group Areas Act, No. 41 of 1950, has uprooted hundreds of thousands of families from their homes and dumped them in endless townships of matchbox houses. The effects of this Act on communities include the gradual breakdown of the supportive extended family system, increased living and transport costs, an increase in the number of women compelled to work, and large numbers of unsupervised children roaming the streets. Children cannot remain unaffected by the trauma caused by this legislation.

(b) The 'pass laws' (including influx control legislation)[4] can make African parents criminals and cause African children to go to prison with their mothers simply because they do not have a 'pass' to 'white South Africa'.

(c) The migrant labour system denies thousands of African children a normal family life for all but a few weeks of each year in their childhood.

(d) The education system blatantly discriminates against blacks.

(e) Many other socio-economic facts of black township life, such as housing shortages and over-crowded living conditions, high unemployment, poverty, and inadequate services and facilities, all affect the lives of township children.

The effect of such laws is that a disproportionate number of black children come into contact with the criminal justice system. A further effect is that many black children naturally learn to disrespect laws that discriminate against them. This disrespect has been extended to many other laws forbidding criminal activities which black children no longer regard as wrong. For example, many black children scorn capitalism, as it appears to favour only whites so that the theft of whites' goods is justified as 'redistribution' or 'repossession' and no longer bears the stigma of theft. As described below, the actual implementation of these laws further erodes a black child's faith in the administration of justice in general and in the courts themselves.

Juvenile and Children's Courts

The general welfare of children is protected by the Children's Act, No. 33 of 1960, which, in brief, prohibits anyone from permitting a child in his or her care to be ill-treated or neglected (Section 18 (1)). Any person legally liable to maintain a child must provide the child with adequate food, clothing and medical care (Section 18 (2)). The Child Care Act, No. 74 of 1983, imposes a similar duty of care and support (Chapter 8). This duty would therefore shift to prison and police officials during any period that a child was in their care, unless any such duty was specifically excluded by legislation. For example, security legislation permits the use of solitary confinement which, it is submitted, would constitute emotional neglect if committed by a parent.

There are two entirely different and separate courts concerned with children: the *juvenile court*, which deals with children charged with criminal offences; and the *children's court*, which conducts enquiries to determine whether a child is 'in need of care'.[5]

Most children are sent to prisons or police cells as a result of their alleged criminal behaviour even though some of these children who are young or who have committed petty offences may finally be transferred to a child-care school instead. Discussion is therefore limited to the juvenile court and its enforcement of legislation that permits the imprisonment of children.

The juvenile court is an ordinary criminal court. Children accused are essentially treated in the same way as adult accused. The only differences between a juvenile court and an ordinary criminal court are: juvenile trials are held 'in camera'; parents or guardians may assist their children in the proceedings; and there are alternative sentences available for children.

The Positive Law

The Criminal Procedure Act

The Criminal Procedure Act, No. 51 of 1977, governs criminal proceedings from the time of arrest to conviction or acquittal. This Act has special provisions aimed at protecting the child accused. A brief discussion of this legislation and trial proceedings illustrates the aims of this Act and its practical application. The writer will argue that in practice those safeguards fail to protect children due to both loopholes in the legislation and circumstances peculiar to each case.

In order to secure the attendance of an accused in court, the police may arrest the accused or issue a notice ordering him or her to appear in court (Section 38). If the accused is arrested, he or she may be released on warning or on bail, or be given written notice to appear in court (Sections 59, 60, 72, and 56). If the accused is not so released, he or she must appear before a court within forty-eight hours of arrest, when the court may grant bail or otherwise authorize his or her further detention (Section 50(1)). To refuse an accused bail, the court must have reason to believe that he or she will not appear for trial or will interfere with the state's investigation of the case. An accused may appeal against the decision to refuse bail, the amount of the bail or the conditions imposed upon the granting of bail (Section 65). There are additional alternatives to pre-trial detention for children: the police and/or court may place a child in a 'place of safety' or in the care of his or her custodian, who is then obliged to ensure the child's presence in court on the trial date (Sections 71(1)(b) and 72(2)(b)).

The power to release a child into his or her parents' custody is only a discretionary one. Furthermore, the court is obliged to secure the presence of a child's parents in court only if they live within the same magisterial district as the court and are easily traceable (Section 74(2)). As a result, a child may appear alone in court. A child in such a situation in unlikely to know that he or she may apply for bail or be released into his or her parents' custody. Many children and parents are unable to afford bail.

Due to a chronic shortage of children's homes and 'places of safety', particularly for black children, the option of such alternative placement is not a viable one in most circumstances. In many rural areas, referral to a 'place of safety' would mean a long journey and therefore be impractical. Furthermore, since a 'place of safety' includes a police cell, thousands of children are kept in police cells as an alternative to prison. Conditions in police cells are no better than in prison. If the legislature intended the placement of children in prison only where necessary, it has failed to effect this intention.

In the writer's view, the most fundamental flaw in the legislation is the lack of automatic legal representation for children. Although an accused has a right to a lawyer from the time of arrest, there is no duty on the court to inform the accused of this fact. The state provides free legal counsel only in cases involving capital offences. Children have seldom heard of the legal aid services available and these are limited anyway. Most children are simply unaware of their right to a lawyer. They may also not contemplate instructing an attorney for fear of the expense or they may be ignorant of the procedure for doing so. Many are sceptical of any assistance in a system which they perceive as discriminating against them.

The fact that a parent may assist a juvenile in court proceedings offers little consolation, as many parents themselves are just as ignorant as their children of the rights of the accused and the technical complexities of criminal procedure. Without legal assistance, a child and his or her parents are, for example, unaware of the consequences of a mistaken plea of guilty, or a statement outlining his or her defence to support a plea of not guilty.[6] A child cannot be expected to rely on 'the system's' own court officials for assistance within and against that same system.

One of the most important provisions for children in the Criminal Procedure Act is the conversion procedure whereby a juvenile court trial may be converted into a children's court enquiry (Section 254). This procedure may be used when it appears to the court that the child is in fact 'in need of care' and should be dealt with as such. In theory this procedure should protect all those children whose alleged criminal conduct is in reality a manifestation of some form of neglect. The effect of the conversion procedure is to remove the child from the criminal justice system and therefore remove the possibility of a criminal record. Yet, in practice, this protection is ineffective. The presiding officer may be unaware of the facts that indicate that a child might be 'in need of care'. Some court officials erroneously believe that probation services achieve the same purpose, though the probation services are not extensively used either. Furthermore, the conviction results in a criminal record for the child. The shortage of facilities for children 'in need of care' also discourages court officials or social workers from dealing with the child in terms of this provision. This is particularly true for African children.

Upon conviction by a juvenile court, a child may receive one or a combination of the following sentences (Section 276):

1) the death sentence (Section 277(1))[7];
2) imprisonment;
3) commital to an institution established by law;
4) a fine;
5) whipping.

The alternative sentences especially for juveniles are (Section 290):

1) probation under the supervision of a probation officer;
2) placement in the custody of any suitable person; or
3) reform school: if the reform school is full, the child may be temporarily accommodated in a 'place of safety' or place of detention.

Despite the choice of several welfare dispositions intended for the benefit of child offenders, in practice these are not sufficiently utilized by the courts. The shortage of probation officers, children's homes, 'places of safety', and reformatories severely curtails the use of these options. Furthermore, probation reports are not obligatory in juvenile trials and it is submitted that magistrates are not qualified to decide a child's disposition without such professional assistance. Certain options, such as reformatories, are not always an improvement on prisons, and children may spend far longer periods in reformatories than in prison for the same offence.

Generally the court has a discretion as to the length of the prison term imposed. Compulsory minimum sentences are not mandatory for children, while prison and reform school sentences are subject to review in certain circumstances (Section 302). Although the accused may submit a written statement to the reviewing judge (Section 303), an unassisted child is unlikely to be able to draft a suitable statement even if he or she were aware of such a right. Similarly, an unrepresented juvenile will probably be unaware both of the right to appeal against the conviction and/or sentence and of the procedure for doing so. The expense of legal assistance further eliminates a child's chances of appeal.

In sum: the discretion of the courts and police, practical difficulties in the implementation of alternative welfare sentences, the technical complexity and inadequate provisions of the law itself, cause the Criminal Procedure Act to provide little real protection to children in the criminal justice system (McLachlan 1984: Section 4, 29).

Security legislation

In 1982 the security laws were consolidated with the enactment of the Internal Security Act, No. 74 of 1982. Security legislation, aimed at 'the protection of State security', has been severely criticized as a violation of human rights and the fundamental principles of criminal justice.[8] The Act concerns 'terrorism', 'subversion', 'sabotage', and 'communism'.[9] There are few procedural safeguards against abuse by security officials and/or the executive. The courts may not review the legislation itself and they are essentially excluded from the enforcement of security measures.

Children are given no special protection under security legislation. Only in 1982 were alternative sentences for juveniles convicted of security offences introduced, even though many of the security laws imposed mandatory minimum prison terms. Over the years numerous allegations have been made about abuse perpetrated in terms of these laws. Detainees have reported various torture methods, such as sleep deprivation for long periods, electric shocks, suffocation, assaults with batons, hose pipes and gun butts, mid-air suspensions, assaults on genitals, interrogation sessions while naked and/or hooded, injections with unknown substances, teargassing, death threats and threats against family and friends.[10] Between 1963 and October 1985 eighty-three people had died in detention (*Weekly Mail*, 25-31.10.85), and in 1985 a twelve-year-old boy died mysteriously within hours of his arrest (*Star*, 9.7.85).

The Internal Security Act ostensibly introduced certain procedural protections for the benefit of detainees. Examples of the new safeguards are: visits by a magistrate or district surgeon; the requirement of ministerial approval of detention for more than thirty days; a limited review mechanism that comes into effect after six months of detention; police authorization of visitors other than state officials; and the review of all preventive detentions and banning orders.[11]

In practice these provisions have had little, if any, effect. They essentially concern the trial stage and not the pre-trial stage, which is the period of concern for detainees. Similarly, the introduction of alternative sentences for juveniles serves little purpose unless the child is brought to trial. Many detainees are never charged despite lengthy periods in prison cells. Furthermore, the limited existence of these provisions in previous legislation was ineffective. Officials such as magistrates and district surgeons, who presumably provide the 'independent' checks, are all state employees and are therefore regarded by most detainees as part of 'the system'.[12]

Emergency regulations

At the time of writing the declaration of a partial state of emergency has probably been the most common reason for the detention of children since its commencement in July 1985.[13] These regulations constitute an extension of the inroads made upon the basic principles of criminal justice and the individual's rights by security legislation. The potential for abuse of these powers by the authorities is even more disturbing than that in security legislation provisions, as so many children have been detained since the emergency was declared.

In brief, the aspects of detention in terms of these regulations that are particularly disquieting with respect to children are:

1) that parents and relatives are not informed of the child's detention and/or whereabouts;
2) the possibility of indefinite detention with no right of representation for the detainee;
3) that a child has no right to visits by his or her parents or relatives;
4) that no provision is made for the inspection of juvenile cells by persons independent of 'the system', such as medical practitioners, social workers, lawyers, and religious ministers;
5) that unrepresented and unaccompanied minor children are subjected to lengthy interrogation periods;
6) the use of solitary confinement; and
7) the provision of a civil and criminal indemnity to protect the actions of state officials unless the aggrieved person can rebut the presumption in favour of the state that such actions were conducted in good faith (Regulation 11: Proclamation No. R121, 1985).

From the writer's experience, the allegations made by child detainees released from detention substantiate the critics' fears. Children as young as eleven years old have echoed the reports of torture described in the preceding section. One can only speculate on the psychological effects suffered and still to be suffered by the large number of children that have spent time in detention.

Children have not only suffered in prison and police cells in terms of these regulations but also in the townships. Hundreds of children have been teargassed, sjambokked, shot and injured, maimed or killed. Township life is becoming increasingly violent and the brutalizing effect this must have upon so many young black children is sure to augment future prison statistics.

Conditions in Prison

The Prisons Act

Officially conditions in prisons and police cells are governed by the Prisons Act, No. 8 of 1959, as amplified by the Consolidated Prison Regulations. In terms of the Prisons Act a juvenile is someone under the age of twenty-one years (Section 1), and prisons are established for, *inter alia*, the 'detention, treatment and training' of juveniles (Section 20(1)(b)). Only a few provisions apply specifically to juveniles, so that there is little difference between the treatment of adults and children.

Unconvicted prisoners under the age of eighteen years should not be held in prison or police cells unless this is necessary and no suitable place of detention is available (Section 29(1)). They may not be in prison with anyone older than twenty-one unless such inmate is a co-accused or the association would not be detrimental to the child (Section 29(3)). Pending their removal, juveniles should be kept separately from older and more hardened criminals (Regulation 137). Females under the age of eighteen must be placed under the supervision of women warders (Section 29(4)).

The aim of these provisions is surely to protect child prisoners from the physical danger posed by other cell-mates and to prevent the furtherance of their 'criminal education' under the tutelage of 'more experienced criminals'. It is therefore unfortunate that the Prisons Act's definition of 'juvenile' includes people in the eighteen to twenty-one age group, as this admits many hardened and tough gang members into the juvenile cells, who pose just as great a threat to the young prisoner as any adult.

Apart from the provisions above, which concern only juveniles, the remainder of the Act treats adults and children alike. Prisoners have certain rights, not as yet fully defined by the courts, and some privileges. The latter depend upon state authority and may be withdrawn without reason and/or without a hearing. Examples of basic rights are rights to food, clothing, accommodation and medical aid.

Prisoners are entitled to a copy of the Prisons Act (Section 85) and they may apply for court orders against prison officials relating to their prison conditions. The head of the prison must see each prisoner daily and attend to complaints (Regulation 103(1)). Prisoners have a right to medical attention and cells have to comply with certain minimum standards (Regulation 97(1)). Each prisoner should be given a set of sufficient clothing (Regulation 115). Chaplains may visit prisons to attend to a prisoner's religious needs (Regulation 108(1)(a)) and a prisoner's relationship with his or her family is encouraged as an important part of the rehabilitative objective (Regulation 110(1)). Prisoners also have a limited right to consult their lawyers (Regulation 123).

Each prisoner should exercise outside every day and the period of such exercise depends upon his or her physical condition or age (Regulation 113). The period should not be reduced as a form of punishment.[14] Prison food should have a certain nutritional value according to a prescribed diet scale and there should be a reasonable variety of well-prepared food (Regulation 114(1)).

There appears to be a discrepancy between these provisions and practice. The most common complaint made by children released from prison concerns food. They describe the monotonous regularity of *pap* (porridge), tea, and bread and many complain that they were always hungry. It is not uncommon for children to resort to 'selling themselves' to other inmates in return for additional food. Many children also deny that they were ever taken outside for exercise.

Prisoners may be punished for contraventions of the Act and Regulations (Section 54). Possible punishments include the deprivation of one or two meals, corporal punishment of a maximum six strokes for males under forty years, solitary confinement for a maximum of thirty days, or a combination of solitary confinement and periods of reduced, spare, and full diets. A prisoner may be deprived of one or two meals without a hearing. There is a limited review of certain punishments.

The writer submits that it is time the authorities replaced these archaic forms of punishment with more effective disciplinary measures in line with modern-day child-care practices. The forms of punishment currently used are an indication of the retributive and punitive attitude of the criminal justice system towards children. The Supreme Court has held that a juvenile should not be given a punishment which might affect his health, such as a spare diet or solitary confinement, unless there was an element of viciousness or cruelty in the offence.[15] The use of solitary confinement for children, the deprivation of meals, and the excessive use of corporal punishment, which are permitted by law, cannot be in the interests of the normal, all-round development of children in prison.

Unconvicted prisoners have additional rights which are of particular importance for children. Subject to certain restrictions, they have a right to write and receive letters, have visitors, and receive food delivered to the prison (Section 82(d)). They may wear their own clothes (Section 83) and may purchase stationery and approved reading material from outside sources.[16]

Most parents and children are ignorant of the limited rights and privileges available to prisoners, especially awaiting-trial prisoners. Parents often state that they are refused visits to their awaiting-trial children held in police cells. The police may restrict such visits but they are not entitled to deprive children of their visiting rights altogether. Policemen are either ignorant of such rights or abuse their position by such refusals. If more people, particularly social workers, teachers, doctors, and parents were aware of these rights, they could advise child prisoners and assist their families in enforcing their rights.

Prison gangs

One of the most horrifying aspects of prison life for anyone, and especially children, must be the network of gangs that proliferates in the prison world. Inevitably, at some stage of prison life, either as an awaiting-trial or sentenced prisoner, a child will be confronted by the violent reality of powerful and organized prison gangs.[17]

It appears that such gangs have developed in response to the prison sub-culture and hardships of prison life. The circumstances of prison life, namely the large numbers of male prisoners, overcrowding, isolation from family and friends, boredom, powerlessness, frustration, and spartan living conditions, cause intense competition and rivalry between the gangs, who fight for extras such as food, tobacco, drugs, money, clothes, or sex. Assaults, stabbings, theft, and homosexual rape are common features of gang-life.

The members of each gang are organized into a quasi-military hierarchy subject to a rigid disciplinary code with set methods of punishment. Gang punishments are violent and brutal and may include death. Prison officials have finally admitted that they cannot guarantee the protection of prisoners from gangs.

Conclusion

It is submitted that in virtually every aspect the legal system fails to provide support and protection to the thousands of children that are swept up in its network of laws, courts, prisons, and police cells. The laws not only permit the incarceration of children in adult penal facilities, but provide so many loopholes to the ostensible safeguards as to render these of minimal effect. Experiences in prisons and police cells are frequently such violent, frightening, and lonely ones for children that they may cause severe emotional, physical and mental damage to the child concerned.

The writer believes that, as a result, thousands of children are quickly losing all respect for the entire legal system: its laws, which they perceive as unjust and/or racist in content or effect, and its courts and officials, whom they believe implement an inherently unfair system. That an unrepresented and unassisted child must fend for himself or herself within such a legal envioronment is both a serious indictment of the South African system of justice and a reflection of the low position of children in the state's list of priorities.

Notes

1. The extracts are taken from statements recorded by the author during 1985. The statements were obtained during the course of independent research.
2. See further McLachlan (1984) Section 3, 17-20.
3. In *S v Dyk* 1969 (1) SA 601 at 603 the review court stressed that the crucial test is the state of mind and general appreciation at the time the offence was committed.
4. Blacks (Abolition of Passes and Co-ordination of Documents) Act, No. 67 of 1952; Black (Urban Areas) Consolidation Act, No. 25 of 1945.
5. As defined in Section 1 of Act 33 of 1960.
6. For example, in certain circumstances the court may convict an accused who pleads guilty without further enquiry into the facts (Section

112(1)(a)). If the court believes an accused may not be guilty, a plea of not guilty must be recorded but any admission made prior to the change of plea is proof in court of the admission (Section 113). Where an accused pleads not guilty, the court may ask the accused to make a statement outlining the basis of his or her defence. If the accused refuses, the presiding officer may question the accused to establish which allegations are disputed and which may be recorded as admissions (Section 115).

7. In terms of Section 277(2) the court is not obliged to impose the death sentence on a person under the age of eighteen convicted of murder.

8. See generally Mathews (1971).

9. Sections 54(1), 54(2), 54(3), and 55 read with Section 1(iv), respectively.

10. For example, in 1982 the Detainees' Parents Support Committee submitted a memorandum to the Minister of Law and Order alleging the torture of detainees — see further Randall (1982: 253).

11. For a more detailed discussion of the Internal Security Act, see Dugard (1982: 593).

12. In accordance with an agreement concluded between the Medical Association of South Africa (MASA) and the government during October 1985, MASA is to establish a panel of doctors who will be available to political detainees who wish to obtain a second medical opinion in addition to that of the district surgeon. The detainee may choose a doctor from the panel at his or her own cost. See further *Star*, 22.10.85.

13. The emergency regulations were promulgated in terms of Section 3(1) of the Public Safety Act, No.3 of 1953. On 11 February 1986 the Minister of Law and Order disclosed in parliament that between 21 July 1985 and 31 January 1986 2 106 children under the age of sixteen had been detained under these regulations (*Cape Times*, 12.02.86).

14. This was held in *Cassiem and Another v Commanding Officer, Victor Verster Prison and Others* 1982 (2) 547 (C) at 550.

15. See *S v Diedericks*, 1967 (3) SA 157 (C) at 159.

16. Regulation 132(5) read with 133, 135(2) and 136(2).

17. See further Haysom (1981).

The End of Childhood:
An Anthropological Vignette

Eleanor Preston-Whyte and Jennifer Louw

The anthropological perspective is an avowedly cultural and cross-cultural one (Beattie 1964; Geertz 1973, 1983). In South Africa, where cultural difference is entrenched in the dominant structures of white political ideology and government practice, an approach which focusses upon the differences between South Africans rather than upon their common citizenship may well be regarded by opponents of the contemporary regime as both insensitive and even dangerous in providing support for notions of racial separation. Used circumspectly, however, we would argue that a cross-cultural perspective has considerable value in revealing not only differing cultural nuances, but also some of the glaring inequalities in South African life. By focussing, not on the details of cultural difference for their own sake, but upon comparative cultural strategies for dealing with common problems and crises, this perspective should serve to draw attention both to conflicts and inconsistencies in the macro-level social formation which places some of its constituent cultural groups or categories at a structural disadvantage relative to others, and also to how aspects of cultural tradition may be adapted to meet current problems in a unique and constructive manner.

In describing and analysing what happened to a Zulu schoolgirl who became pregnant — the crisis which brought about 'the end of childhood' referred to in the title of this chapter — we have a number of objectives. First to draw attention to the lack of institutional social security provisions for coping with a crisis which has become a recurrent feature of the lives of black[1] teenagers and their parents. Though similar pregnancies occur amongst whites, they are by no means as frequent, and the crisis tends to be somewhat cushioned by relative wealth and the availability of some state welfare facilities. There are also differences in the way teenage pregnancies are treated in black and white families, and we will explore, secondly, one set of Zulu cultural responses which seek to contain the problem in a ritual manner derived from, but by no means identical with, the way in which it is reported to have been dealt with in the past. Turning, thirdly, to long term social structure, we shall argue that the frequency of teenage pregnancies and the way they are dealt with at a practical level — whether marriage occurs or not, who cares for and rears the children concerned — contributes to the prevalence of three- or even four-generational households amongst black South Africans. These factors lead also to the development of what are referred to in the literature as female-headed or female-linked domestic units (Dubb 1974; Pauw 1963; Preston-Whyte 1978).

Our method will be to examine one case in detail, reviewing the steps taken before and after the birth of the child and the ensuing re-arrangements in the families of the young parents over some two and a half years.[2] During this period the baby was taken by his paternal grandmother to live on the premises of her white employers. Since the objective of this book is to examine the various nuances of childhood in South Africa, we shall conclude by changing the focus of our attention from the young parents to the growing child and shall give some impressions of what it is like for a black child to live with, yet effectively separate from, a white family for whom his or her parent or guardian is working. This is an experience common to many thousands of black South Africans whose parents were or are resident domestic servants or farm labourers. Encapsulated within this experience of childhood, we feel, lies something of the essence of the paradoxes, indignities and very real human suffering inflicted upon blacks by the apartheid system.

We cannot, of course, claim that the case we describe can represent all or even a majority of similar cases in all their varied detail. We do feel, however, that in outline it illustrates dramatically some of the fundamental and recurrent features of black South African life which are not usually appreciated by white South Africans. Taking the issue of schoolgirl pregnancies alone, it is seldom realized that, to quote a nursing sister at one large polyclinic serving both an urban area and a rural hinterland in KwaZulu, about half of all first babies are born to girls still at school (quoted in Craig 1980; Craig and Richter-Strydom nd.: 15). A black social worker covering the same area commented recently that 'illegitimate births [have] become the order of the day, particularly in the urban environment'[3] (Khanyile 1974). While there is considerable concern amongst these doctors and nurses who come into daily contact with this situation and also amongst black community and church leaders, most research has so far concentrated on the causes of the problem, rather than upon how the crisis is dealt with or how it affects longer-term social relations and domestic structures.

It is of interest and possible practical significance that in the case reported here, where the father of the child was known and was willing to acknowledge paternity, indigenous control mechanisms came into operation to cope with the problem. Money and two goats referred to as *imigezo* (singular *umgezo* from -*Geza* to wash or to purify, hence purification beast[4]) were presented by the boy's family to the relatives of the girl in a small domestic ritual which, we shall suggest, served to 'normalize' and even institutionalize the crisis precipitated by the youthful pregnancy. It brought the families of the girl and boy together for discussion and relatively amicable interaction and, most important, it helped to 'place' the coming child in a social sense. Despite the fact that the parents did not marry immediately, and no marriage negotiations were begun for at least two years, those responsible for the child's conception and future care were clearly and publicly indicated at the ceremony. The families continued to interact, and over the two years since the birth have taken differing shares in the responsibility of caring for the child. It was the mothers of the young parents who bore the financial burden of the pregnancy and birth and it is the mother of the father who is now caring for the baby; the young parents are still not married and the child's mother is training as a nurse-aide. We believe that what happened, in terms of both the handing over of the *imigezo* beasts and the subsequent structural arrangements for taking care of the child, represent a typically Zulu cultural response to a contemporary problem faced at one time or another by a very high proportion of black parents and children. This response is in contrast to what happens in the white community, where abortion, adoption, or speedy marriage are the more usual ways of dealing with the same crisis.

In the case study which follows some readers may be struck by the relatively advanced ages of the young parents; here is another contrast between black and white in South Africa. White couples approaching and in their twenties are not regarded as 'children'. Most have left school and are working or training for their future careers. Schooling starts some two years later for black children than it does for their white counterparts and many miss a year or two of schooling due to lack of money or because they fall victim to high failure rates. It is thus not unusual for black youths to be in their twenties and still at school. The lack of job opportunities exacerbates the situation and, indeed, many black parents have living in their houses children who are well over twenty but who are still dependent on them both financially and, because they are not married, in terms of responsibility. While these individuals are regarded as, and even spoken of as children in the black community, to use the term 'children' for them is, in many ways, a misnomer. Most are mature not only in sexual terms but, as recent events have shown, in their active and critical involvement in the political confrontations of day-to-day township life. Let us now turn to our case study.

Background Events

The story begins in late 1982 when Grace P, who was then twenty-one[5] and in her final year at a large KwaMashu high school, realized that she was pregnant. Her boyfriend, Amos D, was nineteen years old and in the same form. Both were sitting their matriculation (school-leaving) examinations and both were, as they put it, 'hoping to go on for further study' the next year. Grace wanted to be a nurse; Amos had not yet decided what to do and he was seriously hampered by lack of funds. His mother, Mrs Maria D, was divorced and supporting him and three younger children entirely from her small salary as a resident domestic worker in Durban. The children lived with Mrs D's widowed mother in Durban's KwaMashu Township in a four-roomed house which was allocated to Mrs D's father before he died and for which Mrs D now paid the rent. This house was frequently full to overflowing, as Mrs D's sister, together with her six children, invariably stayed there when her husband, who was often out of work, was unable to provide them with adequate support. Grace and her mother, Thembi, who had not married, were staying nearby with Thembi's sister and her husband, so that Grace could attend school in KwaMashu and Thembi be able to keep her job as a non-resident domestic worker in Durban. Their permanent home was at Umzinyati, a rapidly developing peri-urban area forty kilometres from Durban. There, in her deceased father's house, lived Thembi's widowed mother together with Petros, Thembi's eldest brother and head of the household, his wife and three children, a single brother, another unmarried sister and her two children, and Thembi's four other children, a total of fourteen people in all. Thembi and Grace usually visited Umzinyati over weekends and Grace, although schooling in the township, was regarded at Umzinyati as one of the young girls of the local neighbourhood. Her pregnancy was viewed very seriously by her grandmother and her mother's brother. It was reported to the *induna* and chief and it was considered to be defiling for all the girls of a similar age in the neighbourhood with whom Grace had grown up, and with whom she was still close friends.

It is important to point out that although the density of settlement is increasing rapidly, Umzinyati is still a 'rural area' in organizational terms, and indigenously-based forms and processes of political control obtain there, as do some other structural features such as the organization of girls between puberty and marriage (*izintombi*) into recognized age groups under a designated leader (*ighikize*). Though the P family belong to the African Congregational Church, they accepted the fact that Grace's pregnancy as an unmarried girl had brought 'trouble and disgrace' on their home and girls of the neighbourhood, and also the community at large. 'Bad luck' might result and, as they put it, 'something had to be done'. Normally the man responsible for such a pregnancy or his family has to provide at least one goat for purification (in this case the Ps demanded two goats, one for cleansing the household and the other for their ancestors), R20 for the girls of the neighbourhood to be spent as they wish (usually on a 'party'), and R10 for the chief to inform him that the girl is no longer a virgin. Although living in KwaMashu, Mrs D accepted the necessity of this procedure and pointed out that she felt duty-bound to provide what was asked because, to quote her, 'Amos is my son and not working, so I must pay for him'.

Mrs D did not hear of the pregnancy from Amos, nor from Grace's kin. A younger son, Lloyd, told her: 'Amos just ran away . . . .' As is usual in these cases, she had not previously met Grace nor even been aware of her existence. Many writers have commented on the fact that early love affairs and sexual encounters between today's black teenagers are kept from their parents (De Haas 1984: 54; Craig and Richter-Strydom nd.: 3).[6] This is said to be in keeping with 'tradition', in that it was a girl's age mates and the older girls who supervised early courting activities (Krige 1936: 104-106). Mrs D demanded that the girl be brought to her: 'If I didn't like her, I shouldn't have paid'. Grace and an elder sister[7] arrived and later her mother visited Mrs D. 'Everyone was in tears. I cried, she [Thembi] cried and we all cried . . . they were so young and just sitting for exams.' Thembi then made the Ps' expectations known and Mrs D was left to wonder how she would gather enough money to meet them. She managed to arrange with her employers for her salary to be paid early, and was also given a loan of R50 by them. At the time none of her children were earning money, and her salary of R120 per month was usually exhausted by the rent of the KwaMashu home and by feeding, clothing, and educating her children. The goats together cost R140, plus R1 for delivery to Mrs D's mother's home in KwaMashu. Fortunately Mrs D did not have to pay for transport to Umzinyati[8] but, had she been forced to hire a taxi, it would have added approximately another R25 to the already large amount of R141.

Before embarking on a description of the ceremony at which the goats and money were handed over, we must examine briefly the conceptual background against which it was all planned and executed. Zulus recognize a number of situations which cause individuals to be in a state of ritual danger or impurity and as a result of which they are vulnerable to misfortune. These states must be rectified for the sake of the individual concerned and because the contamination may spread to others. Purification or 'washing' (*ukugeza*) ceremonies serve this purpose (Ngubane 1977: 77-99; Raum 1973: 524). The particular danger which results from the pregnancy of a young girl was documented by earlier writers (see Krige 1936: 105-106; 157-58) and has been well described by Vilakazi (1962) who worked amongst the Nyuswa-Zulu of the Valley of a Thousand Hills in the 1960s. Since the Valley is fairly close to Umzinyati, we quote at some length from Vilakazi (1962: 55-66):

> Both among traditionalists and the Christians, premarital pregnancy, as such, is considered a ritually dangerous state for both the family and its girls and for girls of the neighbourhood. A girl who has become pregnant has, by such an act, 'soiled' i.e. *ngcolisa'd* the girls of the whole neighbourhood, and has given a bad example to them. They must, accordingly, be cleansed or washed with a goat . . . Premarital pregnancy brings with it what people call *umkhokha* or *ukhondolo olubi*. The

umkhokha is a train of ugly, unpleasant consequences which a person brings with him e.g. from the committal of a crime; or it might be called a hotbed of contagious disease. *Ukhondolo* carries with it the connotation of a proclivity to crime. Used in the context of premarital pregnancy, these words mean a ritual taint which predisposes the girls of the family, and, indeed, of the whole community to premarital pregnancy.

Ngubane, working in the same area some fifteen years later, found essentially the same beliefs operative, but adds that 'pregnancy is supposed to happen within the context of marriage, and even then it is polluting, but if it happens before marriage its pollution takes a new dimension. It is considered as having "opened the way for further misfortunes"' (1977: 80). Sibiya (1981), writing of marriage negotiations and payments in the modern context of wider KwaZulu, mentions the same 'contagious ill luck' (*ukhondolo olubi* or *umkhokha*) believed by traditionalists to be associated with the loss of virginity before marriage. Raum (1973: 452) likened it to shame or disgrace on the part of the girl, who, to quote one of his informants, 'has *amahloni*: she doesn't walk about, but hides at home. In the past she no longer mixed with her age mates, and they were beaten severely for not watching her better. The girl can no longer cook food for her brothers, for her hands are "unclean"'. Both Raum and others have described how, in the past, the girl's age mates might assault her and her lover, and how they would go in anger to the home of the boy, take a beast or a goat, kill it and use the stomach contents for cleansing (Raum 1973: 452; Krige 1936: 158; Vilakazi 1962: 56). Raum's informant added that the girls could not eat the meat of the animal used in cleansing, but that it was eaten by an old woman of the boy's home who was past childbearing 'and had no need of cleansing'. Similarly, Sibiya notes that the girls 'after washing themselves, leave the goat or the money to be picked up by old women who are believed to be immune from the pernicious effects of the ill-luck transposed into the money or goat' (1981: 148).

A number of additional points require some clarification and emphasis. It was Grace's *pregnancy* which precipitated the crisis we are discussing. However, two separate issues were in fact at stake — her seduction and her impregnation. Both were and are actionable in Zulu law (Bekker and Coertze 1982: 339-53). Today, as few mothers examine their daughters for evidence of intercourse, it is usually pregnancy which precipitates action. In discussions of the *imigezo* for Grace, however, the distinction was, as we shall see, consistently made. In considering the liability of Amos and his family for both the seduction of a virgin and her pregnancy, another distinction was drawn. The *umgezo* beast is only part of a dual system of what is referred to as 'damages' (*inhlawulo* or *amademeshe*) due to the father or guardian of an unmarried girl who is seduced and made pregnant. The concept of damages is essentially a legal one and is written into the Natal Code of Law for many different types of 'damage' or insult. Where the term *umgezo* is used, however, it is often understood to be informal damages for seduction and the payments are essentially obligations of a moral type which cannot be enforced by law. In addition, one or possibly two or more beasts can be and often are sued for in the courts. The first is the so-called 'mother's beast' (*ngquthu*) which is said to represent the girl's virginity (Bekker and Coertze 1982: 385) and which is the mother's property alone. Under the Natal Code another beast can be claimed for any pregnancy, whether to term or not. In some places this is referred to as the *mvimba* (Bekker and Coertze 1982: 343), though it is also called the 'father's beast'. In the case of Grace's pregnancy, discussion about these two beasts was not begun until the goats for the purification had been handed over. It is important, finally, to realize that the *umgezo* and the two other beasts are not seen as part of marriage payments (ilobolo). They are part of damages and quite separate from *ilobolo*. They must be paid *before* a marriage is mooted, and even if it is not. However, should marriage follow, the *mvimba* beast may be deducted from the *ilobolo*.

It is thus clear, both from the literature and from the case before us, that Zulu Christians and Zulu traditionalists alike recognize premarital pregnancy as a potentially disruptive situation. Christians often speak of 'bad luck' but may not go to the lengths of attacking the boy concerned. Similarly, because they do not wish to be overtly associated with traditional cosmology, they may not, in speaking of the issue, distinguish *umgezo* from the general *amademeshe* due to the girl's guardian. Amos and Grace and their families are all staunch Christians and, although they spoke of 'bad luck' when explaining why *umgezo* had to be given, they were not clear as to the nature and extent of the possible mystical repercussions of Grace's pregnancy. Thembi spoke of Grace as being *umkhokha* but thought this state would be confined to the family. However, she claimed *umgezo* openly, and the girls of the neighbourhood and the chief were actively involved through the payment of money to them. In addition, though Amos was himself not actually attacked, the Ps' attitude to the D party was, as we shall see, hostile, and there was talk of 'fighting the boy'.

Handing over the Imigezo

The *imigezo* goats were handed over in mid-December, 1982, the event being arranged within two weeks of Mrs D being told of Grace's pregnancy. Neither Mrs D nor Amos were present at the ceremony at which a close family friend, Mr N, acted and spoke on behalf of Mrs D's household.[9] Mrs D's mother, Mrs M, attended, but Mrs D claimed that she herself was afraid to go as it was her son 'who had made trouble with Grace's family . . . they might fight with me . . .' Amos could not enter the P home until after the purification. Before leaving for Umzinyati the goats were brought into the lounge of Mrs D's mother's house in KwaMashu, where Mr N spoke to Mrs D's paternal ancestors, informing them of what was being done. Mrs D explained that as she was divorced and no longer part of her ex-husband's family (*umndeni*),[10] her own ancestors look after the children and would 'explain' to her ex-husband's ancestors what was happening.

The journey to Umzinyati over untarred roads took about thirty minutes. The party (which included, besides Mr N and Mrs M, the two researchers) was met by Thembi's brother, Petros P, and a George P, the son of a half-brother of Thembi and Petros P. They were joined by a third brother, James, but it was Petros P who, as household head, received the party and the goats on behalf of his and Grace's mother's *umndeni*. The goats were penned outside the yard, one in particular not being allowed to enter the homestead precincts, and the visiting party was ushered into the front room of the house and left for a few minutes before the three P men entered and proceedings began. At first the atmosphere was tense and the Ps' anger at the pregnancy was openly voiced. However, as he told us, Mr N had come prepared to be conciliatory, and he saw his role as that of a mediator and go-between who would draw the two families together, if not in marriage, at least in long-term friendship and co-operation. Indeed, following Fortes (1969: 219-49), we may suggest that what was established that day was rather more than mere friendship; it was a state of *amity* between two bodies of kin. Because a marriage had not taken place, this relationship was, of necessity, different in kind from that of conventional kinship. Being focussed on the coming child and the public recognition of his cognation to both parties, it was, however, strong enough to entail the expectation and later fulfilment of critical rights, duties, and obligations between the parties concerned. It should be noted also that the behavioural conventions and, indeed, the cultural model for interaction once the *imigezo* had been handed over was that normally adopted in Zulu marriage negotiations and, although it was clear that marriage was not an issue that day, its possibility was not ruled out for the future.

Taking the initiative and addressing Mr Petros P, Mr N began: 'This boy [Amos] is a thief for what he has done to the girl's family'. Mr P responded aggressively by saying that as Mr N knew what the trouble was, he should know well what to do — namely pay *inhlawulo* (damages) for the pregnant girl 'since the girl has never slept with any man, so you are liable for everything; you seduced her first and then you made her pregnant — now you have to pay for seduction and pregnancy'. Mr N agreed, saying, 'That is why I came here; my son said he made a certain woman pregnant. I come to cry to you not to kill me, but to see the brighter side of it and to make a relationship and to unite the families even though not married.' Apparently mollified, Mr P agreed that Mr N had come so that both sides could rejoice and be one family. Mr N quickly underlined his points as follows:

> Even though we know we've done you wrong, Mr P, we haven't come just for paying *inhlawulo*, but to unite our families; even if our son might not marry her, but we'll always be a united family. Since you know the younger generation never want to marry the girls they make pregnant, so whenever we meet each other in the street we should greet each other even if our kids are no longer in love — also not be enemies to each other. We would like you to bring forth what we have brought here [the goats] to the forefathers [*abadala*].

Thus was a commitment stated on the part of Amos's family. It was accepted by the P family when, over cool drinks and cake served by the women of the house, the talk turned to practicalities.[11] Just before this, Mr N explained to us in an aside just how difficult Mr P had been in the beginning. 'Firstly he nearly gave me a kick so we would have had to fight, but now he is talking straight and the way is clear . . . he wants me to show him the goods [*izimpahla* — referring to the goats] . . .' The first goat, he explained, was to cleanse the household (*ingezamuzi*) and to put matters right between the two families. Thembi, in response to questioning later, added that the *ingezamuzi* goat was also to remove from Grace the ritual impurity (*umkhokho*) which her pregnancy had precipitated. This goat was both kept outside the yard and slaughtered outside the precincts of the home. The second goat, Mr N said, 'is for the boy, that when he comes to the mother of the baby he can eat food in front of the girl's mother.' The terminology used by Mr N was that of marriage — the girl being referred to as *umakoti* (bride) and the boy as *umkhwenyane* (son-in-law). Though the animosity shown by Mr P was understandable in the circumstances, it was also conventional in that it echoed the normal expression of tension between the families of the prospective bride and groom which occurs in most marriage preliminaries and which a skilful *umkhongi* or go-between has to manage (Krige 1936: 126-28; De Haas 1984: 92). Responding to the manifestations of this conventional aggression on the P side was the expected restraint observed by Mr N and his careful manoeuvring to bring together the two previously unacquainted and potentially hostile groups by stressing their future involvement through their relationship to the coming child. The emphasis was on the fact that, with his or her cognation to both families, the baby would serve to unite them even if a marriage did not take place. Mr N also made the point clearly that since pregnancy without marriage is by no means an unusual occurrence in the social climate of today, the families should not be enemies if the young parents did not continue their relationship.

It must be noted that the second goat, which was subsequently allowed into the yard and which Thembi acknowledged was not customary or even strictly obligatory, was intended for the ancestors, though Mr N spoke of it as serving to ease the future role of Amos in Grace's household. It was to allow Amos, when he visited the baby, to eat in front of the girl's mother and to be 'respected' and 'heard' on such visits. The goat for the ancestors would, Mr N said, bind and pull Amos's and Grace's families together. The word used here was *ukumkhunga*, from -*khunga*, to tie or bind up. Despite the hurt done to the family, clearly the way was open for the acceptance of damages, and for marriage if the boy wanted it. Indeed, Mr P said the girl had used 'sweet words' when telling them of Amos's intention to come to pay *inhlawulo*, and by using the term *umkhwenyana*, Mr N was honouring Amos and his people.

At this point the men repaired outside to view the animals. On their return a number of women of the P *umndeni*, including Thembi and her mother and Grace herself, came into the lounge. Eight of Grace's age mates (including the two sisters just older and younger than her and two of her mother's brother's daughters) were also present. The time had come to get down to the business of negotiating what was due to Grace's people over and above the two purification goats. Mr N offered R10 for the chief and R10 for the *izintombi* (girls from puberty to marriage) but Mr P insisted on R20 and another 20 cents in the form of two 10 cent pieces for the girls, as well as the R10 for the chief. The money for the girls was passed to Mrs M to give to their leader and the money for the chief was given to one of the men to pass on to him. When the money had been duly paid, Mr P commented: 'It is not the first time that a girl does such a thing, and what has just been done is one of our *isiko* [customs], to pay *inhlawulo* and money for the washing of the girls of the district.' He went on to emphasize that the money so far given was not for the family, but for the 'girls' and the chief. What was due to the P family (that is, the rest of the legally enforceable 'damages') was still to be paid. 'Thembi is demanding her "cow" [*ngquthu*], but because everyone knows how expensive a beast is, she will be satisfied with R250 for her beast and R200 for the "father's" beast.' Again Mr N, acting for Amos's mother, accepted the claim, but asked for time to pay as he pointed out that Mrs D was divorced and as her ex-husband 'can't even buy a sack of mealie-meal', she had to care for the children and also pay all the *inhlawulo* herself.

While this claim was being presented, proceedings moved subtly into another phase. Information was sought and given on the D family and the circumstances of Mrs D and Amos himself. Mr N pointed out that it was Amos who should have been responsible for paying a cow, to which he referred as *inkomo yokubonga*: 'He [Amos] should leave school and work — he started things and he should finish them and not be a burden to his mother.' Mr P agreed, but added, 'Even this girl is not having a father, she is becoming a burden . . . .' to which Mr N quickly replied, 'Just look at that, they're making mistakes, and they're creating big problems for both families.' Then he went on, 'If the boy can't pay for the cow he should go and borrow from the neighbours and try and pay. Since the boy is a bit educated he'll get a better job, he won't be loading the trolley, he'll be inspecting the people . . . .' Finally Mr N thanked Mr P for his kindness and understanding and promised that either he or the boy would bring them the first R200 when possible: 'Will you please give me a chance so that we won't quarrel?'

It was then the turn of Mrs M to thank the P family for what she termed their braveness, kindness, and understanding, 'since the children took themselves to school to learn something, they forgot about books and taught themselves something else . . . .' She then commented, like Mr N, on the fact that Grace's pregnancy was by no means an unusual occurrence amongst black people and she mentioned that it is a common situation in the township in particular. However, she stressed that it was no good simply to blame town life as 'we were born in rural areas and know about the customs. If we were 'Mashu' people we're not going to come and explain what happened, we'd just sit and wait for you to come and take us to court, and then say "the boy's not working . . . ." If we did not come to you, you were going to hate us, then your daughter was going to give birth again to another child and it was going to be our problem again. Then people were going to say, "Do you know that you're having a kid from the tree?"'[12] She ended by saying, 'We should pray that the children should be united as one, so if we pray, we might bring them together, if they were not together before.'

Mr P responded by thanking her and saying he understood the position well and would not make excessive demands. 'It would be bad for me to overcharge you, because we often have such accidents, it might happen to me one day, and you do the same . . . . I know you are poor, in the same way that I am.' It was Mr N, the spokesman and conciliator, who had the last word, bringing out the essentially positive features of the situation. 'Your words are good. They will make a house, and they will live for ever . . . .' He then called on the ancestors to bless everyone concerned.

After a meal the ceremony was completed when everyone came into the lounge and joined in a Christian hymn and prayer. Hands were shaken all round; the departing guests were escorted to the Kombi; farewells were waved. Later we asked Mrs D how she would find the R450 for the two beasts. She replied that Amos would have to find work. Indeed, it was for him the end of childhood and the beginning of adult responsibilities. For Grace, the birth of her baby would similarly signal the end of childhood and the start of her role as a mother.

The *ingezamuzi* goat was slaughtered soon after the visitors left. The gall was sprinkled on the ground and the intestines were left for the dogs to eat. The meat was eaten by everyone in the homestead, including some neighbours. The skin was kept and dried to be used for sitting on in future. The second goat was killed a few weeks later and was eaten by the P family alone. 'It was for the *umndeni* to eat as the goat was for our ancestors,' said Thembi. Mr Petros P officiated as the head of the homestead and called on the ancestors in what Thembi described as 'the usual or general way'. No specific ancestors were named. Some of the gall was sprinkled on Grace's toe to show the ancestors 'that she is a woman'. The gall bladder was kept and a *isiphandla* (bracelet) was made from the skin, which Grace wore for a few days 'to show everyone *ugezo* had been done'. The rest of the skin was hung in Thembi's mother's house. The girls subsequently used most of the money given to them to buy cakes and lemonade for a party which they enjoyed greatly.[13] On the morning following the presentation of the *imigezo* they had taken the two 10 cent pieces to the river and used them as 'soap' when washing. The coins were then thrown away on the river bank for 'an old woman' to pick up, recalling the descriptions given by earlier writers of the symbolic casting away of ritual defilement. When pressed as to the meaning of her actions, Grace, however, merely commented that she and her age mates had been told 'to wash that way in order to get rid of the bad luck and finish the business'.

Interpreting the Rituals of the Imigezo

We must pause in our saga to comment on the ritual aspects of the handing over of *imigezo* for Grace's pregnancy, and the interpretation which we offer gives the events described above a central role in dealing with or containing the crisis precipitated by the pregnancy. It will be remembered that all concerned emphasized that *umgezo* had to be paid and, indeed, from the point of view of the major actors in the social drama — Grace, Amos, Mrs D, Thembi, and Mr P — and also the wider social groupings, that is the two families, the girls of Grace's age at Umzinyati, and the whole local community there, the payment was a social event of some importance which stressed *positive* as well as negative aspects of the pregnancy. We suggest that it helped to provide a resolution to the situation of uncertainty and disorder brought about by the pregnancy and that it also laid the foundation for future order and amicable interaction of all concerned. The notions of ritual impurity (or, in the modern Christian metaphor, 'bad luck') are, we think, a way of expressing negative reactions to social disorder, and the ceremony of washing and purification is one of the practical mechanisms for dealing with that disorder and attempting to return the actors to 'normality'. This interpretation is in keeping with analyses of ritual suggested by such writers as Durkheim (1912), Gluckman (1965: 247), and Wilson (1957), and we make no apologies for its functionalist tone. We believe that there are indeed certain social situations which, because of their potentially disruptive nature, have to be contained and coped with in the interests of orderly social existence, and ritual or ceremonial is often an effective way of doing this. The fact that youthful pregnancies are so frequent in contemporary South African black society makes them not 'normal' in the sense of being acceptable or liked, but 'normal' in that there are recognized ways of responding to and dealing with the crisis. Though by no means always paid (especially when the father of the child is not known, or refuses to acknowledge responsibility),[14] when it is, the *umgezo* and the ceremonies surrounding its presentation serve to stabilize the situation and lay the foundation for future order. In support of this view we draw attention to some points which emerged clearly from the above description.

For Grace the ceremony was a *rite de passage* in something of the original sense used by Van Gennep (1960). The anointing of her toe with the gall of the ancestral goat signalled that her passage from childhood to adulthood, if not complete, was well under way. She was leaving behind, however, not only childhood but, through the various washing rituals and especially the use and abandonment of the 20 cents at the stream, both the pollution and the marginal and uncertain state which her unexpected pregnancy had precipitated. The danger which this might have brought to the family and to the other girls of her age was neutralized through the killing of the *ingezamuzi* goat and the subsequent holding of the 'party' using the girls' R20. Finally, the wearing of the *isiphandla* made from goatskin indicated that, as far as possible, all correct formalities had been observed; even the chief was aware of the situation through the payment to him of a R10 'fine'.

What was particularly striking throughout the events described was the balance between the negative and positive aspects of the situation. The ceremony was held so that the 'bad luck' could be expunged, but there was a continual emphasis in the rituals of speech and action on the more positive side of the affair. Grace's fertility and especially her bringing of a young man to pay damages and possibly later *ilobolo* were a matter for congratulation, for the 'sweet words' about which Mr P spoke. Although he was not personally present, Amos was made known to the P family and the way was opened up for him to visit

Grace and the baby. The information given about him was favourable — that he was 'educated' and would one day hold a supervisory job. His family was a decent one and his antecedents acceptable. Though his family came from KwaMashu, they knew how things 'should be done' and clearly did them in the right way. Indeed, reparation for both the seduction and pregnancy was well in progress and the use of the terminology usual in marriage situations was indicative of a hope and willingness for this final tie to develop out of the present disorganized and unsatisfactory situation. Perhaps most important of all, however, the social position of the coming child was addressed. It was not only that its parentage was established and acknowledged publicly by the D family; responsibility for its care was placed squarely on the shoulders of Amos's family as well as that of Grace. It was indicated that Amos would be welcome to visit Umzinyati in the future and the promise was made by his family of damages and of the visits to pay these. Continued interaction between the two families was thus, as far as possible, ensured. The focus of attention was mostly on the future, and though the coming baby was not directly mentioned, the ambiance was of mutual co-operation. In summary, the baby was due to come into the world with a fixed and recognized social position, with people responsible for caring for and supporting him, and with social circumstances as far as possible normalized, and the immediate crisis of youthful pregnancy, to some extent at least, weathered and contained.

The handing over of the *imigezo* was the occasion also of the first *formal* meeting between the kin of Amos and Grace, and cultural tradition provided all concerned with a model of how to behave towards each other, both then and in the future. The situation was a delicate one; the distress generated by Grace's pregnancy was well expressed by Mrs D when she commented on how she and Thembi had both cried at their first meeting, and by the fact that neither she nor Amos went to the P house to present the goats. It was left to Mr N to smooth the way. In doing this, he drew on two elements of Zulu cultural tradition — the provision by Amos's family of the means of purification for Grace, her family and her age-mates, and the formalities and conventions of normal marriage negotiations. The tensions and animosities generated by the situation were simultaneously allowed expression and kept under control by the adoption of conventional phrases, the use of a go-between, and the hope of both parties that a marriage might eventuate. A sizeable dose of practicality informed the actions of both sides. 'It may happen to me one day,' said Mr P, and the purpose of the second goat was stated explicitly to be that of binding the two families together even if a marriage did not follow. Thus were the foundations laid for co-operation, at best in a future marriage, but at least in respect to the birth of the coming child. Hence also Mr N's speech quoted above (p.369), in which he emphasized that the two families would always be united and should greet each other and not be enemies.

To us it seems clear that what this series of relatively simple and largely domestic rituals achieved was the creation of bonds between the two families concerned which were stronger than those of friendship, but which, because a marriage was still in doubt, could not be of the sort usually associated with birth. The rituals also achieved the ending of childhood in the creation of a new procreative domestic unit. Indeed, as the rest of the case will show, the bonds forged on the day when the goats were presented have stood up well to the test of time, and the financial and emotional demands made of both families by the birth and rearing of the child. It is for this reason that the word *amity* as used by Fortes (1969: 241, 249) is, we think, appropriate to the situation, for it describes a relationship which is different to (and less than) kinship, but one which is more than mere friendship. What Fortes terms the axiom of amity presupposes an additional nuance to that of normal friendship; in this case this was provided by the mutual acknowledgement of the paternity of the coming child, and of certain responsibilities for its care on the part of both families. Adding to the strength of the new relationship was, of course, the possibility of marriage and the transformation of the ties of amity into those of affinity.

Many, many black South African families face the crisis of premarital pregnancy, and we suggest that what institutions such as *umgezo* achieve in the contemporary situation is the creation of functional bonds which will bridge the gap left by delays in, and often the failure of, marriage to follow conception. Cultural traditions, whatever may have been their forms and uses in the past, may thus provide potent symbols and fruitful models for coping with today's problems.

For many black families the ability to involve the father of an illegitimate baby and his kin in the support and care of the growing child is vital, due both to relative poverty and to very real practical difficulties experienced in rearing such children. Welfare provisions for black women with no support are virtually non-existent and women who cannot rely on the financial support of a husband have to earn their own living. In many cases this necessitates leaving small children alone or in the care of parents or siblings. The nature of some of these problems and how they may be dealt with is well illustrated as we continue our story.

Subsequent Events

The baby, a boy who was called Thulani, was born on 28 February 1983. For some time Grace and the baby remained at Umzinyati with her maternal grandmother. Amos and Mrs D contributed 'as much as they could' for clothing, and Thembi kept a record of all that she or her mother paid out so that she could be reimbursed by Mrs D or Amos. Grace often brought the child to visit KwaMashu 'to remind the father', and even visited Mrs D's place of employment to show him to her employers. At one time when the child was ill, Mrs D was telephoned to go to Umzinyati to fetch him and take him to hospital in Durban. The P family have, indeed, been fairly demanding, but Mrs D does not appear to resent the calls on her time and pocket, and the obligations established by the *imigezo* are being fulfilled by her and Amos.

Both Amos and Grace had passed their matriculation examinations at the end of 1982, but it was not until June that Amos got an unskilled job in a factory paying R52 per week. When the baby was about six months old, Grace began a course as a nurse-aide and later got a job at a white old-age home in Durban. Her hours are irregular and it has been impossible for her to care for the baby or have him with her at the home. At first he remained with Grace's maternal grandmother at Umzinyati but the old lady complained that she already had too many children to care for. During this period Thembi established herself and her children in a new shack area on the outskirts of KwaMashu. At much the same time Mrs D, with the help of her employers, got a house at Ntuzuma, an extension of KwaMashu. Her daughter, Nomusa, finished school at the end of 1983 and began a secretarial course in 1984 but could find no work. The second son, Lloyd, did a carpentry course and was apprenticed, earning R30 per month. Despite the cost of the rent of the new house and outlays on furniture, Mrs D and Amos still managed to save the R200 for the one beast which was promised to the family, and this money was paid in mid-1983. The outstanding R250 for the *ngquthu* beast was collected and handed over in mid-January 1985, thus at least clearing the amount asked for by Thembi's brother in damages.

As soon as Mrs D moved into her house at Ntuzuma, the P family began to be more insistent that she have Thulani to live with her. Thembi pointed out that neither she nor Grace could care for the baby as both were working, and it was decided that Nomusa should look after him. This did not work out well and in desperation Mrs D asked her employers if she could have the child on their premises. This meant a double load for Mrs D, as she had to care for the baby, who was then about a year old, and do all her usual work. Over weekends, when she was off duty, she had her own home to set to rights. Nomusa and Lloyd were, however, there on Sundays to help with the baby, and Grace became a frequent visitor, taking over the cooking as any *makoti* (bride) might when visiting the home of her affines. At one time Mrs D contemplated employing an 'old lady' to care for the baby during the week, but found the necessary R40 a month prohibitive. Thulani now appears to have become a fixture at Mrs D's place of employment. He is much loved by her employer's children, who play 'nanny' to him after school and when they are on holiday. This gives Mrs D some time to get on with her work. However, Thulani is growing fast. He is no longer a sedentary baby but wanders around getting into mischief, and Mrs D is continually under the strain of fearing that he may break something in her employer's home. When the adults return home from work, she tries to keep him as quiet as possible, but since her room adjoins the main house, it is difficult for Thulani not to disturb the family if he cries or even laughs and sings in the evenings.

The situation at the time of writing was that the D family were looking into the future. Mrs D, when interviewed just before the R250 for the *ngquthu* beast was due to be handed over, said that Amos now wanted to begin paying *ilobolo*. 'But it is his business, he must pay . . . he loves the baby very much and unless he starts paying, it can't be registered in his name . . . at any time Grace can come and take Thulani away . . . I don't know if he loves Grace . . . they're still seeing each other, but he loves Thulani very much.' She might have said that she too loves the toddler and quite clearly enjoys having him with her, even if it means extra work. Ideally, she would like to keep him at the Ntuzuma home — and have Grace there as *makoti* to care for him, the home, and her other children. Once *ilobolo* arrangements have been agreed upon and 'some' paid, she thinks 'the girl will come over . . . we don't have to pay all at once . . . it may be eight or nine cows or more . . . .' With R200 as the going rate per cow, it seems a monumental task for Amos to save the full bride-wealth. Well-paid employment is difficult to come by, and each year a new generation of school leavers come on to the job market. Amos cannot afford to leave his job to get further qualifications, although Grace is now studying for a higher nursing-aide examination and may eventually prove an economic asset, especially if one of her sisters comes to help with the baby while she is at work. However, the immediate problem facing the D family was to raise enough cash to open marriage negotiations. Petros was demanding 'a large goat', R100, and two bottles of whisky as *imvulamlomo*.[15] This will probably total just under R200 and Mrs D commented, 'Marriage is a very heavy thing . . . .' Her salary increase to R40 per week hardly seems likely to accommodate its demands and she was showing signs of stress and anxiety.

We now turn to speculate upon what the future may hold for the protagonists in our Social Drama (Turner 1957) and, in so doing, provide some comment upon what the case reveals about the nature and development of contemporary Zulu domestic groupings and, in particular, those headed by women.

Premarital Pregnancy, Marriage, and Female-headed Households

The initial question is whether Amos and Grace will indeed marry. It seems likely that the *imvulamlomo* will be paid and *ilobolo* payments initiated; whether they will be concluded is another matter and at what point, if any, Thembi and Petros will allow Thulani and Grace to move over to the D family remains to be seen. If a marriage does not occur, Thulani will eventually retain his mother's father's name and remain the responsibility of her family, with her uncle, Petros, as his legal guardian. Should Grace marry somebody else, Thulani may go with his mother, but it is more likely that he will remain with the P family, possibly under the care of Thembi's mother. In either case the D family will, over time, probably see less and less of the child, and the burden of care and support will shift entirely to the P family. If Grace does not marry, we have the basis for the development of a functioning domestic group made up of consanguineally-related women who live together and co-operate in providing a home for their children. Let us examine this possibility more fully.

Thembi herself has five children, and it seems unlikely that she will marry. At the time of Grace's pregnancy, Thembi's sister was also unmarried with children, and both were relying on their widowed mother to care for the children 'in the country' at Umzinyati while they worked to support them in town. This situation is symptomatic of the trend, to which one of us has already drawn attention (Preston-Whyte 1978: 60), for many African working women to be unable to live permanently in the homes and with the children they are supporting. Their role is that of migrants whose work enforces absenteeism upon them. The birth of Thulani, furthermore, threw the emphasis in child care and support on three generations of unattached consanguineally-related women — Thembi, who had not married, her widowed mother, and her unmarried daughter. At the time of the *imigezo* payment, this unit was still embedded within a relatively normal extended family structure, with Thembi's eldest brother as head. As his own nuclear family was increasing in size, however, his money was naturally channelled to support them, leaving Thembi and her unmarried sister to earn money to support their children. The building of her own home can be seen as a positive move by Thembi towards independence, as well as a strategy for getting closer to Durban and work opportunities. The latter, of course, is the *sine qua non* for successfully operating a working household in the absence of permanent male support. If Grace does not marry and other daughters of Thembi have children but do not marry or are widowed or divorced, the new home could provide the necessary base for a fully developed female-headed and female-linked family: one in which women not only provide support, but also take the major decisions; one which, indeed, is fully matrifocal in the original sense used by R.T. Smith (1956).[16] Thembi is, furthermore, an example of the 'new breed' of African women who, to quote Pauw, 'never get married, but nevertheless families develop around them which never pass through a stage of being a complete elementary family' (1963: 140).

Mrs D's family is also both female-headed and matrifocal, but came about in a different manner and may develop along very different lines. It was Mrs D's divorce which forced her to seek a home for her children with her parents. Her sister, though married, repeatedly brought her six children to seek refuge in the KwaMashu house. Since both the sister and her husband seemed incapable of keeping regular employment, it was usually Mrs D who supported the whole household, with the help of her mother's pension. At last the burden was so great that Mrs D removed her children from the house, leaving them temporarily with her mother's brother and later renting a house of her own at Ntuzuma. How she acquired and furnished this home is another story, but her manoeuvering, strategizing, and eventual success show her as a true matriarch (Smith 1956; Dubb 1974), the head and centre of a domestic unit in which adult or mature men at present play no decision-making role. It is true that Amos and Lloyd bring in wages each month, but it is Mrs D who decides how the money should be spent. 'Amos gives his money to me . . . so does Lloyd and now Nomusa when she is working temporarily. She also gives me her money. None of them are married and all live in my house . . . if Amos marries it will be different, but he still has to collect the *ilobolo*', she explained. If, indeed, Amos and Grace do marry and come with Thulani to live in the Ntuzuma home, and if Nomusa marries and leaves it, the home will take on the appearance of three-generational patriarchal extended households usual in Zulu society even today (Dubb 1974: 455-60). Mrs D will, however, for many years surely play a fairly dominant role in both support and decision-making. Grace may find the influence of her mother-in-law restrictive, but the paucity of accommodation for blacks, and particularly for young married couples, and the costs of setting up an independent domestic unit will probably inhibit movement out of Mrs D's home. Since the house is registered in Mrs D's name and the deposit was paid by her employers, she is likely to retain her position as effective head and decision-maker for some time to come. Her household is thus an example of the type of female-headed domestic group which results from the failure of marriage and represents, in reality, merely one possible stage in the developmental cycle of many contemporary Zulu households initiated by marriage (Fortes 1958; Pauw 1963: 139-40).

The case of Amos and Grace and their son Thulani demonstrates certain recurrent features of the childhood of many black children in South Africa. Continual moves occur. These are not only from country to town and from one house to another, but from one set of relatives to another, or from relatives to friends, or to the premises of employers. Long or permanent absences of male support figures, and even of mothers who must work and live elsewhere to support their children, are common. What is also strikingly illustrated by our case is that female-headed or female-linked units in which many children spend time do not necessarily continue to exist over time as fixed or corporate entities; male support comes and goes and marriage is still the ideal for most people, as the *ilobolo* negotiations for Grace and Amos indicate.

For many African women, however, marriage does not occur (Preston-Whyte 1981), and for those who bear children financial support is always a problem. In theory, and often in practice in Zulu society, it is the mother and her consanguineal kin who (despite damages) bear the major burden of support in the case of premarital births. What this case has shown clearly, however, is that where the father is known, his close kin may not be averse to contributing to the child's support, certainly in the early years, and may even *wish* to assume full structural responsibility through marriage with the mother. It seems to us likely that this attitude and responsibility have been largely neglected by writers on the problems of premarital pregnancies amongst black women, though Moeno (1977) and, long before her, Krige (1936b) did point out that at least a proportion of births to unmarried women were followed by marriage. The high social value which is placed upon fertility and birth in Zulu society makes, perhaps, for a different situation from that in the white community, where premarital pregnancies are (or were a decade or so ago) usually viewed in completely negative terms. Children are also valued in and for themselves in Zulu society, and Mrs D's struggle to keep Thulani indicates, we think, something of this value. This is not to say that we do not recognize that many black children are neglected, particularly in cases where they were not planned and where they put severe strain on household budgets, or where there is literally no 'family' (be it male- or female-headed) to absorb and care for them (Loening 1981). Thulani is, indeed, one of the fortunate children who has a clearly indicated place in society, the warm and loving care of both parents and of paternal and maternal grandmothers who are earning money for his support. What is significant is that on both Thulani's mother's and his father's side, women play, and seem likely to continue to play, a dominant role in his support and care.

Drawing together the threads of what has been suggested by our case, it seems to us that the essence of black household structures is complexity and variety. The basic marriage link may be absent and, even when present, does not provide lifelong security due to such factors as inadequate or even non-existent financial support from males, divorce, widowhood, and premarital pregnancy. As a result, the nuclear and extended family based on male-female dyads,[17] and also female-headed households are not merely stages in developmental terms, but are *alternatives* to which, in addition, other kin may be added when and for as long as necessary. Individual adults can live on their own — perhaps as domestic servants on employers' premises, perhaps in hostels or in rented rooms, but when children are involved some wider domestic organization is needed. The old sociological truism that the major function of the family is to care for and socialize children still applies, but with different and often changing actors: where male/female conjugal dyads do not exist, female consanguineal dyads (or triads, etc.) may suffice. For anyone familiar with the growing literature on domestic units headed by and composed largely of women both in South Africa and in other parts of the world, these remarks will echo closely the functions widely attributed to these units and also their flexibility (Adams 1960; Blumberg and Garcia 1977; Smith 1956; Solien de Gonzalez 1969; Stack 1970, 1974; Young, Wolkowitz and McCullagh 1981).

The high 'rate' of births to unmarried black women in South Africa is a factor which contributes to the development of female-headed households and gives both them and also conjugally-based households a tendency to be three or even four generational (Pauw 1963). The many factors which in their turn contribute to the large number of pregnancies among young black women in urban areas have been discussed in full in a number of places (Khanyile 1974; De Haas 1984; Craig and Richter-Strydom nd., 1983; Rip and Schmidt 1977). It will suffice to mention some of those which stem directly from the type of social environment in which many black teenagers are reared in town, a milieu in striking contrast to that of most white teenagers.

In many black families both parents are working and in female-headed households it is virtually inevitable that the responsible and able-bodied adult women may have to spend long hours either at work or in informal money-making. If the latter does not take them away from home, it may bring large numbers of men to the house in order to buy food and drink. Children are thus either left alone at home for most of the day or soon become involved in helping their mothers make money. This brings girls in particular into contact with adult men, many of whom have money to spare not only for drink or food, but also to 'spoil young girls'. The attractions of older men who flatter girls and give them 'a good time' are often spoken of both by teenagers and their worried mothers. This type of problem aside, organized recreational facilities for all, and particularly for teenagers, are poorly developed in urban areas and there is little formal provision for either entertainment or supervision during the time when children are not in school. High levels of unemployment, especially among recent school leavers and school 'drop-outs', means that large numbers of teenagers are at home with nothing to do during the day or in the evening. Many parents, furthermore, cannot afford to keep their children at school, and teenagers often have to skip a year or two of education. This, together with the late age of school entrance compared to whites, and high failure rates in most standards, means that scholars are, as we have seen, often nearer twenty and many over twenty by the time they leave school. Sexual experimentation and involvement appear to begin at an early age and peer group pressure is often against the maintenance of virginity for both sexes. There is, in addition, a virtual absence of formal sex education at school and reluctance amongst parents to broach the subject with their children. 'We mothers tell them nothing', said Mrs D, 'except not to have boyfriends and what is that when everyone does, and people laugh at the girls who don't . . . ?' To reiterate her mother's words when the *imigezo* were handed over, 'since the kids took themselves to school to learn something, they forgot about books and taught themselves something else . . . . '

Such is the social environment of black 'childhood' in most South African urban areas. We contend that it is dramatically and shockingly different from that experienced by many of the sheltered and indulged white children of our acquaintance.

Apartheid at First Hand: Growing Up on White Premises

> The one thing for which I always remember the Singer family is their dog and the fuss they made about it. They'd let me wait in the kitchen while Mrs Singer collected the articles of washing. 'The girl' as they called their maid, who must have been about twenty-five, gave the dog fresh tea after breakfast. I often sat there, *my mouth flowing with saliva at the warm aroma of coffee and eggs and ham which were foreign down our way* (Mphahlele 1959: 69) (Author's emphasis).

In this quotation from *Down Second Avenue*, Ezekiel Mphahlele allows us a glimpse of one of the most poignant experiences of black childhood in South Africa — seeing at first hand what life is like on the other side of the racial divide. Before they leave school and enter the labour market, black children raised in townships or in black rural areas seldom experience the enormity of the gulf between black and white lifestyles. For the children of domestic servants and farm labourers, the experience is often part of growing up. Let us look at it from Thulani's point of view.

In mid-1984, when he went to live with his paternal grandmother on the premises of her white employers in Durban, Thulani began to live what could be described as a 'double life'. During the week he and Mrs D live in her small room attached to the white employer's house and on Friday, when his grandmother goes 'off duty' for the weekend, they journey to her home on the distant fringes of KwaMashu at Ntuzuma. Since they usually leave the employer's home at about 4 or 5 p.m. and the journey takes between two and two and a half hours, depending on the buses, they invariably arrive after dark. Until he was too big, Thulani was often carried on Mrs D's back while she walked to and waited for the bus. Now she alternatively carries and encourages him to walk when she is exhausted. In contrast to the brightly-lit house in Durban, the Ntuzuma home is without electricity. There is only a small primus stove to cook on and no running water, either hot or cold. Mrs D and Thulani usually arrive not only worn out, but dusty from bad, untarred roads and crowded, often dirty buses. Sometimes Thulani is so tired he just falls into bed — usually with one of Mrs D's other children or with her sister's children, as there are not enough beds for everyone. On other occasions he is kept awake by his young father, 'aunty' (that is, father's sister), and even by his mother who may be visiting and who may not have seen him for a month or more. All are happy to welcome and play with him. The house is often very crowded, especially if Mrs D's sister's children are there, but sometimes it is virtually empty if Nomusa and Amos are late or have got temporary night work. All round him people are laughing and talking loudly, and the radio blares out. Often the neighbours are even more rowdy than his own family and drunks sometimes bash on the doors and windows. Their area is, however, fairly quiet and safe compared with many elsewhere in KwaMashu and the surrounding shack areas. Early on Monday morning their journey to Durban begins again. Mrs D has to have Thulani up, washed, and dressed by 5.30 a.m. in order to catch the bus to town and be at work just after 8 o'clock. In winter it is dark until at least 6.30 a.m. and dressing is done by candlelight. There are no street lights on the way to the bus-stop, but at least it is getting light and not, as on the homeward journey, getting darker as time goes on. Walking to and from the buses in the dark township is dangerous and can be very frightening for a small child. Sometimes either his father or aunty walk to the bus with Thulani and his grandmother. Usually, however, they have to leave earlier than Mrs D, as they have further to travel and must be at work by 7.30 a.m. Mrs D tries to clean up and tidy the home before she leaves, especially if she knows Nomusa is not going to be home till evening. She herself will not return until Friday evening unless there is a family crisis. Clearly Mrs D spends very little of her life enjoying the home she has struggled to get and for which she has to remain in employment in order to meet the domestic budget.

Once over the employer's threshold, the tenor of life is physically very different from that at Ntuzuma. Thulani always has the comforting presence of Mrs D, but she is often harassed and rushed with her work. This entails cleaning a fairly big four-bedroomed house and washing, ironing, and cooking for a family of four; the employer in her turn works full-time and often leaves home at 7.30 a.m., to return only after 5 p.m. in the evening. Instead of his father and aunty and Mrs D's other children, he has only the white employer's two teenage children with whom to play. While it is true that they are very fond of him and the girl of twelve plays with him a lot when she is at home, there are subtle constraints and unwritten rules of behaviour which affect what Thulani can do and how he must behave. Though living effectively in a white household, he can never be *of* the white family in any real sense. It is not just that he is not a relative; it is that he is, first and foremost, black in a society in which colour creates the deepest divisions. Second, he is the grandson of an employee and, more than that, he is the grandson of a domestic *servant* who is dressed in cap and apron to show her subordinate position in society. The children of the white household call her by her first name and though, at least when their parents are within earshot, they are not overtly rude to her, their friends sometimes are. Many white children swear at servants and take liberties they would not dream of attempting with other adults. As Thulani grows up he will see this behaviour and experience the humiliation of his beloved grandmother.

Looking at the situation from one point of view — that often taken by whites — Thulani could be seen as very fortunate. In contrast to many black children, he is well fed and comfortably housed. The children of the white employer genuinely enjoy having him with them;

when he stays at Ntuzuma they beg Mrs D to fetch him and when he is sick they encourage their mother to get medicines for him. At Christmas he gets a gift from them wrapped as lovingly as any for their family and friends. They play with him a lot when they are at home, while the other adults in the household and visitors smile at him, chuck him under the chin, and sometimes give him sweets or pocket money. He watches television at night when the employer's children have the set on and he plays on the lawns of the employer's home during the day. There is, however, another side to the situation.

As a baby Thulani was fully indulged, but as he grows into toddlerhood he is being made aware of subtle differences between him and the white children of the house. The lawns are not his; he is there on sufferance, usually only till the white employers come home in the afternoons. If the white children are out, or are not watching television, he has to sit in his grandmother's room or in the kitchen. He may not take the toys belonging to the white girl home and those he plays with during the day have to go back to her room at night. It is true that she gives him many of her old toys, but somehow they are usually the broken ones. He is not called out to meet guests as are the white children; when they are given presents or treats by friends and parents, he is overlooked as he sits in the kitchen or peers in at the lounge door. His grandmother insists that he be quiet and respectful when the white adults are present and when games with her employer's children become rowdy, she hastens to quieten the three of them. When there is a dinner party or guests, it is a great strain to keep Thulani amused and quiet. This is the other side of his life in the white home, one which will loom larger as he grows older. He will eventually go to different and relatively poorly-equipped schools compared with that of the white children with whom he now plays. Indeed, when he begins school he will have to leave the room on the property of the white employer and live full-time at Ntuzuma. Who will then look after him is still to be negotiated, and if his parents do not marry and Nomusa gets a full-time job, it seems likely that he will join the ranks of young school children who take themselves to school and return to an empty house when they have finished their lessons for the day. Unlike the children of his grandmother's employer, he will not have even the benefit of Mrs D's presence to welcome him and provide him with food and company in the afternoons.

These are some of the paradoxes of life in South Africa. For children reared on the premises of white employers like Thulani, and even for those who, like Mphahlele when he was a boy, merely call at white homes in order to collect washing or to visit relatives, childhood may be the time when they are introduced in an extremely hurtful way to the stark realities of the apartheid regime. It is indeed ironical that childhood is conceptualized in much Western thought and literature as a time of innocence and idyllic irresponsibility, when the individual is protected from the harsh realities of life. On this reading few black children in South Africa can be said to experience childhood in any but the most attentuated form.

Notes

1. The use of the word 'black' here and throughout this chapter means African, though what is said of Africans applies very largely also to coloured people.
2. The case came to our notice in late 1982 when one of us (Louw) was looking for a topic for a third-year research project for the following year. The other (Preston-Whyte) was supervising these projects and it was decided to work together on the case. A Master's student, M. de Haas, also joined the investigation, and she and Louw attended the ceremony which is reported here. It is also discussed by De Haas (1984: 66-67). The case was then followed up by Preston-Whyte and Louw until the start of 1985. It falls, therefore, into the type of research data often referred to as an 'extended case' (Van Velsen 1967) and qualifies also as a social drama (Turner 1957). The ceremony was conducted in Zulu; a tape recording was made and later transcribed and translated. We would like to acknowledge the helpful comments of Professor W.J. Argyle on the manuscript and we are indebted to him for the suggestion that Fortes's 'Axiom of Amity' might be an appropriate notion to describe the relationship established by the passing of the *imigezo*.
3. While statements of this sort are made by people in touch with both black teenagers and maternity services for blacks, and certainly reflect fast-held beliefs, figures to substantiate these claims are difficult to come by and to assess accurately. Births to unmarried African women are not given separately in published census data and, though purely local studies tend to support the observation, it is not possible to compare the national situation amongst Africans with that amongst white, coloured and Indian South Africans (Rip 1966). Illegitimacy amongst Africans seems to have been the focus of more research on the Reef than in other parts of the country and more work has been done in urban than in rural areas. Coertze (1969) reported in the late 1960s that 55 per cent of

births in Atteridgeville were what he termed illegitimate, while Mostert and Du Plessis (1972) found in a fertility study of both Atteridgeville and Mamelodi, published in the early 1970s, that 50.3 per cent of a sample of 1 001 women had borne at least one illegitimate child. These births formed 23 per cent of live births and 17 per cent of the expected number of children at family completion. Rip and Schmidt (1977: 5), working somewhat later in Mamelodi, found that of a complex three stage sample the average number of illegitimate births per family was 1.77. They amassed a fair amount of data on the general topic of illegitimacy and were aware also that definitions of illegitimacy are culture-bound: that in a proportion of the cases which they calculated as illegitimate, it was likely that the people concerned did not classify the birth this way, as bridewealth negotiations were underway or the couple subsequently married.

Turning to KwaZulu and Natal, and specifically to Durban and its surrounding areas, we are fortunate in having access to a number of studies carried out by researchers from the University of Natal Medical School, four of which were undertaken at maternity and antenatal clinics attached to the KwaMashu Polyclinic where the schoolgirl about whom we are writing had her baby, and one at a clinic attached to the King Edward VIII teaching hospital. These sets of figures suggest similar trends and we are greatly indebted to Professor S.M. Ross of the Department of Obstetrics and Gynaecology at the University of Natal for allowing us to use the previously unpublished KwaMashu figures, and for helping us to interpret them. For clarity, we list the findings separately below. Some findings are reported in Ross (1984).

KwaMashu Study One
In 1978 an investigation was made of 250 women who attended the maternity section of the KwaMashu Polyclinic for the birth of their first child (primigravidae). Twenty-eight (11.2 per cent) were married, 222 (88.8 per cent) were single, and of the single women, 117 (52.7 per cent) were aged 18 or less. Though in only one case (3.6 per cent) had the married woman not planned to fall pregnant, 197 of the single women (88.7 per cent) reported not having planned the birth (Ross, personal communication).

KwaMashu Study Two
In an investigation of 181 primigravidae undertaken at the same clinic as background to a study of the problems of schoolgirl pregnancies, Craig (1980) found that no less than 99 (55 per cent) of the women were at school when the pregnancy began.

KwaMashu Study Three
One hundred women having their second child at the clinic were

investigated. Thirty-five were married, 65 unmarried. Seven of the single women were 18 years of age or younger. In 18 cases the child had a different father to the woman's first child (Ross, personal communication).

KwaMashu Study Four
In 1981, 856 women attending antenatal clinics attached to the KwaMashu Polyclinic were considered. Three hundred and thirty-six (39 per cent) were 18 years or less and 181 (51 per cent) were at school. The exact ages of the girls under 18 are as follows:

18 years	95
17 years	90
16 years	10
15 years	32
14 years or less	9

Conclusions from the above
In the late 1970s and early 1980s a high proportion (possibly between 60 and 80 per cent) of first and second babies delivered at selected black maternity clinics north of Durban were born to single women. Not only were many of the mothers under 18 but about 50 per cent were at school when the pregnancy occurred. These figures are confirmed by the findings of Larsen and Van Middelkoop (1982), who undertook similar investigations of 118 women who gave birth at the King Edward VIII hospital situated in Durban itself. Though women from KwaMashu and its environs also attend this hospital, it is a referral hospital for serious cases and is therefore likely to tap a different attendance to the KwaMashu Polyclinic. In this case seventy (59 per cent) of the women were single and another twenty-one (18 per cent) were having bridewealth paid for them, making 77 per cent who were not formally married. Twenty-six (22 per cent) were married or widowed and in one case no information was available. If we exclude the women for whom bridewealth was being paid, it is clear that nearly 60 per cent of the women were single when birth took place. This is much in keeping with the findings of KwaMashu Study Three, though lower than KwaMashu Study One, where 88.8 per cent were single. The reasons for the differences may lie in the fact that in the latter study the issue of bridewealth payment was not enquired into and in the King Edward study the sample itself seems to have had a bias towards married women, in that the investigators were interested in the differences between women who had attended an antenatal clinic and those who had merely arrived for delivery. Twenty-eight per cent of the 'booked' mothers were married as against 12 per cent of the unbooked mothers, but 67 of the 118 women studied were 'booked', and only 51 'unbooked'.

The niceties of these arguments cannot however detract from the fact that a very high proportion of African women are single when they visit maternity clinics. We have unfortunately no way of counting the number of births to African unmarried women which occur at home. The onus is on the parents to register the child but this is not always done and the age distribution of women giving birth at home is unknown.

4. In most other cases of a similar nature which we have encountered, only one goat, or the stomach contents of a beast which was bought from a butcher, were given. This is then referred to as *umgezo* — the purification beast. Since two goats were involved in this case, the plural form is used in the description of events.

5. Grace is in many ways unusual: the majority of schoolgirl pregnancies occur earlier, both in terms of age and standard achieved at school. In the following table the educational standards of women investigated in Ross's KwaMashu Studies One and Three (1984) give some idea of the broader context.

Kwa-Mashu Study One *(250 women having first baby)*			Kwa-Mashu Study Three *(100 women having second baby)*	
	No.	%		No. & %
No education	22	9	No education	15
Education achieved or in progress:			Education achieved or in progress:	
Std. 1	6	2	Std. 1	2
Stds. 2-4	44	18	Stds. 2-4	21
Stds. 5-7	85	34	Stds. 5-7	37
Stds. 8-10	74	30	Stds. 8-10	18
Matric passed	13	5	Matric passed	5
Post Matric (teachers)	6	2	Teachers	2
	250	100		100

6. Interesting confirmation of this comes from further figures reported by Ross (personal communication), who found that 45 per cent of a sample of black medical students at the University of Natal had received their knowledge of sexual matters 'from books', 30 per cent from friends, 20 per cent at high school. In only 2 per cent of the cases had the student been informed by parents and in none by church groups or pastors. Similarly only 15 per cent of nursing staff claimed to provide sex education for their children. Craig (1980) found in her study of 99 pregnant school girls at the KwaMashu Polyclinic that 26 per cent had got no instruction or even knowledge from home and even the 67 per cent who had learnt 'something' at home reported it to have been purely negative, of the 'boys get girls into trouble' variety. Forty-nine per cent had got some knowledge from friends. Ninety-five per cent reported that the

church simply preached against sex but gave no advice or information on the topic.

7. In fact the daughter of Grace's mother's brother Petros, but an older girl than Grace.

8. Louw and De Haas provided the transport.

9. Since Mrs D is divorced and her father dead.

10. The word *umndeni* was used explicitly in its wide and all-inclusive meaning of family or local agnatic group.

11. Mrs D thought that this would not have taken place had the researchers not been present. 'It was politeness for the white visitors . . . normally it is just to get the business over'.

12. Euphemism for 'with no known father'.

13. There does not seem to have been anything unusual about this act. No special place was chosen and no formality accompanied it.

14. We do not know how prevalent the giving of *umgezo* in the form of money or a goat may be in urban areas. Research in a rural area, however, suggests that both are frequent and expected behaviour. In a stable and fixed community, responsibility for pregnancy may be easier to assign than in the fluid social situation of township or shack areas. The P family were fortunate that Mrs D acknowledged her 'responsibility to pay'. There was no way in which they could have forced her to produce the *imigezo* beasts, though they could have sued for the *ngqutu* beast and the *mvimba* in the courts. In this respect figures provided by Professor Ross (personal communication) are useful. In a small investigation of 33 primigravidae aged 17 or less, he found that damages had been paid in six cases, while in five other cases they had been partly paid. *Ilobolo* had been paid in one case. Thus in 35 per cent of the cases the young women's parents or guardian had been recompensed in some degree for impregnation. Unfortunately his study does not distinguish the passing of a purification beast (*umgezo*) from the 'damages' legally claimable in court.

15. This represents gifts to open marriage negotiations.

16. For a summary of Smith's position and also of the terminological confusion present in the literature on female-headed households and families, see Preston-Whyte (1978).

17. That is, interacting couples.

Afterword

Pamela Reynolds

The book brings to the attention of readers the plight of children in South Africa and the multiplicity of their experiences. In part it celebrates children's creativity, resilience and enterprise even in the face of great disadvantage. In part, it mourns for their suffering and places on record society's culpability. In part it calls for a deeper understanding of and firmer action by society on their behalf and in accord with their needs and wishes.

Anna Freud (1982: 299) said, 'there are in our world many phenomena which tax or defy our understanding, the phenomenon of childhood having high priority among them'. Understanding is not easily acquired for a number of reasons. One is that childhood is a continuing metamorphosis: 'the category of childhood is concretely descriptive of a community which though relatively stable in its structure is by definition only fleeting in its particular membership' (Jenks 1982: 11). Besides, the needs of children alter over time and in relation to variations in social, economic, moral, and political conditions: the status of childhood 'is constituted in particular socially located forms of discourse' (Jenks 1982: 23). Another reason is that children do not have formal institutions that they have shaped to represent their views. A fourth reason is that their codes are not easily transcribed by adults. A fifth is that adults too often begin their investigation of children's society with preconceptions or they use inappropriate research tools. Finally, research on children can conflict with vested interests: for example, those of a government attempting to obscure the truth; those of organizations unwilling to countenance the results of their practices; or those of individuals who refuse to accept their responsibilities.

The Rights of Children

We need to consider where an understanding of the contexts of childhood in South Africa can lead. Should a charter of children's rights be drawn up and appropriate laws passed? Do children have rights? If so, who should crystallize them and on the basis of what information and whose analysis? Current debate on children's interests centres on their rights. Opinion tends to polarize around the issue of their protection versus their rights.

Freeman (1983: 19) distinguishes between the two orientations, saying that the former stresses the provision by society of supposedly beneficial objects, environments, services, experience, etc. for the child; the latter stresses those potential rights which would allow children to exercise control over their environments, to make decisions about what they want, to have autonomous control over various facets of their lives. The former corresponds broadly to child-saving notions of 'giving children what is good for them'; the latter conforms to the idea propagated by child liberationists who want children to have greater autonomy so that they are given the freedom to decide 'what is good for themselves'.

Two fundamental problems that typically confront policy makers trying to make rational decisions about the best interests of children are outlined by Mnookin (1985: 16-17). The first, which he calls the prediction problem, is that it is often exceedingly difficult to predict the consequences of alternative children's policies. The second, the value problem, arises from the difficulty of selecting the criteria that should be used to evaluate the alternative consequences. He comments that the choice of criteria is inherently value-laden; all too often there is no consensus about what values should inform this choice. These problems are not unique to children's policies, but they are especially acute in this context because children themselves often cannot speak for their own interests. Mnookin feels that, 'very young children are often entirely unable to articulate their own preferences. And though older children may have much to say, their inexperience and immaturity often cause adults to doubt children's capacity to decide what is in their own interests.'

Mnookin (1985: 13) notes further that there are two basic difficulties involved in giving practical content to constitutional rights where children's rights are at issue. He says that,

> First, because children lack adult capacity and maturity, giving children the *same* rights and obligations as adults would often do them a substantial disservice. They may need special protection . . . . however, not all children are part of families, and our traditions emphasize the primacy of the parental role in childrearing. The rights of children cannot be defined without reference to their parents. But . . . it may not always be clear which adult is entitled to deference as a 'parent'. Nor is it clear who should prevail when the 'rights' of parents and the needs of children collide.

Some of the problems arise from the fact that children often lack the ability to define and defend their own interests. Gross and Gross (1977: 7) observe that 'the rights of children is an abstract, general, legalistic concept. It is an idea, an ideal, at best an affirmation of principle. It does not help children until it is put into practice. If it is ignored, obstructed, or prevented it does no good; in fact, it may do harm, because many people will take the words for the act and think that because the words have been spoken the condition of children's lives has changed.'

Children's rights have been embraced enthusiastically by writers, commissions, legislatures and judges, says Freeman (1983: 279) in his book *The Rights and Wrongs of Children*. However, he adds, 'only the most cursory thought has been given to what is meant by the phrase, and what the implications of children's rights are . . . . Thinking about children's rights has concentrated on policies, not principles. This is doubly unfortunate for moral and political theory has so much to offer . . . . but in general the impact of contemporary moral and political thinking on those concerned with children's rights has been minimal.'

Academics have a duty to children. They ought to ensure that research efforts and funding priorities are focussed on theoretical and methodological issues that reflect the interests of children. Knowledge is power and, according to Giddens (1979: 244), studies of existing society constitute a potential intervention within that society. We should concern ourselves with the question of who possesses awareness (and thus power) and what it is that we do not know about the conditions and consequences of actions as they affect children.

Action on behalf of children is difficult to follow through even where concern and commitment are fairly widespread. Freeman (1983: 279) gives a gloomy summation of what Britain achieved in the three years following the International Year of the Child (1979): 'child poverty is worse, youth unemployment greater, more children are locked up than in 1979. Many of the issues remain the same. The debate about corporal punishment has got no further.' It is much more difficult to be optimistic about South Africa's care of children over the next decade. The country negates every one of the ten articles of the United Nations Declaration of the Rights of the Child. It is worth recalling that the Preamble to the Declaration begins with the clause: 'whereas mankind owes the child the best that it has to give . . . .'

The Right of a Child to Live with His or Her Parent

There is one right that should be enshrined in the nation's constitution and assured by law and its strict implementation, and that is the right of a child to live with his or her mother and father. How extraordinary that there is a country that legislates against this fundamental right: a country that enforces through vast, complex machinery at enormous cost the separation of child and parent. Given the high rate of divorce in South Africa and the destruction of family life, many children cannot live with both parents, but legislation such as that which controls movement of people and access to housing and jobs should not determine with whom the child may or may not live nor where.

Children and Unemployment

During the nineteenth century in Europe and the United States of America there was a population growth of only one per cent per annum while industrial jobs were being created at between two and three per cent per annum. As a result, labour was imported to industrial growth areas. In these countries jobs were created around small units, using little capital, and low and variable wages were paid. South Africa's industrial growth pattern is different. Almost half the population is under fifteen years old and the population growth rate is over three per cent per annum: already there is a high dependency ratio. The number of people on the labour market is increasing by over five per cent per annum. South Africa's industrial complex is characterized by high technology, high capital outlay per job, and a considerable amount of legislation and trade union activity surrounding wage conditions and job security. There will be a difficult passage of many years before the formal sector can employ everybody.

Earlier this century China faced the same problem. The solution there was to keep people in the countryside on communal farms with only small private plots of land, working many more days a year for low marginal returns per day in order to improve real living standards. South Africa has neither the political system nor the organizational capacity to pursue that option now. South Africans expect to participate in a modern, urban-based society. There seems to be no choice for the state except to redistribute wealth, notably through health, education, and housing. Children are already growing up in a society of high unemployment. Even if South Africa experiences high growth rates the problem of creating jobs will remain.

In a country in which family structures have been deliberately undermined, it is imperative that attention be paid to the establishment and nurture of community support systems.

Generations

This book has barely touched on the complexity and variety of children's experiences in South Africa. There is so much more that needs to be explored: in the experience of children in other ethnic communities — for example, Portuguese, Chinese, Greek; in the various forms of initiation through which many are made to pass; in particular forms of coercion like being forced to marry a man chosen by kin; in times of stress when they face political choices of momentous consequence; in making moral choices to do with religious affiliation or community cooperation.

We end with a reminder about the possibility of rejuvenation that the cycle of generations offers society. Culture is developed by individuals who come into contact anew with the accumulated heritage. A fresh contact always means a changed relationship of distance from the object and a novel approach in assimilating, using, and developing the existing material. An individual's attitude towards the heritage handed down by his predecessors is a novel one. In Mannheim's words (in Jenks 1982: 263), 'the continuous emergence of new human beings certainly results in some loss of accumulated cultural possessions; but, on the other hand, it alone makes a fresh selection possible when it becomes necessary; it facilitates reevaluation of our inventory and teaches us both to forget that which is no longer useful and to covet that which has yet to be won'.

References

Aboud, F.E. and Skerry, S.A. 1984. 'The development of ethnic attitudes: a critical review', *Journal of Cross-Cultural Psychology*, 15, 3-34.

Abrahams, I. 1955. *Birth of a Community: A History of Western Province Jewry from Earliest Times to the End of the South African War, 1902* (Cape Town Hebrew Congregation, Cape Town).

Adam, B.D. 1978. 'Inferiorization and "self-esteem"', *Social Psychology*, 41, 47-53.

Adam, H. and Giliomee, H. 1979. *The Rise and Crisis of Afrikaner Power* (David Philip, Cape Town).

Adams, R.N. 1960. 'An enquiry into the nature of the family' in *Essays in the Science of Culture*, edited by B.E. Dole and R.L. Carneiro (Y. Cromwell Co., New York).

African Self Help Association. 1982. *Annual Report, 1981 – 1982* (Johannesburg), 3.

Anti-Slavery Society. 1983. *Child Labour in South Africa: A General Review*, Child Labour Series, Report No.7 (Anti-Slavery Society, London).

Ardener, E. 1972. 'Belief and the problem of women' in *The Interpretation of Ritual*, edited by J.S. La Fontaine (Tavistock, London).

Ardener, S. (ed.). 1978. *Defining Females* (Croom Helm, London).

Arens, L.J., Molteno, C.D., Marshall, S.R., Robertson, W.I., and Rabkin, J. 1978. 'Cerebral palsy in Cape Town — a comparative 12-year retrospective study', *South African Medical Journal*, 53, 319-24.

Argus, Cape Town (daily evening newspaper).

Argyle, J. 1977. 'The myth of the elementary family: a comparative account of variations in family household structure amongst a group of South African whites', *African Studies* 36, 2, 105-18.

Ariès, P. 1962. *Centuries of Childhood* (Jonathan Cape, London).

Arkin, A. 1985. 'The contribution of South African Jewry to contemporary South African economic life', *Jewish Affairs*, 40, 1, 24-30.

Asher, S.R. and Allen, V.L. 1969. 'Racial preference and social comparison processes', *Journal of Social Issues*, 25, 157-66.

Auerbach, F.E. 1965. *The Power of Prejudice in South African Education* (Balkema, Cape Town).

Bachmayer, T. 1985. 'Struggling with unemployment', *Critical Health*, 12, 19-24.

Bagley, C. 1979. 'Self-esteem as a pivotal concept in race and ethnic relations', *Research in Race and Ethnic Relations*, 1, 127-67.

Bamford, F.N. 1980. 'The school health service: organization' in *Child Health in the Community*, edited by R.G. Mitchell (Churchill Livingstone, Edinburgh).

Banks, W.C. 1976. 'White preference in blacks: a paradigm in search of a phenomenon', *Psychological Bulletin*, 83, 1179-86.

Barling, J. 1981. 'Developmental trends in children's psychological conservatism: a failure to replicate', *Journal of Genetic Psychology*, 138, 143-44.

Barling, J. 1982. 'Developmental trends in psychological conservation: rejoinder to Powell and Stewart', *Journal of Genetic Psychology* 140, 311-12.

Barling, J. and Fincham, F. 1978. 'Locus of control beliefs in male and female Indian and white schoolchildren in South Africa', *Journal of Cross-Cultural Psychology*, 9, 227-35.

Barling, J. and Fincham, F. 1979. 'Cultural and sexual effects on psychological conservatism in children', *Journal of Social Psychology*, 107, 15-21.

Beals, A. 1967. *Culture in Process* (Holt, Reinhart and Winston, New York).

Beattie, J. 1964. *Other Cultures: Aims, Methods and Achievements in Social Anthropology* (Cohen and West, London).

Becker, R. 1983. 'The sexual division of labour and its implications for trade union organization', unpublished BA Hons. thesis, University of the Witwatersrand, Johannesburg.

Beitz, J. 1960. 'An investigation of race awareness and attitude in white South African children aged 3 – 10 years', unpublished BA Hons. thesis, University of the Witwatersrand, Johannesburg.

Bekker, J.C. and Coertze, J.J. 1982. *Seymour's Customary Law in Southern Africa*, fourth edition (Juta, Cape Town).

Berkowitz, J. 1984. 'Juvenile justice in South Africa: the reformatory institution — "Rehabilitation or Control?"', unpublished research paper, Institute of Criminology, University of Cape Town, Cape Town.

Bhana, K. and Bhana, A. 1975. 'Colour concept attitudes among Indian preschool children as a function of black nannies', *Journal of Behavioural Sciences*, 2, 115-20.

Blumberg, R.L. and Garcia, M.P. 1977. 'The political economy of the mother-child family: a cross-cultural view' in *Beyond the Nuclear Family Model*, edited by L. Lenero-Otero, Sage Studies in International Sociology, 7 (Sage, London).

Boberg, P.Q.R. 1977. *The Law of Persons and the Family* (Juta, Cape Town).

Brand, E.S., Ruiz, R.A. and Padilla, A.M. 1974. 'Ethnic identification and preference: a review', *Psychological Bulletin*, 81, 860-90.

Buijs, G. 1978. 'Kinship in a changing society: extra familial kinship among Indians living on a sugar estate in Natal', unpublished MA thesis, University of Natal, Durban.

Buijs, G. 1980. 'The role of the Mother Goddess Mariamma in Natal', *Religion in Southern Africa*, 1, 1, 1-9.

Buijs, G. 1981. 'An analysis of some factors affecting religious commitment in a South African Indian community', *Religion in Southern Africa*, 2, 2, 25-33.

Burman, S.B. 1983. 'Roman-Dutch family law for Africans: the Black Divorce Court in action', *Acta Juridica 1983*, 171-89.

Burman, S.B. 1984. 'Divorce and the disadvantaged: African women in urban South Africa' in *Women and Property / Women as Property,* edited by R. Hirschon (Croom Helm, London).

Burman, S.B. and Barry, J. 1984. 'Divorce and deprivation in South Africa', *Second Carnegie Inquiry into Poverty and Development in Southern Africa*, conference paper no. 87 (SALDRU, University of Cape Town, Cape Town).

Butler-Adam, J.F. and Venter, W.M. 1984. *Indian Housing Study in Durban and Pietermaritzburg*, 5 vols., Natal Town and Regional Planning Main Series Report 58 (Institute for Social and Economic Research, University of Durban-Westville, Durban).

Cape Times, Cape Town (daily morning newspaper).

Cameron, M.A. July 1984. 'School health education project', unpublished report, Department of Community Medicine, University of Cape Town.

Centre for Intergroup Studies. 1980. *District Six*, occasional paper no. 2 (CIGS, University of Cape Town).

Charlton, N.C.J. 1975. 'Afrikaners as viewed by English-speaking compatriots' in *Looking at the Afrikaner Today*, edited by H.W. van der Merwe (Tafelberg, Cape Town).

Child Safety Centre. 1984. 'Child Safety Centre report', unpublished data, Red Cross War Memorial Children's Hospital, Cape Town.

Chisholm, L. May 1982. 'Training for capital: De Lange Reports', *Perspectives in Education*, 3-20.

Chisholm, L. 1984. 'Redefining skills: black education in South Africa in the 1980s', in *Apartheid and Education*, edited by P. Kallaway (Ravan Press, Johannesburg).

Chisholm, L. 1985. 'The pedagogy of Porter Reformatory in the Cape Colony, 1882 – 1910', postgraduate seminar paper, African Studies Institute, University of the Witwatersrand, Johannesburg.

Christie, P. 1985. *The Right to Learn — The Struggle for Education in South Africa* (SACHED/Ravan Press, Johannesburg).

Christie, P. and Collins, C. 1984. 'Bantu education: apartheid ideology and labour reproduction' in *Apartheid and Education*, edited by P. Kallaway (Ravan Press, Johannesburg).

Clark, K.B. and Clark, M.K. 1939. 'The development of consciousness of self and the emergence of racial identification in negro preschool children', *Journal of Social Psychology*, 10, 591-99.

Clark, K.B. and Clark, M.K. 1947. 'Racial identification and preference in negro children' in *Readings in Social Psychology*, edited by T.M. Newcomb and E.L. Hartley (Holt, New York).

Cloete, M. 1983. 'Maternity rights and benefits', research project for Industrial Sociology III, University of the Witwatersrand, Johannesburg.

Cobb, J. 1984. *Babyshock: A Mother's First Five Years* (Arrow Books, London).

Cock, J. 1980. *Maids and Madams* (Ravan Press, Johannesburg).

Cock, J. September 1981. 'Disposable nannies: domestic servants in the political economy of South Africa', *Review of African Political Economy*, 21, 63-83.

Cock, J., Emdon, E., and Klugman, B. 1984. 'Child care and the working woman: a sociological investigation of a sample of urban African women', *Second Carnegie Inquiry into Poverty and Development in Southern Africa*, conference paper no. 115 (SALDRU, University of Cape Town, Cape Town).

Coertze, R.D. 1969. *Atteridgeville: 'n Stedelike Bantoe Woonbuurt* (Pretoria University, Pretoria).

Coetzee, J.C. 1975. *Onderwys in Suid-Afrika, 1652 – 1970* (HAUM, Pretoria).

Community Arts Project (CAP), Stroller Project — a documented photographic exhibition put together by Jenny Altschuler, Costa Christie, and Pam Warne, entitled 'Another Street'.

Conquest, R. 1970. *Nation Killers: The Soviet Deportation of Nationalities* (Macmillan, London).

Cooper, C. *et al.* 1984. *Survey of Race Relations in South Africa 1983*, vol. 37 (South African Institute of Race Relations, Johannesburg).

Cooper, C. *et al.* 1985. *Survey of Race Relations in South Africa 1984*, vol. 38

(South African Institute of Race Relations, Johannesburg).

Craig, A.P. 1980. 'A preliminary investigation into some of the factors associated with pregnancies among urban Zulu school children', unpublished MA dissertation, University of Natal, Durban.

Craig, A.P. and Richter-Strydom, L.M. No date. 'Unplanned pregnancies amongst urban Zulu school children: a summary of the salient results from a preliminary investigation', occasional paper from Department of Psychology, University of Natal, Durban.

Craig, A.P. and Richter-Strydom, L.M. 1983. 'Unplanned pregnancies among urban Zulu schoolgirls', *South African Medical Journal*, 63, 452-55.

Creber, J.W.P. 1972. *Lost for Words: Language and Educational Failure* (Penguin, Harmondsworth).

Crystal, D. 1980. *A First Dictionary of Linguistics and Phonetics* (Andre Deutsch, London).

Current Population Survey: unpublished tabulations. These were compiled from the March 1980 returns and data tapes in the Central Statistical Service by C.E.W. Simkins in 1980 and 1981. Tabulations in the possession of Simkins.

Dallos, R. and Sapsford, R.J. 1981. 'The person and group reality' in *Crime and Society*, edited by M. Fitzgerald, G. McLennan, and J. Pawson (Routledge and Kegan Paul, London).

Danziger, K. 1957. 'The child's understanding of kinship terms: a study of the development of relational concepts', *Journal of Genetic Psychology*, 91, 213-32.

Davey, A. 1983. *Learning to Be Prejudiced: Growing Up in Multi-Ethnic Britain* (Edward Arnold, London).

Davey, D.A. 1983. 'Introduction' in *Annual Report of the Department of Obstetrics and Gynaecology, University of Cape Town, 1983* (Department of Obstetrics and Gynaecology, Medical School, University of Cape Town, Cape Town).

Davies, J. 1984. 'Capital, state, and educational reform in South Africa' in *Apartheid and Education*, edited by P. Kallaway (Ravan Press, Johannesburg), 341-70.

Davis, A. 1982. *Women, Race and Class* (The Women's Press, London).

Dean, E., Hartmann, P., and Katzen, M. 1983. *History in Black and White* (UNESCO, Paris).

Deeny, J.D., Walker, M.J., Kibel, M.A., Molteno, C.D., and Arens L.J. 1985. 'Tuberculous Meningitis in children in the Western Cape', *South African Medical Journal*, 85, 75-78.

De Groot, W.A. 1978. 'Kleurbewustheid en groepsidentifikasie onder groepe Kleurlingkinders', unpublished MA thesis, Rand Afrikaans University, Johannesburg.

De Haas, M.E.A. 1984. 'Changing patterns of black marriage and divorce in Durban', unpublished MA thesis, University of Natal, Durban.

De Jong, G. and Pattinson, R.C. 1984. 'A clinical analysis of stillbirths at Tygerberg Hospital' in *Proceedings of the Third Conference on Priorities in Perinatal Care of South Africa* (mimeo, Department of Paediatrics, Johannesburg Hospital, Johannesburg), 1-7.

De Klerk, W.A. 1975. *The Puritans in Africa: A History of Afrikanerdom* (Penguin, Harmondsworth).

Della Pergola, S. 1977. 'Emigration. Advance report no.2', *South African Jewish Population Study* (Institute of Contemporary Jewry, Hebrew University, Jerusalem).

Department of Statistics. 1970, 1980. *Population Census*, Various Reports (Government Printer, Pretoria).

Department of Statistics. 1982. *Marriages and Divorces: Whites, Coloureds and Asians, South Africa*, report 07-02-16 (Government Printer, Pretoria).

Department of Statistics. 1983. *Report on Births: Whites, Coloureds and Asians 1980*, report 07-01-08 (Government Printer, Pretoria).

Detainees Parents' Support Committee Report. November 1985. (DPSC, Johannesburg).

De Villiers, V.P. 1985. 'Tienderjarige swangerskappe in die Paarl-hospitaal', *South African Medical Journal*, 67, 301-02.

Dickens, C. 1839. *Nicholas Nickleby* (Chapman and Hall, London).

Dreyer, H.J. 1980. *Adolescence in a Changing Society* (Academia, Pretoria).

Dryden, J. 1886. 'The Hind and the Panther' in *The Poetical Works of John Dryden*, The Globe edition, edited by W.D. Christie (Macmillan, London).

Dubb, A.A. 1972. 'Changes in ethnic attitudes of Jewish youth in Johannesburg', *Jewish Social Studies*, 34, 1, 58-72.

Dubb, A.A. 1974. 'The impact of the city', in *The Bantu-Speaking Peoples of Southern Africa*, edited by W.D. Hammond-Tooke (Routledge and Kegan Paul, London).

Dubb, A.A. 1979. 'The impact of the city', in *South Africa: Sociological Analyses*, edited by A.P. Hare, M.H. Von Broembsen, and G. Wiendienck (Oxford University Press, Cape Town).

Dubb, A.A. 1985. 'The South African Jewish population at the beginning of the Eighties', *Jewish Affairs*, 40, 12, 65-76.

Dubb, A.A., Della Pergola, S., and Tal, D. 1978. 'Educational attainment and languages. Advance report no.6', *South African Jewish Population Study* (Institute of Contemporary Jewry, Hebrew University, Jerusalem).

Dugard, J. November 1982. 'A triumph for executive power – an examination of the Rabie Report and the Internal Security Act 74 of 1982', *South African Law Journal*, 99, Part 4, 589-604.

Duncan, S. 1983. 'Aspects of family breakdown', *Work in Progress*, 27, 37.

Du Preez, J.M. 1982. ''n Kommunikatiewe studie van geskrewe secondêre onderrigsmateriaal in Suid-Afrika', unpublished MA thesis, University of South Africa, Pretoria.

Du Preez, J.M. 1983. *Africana Afrikaner: Master Symbols in South African School Textbooks* (Librarius, Alberton).

Durkheim, E. 1912. *The Elementary Forms of the Religious Life* (Allen and Unwin, London).

Du Toit, B. 1955. 'Beperkte lidmaatskap', unpublished MA thesis, University of Stellenbosch, Stellenbosch.

Ebrahim, G.J. 1983. *Nutrition in Mother and Child Health* (Macmillan Press, Hong Kong).

Edelstein, M.L. 1974. *What Do the Coloureds Think?* (Labour and Community Consultants, Johannesburg).

Editorial. 1985. 'Adolescent pregnancy', *South African Medical Journal*, 67, 27.

Eekelaar, J. and Clive, E. 1977. *Custody after Divorce* (Centre for Socio-Legal Studies, Oxford).

Elkind, D. 1962. 'Children's conceptions of brother and sister: Piaget Replication Study V', *Journal of Genetic Psychology*, 100, 129-36.

Elliot, G.A. and Tyson, G.A. 1983. 'The effects of modifying colour-meaning concepts on the racial attitudes of black and white South African preschool children', *Journal of Social Psychology*, 121, 181-90.

Epidemiological Comments. 1985. 'Tuberculosis', 12, 5, 5.

Epidemiological Comments. 1985. 'Immunization', 11, 12, 16.

Epstein, L. and Tamir, A. 1984. 'Health-related behaviour of adolescents: change over time', *Journal of Health Care*, 5, 91-95.

Erasmus, H.J., Van der Merwe, C.G., and Van Wyk, A.H. 1983. *Lee and Honorè's Family, Things and Succession*, second edition (Butterworths, Durban).

Evans, D., Bowie, M.D., Hansen, J.D.L., Moodie, A.D. and Van der Spuy, H.W. 1980. 'Intellectual development and nutrition', *Journal of Pediatrics*, 97, 358-63.

Fanon, F. 1968. *Black Skin White Masks* (Grove Press, New York).

Favis, M. 1983. 'Black women in the South African economy', unpublished research paper, Durban.

Fincham, R.J. and Thomas, G.C. 1984. 'Nutritional intervention: a Ciskei and Eastern Cape perspective', *Second Carnegie Inquiry into Poverty and Development in Southern Africa*, conference paper no. 213 (SALDRU, University of Cape Town, Cape Town).

Fisher, S. 1984. 'Measles and poverty in Port Elizabeth', *Second Carnegie Inquiry into Poverty and Development in Southern Africa*, conference paper no. 172 (SALDRU, University of Cape Town, Cape Town).

Fortes, M. 1958. 'Introduction' to *The Developmental Cycle in Domestic Groups*, edited by J. Goody (Cambridge University Press, London).

Fortes, M. 1969. *Kinship and the Social Order: The Legacy of Lewis Henry Morgan* (Aldine Publishers, London).

Foucault, M. 1980. *Power/Knowledge: Selected Interviews and Other Writings 1972 – 1977*, edited by C. Gordon (The Harvester Press, Brighton).

Fox, D.J. and Jordan V. 1973. 'Racial preference and identification of black, American, Chinese, and white children', *Genetic Psychology Monographs*, 88, 227-86.

Frankental, S. 1984. 'Some reflections on the status of Jewish studies in South Africa', *Jewish Affairs*, 39, 3, 25-29.

Freeman, M.D.A. 1983. *The Rights and Wrongs of Children* (Frances Pinter, London).

Freud, A. 1982. *Psychoanalytic Psychology of Normal Development 1970 – 1980* (The Hogarth Press, London).

Friedlander, A. and Power, D.J. 1982. 'A study of handicapped children in a typical urban community in Cape Town', *South African Medical Journal*, 60, 873-76.

Gardiner, M. 1984. 'Redefining education: the White Paper on the provision of education', *Africa Perspective*, 24, 3-19.

Geber, B.A. and Newman, S.P. 1980. *Soweto's Children: The Development of Attitudes* (Academic Press, London).

Geertz, C. 1973. *The Interpretation of Cultures* (Basic Books, New York).

Geertz, C. 1983. *Local Knowledge* (Basic Books, New York).

Genovese, E.D. 1976. *Roll, Jordan, Roll: The World the Slaves Made* (Vintage, New York).

Gerwel, G.J. 1983. *Literatuur en Apartheid: Konsepsies van 'gekleurdes' in die Afrikaanse Roman tot 1948* (Kampen, Kasselsvlei).

Giddens, A. 1979. *Central Problems in Social Theory: Action, Structure and Contradiction in Social Analysis* (Macmillan, London).

Giddens, A. 1981. *A Contemporary Critique of Historical Materialism — Power, Property and the State* (Macmillan, London).

Gilbert, J.P. 1971. 'Computer methods and kinship studies' in *Explorations in Mathematical Anthropology*, edited by P. Kay (MIT Press, Massachusetts).

Glover, C., Schärf, W. *et al.* 1981. 'Scrap-collecting', video documentary, Community Video Resource Association, Cape Town.

Gluckman, M. 1965. *Politics, Law and Ritual in Tribal Society* (Basil Blackwell, Oxford).

Goldberg, A. 1985. 'Reflections on a congress', *Jewish Affairs*, 40, 6, 12-17.

Gonzalez, N. Solien de. 1969. *Black Carib Household Structure* (University of Washington Press, Seattle and London).

Goodman, M. 1964. *Race Awareness in Young Children*, second edition (Collier, New York).

Graal, M.B. and Schmeets, I.O.L. 1983. *Measuring Health in the Gelukspan District, Bophuthatswana, March-June 1983* (Department of Epidemiology, Erasmus University, Rotterdam).

Grace, H.J., Gray, R. and Conradie, J.D. 1981. 'Prenatal detection of neural tube defects by maternal serum and fetoprotein assay', *South African Medical Journal*, 60, 319-24.

Grant, J.P. 1984. *State of the World's Children 1984* (published for UNICEF, Oxford University Press, London).

Grant, J.P. 1985. *State of the World's Children 1985* (published for UNICEF, Oxford University Press, London).

Greenberg, S.B. 1981. 'Economic growth and political change', paper submitted to the Study Commission on United States Policy Toward Southern Africa.

Gregor, A.J. and McPherson, D.A. 1966. 'Racial preference and ego-identity among white and Bantu children in the Republic of South Africa', *Genetic Psychology Monographs*, 73, 217-53.

Grobbelaar, J.A. 1984. *Projections and Analysis of the South African Population for the Period 1980 – 2015* (Institute for Futures Research, University of Stellenbosch, Stellenbosch).

Gross, B. and Gross, R. (eds.). 1977. *The Children's Rights Movement* (Andover Press, New York).

Hahlo, H.R. 1975, 1985. *The South African Law of Husband and Wife*, fourth and fifth editions (Juta, Cape Town).

Hall, S. and Jefferson, T. (eds.). 1976. *Resistance through Rituals* (Hutchinson, London).

Hamill, P.V.V., Drizd, T.A., Johnson, C.L., Reed, R.B., Roche, A.F., and Moore, W.A. 1979. 'Physical growth: National Center for Health Statistics percentiles', *American Journal of Clinical Nutrition*, 32, 607-29.

Hammel, E. and Laslett, P. 1974. 'Comparing household structure over time and between cultures', *Comparative Studies in Society and History*, 16, 1, 73-109.

Hammond-Tooke, W.D. 1969. 'The present state of Cape Nguni ethnographic studies' in *Ethnological and Linguistic Studies in Honour of N.J. van Warmelo*, Ethnological Publications, 52 (Department of Bantu Administration and Development, Pretoria).

Hanekom, C. 1975. *Krisis en Kultus* (Academia, Cape Town).

Hansard, South African Parliament, House of Assembly.

Hansen, J. 1984. 'Food and nutrition policy with relation to poverty: the child malnutrition problem in South Africa', *Second Carnegie Inquiry into Poverty and Development in Southern Africa*, conference paper no. 205 (SALDRU, University of Cape Town, Cape Town).

Hardman, C. 1973. 'Can there be an anthropology of children?', *Journal of the Anthropological Society of Oxford*, 4, 11, 85-99.

Haviland, S., and Clark, E. 1974. 'This man's father is my father's son: a study of the acquisition of English kin terms', *Journal of Child Language*, 1, 23-47.

Hay, I.T., Ellis, J.B. and Shipham, S.O. 1984. 'Weight/cause specific mortality at GaRankuwa' in *Proceedings of the Third Conference on Priorities in Perinatal Care in South Africa* (mimeo, Department of Paediatrics, Johannesburg Hospital, Johannesburg), 21-26.

Haysom, N. 1981. *Towards an Understanding of Prison Gangs* (Institute of Criminology, University of Cape Town, Cape Town).

Heaven, P.C.L. 1978. 'The social attitudes of a group of South African children', *South African Journal of Psychology*, 8, 30-34.

Hellig, J. 1984. 'Religious expression' in *South African Jewry: A Contemporary Survey*, edited by M. Arkin (Oxford University Press, Cape Town).

Henning, P.A. and Beyers, N. 1984. 'Tygerberg Hospital: neo-natal statistics 1983' in *Proceedings of the Third Conference on Priorities in Perinatal Care in South Africa* (mimeo, Department of Paediatrics, Johannesburg Hospital, Johannesburg), 8-13.

Herman, A. and Wyndham, C.H. 1985. 'Changes in infant mortality rates of whites, coloureds and urban blacks in RSA over the period 1970-1983', unpublished paper, South African Medical Research Council, Johannesburg.

Herrman, L. 1935. *A History of the Jews in South Africa* (Gollancz, London).

Hill, A. 1983. 'Materialist feminism and South Africa: the position of black working women in contemporary Cape Town', unpublished BA Hons. thesis, University of Cape Town, Cape Town.

Hoffman, M.A., Durcan N.M., and Disler P.B. 1984. 'Breastfeeding in a socio-economically disadvantaged area of Cape Town', *South African Medical Journal*, 66, 64-67.

Horowitz, R.E. 1939. 'Racial aspects of self-identification in nursery school children', *Journal of Social Psychology*, 7, 91-99.

Hraba, J. and Grant, G., 1970. 'Black is beautiful: a re-examination of racial preference and identification', *Journal of Personality and Social Psychology*, 16, 398-402.

Human Sciences Research Council. 1981. *Education Provision in the RSA* (HSRC, Pretoria) (De Lange Report).

Human Sciences Research Council, Main Committee. 1985. *The South African Society: Realities and Future Prospects.* An investigation into intergroup relations (HSRC, Pretoria).

Hund, J. and Kotu-Rammopo, M. July 1983. 'Justice in a South African township: the sociology of *makgotla*', *Comparative and International Law Journal of Southern Africa*, 16, 179-208.

References 409

Hunter, M. 1936. *Reactions to Conquest. Effects of Contacts with Europeans on the Pondo of South Africa* (Oxford University Press, London).
Hurlock, E.B. 1972. *Child Development*, sixth edition (McGraw-Hill, Kogakusha Ltd, Tokyo: International Student Edition).

Independent Television Network (ITN), 18 April 1985. Channel Four Evening News, Britain.
Irwig, L.M. and Ingle, R.F. 1984. 'Childhood mortality rates, infant feeding and use of health services in rural Transkei', *South African Medical Journal* 66, 608-13.

Jackson, B. and Jackson, S. 1979. *Childminders* (Penguin, Harmondsworth).
Jacobs, M. 1984. 'Childhood head injuries and poverty', *Second Carnegie Inquiry into Poverty and Development in Southern Africa*, conference paper no. 179 (SALDRU, University of Cape Town, Cape Town).
Jenks, C. (ed). 1982. *The Sociology of Childhood. Essential Readings* (Batsford, London).
Jithoo S. 1978. 'Complex households and joint families amongst Indians in Durban' in *Social System and Tradition in Southern Africa* edited by J. Argyle and E. Preston-Whyte (Oxford University Press, Cape Town).

Kallaway, P. (ed). 1984a. *Apartheid and Education: The Education of Black South Africans* (Ravan Press, Johannesburg).
Kallaway, P. 1984b. 'An introduction to the study of education for blacks in South Africa', in *Apartheid and Education* edited by P. Kallaway.
Katz, M. 1980. 'The history of Jewish education in South Africa 1841 – 1980', unpublished PhD thesis, University of Cape Town, Cape Town.
Katz, P.A. 1976. 'The acquisition of racial attitudes in children' in *Towards the Elimination of Racism* edited by P.A. Katz (Pergamon, New York).
Katz, P.A. and Zalk, P.R. 1974. 'Doll preferences: an index of racial attitudes?', *Journal of Educational Psychology*, 66, 663-68.
Kemp, M. 1984. 'Poverty and contraception — family planning in the Western Cape', *Second Carnegie Inquiry into Poverty and Development in Southern Africa*, conference paper no. 178 (SALDRU, University of Cape Town, Cape Town).
Khanyile, J. 17 August 1974. 'Illegitimacy: its social origin and present difficulties in an African society', paper presented at the Joint Council for African Life, Durban.
Kibel, M.A. and Epstein, L. Forthcoming 1986. 'Adolescent health', editorial, *South African Medical Journal*.
Kimble, J. and Unterhalter, E. 1982. 'ANC women's struggle 1912 – 1982', *Feminist Review*, 19, 11-35.
Kingsley, C. 1863. *The Water Babies* (Macmillan, London and Cambridge).

Klevansky, I.H. 1982. *The Kugel Book* (Jonathan Ball, Johannesburg).

Knobel, G.J., De Villiers, J.C., Parry, C.D.H., and Botha. J.L. 1984. 'The causes of non-natural deaths in children over a 15-year period in greater Cape Town', *South African Medical Journal*, 66, 795-805.

Kolman, S.A. 1979. 'Family variables related to ethnocentrism in children: a literature review', *Ethnic Groups*, 2, 93-107.

Kotze, H.J. 1985. 'Mass media and the matriculant mind: a case study of political socialization in South Africa', *Communicare*, 4, 2, 26-37.

Kotze, H.J. and Norval, A.J. 1983. ''n Kruis-kulturele studie in politieke sosialisering', *South African Journal of Sociology*, 14, 1, 17-25.

Krige, E.J. 1936a. *The Social System of the Zulus* (Longman, London).

Krige, E.J. 1936b. 'Changing conditions in marital relations and parental duties among urbanized natives', *Africa*, 2, 1-23.

Kuper, H. 1960. *Indian People in Natal* (University of Natal Press, Pietermaritzburg).

La Hausse, P. 1982. 'Drinking in a cage: the Durban system and the 1929 beer hall riots', *Africa Perspective*, 20, 63-75.

Lambert, W.E. and Klineberg, O. 1968. *Children's Views of Foreign People: A Cross-National Study* (Appleton-Century-Crofts, New York).

Landes, D.S. 1972. *The Unbound Prometheus — Technological Change and Industrial Development in Western Europe from 1750 to the Present* (Cambridge University Press, Cambridge).

Larsen, J.V. and Van Middelkoop, A. 1982. 'The "unbooked" mother at King Edward VIII hospital, Durban', *South African Medical Journal*, 62, 483-86.

Laslett, P. 1965. *The World We Have Lost* (Methuen, London).

Laslett, P. 1972. *Household and Family in Past Time* (Cambridge University Press, Cambridge).

Lasovsky, S. 1982. 'The relationship between self-esteem and black-consciousness in the "coloured" population of the Western Cape', unpublished BA Hons. thesis, University of Cape Town, Cape Town.

Leahy, R.L. 1983. *The Child's Construction of Social Inequality* (Academic, London).

Lerner, R.M. and Buehrig, C.J. 1975. 'The development of racial attitudes in young black and white children', *Journal of Genetic Psychology*, 127, 45-54.

Le Roux, P. 1963. 'Should domestic servants be abolished?', *Jaarblad*, Klerksdorp Hoërskool, 32.

Lever, H. 1978. *The South African Society* (Jonathan Ball, Johannesburg).

LeVine, R. and Price-Williams, D. 1974. 'Children's kinship concepts: cognitive development and early experience among the Hausa', *Ethnology*, 13, 1, 25-44.

Lipschitz, M. 1985. 'Housing and Health', *Critical Health*, 12, 25-30.

Loening, W.E.K. 1981. 'Child abuse among the Zulus: a people in cultural transition', *Child Abuse and Neglect*, 5, 3-7.

Louden, D. 1981. 'A comparative study of self-concept among minority and majority group adolescents in English multi-national schools', *Ethnic and Racial Studies* 4, 153-74.

Lyons, J. 1981. *Language and Linguistics* (Cambridge University Press, Cambridge).

MacCrone, I.D. 1937. *Race Attitudes in South Africa* (Oxford University Press, London).

Mahler, H. 1985.'Healthy youth: our best resource', *World Health*, 1, 83.

Malcolm, D. 1983. 'Pre-school child care facilities in Alexandra township: an investigation into the reproduction of labour', unpublished BA Hons. thesis, University of the Witwatersrand, Johannesburg.

Malherbe, V.C. 1985. 'Should special attention be given to "black history"?', tape and transcript, privately held.

Mann, J.W. 1971. 'Attitudes towards ethnic groups' in *South Africa: Sociological Perspectives* edited by H. Adam (Oxford University Press, London).

Marsden, D. and Jackson, B. 1962. *Education and the Working Class* (Routledge and Kegan Paul, London).

Marshalkowitz, J. 1985. 'Patterns of adolescent mortality in Israel 1974 – 80', unpublished MB.Bch. thesis, Hebrew University Medical School, Jerusalem.

Marwick, M. 1978. 'Household composition and marriage in a Witwatersrand African township' in *Social System and Tradition in Southern Africa* edited by J. Argyle and E. Preston-Whyte (Oxford University Press, Cape Town).

Mathews, A.S. 1971. *Law, Order and Liberty in South Africa* (Juta, Cape Town).

McCarthy, J.D. and Yancey, W.L. 1971. 'Uncle Tom and Mr Charlie: metaphysical pathos in the study of racism and personal disorganization', *American Journal of Sociology*, 76, 648-72.

McIntyre, D. 1984. 'An economic appraisal of the provision of education and technical training in South Africa', unpublished BA Hons. thesis, University of Cape Town, Cape Town.

McLachlan, F. 1983. *The New Child Care Act — in the Best Interest of Family, Parent or Child?*, research report (Institute of Criminology, University of Cape Town, Cape Town).

McLachlan, F. 1984. *Children in Prison in South Africa* (Institute of Criminology, University of Cape Town, Cape Town).

Mead, M. 1978. *Culture and Commitment: The Relationship between the Generations in the 1970s* (Anchor Books, New York).

Medical Officer of Health. 1985. *Annual Report 1984* (City of Cape Town, Cape Town).

Meer, F. 1969. *Portrait of Indian South Africans* (Avon House, Durban).

Meij, L.R. 1966. 'The Clark Dolls Test as a measure of children's racial attitudes: a South African study', *Journal for Social Research*, 15, 25-40.

Melamed, L. 1968. 'Race awareness in South African children', *Journal of Social Psychology*, 76, 3-8.

Melamed, L. 1970. 'Ethnic attitudes of South African children', *South African Journal of Psychology*, 1, 13-17.

Milner, D. 1973. 'Racial identification and preference in black British children', *European Journal of Social Psychology*, 3, 281-95.

Milner, D. 1983. *Children and Race: Ten Years On* (Ward Lock International, London).

Milner D. 1984. 'The development of ethnic attitudes' in *The Social Dimension,* edited by H. Tajfel (Cambridge University Press, Cambridge), vol. 1.

Milroy, L. 1980. *Language and Social Networks* (Basil Blackwell, Oxford).

Mink, R. 1984. 'Education' in *South African Jewry: A Contemporary Survey,* edited by M. Arkin (Oxford University Press, Cape Town).

Mnookin, R.H. 1985. *In the Interests of Children. Advocacy, Law Reform, and Public Policy* (W.H. Freeman, New York).

Moeno, N. 1977. 'Illegitimacy in an African urban township', *African Studies*, 36, 1, 43-47.

Moerat, F. 1983. 'A study of newsvendors in the Cape Peninsula', unpublished research project, SHAWCO, Elsies River.

Moller, V. and Schlemmer, L. 1977. *The Situation of African Migrant Workers in Durban: Brief Report of a Preliminary Survey Analysis* (Research Report Series, Centre for Applied Social Sciences, University of Natal, Durban).

Molteno, C.D. March 1985. 'The relationship between growth and social milieu: a longitudinal study involving coloured children in Cape Town', paper presented at the Fifth Biannual National Congress of the South African Association of Child Psychology, Psychiatry and Allied Disciplines, Cape Town.

Molteno, C.D., Hollingshead, J. and De Waal, R. 1982. 'Management of handicapped children in the Cape Peninsula', unpublished report, Child Health Unit, University of Cape Town, Cape Town.

Molteno, C.D., Hollingshead, J., Moodie, A.D., Willoughby, W., Bowie, M.D., Bradshaw, D., and Pretorius, J.P.G. 1980. 'A study on child development in Cape Town', *South African Medical Journal*, 58, 729-32.

Molteno, C.D., Kibel, M.A., and Van Zyl, J.S. August 1985. 'Early childhood mortality in the Matroosberg Divisional Council Area', paper presented at the Research Day, Department of Pediatrics, University of Cape Town.

Moodie, M.A. 1980. 'The development of national identity in White South

African schoolchildren', *Journal of Social Psychology*, 3, 169-80.

Moody, D. 1975. *The Rise of Afrikanerdom: Power, Apartheid and the Afrikaner Civil Religion* (University of California Press, Berkeley).

Moosa, A. 1984. 'The health of children in South Africa: some food for thought', *The Lancet*, 1, 8380, 779-82.

Morifi, M. 1984. 'Life among the poor in Philipstown', *Second Carnegie Inquiry into Poverty and Development in Southern Africa*, conference paper No. 33 (SALDRU, University of Cape Town, Cape Town).

Morland, J.K. 1966. 'A comparison of race awareness in Northern and Southern children', *American Journal of Orthopsychiatry*, 36, 22-31.

Morley, D. 1973. *Paediatric Priorities in the Developing World* (Butterworths, London).

Morris, A. 1985. 'The "class-blind" approach to South African schooling: a reappraisal', unpublished seminar paper, Centre for African Studies, University of Cape Town, Cape Town.

Morris, P. February 1985. 'Black housing — weapon of apartheid — what will change?', *Sash*, 27, 4, 7-13.

Mostert, W.P. and Du Plessis, J.C. 1972. *Die Gesinsbouproses by Bantoes in die Munisipale Gebied Pretoria* (Instituut vir Sosiologiese Navorsing, Pretoria).

Mphahlele, E. 1959, 1965. *Down Second Avenue* (Faber & Faber, London).

Mullins, A. 1982. 'Working women and the dual shift: the case of a sample of women in the laundry, drycleaning, and dyeing industry', unpublished BA Hons. thesis, University of the Witwatersrand, Johannesburg.

Mullins, A. 1983. 'Working women speak', *Work in Progress*, 27, 38-40.

Murray, C. 1976. 'Keeping house in Lesotho. A study of the impact of oscillating migrants', unpublished PhD thesis, University of Cambridge, Cambridge.

Nasson, B. 1983a. 'The defence of inequality: schooling and the state, with particular reference to South Africa', *Journal of Education with Production*, 2, 1, 49-71.

Nasson, B. 1983b. *Education and Poverty: Some Perspectives*, SALDRU Policy Paper No. 2 (SALDRU, University of Cape Town, Cape Town).

Nasson, B. 1984a. 'Bitter harvest: farm schooling for black South Africans', *Second Carnegie Inquiry into Poverty and Development in Southern Africa*, conference paper no. 97 (SALDRU, University of Cape Town, Cape Town).

Nasson, B. 1984b. 'More chaff than wheat: South African farm schooling', unpublished paper delivered at the Yale-Wesleyan Universities Southern African Research Program Workshop, Brown University.

Nasson, B. 1984c. 'White farm schools — the educational Cinderella', *Matlhasedi Education Bulletin*, 3, 2-3, 40-41.

Nasson, B. 1984d. 'Ambiguous hope: education and poverty', *Social Dynamics*, 10, 2, 1-19.

New Haven Register, New Haven (daily evening newspaper).

Ngubane, H. 1977. *Body and Mind in Zulu Medicine* (Academic Press, London).

NICRO. 1974. *Vagrancy, a Limited Study of Vagrants in the Metropolitan Area of Cape Town*, research report, National Institute for Crime Prevention and Rehabilitation of Offenders, Cape Town.

Oakley, A. 1979. *Becoming a Mother* (Martin Robinson, Oxford).

Oakley, A. 1980. *Women Confined* (Martin Robinson, Oxford).

O'Meara, D. 1983. *Volkskapitalisme: Class, Capital and Ideology in the Development of Afrikaner Nationalism, 1934 – 1948* (Cambridge University Press, Cambridge; Ravan Press, Johannesburg).

Omond, R. 1985. *The Apartheid Handbook* (Penguin, Harmondsworth).

Parenzee, D. 1985. *Driven to Work* (Ravan Press, Johannesburg).

Patterson, S. 1957. *The Last Trek: A Study of the Boer People and the Afrikaner Nation* (Routledge and Kegan Paul, London).

Pauw, B.A. 1963, 1973. *The Second Generation: A Study of the Family Among Urbanised Bantu in East London* (Oxford University Press, Cape Town).

Pelzer, A.N. 1979. *Die Afrikaner-Broederbond: Eerste 50 Jaar* (Tafelberg, Kaapstad).

Pettigrew, T.F. 1978. 'Placing Adam's argument in a broader perspective: comment on the Adam paper', *Social Psychology*, 41, 58-61.

Piaget, J. 1928. *Judgement and Reasoning in the Child* (Kegan Paul, London).

Piaget, J. 1976. *The Child and Reality. Problems in Genetic Psychology*, translated by A. Roslin (Penguin, Harmondsworth).

Pillay, P.N. 1984. 'The development and underdevelopment of education in South Africa', *Second Carnegie Inquiry into Poverty and Development in Southern Africa*, conference paper no. 95 (SALDRU, University of Cape Town, Cape Town).

Pinnock, D. 1980. 'Elsies River', research project, Institute of Criminology, University of Cape Town, Cape Town.

Pinnock, D. 1982. 'Towards an understanding of the structure, function and history of gang formation in greater Cape Town', unpublished MA thesis, University of Cape Town, Cape Town.

Pinnock, D. 1984. *The Brotherhoods* (David Philip, Cape Town).

Pitchford, R.J. 1981. 'Bilharzia in South Africa', paper presented at Bilharzia Symposium, Pretoria, 11-13 May.

Platzky, L. and Walker, C. 1985. *The Surplus People. Forced Removals in South Africa* (Ravan Press, Johannesburg).

Porter, J.D.R. 1971. *Black Child, White Child* (Harvard University Press, Cambridge, Mass.).

Power, D.J. 1977. 'A study of the prevalence of severe mental retardation among coloured children in an urban community', *South African Medical Journal* 52, 30-34.

Press, L., Burt, I., and Barling, J. 1979. 'Racial preferences among South African white and black preschool children', *Journal of Social Psychology*, 107, 125-26.

Preston-Whyte, E.M. 1978. 'Families without marriage', in *Social System and Tradition in Southern Africa*, edited by W.S. Argyle and E.M. Preston-Whyte (Oxford University Press, Cape Town).

Preston-Whyte, E.M. 1981. 'Women migrants and marriage', in *Essays on African Systems of Marriage in Southern Africa*, edited by E.J. Krige and J. Comaroff (Juta, Cape Town).

Rakoff, V. 1949. 'An investigation into some aspects of the race attitudes of Cape coloured school children in the secular schools of the Cape Peninsula', unpublished MA thesis, University of Cape Town, Cape Town.

Randall, P. (ed.). 1983. *Survey of Race Relations in South Africa 1982*, vol. 36 (South African Institute of Race Relations, Johannesburg).

Rand Daily Mail, Johannesburg (daily morning newspaper).

Raum, O.F. 1973. *The Social Function of Avoidances and Taboos Among the Zulu* (De Gruyter, Berlin).

Reader, D.H. 1966. *Zulu Tribe in Transition* (Manchester University Press, Manchester).

Reilly, P. and Hofmeyr, F. 1983. *Pre-primary Education in the Republic of South Africa* (HSRC, Pretoria).

Resnick, M., Blum, R.W., and Hedin, D. 1980. 'The appropriateness of health services for adolescents. Youths' opinions and attitudes', *Journal of Adolescent Health Care*, 1, 137-41.

Reynolds, N. 1984. 'Citizens, the state and employment: public works as the core of a rural development strategy', *Second Carnegie Inquiry into Poverty and Development in Southern Africa*, conference paper no. 234 (SALDRU, University of Cape Town, Cape Town).

Richman, N., Stevenson, J., and Graham, P. 1982. *Preschool to school: a Behavioural Study* (Academic Press, London).

Ridd, R.E. 1981. 'Position and identity in a divided community: colour and religion in District Six, Walmer Estate, Woodstock area of Cape Town', unpublished DPhil thesis, Oxford University, Oxford.

Rip, C.M. 1966. *Contemporary Social Pathology* (Academia, Pretoria).

Rip, C.M. and Schmidt, J.J. 1977. *Black Pre-marital Illegitimacy in Pretoria*, Human Sciences Research Council Research Finding no. S-N-100 (HSRC, Pretoria).

Rip, M.R., and Tibbit, L. 1984. 'The effect of birth weight on infant mortality in a Western Cape metropolitan area', *Second Carnegie Inquiry into*

Poverty and Development in Southern Africa, conference paper no. 176 (SALDRU, University of Cape Town, Cape Town).

Robertson, B.A. and Hayward, M.A. 1976. 'Transcultural factors in child abuse', *South African Medical Journal*, 50, 1765-67.

Robertson, I.W. 1980. 'Health services for children' in *Notes on the Promotion of Child Health in Southern Africa* edited by M.A. Kibel (Institute of Child Health, University of Cape Town, Cape Town).

Ross, J.A. 1979. 'Language and the mobilization of ethnic identity' in *Language and Ethnic Relations* edited by H. Giles and B. Saint-Jacques (Pergamon Press, Oxford).

Ross, S.M. 1984. *Health for All by the Year 2000: Possibility or Pipe-dream?* (University of Natal Press, Pietermaritzburg).

Ryan, E.B. 1979. 'Why do low-prestige varieties persist?' in *Language and Social Psychology* edited by H. Giles and R. St Clair (Basil Blackwell, Oxford).

Saron, G., and Hotz, L. (eds.). 1955. *The Jews in South Africa: A History* (Oxford University Press, Cape Town).

Schärf, W. 1984. 'The impact of liquor on the working class (with a particular focus on the Western Cape). The implication of the structure of the liquor industry and the role of the state in this regard', unpublished MSocSc thesis, University of Cape Town, Cape Town.

Scheffer, P. 1983. *Afrikaans en Engels onder die Kleurlinge in die Kaapprovinsie, en in Besonder in die Skiereiland* (HSRC, Pretoria).

Schlemmer, L. and Stopforth, P. 1974. *Poverty, Family Patterns and Material Aspirations among Africans in a Border Industry Township* (Institute for Social Research, University of Natal, Durban).

Seagrim, G. and Lendon, R. 1980. *Furnishing the Mind. A Comparative Study of Cognitive Development in Central Australian Aborigines* (Harcourt Brace Janovitch, New York).

Sennett, R. and Cobb, J. 1972. *The Hidden Injuries of Class* (Vintage, New York).

Shah, A.M. 1964. 'Basic terms and concepts in the study of the family in India', *Indian Economic and Social History Review*, 1, 3, 1-36.

Shah, A.M. 1974. *The Household Dimension of the Family in India* (University of California Press, Berkeley).

Shain, M. 1983. *Jewry and Cape Society: The Origins and Activities of the Jewish Board of Deputies for the Cape Colony* (Historical Publications Society, Cape Town).

Sheridan, M.D. 1968. 'The development progress of infants and young children', *Ministry of Health Report*, 20, 102 (HMSO, London).

Shimoni, G. 1980. *Jews and Zionism: The South African Jewish Experience 1910 – 1967* (Oxford University Press, Cape Town).

Short, A. 1984. 'The role of preschool education in relation to the problems of the poor', *Second Carnegie Inquiry into Poverty and Development in Southern Africa*, conference paper no. 103 (SALDRU, University of Cape Town, Cape Town).

Sibiya, J. 1981. 'Contemporary trends in marriage and its preliminaries among the Abakwamkwanazi', unpublished MA thesis, University of Zululand.

Simkins, C.E.W. 1983. *Four Essays on the Past, Present and Possible Future of the Distribution of the Black Population of South Africa* (SALDRU, University of Cape Town, Cape Town).

Simkins, C.E.W. 1984a. 'Can the state achieve educational equality?', *Die Suid-Afrikaan*, Lente, 16-17.

Simkins, C.E.W. 1984b. 'A demographic base for the simulation of income distribution and poverty among black South Africans since 1960', unpublished PhD thesis, University of Natal, Pietermaritzburg.

Simmons, R.G. 1978. 'Blacks and high self-esteem: a puzzle', *Social Psychology*, 41, 54-57.

Sinclair, J. 1982. 'Divorce in South Africa — principles and practice', paper presented at the Fourth World Conference of the International Society of Family Law, Harvard.

Smart, R.D. 1981. 'Down Syndrome in the Cape Peninsula and the value of amniocentesis as a preventive measure', *South African Medical Journal*, 59, 670-72.

Smith, R.T. 1956. *The Negro Family in British Guiana* (Routledge and Kegan Paul, London).

South African Catholic Bishops' Conference. 1984. *Report on Police Conduct during Township Protests: August-November 1984* (SACBC, Pretoria).

South African Conference on Dagga. September 1983. Unpublished report, University of Natal, Durban.

South African Jewish Board of Deputies. 1950. *South African Jews in World War II* (SAJBD, Johannesburg).

Sowetan, Johannesburg (daily morning newspaper).

Spencer, M.B. 1984. 'Black children's race awareness, racial attitudes and self-concept: a reinterpretation', *Journal of Child Psychology and Psychiatry*, 25, 433-41.

Spiegel, A. 1980. 'Changing patterns of migrant labour and rural differentiation in Lesotho', *Social Dynamics*, 6, 2, 1-13.

Spiro, E. 1971. *Law of Parent and Child*, third edition, with 1979 supplement (Juta, Cape Town).

Stack, C.D. 1970. 'The kindred of Viola Jackson: residence and family organization in an urban black American family' in *Afro-American Anthropology: Contemporary Perspectives*, edited by N.E. Whittenan and J.F. Szwed (The Free Press, New York).

Stack, C.D. 1974. *All Our Kin: Strategies for Survival in a Black Community*

(Harper and Row, New York).

Star, Johannesburg (daily evening newspaper).

Stein, H. 1982. *The Sick Black Child* (Witwatersrand University Press, Johannesburg).

Stellman, J. 1977. *Women's Work, Women's Health. Myths and Realities* (Pantheon Books, New York).

Steyn, A. 1982. 'Gesinsosiologie in Suid-Afrika', *Humanitas*, 8, 2, 89-104.

Steyn, A. and Rip, C.M. 1968. 'The changing urban Bantu family', *Journal of Marriage and the Family*, 30, 499-517.

Stoch, M.B. and Smythe, P.M. 1976. '15-year developmental study on effects of severe undernutrition during infancy on subsequent physical growth and intellectual functioning', *Archives of Diseases of Childhood*, 51, 327-36.

Stokes, R.G. 1975. 'Afrikaner Calvinism and economic action: the Weberian thesis in South Africa', *American Journal of Sociology*, 81, 1, 62-81.

Sunday Star, Johannesburg (Sunday newspaper).

Sunday Times, Johannesburg (Sunday newspaper).

Sunkler, B. 1976. *Zulu Zion and some Swazi Zionists* (Gleerups, with Oxford University Press, Oxford).

Super, C.M. 1976. 'Environmental effects on motor development: the case of "African infant precocity"', *Development Medicine and Child Neurology*, 18, 561-67.

Surplus People Project. 1983. *Forced Removals in South Africa: Surplus People Project Reports, The Eastern Cape*, second edition, vol. 2 (SPP, Cape Town).

Tamir, A., Wolff, H., and Epstein, L. 1982. 'Health-related behaviour in Israeli adolescents', *Journal of Adolescent Health Care*, 2, 261-65.

Tapper, T. and Salter, B. 1978. *Education and the Political Order: Changing Patterns of Class Control* (Macmillan, London).

Theron Commission. 1976. *Report of the Commission of Inquiry into Matters Relating to the Coloured Population Group*, R.P.38-1976 (Government Printer, Pretoria).

Thomas, T. 1982. *Their Doctor Speaks*, re-issue (Dr Mary Roberts, Cape Town).

Thompson, E.P. 1980. *Writing by Candlelight* (Merlin, London).

Thompson, L.M. 1952. 'Indian Immigration into Natal', *Archives Year Book of South African History*, vol. 2.

Tötemeyer, A. 1984. 'The racial element in Afrikaans children's literature', unpublished D Phil thesis, University of Stellenbosch, Stellenbosch.

Trudgill, P. 1975. *Accent, Dialect and the School* (Arnold, London).

Turner, V.W. 1957. *Schism and Continuity in an African Society* (Manchester University Press, Manchester).

UNISA, Bureau of Market Research. 1981a. *Income and Expenditure Patterns of Black Households in Venda, 1980*, Research Report 80 (BMR, Pretoria).

UNISA, Bureau of Market Research. 1981b. *Income and Expenditure Patterns of Black Households in Transkei, 1980*, Research Report 90 (BMR, Pretoria).

UNISA, Bureau of Market Research. 1981c. *Income and Expenditure Patterns of Urban Black Households in Pretoria, 1980*, Research Report 94.1 (BMR, Pretoria).

UNISA, Bureau of Market Research. 1981d. *Income and Expenditure Patterns of Urban Coloured Multiple Households in the Cape Peninsula, 1980*, Research Report 94.2 (BMR, Pretoria).

UNISA, Bureau of Market Research. 1981e. *Income and Expenditure Patterns of Urban Black Multiple Households on the East and West Rand, 1980*, Research Report 94.3 (BMR, Pretoria).

UNISA, Bureau of Market Research. 1981f. *Income and Expenditure Patterns of Urban Indian Multiple Households in Durban, 1980*, Research Report 94.5 (BMR, Pretoria).

UNISA, Bureau of Market Research. 1981g. *Income and Expenditure Patterns of Urban Black Multiple Households in Durban, 1980*, Research Report 94.6 (BMR, Pretoria).

UNISA, Bureau of Market Research. 1981h. *Income and Expenditure Patterns of Urban Black Multiple Households in Johannesburg, 1980*, Research Report 94.7 (BMR, Pretoria).

Van Coeverden de Groot, H.A. and Van der Elst, C.W. 1983. *Annual Report of the Department of Obstetrics and Gynaecology, University of Cape Town, 1983* (Department of Obstetrics and Gynaecology, University of Cape Town, Cape Town).

Van den Berghe, P. 1979. *Human Family Systems* (Elsevier, Amsterdam).

Van der Merwe, C.F. 1969. *Die Afrikaanse Landelike en Stedelike Gesin: 'n Vergelykende Ondersoek*, Research Report S-1 (HSRC, Pretoria).

Van der Vliet, V. 1984. 'Staying single as a strategy against poverty', *Second Carnegie Inquiry into Poverty and Development in Southern Africa*, conference paper no. 116 (SALDRU, University of Cape Town, Cape Town).

Van Gennep, A. 1909, 1960. *The Rites of Passage*, translated by Vizedom and Caffee (University of Chicago Press, Chicago).

Van Velsen, J. 1967. 'The extended-care method and situational analysis' in *The Craft of Social Anthropology*, edited by A.L. Epstein (Tavistock, London).

Van Warmelo, N.J. 1931. *Kinship Terminology of the South African Bantu*,

Ethnological Publications, 2 (Department of Native Affairs, Pretoria).

Van Warmelo, N.J. 1935. *Preliminary Survey of the Bantu Tribes of South Africa*, Ethnological Publications (Department of Native Affairs, Pretoria).

Vaughan, G.M. 1964. 'The development of ethnic attitudes in New Zealand school children', *Genetic Psychology Monographs*, 70, 135-75.

Vaughan, G.M., 1978. 'Social change and intergroup preferences in New Zealand', *European Journal of Social Psychology*, 8, 297-314.

Vilakazi, A. 1962. *Zulu Transformations* (Natal University Press, Pietermaritzburg).

Walker, C. 1982. *Women and Resistance in South Africa* (Onyx Press, London).

Ward, S.H. and Braun, J. 1972. 'Self-esteem and racial preference in black children', *American Journal of Orthopsychiatry*, 42, 644-48.

Weekly Mail, Johannesburg (weekly newspaper).

Weitzman, L.J. and Dixon, R.B. 1979. 'Child custody awards: legal standards and empirical patterns for child custody, support and visitation after divorce', *UCD Law Review*, 12, 2, 473-521.

Welburn, V. 1980. *Postnatal Depression* (Fontana Paperbacks, Glasgow).

Wessels, T.I., Hoek, B.B., and Van Niekerk, C.H. 1984. 'Factors associated with neonatal mortality at Pelonomi Hospital, Bloemfontein, 1 January 1983 – 31 December 1983' in *Proceedings of the Third Conference on Priorities in Perinatal Care in South Africa* (mimeo, Department of Paediatrics, Johannesburg Hospital, Johannesburg), 14-16.

West, M. 1975. *Bishops and Prophets in a Black City: African Independent Churches in Soweto, Johannesburg* (David Philip and Rex Collings, Cape Town).

Westcott, D. 1984. 'Sexual abuse of children', *South African Medical Journal*, 65, 895-97.

Whisson, M. 1976. 'The significance of kinship in a Cape peninsula township', *African Studies*, 35, 3-4, 253-71.

Whitehead, F. 1984. 'Racial awareness of South African primary school-children', unpublished BA Hons. thesis, University of Cape Town, Cape Town.

White Paper. 1981. *Report of the Commission of Inquiry into Labour Legislation*, Q.81 (Government Printer, Pretoria).

White Paper on the Provision of Education in RSA. 1983. R.P.72-1983 (Government Printer, Pretoria).

White Paper on Statistical/Economic Review in Connection with the Budget Speech 1985/86. 1985. W.P.B-85 (Government Printer, Pretoria).

Whittaker, D.E., Le Roux, I., and Disler, P. 1985. 'The estimated cost effectiveness of a nutritional rehabilitation day centre in an urban squatter community: Philani Crossroads, Cape Town', *South African Medical Journal*, 68, 174-76.

Wiehahn Commission. 1981. *Report of the Commission of Inquiry into Labour Legislation*, R.P.27-1981, part 5: Industrial Relations (Government Printer, Pretoria).

Wilkins, I. and Strydom, H. 1978. *The Super-Afrikaners: Inside the Afrikaner Broederbond* (Jonathan Ball, Johannesburg).

Williams, J.E. and Morland, J.K. 1976. *Race, Colour, and the Young Child* (University of North Carolina Press, Chapel Hill, N.C.).

Williams, J.E. and Morland, J.K. 1979. 'Comment on Banks's "White preference in blacks: a paradigm in search of a phenomenon"', *Psychological Bulletin*, 86, 1, 28-32.

Williams, J.E. and Robertson, J.K. 1967. 'A method for assessing racial attitudes in preschool children', *Educational and Psychological Measurement*, 27, 671-89.

Williams, R. 1965. *The Long Revolution* (Penguin, Harmondsworth).

Williamson, B. 1982. *Class, Culture, and Community: A Biographical Study of Social Change in Mining* (Routledge and Kegan Paul, London).

Wilson, F. 1972. *Migrant Labour in South Africa* (SPRO-CAS, Johannesburg).

Wilson, G.D., Nias, D.K.B., and Insel, P.M. 1972. *Manual for the Children's Scale of Social Attitudes* (Children's Studies Ltd., London).

Wilson, M. 1983. 'Ethnic attitudes of South African primary school children', unpublished BA Hons. thesis, University of Cape Town, Cape Town.

Wilson, M. 1957. *Rituals of Kinship among the Nyakyusa* (Oxford University Press, London).

Wilson, M. and Mafeje, A. 1963. *Langa. A Study of Social Groups in an African Township* (Oxford University Press, Cape Town).

Wilson, T.D. 1984. 'Health services within Soweto', *Second Carnegie Inquiry into Poverty and Development in Southern Africa*, conference paper no. 170 (SALDRU, University of Cape Town, Cape Town).

Women's Legal Status Committee Study Group on Women in Employment. 1978. Memorandum, Johannesburg.

Work in Progress. 1983. 'Apartheid and family life', *WIP*, 27, 40-42.

World Health Organization. 1981. 'Development of indicators for monitoring progress. Towards health for all by the year 2000', unpublished report, WHO, Geneva.

World Health Organization. 1983. *World Health Statistics Annual 1983* (WHO, Geneva).

Wyndham, C.H. 1980. 'A comparison of the mortality rates of white South Africans with those of the population of England and Wales', *South African Medical Journal*, 57, 729-41.

Wyndham, C.H. 1984a. 'Leading causes of death among children under 5 years of age in the various population groups of the RSA in 1970', *South African Medical Journal*, 66, 717-18.

Wyndham, C.H. 1984b. 'Trends in the mortality rates for the ten leading causes among white, coloured and Asian children under 5 years of age in the RSA, 1968 – 1977', *South African Medical Journal*, 66, 719-25.

Yancey, W.L., Rigsby, L., and McCarthy, J.D. 1973. 'Social position and self-evaluation: the relative importance of race', *American Journal of Sociology*, 78, 338-59.

Yawitch, J. 1983. 'Women in wage labour', *South African Labour Bulletin*, 9, 3, 82-93.

Young, K., Wolkowitz, C., and McCullagh, R. (eds). 1981. *Of Marriage and the Market: Women's Subordination in International Perspective* (C.S.T. Books, London).

Zborowski, M. and Herzog, E. 1962. *Life is with People. The Culture of the Shtetl* (Schocken Books, New York).

Index

Glossary

Words are dealt with only in the form and context in which they appear in the book.

'aanklop'	begging (Afrikaans slang)
abadala	forefathers; ancestors (Zulu)
affine, affinity	person related by marriage, hence marriage relationship
afkoel	cooling off (Afrikaans)
amademeshe	damages (Zulu)
amahloni	shame (Zulu)
ANC	African National Congress
anthropometry	growth as defined in terms of body measurement
ASB	Afrikaanse Studentebond
ASHA	African Self Help Association
AZAPO	Azanian People's Organization
AZASO	Azanian Students' Organization
barmitzvah	name given to male Jewish initiation rite undergone at age 13; the female equivalent is *batmitzvah* (Hebrew)
bawo, bobawo	father; also used for spouses of father's sisters, who are also called 'father' (Xhosa)
bawomkulu	paternal and maternal grandfathers; father's eldest brother (Xhosa)
Betar	acronym of Brit Yosef Trumpeldor — the union of Joseph Trumpeldor (Hebrew)
'bloedsap'	traditional supporter of the SAP (South African Party) in the Smuts era and after: the term is usually used of Afrikaner voters, to distinguish those loyal to the SAP from those who supported the National Party (Afrikaans slang)
'blue train'	methylated spirits (slang)
Bnei Akiva	Sons of Akiva. Religious Zionist movement established in Johannesburg in 1936 (Hebrew)

Boers (or *Boere)*	farmers: traditional name given by themselves and by others to Afrikaners in the aggregate. In some usages it has come to be more loosely applied to members of the security forces (Afrikaans)
'bokslagters'	goat slaughterers: derogatory term applied to poorer Afrikaner tenant farmers who kept goats on their plots (Afrikaans slang)
'bomming'	'bumming', pronounced the Afrikaans way (slang)
'bunnies'	derogatory term for homosexual men (slang)
CAP	Community Arts Project
cognation	descent from common ancestors
COSAS	Congress of South African Students
dadebobawo	father's sister (Xhosa)
dagga	marijuana
'dite'	stroller slang for food
DPSC	Detainees Parents' Support Committee
dyad	relationship linking two people
factor markets	markets in the factors of production — labour and capital
frère	brother (French)
FSAW	Federation of South African Women
FOSATU	Federation of South African Trade Unions
GOBI-FFF	mnemonic for the strategies embodied in a programme of the United Nations International Children's Emergency Fund
gogo	grandmother; familiar term for old woman (Xhosa)
GWU	Garment Workers Union
Habonim	The Builders. Socialist oriented Zionist Scout Movement introduced into South Africa in 1931 by Norman Laurie (Hebrew)
hlonipa	ritual avoidance, respect (Xhosa)
HSRC	Human Sciences Research Council
ighikize	leader of *izintombi* (Zulu)
ilobolo	marriage payments; bridewealth (Zulu)
imigezo	purification beasts (singular *umgezo:* Zulu)
IMR	Infant Mortality Rate: the number of deaths during the first year of life per 1 000 live births
imvulamlomo	gifts to open marriage negotiations (Zulu)
income elasticity of expenditure	the relation of the proportional rise in expenditure to the proportional rise in income, when it occurs
indlu	house (Xhosa)
induna	the headman of a community (Zulu)

ingezamuzi	goat sacrifice to cleanse household (Zulu)
inhlawulo	damages (Zulu)
inkomo	
yokubonga	cow paid in the *ilobolo* intended for the mother (Zulu)
'Inverse Care Law'	those most in need of a service are in the worst position to receive it
ISCOR	Iron and Steel Corporation
isiko	customs (Zulu)
isiphandla	bracelet (Zulu)
ITN	Independent Television Network
izimpahla	things, goods (Zulu)
izintombi	girls between puberty and marriage (Zulu)
kanala	Indonesian word meaning 'please', still used by Cape Town's Muslims
kanina	term used by males exclusively for children of their mothers' sisters (Xhosa)
kashrut	distinction based on Jewish dietary law (Hebrew)
koeksisters	a traditional type of doughnut (Afrikaans)
kombuistaal	kitchen language; patois (Afrikaans)
khokho	male great-grandparents (Xhosa)
kosher	Jewish dietary law observance (Yiddish)
kuduma,	
kudumbom	closest South Indian terms for 'family'
'kugel'	Jewish female stereotype: young person distinguished by her relentless quest for happiness in its most mundane, usually materialistic, social definition (South African Yiddish slang)
kutum	closest North Indian term for 'family'
lobola	marriage payments; bridewealth (Xhosa)
Maginim	Shields: organization for young children in the Progressive Jewish (Reform) Movement (Hebrew)
makoti	bride (Zulu)
makhulu	both paternal and maternal grandmothers; among the Mpondo both grandmothers and grandfathers are called *makhulu* (Xhosa)
malume	mother's brother (Xhosa)
malumekazi	wife of mother's brother (Xhosa)
matrifocal	where the woman is the head of a household, making major decisions and having authority in the unit
MASA	Medical Association of South Africa
mezuzot	parchment scroll in a metal or wooden box attached to the doorposts of dwellings (plural: Hebrew)
mvimba	father's beast, a part of bridewealth (Zulu)

mza, mzala	cross cousins (Xhosa)
mzukulwana	grandchild (Xhosa)
ngcolisa	make dirty, befoul; corrupt (morally) (Zulu)
ngquthu	mother's beast, a part of bridewealth (Zulu)
NICRO	National Institute for Crime Prevention and Rehabilitation of Offenders
PLO	Palestinian Liberation Organization
PAC	Pan African Congress
'parking'	directing motorists to vacant parking places: a form of street begging in which a 'fee' is demanded, sometimes adamantly (slang)
patrilineal	descent through the father's line
patrilocal	residence is centred round male spouse's family
perinatal mortality	stillbirths plus first-week deaths
'pimping'	acting as an informer (slang)
'pinies'	plastic fruit juice containers (slang derived from 'pineapple')
postnatal	existing or occurring after childbirth
postperinatal	from the second week after birth until the end of the first year
primigravida	one who is pregnant for the first time
rights *in geneticem*	husband's rights to the children which his wife bears
rights *in uxorem*	husband's right to require his wife both to sleep with him and to cook and work for him
rite de passage	rite of passage — ceremony to mark a transition in life (French)
rooinekke	red necks: derogatory term applied to the English (Afrikaans)
SABC	South African Broadcasting Corporation
SACBC	South African Catholic Bishops' Conference
SADF	South African Defence Force
sari	length of cotton or silk cloth draped round the body, worn as main garment by Hindu women
SEIFSA	Steel and Engineering Employers' Federation
serial monogamy	where a person has more than one spouse consecutively during his or her lifetime
SFAWU	Sweet, Food and Allied Workers' Union
shul	colloquial name for synagogue (Yiddish)
siyanyova	'we will destroy': a slogan adopted by militant township youths engaging in violence, and hence a collective name sometimes applied to youths with a reputation for

	ruthless violence
soeur	sister (French)
SPCC	Soweto Parents' Crisis Committee
spouse leak	statistical term: the fact that the number of married men enumerated does not quite match the number of married women enumerated
SRC	Student Representative Council
'stroller'	street child (slang)
stryddag	(political) party rally (Afrikaans)
'sugarmummies'	women who proposition young male strollers (slang)
suiwer	pure (Afrikaans)
swaer	brother-in-law (Afrikaans)
'Swart Gevaar'	'Black Danger': the stereotypical fear of black domination attributed to white South Africans, often played on by politicians (Afrikaans)
tiekiedraai	whirling dance movement (Afrikaans)
tzedakah	charity (Hebrew)
ubhuti	brother (Xhosa, derived from Afrikaans)
udadebowawo	father's sister (Xhosa)
udade wethu	older or younger sister (Xhosa)
UDF	United Democratic Front
UIF	Unemployment Insurance Fund
ukhondolo olubi	contagious ill luck (Zulu)
ukugeza	to wash, purify (Zulu)
ukumkhunga	to bond (the two families) together (Zulu)
umakazi	mother's sister (Xhosa)
umakhulu	grandmother (Xhosa)
umakoti	bride (Zulu)
umalume	mother's brother (Xhosa)
umama	mother (Xhosa)
umgezo	purification beast (plural *imigezo*: Zulu)
umkhokha	unpleasant consequences of a misdeed of one individual tainting the rest of the community (Zulu)
umkhongi	go-between in marriage negotiations (Zulu)
Umkhonto we Sizwe	'Spear of the Nation', the military wing of the ANC
umkhuluwe	elder brother (Xhosa)
umkhwenyane	bridegroom (Zulu)
umndeni	family or wider descent group (Zulu)
umninawe	younger brother (Xhosa)
umnt'akwethu	older or younger sister (Xhosa)
umtwanabendlu	child of the house or child of my mother (Xhosa)
umyeni	husband (Xhosa)

usisi	sister (Xhosa, probably derived from Afrikaans)
utata	father (Xhosa)
utatomkhulu	grandfather (Xhosa)
umzi	homestead (Xhosa)
volksfeeste	folk festivals (Afrikaans)
volkspele	folk dances (Afrikaans)
WHO	World Health Organization
Yom Hashoa	Holocaust Day of Remembrance (Hebrew)
YSK	Young Scorpion Kids